# Hannevi'ah and Hannah

# Hannevi'ah and Hannah

## Hearing Women Biblical Prophets in a Women's Lyrical Tradition

Nancy C. Lee

CASCADE *Books* • Eugene, Oregon

HANNEVI'AH AND HANNAH
Hearing Women Biblical Prophets in a Women's Lyrical Tradition



Cascade Books
An Imprint of Wipf and Stock Publishers
199 W. 8th Ave., Suite 3
Eugene, OR 97401

www.wipfandstock.com

ISBN 13: 978-1-62564-900-3

*Cataloguing-in-Publication data:*

Lee, Nancy C.

Hannevi'ah and Hannah : hearing women biblical prophets in a women's lyrical tradition / Nancy C. Lee.

xii + Y p. ; 23 cm. Includes bibliographical references.

ISBN 13: 978-1-62564-900-3

1. Women in the Bible. 2. Women Prophets. 3. Bible. Exodus, XV, 1–21—Criticism, interpretation, etc. 4. Bible. Judges, V—Criticism, interpretation, etc. 5. Bible—Isaiah—Criticism, interpretation, etc. 6. Bible. Jeremiah—Criticism, interpretation, etc. 7. Bible. Lamentations—Criticism, interpretation, etc. 8. Bible. Micah—Criticism, interpretation, etc. I. Title.

BS575 L41 2015

Manufactured in the U.S.A. 09/09/2015

This work is dedicated to the ancestral Hebrew women prophets,
singers, storytellers, and wise women elders,
who entrusted their contributions
and live on in more than memory.

This work is dedicated to the late eminent scholars:

B. Elmo Scoggin

Mishael M. Caspi

John Miles Foley

# Contents

# Preface

It is important to share something of my own social, cultural, and religious location from the outset. Reared, educated, and residing in U.S. culture, and a woman—though living, learning, and moving about regularly in other cultures still shaped by indigenous traditions—means I am shaped by what this entails. As a student of the Hebrew Bible, I have learned most from Jewish scholars and from Christian scholars who have immersed themselves as much as possible in the ancient Hebraic culture(s) and language. Both of these traditions have greatly influenced me as a Christian. Yet, I have a profound respect and appreciation for those who constructively practice the world's indigenous spiritual traditions and world religions, and I also stand with them. I believe we all, including those adhering ultimately to philosophical principles, have something important to contribute to understanding what it means to being fully human, responsible, just, and compassionate in relation to one another, to our kindred spirits in nature, and to the transcendent realm beyond us, that the spiritually inclined call God or Creator or many other names in traditional languages. On the other hand, every culture with its religious or spiritual tradition has its faults and failings which must be critically engaged and criticized.

Besides using oral-poetic, indigenous/postcolonial feminist approaches, this study surely benefits from all the methods and scholarship that has come before, and insights from poststructuralist, new-historical, and postmodern approaches. However, neither the intent nor procedure here, I trust, is to create a methodological 'system' in order to explain everything in or about the biblical texts. This study proposes a 'new' way to rediscover something important about 'the old ways' of Hebraic oral poetic traditional composing, but does not claim to be comprehensive. Moreover, not only do the texts precede theory in this study (if not all presuppositions!), neither is the text all there is in this approach. Biblical lyrics from Hebraic culture and contexts came indeed from real indigenous people with real voices and perspectives, put into writing at some stage. This return to the local and the contextual, as well as a respect for the sophistication of the artistry of indigenous women and men from ancient oral-traditional cultures is central here. And of course the 'hearer' (expanding 'the reader' of texts) is important—as are, one hopes, the oral performers for new contexts. My aim as an investigator is not to stand apart from these traditions but to immerse myself as utterly as possible in them, even though I am still an outsider historically and culturally. Apart from some of the dangerous ideologies occasionally appearing in ancient Hebraic culture (e.g., holy war, misogyny, exclusivism, which have been also practiced by other cultures), it is my firm conviction that retrieving a fuller understanding of the whole Hebraic oral tradition, especially the lyrical, will illuminate much that is desperately needed in our world today.

Nancy C. Lee, PhD

Elmhurst College, Chicago
June 2014

# Acknowledgments

I WISH TO EXPRESS my appreciation first to Elmhurst College for the sabbatical that supported my research for this book, and to my colleagues there, especially women whose leadership and friendship is a constant inspiration. I am grateful to Cascade Books, my editor, K.C. Hanson, Calvin Jaffarian, and numerous other W&S staff for their careful help with a complex manuscript. My profound debt and heartfelt appreciation goes to my professor of Hebrew, the late B. Elmo Scoggin; his inspiration lives on. And for the late Mishael M. Caspi, whose support of me early and later in my career with regard to going against the grain in pursuit of oral tradition and common ground across cultures and religions, I will always be grateful. So too I am grateful to the late John Miles Foley for his affirmation along the way. I want to especially thank dear friends and colleagues in whose communities I have been immersed and graciously welcomed over the years, learning of the power of their cultural traditions—in Croatia, Bosnia-Herzegovina, the Cherokee community, and South Africa.

Important women scholars and teachers, too numerous to mention, have blazed a trail upon which we all make our way. Looking back over the years, I am humbled to realize how many individuals, by their own academic work, word of encouragement, suggestion, or collaboration, have been of support to me along the way. For such for this book, I especially thank Athalya Brenner, Carol Meyers, Mayer Gruber, Walter Brueggemann, Irmtraud Fischer, Steven Bob, Naomi Graetz, Rachel Havrelock, Tim Beal, Julie Claassens, Hendrik Bosman, Jin Han, Marianne Blickenstaff, Chris Franke, Maggie O'Dell, Melody Knowles, Susan Hylen, Laurel Taylor, Shawna Dolansky, Alice Keefe, and Kathy Maxwell. I also thank the Feminist Hermeneutics, and Women in the Biblical World groups at SBL, and the Performance Criticism, Formation of Isaiah, and Lament in

Sacred Texts and Cultures groups. I am especially grateful for collaborations with Christl Maier, Nuria Calduch-Benages, and women colleagues working on the *Bible and Women: An Encyclopaedia of Exegesis and Cultural History.*

Special thanks to Athalya Brenner and to Walter Brueggemann for reviewing parts of this manuscript, and to Ruth Finnegan, all offering their wise feedback. A special thanks to Walter for his steadfast encouragement over time, ever kindling the prophetic imagination and pointing to women's contributions in the Bible. My thanks to Bobby Williamson and Jonathan Kaplan for their work on publication of the Isaiah essay. To Rabbi Steven Bob and Cantor Jennifer Frost, great thanks for their encouragement; and thanks, too, for my enthusiastic students at Elmhurst College, who have patiently listened to this proposal; examined painful, complex charts; and offered helpful feedback along the way. None of these persons should be held accountable for any errors in my judgment or scholarship.

Finally, for their loving support I thank my dear parents, sisters, and family; dear friends; and my loved one: what you have given me is beyond words.

# Abbreviations

| | |
|---|---|
| AB | Anchor Bible |
| ABRL | Anchor Bible Reference Library |
| BA | Biblical Archaeologist |
| BAR | Biblical Archaeology Review |
| BETL | Bibliotheca Ephemeridum theologicarum lovaniensium |
| BDB | F. Brown, S. R. Driver, and C. A. Briggs, *A Hebrew and English Lexicon of the Old Testament* |
| BHS | Biblia Hebraica Stuttgartensia |
| Bib | Biblica |
| BibInt | Biblical Interpretation |
| BibOr | Biblica et orientalia |
| BZAW | Beihefte zur Zeitschrift für die alttestamentliche Wissenschaft |
| CBQ | Catholic Biblical Quarterly |
| *BRev* | *Bible Review* |
| FAT | Forschungen zum Alten Testament |
| FRLANT | Forschungen zur Religion und Literatur des Alten und Neuen Testaments |
| GBS | Guides to Biblical Scholarship |
| HSM | Harvard Semitic Monographs |
| HTR | Harvard Theological Review |
| ICC | International Critical Commentary |
| *IDBSup* | *Interpreter's Dictionary of the Bible: Supplementary Volume* |

| | |
|---|---|
| JAAR | Journal of the American Academy of Religion |
| JBL | Journal of Biblical Literature |
| JNES | Journal of Near Eastern Studies |
| JPS | Jewish Publication Society |
| JQR | Jewish Quarterly Review |
| JR | Journal of Religion |
| JSOT | Journal for the Study of the Old Testament |
| JSOTSup | Journal for the Study of the Old Testament. Supplements |
| JTS | Journal of Theological Studies |
| LXX | Septuagint |
| MT | Masoretic Text |
| NCB | New Century Bible Commentary |
| NICOT | New International Commentary on the Old Testament |
| NJPS | *The New JPS Translation* |
| NRSV | New Revised Standard Version |
| OBT | Overtures to Biblical Theology |
| OTL | Old Testament Library |
| OtSt | Oudtestamentische studiën |
| RB | Revue Biblique |
| SBL | Society of Biblical Literature |
| SBLDS | Society of Biblical Literature Dissertation Series |
| SBLMS | Society of Biblical Literature Monograph Series |
| SBLSymS | Society of Biblical Literature Symposium Series |
| STDJ | Studies on the Texts of the Desert of Judah |
| SubBib | Subsidia Biblica |
| UF | *Ugarit-Forschungen* |
| VT | Vetus Testamentum |
| VTSup | Vetus Testamentum Supplements |
| WBC | Word Biblical Commentary |
| WTJ | Westminster Theological Journal |
| ZAW | *Zeitschrift für die alttestamentliche Wissenschaft* |

# PART 1

# Unnamed Women Prophets in Monarchic Israel

## CHAPTER 1

# Listening for Hannĕvî'ah[1] in First Isaiah and a Women's Lyrical Tradition

*Where can we find women's texts in the Bible?*
*How can they be differentiated from men's texts?*[2]

—ATHALYA BRENNER & FOKKELIEN VAN DIJK-HEMMES

*The Miriamic materials and other similar texts in Hebrew Scripture . . . reveal the presence of a gender-specific tradition, grounded in musical performance, in ancient Israel.*[3]

—CAROL L. MEYERS

*What counts is the world rendered by the text, a world wrought from the reality of Yahweh, who lives in and through the songs of the women.*[4]

—WALTER BRUEGGEMANN

1 Isa 8:3; hereafter Hannĕvî'â. The essence of this chapter I presented as "Listening for Hannĕvî'â, the Woman Prophet, in First Isaiah: A Signature Feature of Biblical Women's Lyrical Tradition" at the SBL annual meeting (Chicago, 2012), Formation of Isaiah session, included in a Festschrift for Walter Brueggemann (Sheffield, 2015).

2. Brenner and Dijk-Hemmes, *On Gendering Texts*, 6.

3. Meyers, "Miriam, Music, and Miracles," 27–48; see also Meyers, *Discovering Eve.*

4. Brueggemann, *Israel's Praise*, 41.

*These world-creating poems that run from Miriam to Mary are preserved in the tradition as the speech of women, who . . . have the capacity to speak an alternative world.*[5]

—WALTER BRUEGGEMANN

*For most of our existence as a species, 'cultural literacy' didn't involve [written] literacy . . . Today the majority of the planet's inhabitants use oral traditions as their primary communicative medium, a fact obscured by Western egocentrism . . . What we haven't been doing is recognizing that our familiar world is actually only one part of an immensely larger and . . . largely unexplored universe of verbal art.*[6]

—JOHN MILES FOLEY

THIS STUDY RESTS ON the possibility that the lyrical compositions in the Bible are less settled regarding male and female creative composers than generally supposed,[7] and a Western view with its "familiar world" of the Bible understands less than it yet needs to hear of the "verbal art" of ancient Hebrew women's lyricizing voices from their indigenous context.

## Aim, Method, and Background

This study will use an oral-poetic approach[8] integrated with feminist/gender-critical and indigenous/postcolonial approaches.[9] The first aim is

5. Brueggemann, "Response to 'The Song of Miriam,'" 297–302.

6. Foley, *How to Read an Oral Poem*, 22–27.

7. Williamson, "Prophetesses in the Hebrew Bible," 75, notes, "The figure of the prophetess was not nearly so unfamiliar in monarchical Israel and Judah as our scant sources initially suggest. The broadly male orientation of our present prophetic texts is therefore to be seen as a later theological construct overlaying an earlier social reality." One may add that androcentric biblical scholarship also passed down for generations the assumption of male-only composers and redactors of biblical texts.

8. Informed by rhetorical critics, including Muilenburg, Brueggemann, and Gitay, and by oral traditional approaches, including Caspi, Niditch, Jaffee, Culley, and Draper.

9. I am guided by Dube, *Postcolonial Feminist Interpretation*, 20–21, in attending to the silencing of women or to their supposed lack of presence, in relation to colonization. This feminist approach leads me to find women's indigenous voices in the Bible yet unattributed. A postcolonial approach prompts an analogy that voices of

to explore whether Isaiah 1–12 with its multiple voices bears evidences of a *women's prophetic lyrical* tradition.[10]

By 'Listening for Hannĕvî'â' in First Isaiah, I do not uncritically aim to identify a particular, historical woman prophet with Isaiah, the attributed male prophet, as responsible for particular lyrics. Rather, more largely, this study seeks to know *whether* and *how* we can discern voices of *real women* lyrical composers at all in the Bible. Did they have a distinctive composing tradition? What might their discourse, long blocked from our ears, have entailed?[11] In the end, women's prophetic lyrics, just as men's lyrics, would be *representations* in biblical texts.

It remains important to adopt a hermeneutic of suspicion when dealing with androcentric biblical texts, cultures, and the history of interpretation. And yet, it is apparent that the Hebraic worldview over time involved a respect for the lyrics of inspired prophets (of men *and also women* as I aim to show), and the desire to preserve their work is obvious. So along with suspicion, let us proceed also with a *hermeneutic of trust*, holding these in tension. Rather than assume that women prophets were completely silenced, let us appreciate the reference to Hannĕvî'â in First Isaiah and search for prophetic women's words embedded in the Isaianic collection.[12] This biblical appellative, refraining from naming a specific woman, allows use of the term for any woman's prophetic voice.[13] Commentators increasingly recognize multiple voices embedded in prophetic books.[14]

---

*indigenous* oral composers *within* the Bible may have also been suppressed, erased, colonized.

10. Differences in the sound patterns of men's and women's speech and in composing, the same language in the same culture, are found in numerous traditional cultures (Jakobson and Waugh, *Sound Shape of Language*, 212–14).

11. Says Foley, *How to Read*, 48, "Oral poetry has left behind recognizable footprints in these silent texts."

12. Taking a feminist approach, Kessler suggests the women prophets' sayings or voices are to be found "in the books of Isaiah, of Jeremiah, of Ezekiel, and the twelve so-called Minor Prophets, that is to say, under the names of male prophets" (Kessler, "Miriam and the Prophecy of the Persian Period").

13. Meyers, *Discovering Eve*, 195–96, suggests biblical women leaders "should be viewed not as the exceptions but rather as the representation of perhaps a larger group of publicly active females whose identity was lost because of the male-controlled canonical process. The female prophets and wisdom figures could not have found their paradigmatic though limited place in the canon if they were not part of an intrinsic acknowledgment of female worth and even authority."

14. Gordon, "Present Trends and Future Directions," 603–4.

James Muilenburg said in his generative commentary on Second Isaiah,

> In ancient Israel language possessed a . . . vitality that is relatively alien to the modern Western mind. The relation between *sound and meaning* was grasped with an immediacy and directness that are best understood by children and poets.[15]

This was not a patronizing or romantic statement, but he emphasized the consummate skill and artistry of the poets.[16] "Words have within them the power and vitality of the speaker, and they are transmitted to those who hear *with ears attuned to their living sources*."[17] In focusing on the power of the poetic, Walter Brueggemann borrowed Walt Whitman's phrase 'finally comes the poet',[18] but he did not limit his treatment only to the male gender of the poet, as Whitman: "Finally shall come the poet, worthy of the name, *the true son* of God shall come singing *his songs*."[19] Instead Brueggemann posed theological and sociopolitical concerns for our modern, cultural dilemma, of "poetry in a prose-flattened world";[20] one might say this in another way—*of indigenous lyrics for a Western world*. This study aims to pull back the curtain behind which androcentric, Western cultures have separated themselves, and throw open a window to hear a *poetry-filled world* with women's lyrics lost, still seeking their hearing today.

A few scholars since the mid-1980s have referred to[21] or made preliminary efforts at searching for the voices of *unnamed* women prophets

15. Muilenburg, *Isaiah 40–66*, 386 (italics added).

16. On the question of defining biblical poetry, historically answered by Jewish and other scholars, see Berlin, *Biblical Poetry through Medieval Jewish Eyes*, 7–15; Meyers, "Miriam, Music, and Miracles," 38, points to the importance of "emic" perspectives—how people in local cultures understand themselves (compared to "etic" studies by outside experts)—which often challenge "preconceived Western notions about male dominance in traditional communities."

17. Muilenburg, *Isaiah 40–66*, 386 (italics added). Biblical Hebrew has tended to be treated as a 'dead language' or an artifact by Western scholars, since it ceased to be an everyday spoken language; however, it is fair to say that biblical Hebrew as an indigenous language of devotion has always remained a 'living language' in some quarters through the generations.

18. Brueggemann, *Finally Comes the Poet*, 6.

19. Ibid. (italics added).

20. Ibid.

21. E.g., Bird, "Images of Women in the Old Testament"; Newsome, *Hebrew Prophets*, 142; Brenner, *Israelite Woman*; Trible, "Bringing Miriam out of the Shadows,"

embedded in the prophetic books.[22] Here I use as criteria three types of textual clues or evidence: (1) Hebrew feminine grammatical indicators, (2) song or lyrical genres associated with women,[23] and (3) distinctive poetic patterns in the Hebrew lyrics of women's attributed (and discerned) voices in comparison to men's poetic patterns. Special attention will be given to dialogical features. Oral poetry in indigenous cultures regularly has multiple voices in lyrical performance.[24]

In the end, this study finds evidence in the Hebrew in a surprising range of poetic texts, including Isaiah, of *a signature feature* of a women's lyrical tradition, unrecognized for much of history, which was suppressed or neglected, and forgotten.

## Critical Text

This study uses Hebrew transliteration of the Masoretic Text (MT)[25] and adopts variants among ancient witnesses helpful to the analysis. The MT remains a basis because the poetic analysis relies on the consonantal text. David Noel Freedman noted that the scribes resisted revisions to the earliest poetry normally seen in prose texts;[26] one may assume prophetic lyrics were carefully preserved as well.[27]

---

14–25, 34; Meyers, *Discovering Eve*; Meyers, *Rediscovering Eve*; Kessler, "Miriam and the Prophecy of the Persian Period," 85–86.

22. Stone, "Second Isaiah: Prophet to Patriarchy," 85–99; McEvenue, "Who Was Second Isaiah?," 213–22; Knauf, "Vom Prophetinnenwort zum Prophetenbuch"; Gruber, "Women's Voices in the Book of Micah"; Lee, "Prophet and Singer in the Fray," 207; Lee, "Singers of Lamentations," 45–46; Lee, "Prophetic 'Bat-'Ammî'"; Cook, "Habakkuk 3, Gender, and War"; and Gafney, *Daughters of Miriam*, 164–65.

23. See Goitein, "Women as Creators," 1–33; Poethig, *Victory Song Tradition*; Brenner and Dijk-Hemmes, *On Gendering Texts*; Caspi and Blessing, *Weavers of the Songs*.

24. Finnegan, *Oral Poetry*, 119, 122, 124; Okpewho, *African Oral Literature*, 133–37.

25. BHS, 1983, Leningrad Codex B19A.

26. Cross and Freedman, *Studies in Ancient Yahwistic Poetry*, viii, xi. Previously, Globe, "Literary Structure and Unity," 508, noted of Judges 5: "it seems highly unlikely that many such additions could have been made without upsetting the balance of the work. It would have taken a poet of genius to make several piecemeal additions in the different styles of the various parts of the poem."

27. Crenshaw suggests by the prophet's followers; "Transmitting Prophecy across Generations"; see also Wilson, "Current Issues."

## Analysis of Prophetic Lyrics within Isaiah 1–12

*Much work still remains to be done on the many ways in which the Isaian poets exploit the resources—especially the sound patterns—of the Hebrew language.* [28]

—Joseph Blenkinsopp

### Isaiah 1

The book of Isaiah opens (Isa 1:2–4)[29] with a judgment oracle against Israel.[30] The prophetic lyrics compel both by rich imagery and, no less important, by the sound of the lyrics. The chart format below tracks and highlights poetic patterns by lining up syllable (and word) sound repetitions, yet still in the order of their unfolding. The extraordinary artistry of the lyricist may put forth a syllable[31] sound that will be repeated very soon, or some lines later, thus repetition also on a metalevel. Here is the coding used (and hereafter):[32]

***ALL CAPS BOLD ITALIC*** (consonants of same root or word repeated)

*ALL CAPS ITALIC* (two or more consonants repeated within syllables or words in proximity, for wordplay)

**Lowercase bold regular** (one consonant's repetition at words' beginning, middle, or end)

***Lowercase bold italic*** (a vowel repeated at ends of words)

28. Blenkinsopp, *Isaiah 1–39*, 78–81.

29. Following the NRSV or NJPS unless otherwise indicated.

30. The historical period of Isaiah son of Amoz, and perhaps of the prophetess associated with him, covers the span of forty to fifty years, beginning ca. 738 BCE (Blenkensopp, *Isaiah 1–39*, 98–105).

31. I am indebted to fluent speakers today of the Cherokee indigenous language with its syllabary and for renewing my realization that the *syllable* is the most basic unit for composition.

32. The necessary 'frame' for the syllable 'house' is the consonant, regardless of vowel pronunciation.

## Isaiah 1

| | |
|---|---|
| *HEAR,* | *ŠIM'*û |
| *O HEAVENS*, and list**en**, O **earth**; | *ŠĀM*ayîm wěha'azînî **ereṣ** |
| **for** *YHWH* has **spoken**: | kî *YHWH* dib**bēr** |
| ***CHILDREN*** | ***BĀNÎM*** |
| I rear**ed** | giddal**tî** |
| and **raised**,[1] | wěrôm**amtî** |
| *BUT THEY* **rebelled** against me. (2) | *WĚHĒM* **pāšě'û** vî |
| **ox** *KNOWS* its owner, | ***YĀDA'*** **šôr** qōnēhû |
| and *THE DONK***ey** its master's trough;[2] | *WAḤĂM***ōr** **'ēvûs** **bě**'ālāyw |
| ***ISRAEL*** | ***YIŚRĀ'ĒL*** |
| does ***NOT KNOW***; | ***LŌ' YĀDA'*** |
| my ***PEOPLE*** do ***NOT*** *UNDERSTAND*. (3) | ***'AMMÎ LŌ'*** hit*BÔN*ān |
| **Ah! Nation sinning**, | **hôy gôy** **ḥōṭē'** |
| ***PEOPLE*** weighed with **iniquity**, | ***'AM*** keved 'āw**ōn** |
| *OFFSPRING DOING EVIL*, | *ZERA' MĔrē'ÎM* |
| ***CHILDREN*** *DOING DESTRUCTION*;[3] | ***BĀNÎM*** *MAŠḥîtÎM* |
| **they** have **forsaken** *YHWH*; | **'oz**v**û** ***'ET-YHWH*** |
| **they** have *DESPISED* Holy One of | *NI'ĂṢ***û** ***'ET***-qědôš |
| ***ISRAEL***; | ***YIŚRĀ'ĒL*** |
| **they** are *ESTRANGED* | *NĀZ***ōrû** |
| (with) anoth**er**![4] (4) | 'āḥ**ôr** |

[1] Author's transl. for greater alliteration.
[2] Author's transl.
[3] Foll. the nuance of the term by Melugin, *New Visions*, 289.
[4] Holladay, "A New Suggestion," 235-37.

Commentators occasionally mention Isaiah's artistry with sound, yet the above arrangement reveals more than an occasional soundplay—rather, a pervasive *doublet sound pattern*, not primarily doublets of words, but doublets of syllables, adjoining or in proximity, sharing two consonants or like-sounding consonants (alliteration), and doublets of vowel sounds (assonance). To name just a few, *šim / šām* (hear O heavens!), *hēm / ḥămōr* (they, donkey), *yāda' / yāda'* (know, know), and *Yiśrā'ēl / zera'* (Israel, offspring). Further, doublet sounds of *šôr / ḥămōr* (ox, donkey) form an inclusio at the end with sounds *nāzōrû / 'āḥôr* (estranged, another).

Sound repetition linked to wordplay of meaning (paronomasia) is common in the prophets,[33] including in Isaiah's represented rhetoric.[34] Sometimes his sound doublet emphasizes parallelism, but other times

33. See Gitay, "Reflections on the Study of the Prophetic Discourse," 213, on the individuality of poet's artistry (in Isaiah 1) related to formulas. On sound repetition in biblical poetry, see Casanowicz, "Alliteration and Kindred Figures," in Jacobs, *Jewish Encyclopedia*, 424–25 and online: http://www.jewishencyclopedia.com/articles/1266-alliteration-and-kindred-figures/; Saydon, "Assonance in Hebrew," 36–50; Sasson, "Wordplay in the Old Testament," 968–70; Watson, *Classical Hebrew Poetry*, 222–50.

34. Exum, "Of Broken Pots"; Gitay, "Reflections on the Study of the Prophetic Discourse"; Gitay, "Effectiveness of Isaiah's Speech"; in Second Isaiah, see Muilenburg, *Isaiah 40–66*.

it breaks out of parallel structure for unexpected, striking meanings. For example, the obvious parallelism is between ox and donkey, but the sound repetition hidden in the Hebrew—'but they' (*wĕhēm)* and 'the donkey' (*waḥămōr*)—hammers home the (often missed) parallel behavior of rebellious children and a donkey. Sound repetitions seen here in Isa 1:2–4 continue across Isaiah 1 but with even greater intensity in *multiples* of two. Even when the genre switches, e.g., in the oracle of salvation and promise in Isa 2:1–4 (also Mic 4:1–3)—the well-known peace lyric—the *doublet sounds persist*.

Scholars often use the terminology of the 'colon' as the smallest segment of Hebrew poetry; yet it is worth loosening the grip on structure to remember that verse numbering with neat cola was 'written in' much later than an originating oral context. For example, Isa 11:5 has two 'cola' (or a bicolon: one colon / one colon):

> Righteousness shall be the belt around his waist /
> and faithfulness the belt around his loins.[35]

In translating and printing Bibles, regular practice is to match parallel *content* of meaning (especially 'righteousness' and 'faithfulness' as a pair). Adele Berlin has shown not only how parallelism works in its rich forms, but also how "sound doublets" engage parallelism.[36] While the above parallelism seems self-evident, in Hebrew the sound repetitions strike a different chord.

| And there will be *righteousness—* | *WĔHĀYÂ* **ṣe**deq |
|---|---|
| a belt around his waist | ***'ĒZÔR*** *MOTNĀ***yw** |
| and (the) faithfulness— | *WĔHĀ'ĔMÛNÂ* |
| a belt around his loins. (Isa 11:5) | ***'ĒZÔR*** **ḥă**lā**ṣāyw** |

In Hebrew, 'belt' (*'ēzôr*) is repeated in parallel, and 'around his waist' and 'around his loins' rhyme in sound; however, 'and there will be' sounds like 'and the faithfulness,' (perhaps *hā* was added to *'ĕmûnâ* by the poet in order to clinch the sound parallel).[37] The *sound* of 'righteousness' (*ṣedeq*) is thereby pushed out there to stand all alone momentarily for emphasis

35. NRSV.

36. Berlin, *Dynamics of Biblical Parallelism*, 27–30.

37. Contra those who emend the text, deleting the definite article because it does not appear with *ṣedeq*, or who do not like the repetition of *'ēzôr*, arbitrarily changing one of them.

in this artistic lyric. Rather than a predictable verse made of two parallel cola (ab/a'b'), the *sound* of the Hebrew rather suggests a verse with an abcd/a'd'cb' pattern, first *setting apart* one sound unit, *ṣedeq* (b), for greatest emphasis, followed by parallelism. Only with the final syllable in the last word of the last line is the *ṣade* sound repeated for closure/inclusio, further emphasizing *ṣedeq*. Here, *what is not* the expected parallel is important. And because English or German—or whatever is one's own primary spoken/receptor language of the translated Bible—is so familiar, we may miss *the indigenous Hebrew poet's inspired artistry*.

## Isaiah 5

Moving along in the opening chapters of Isaiah, Isaiah 5 presents a song (*šîrâ*) of the vineyard setting, whether for a lover or friend, an 'endearment song.' However, the song functions as a parable contributing to a judgment oracle.[38] Thus four different genres are interwoven in these purposeful lyrics. From the Song of Songs, we know the love song genre might involve a dialog of voices. We examine this text closely especially for a woman's voice because of popular genres that women typically sang.[39] Most commentators suggest that male prophets borrowed genres from popular culture and adapted them to serve their oracles. However, there is no reason to exclude the possibility that *women prophets* did not *also adapt genres*—especially women's genres!—in service of their oracles.[40] Let us see what happens if we listen for a woman's voice taking up this song in Isa 5:1–2.

38. Yee, "Form-Critical Study of Isaiah 5:1–7," 30–40.

39. Goitein, "Women as Creators," 19–20. On Isa 5:1–2, Petersen, *Interpreting Hebrew Poetry*, 81–89; such a song could have been composed by a woman or by a man for their beloved.

40. The 'wise woman' of Tekoa speaks an indicting parable to David in 2 Sam 14:5–17; Yee, "Form-Critical Study of Isaiah 5:1–7," 33–35. She speaks prophetically (though Joab put the words in her mouth!).

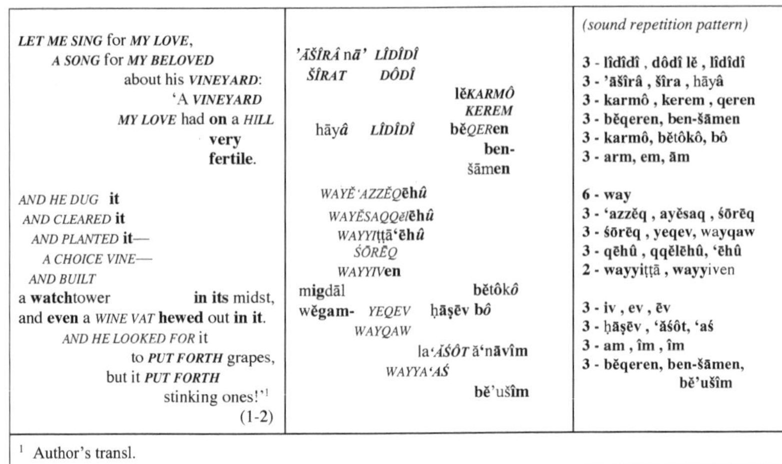

| | | (sound repetition pattern) |
|---|---|---|
| LET ME SING for MY LOVE,<br>A SONG for MY BELOVED<br>about his VINEYARD:<br>'A VINEYARD<br>MY LOVE had on a HILL<br>very<br>fertile. | 'ĀŠÎRÂ nā' LÎDÎDÎ<br>ŠÎRAT DÔDÎ<br>lĕKARMÔ<br>KEREM<br>hāyâ LÎDÎDÎ bĕQERen<br>ben-<br>šāmen | 3 - lîdîdî , dôdî lĕ , lîdîdî<br>3 - 'āšîrâ , šîra , hāyâ<br>3 - karmô , kerem , qeren<br>3 - bĕqeren, ben-šāmen<br>3 - karmô, bĕtôkô, bô<br>3 - arm, em, ām |
| AND HE DUG it<br>AND CLEARED it<br>AND PLANTED it—<br>A CHOICE VINE—<br>AND BUILT<br>a watchtower in its midst,<br>and even a WINE VAT hewed out in it.<br>AND HE LOOKED FOR it<br>to PUT FORTH grapes,<br>but it PUT FORTH<br>stinking ones!'[1]<br>(1-2) | WAYĔ'AZZĔQēhû<br>WAYĔSAQQĕlēhû<br>WAYYIṭṭā'ēhû<br>ŚŌRĒQ<br>WAYYIVen<br>migdāl bĕtôkô<br>wĕgam- YEQEV ḥāṣēv bô<br>WAYQAW<br>la'ĂŚÔT ă'nāvîm<br>WAYYA'AŚ<br>bĕ'ušîm | 6 - way<br>3 - 'azzĕq , ayĕsaq , śōrēq<br>3 - śōrēq , yeqev, wayqaw<br>3 - qēhû , qqĕlēhû, 'ēhû<br>2 - wayyiṭṭā , wayyiven<br><br>3 - iv , ev , ēv<br>3 - ḥāṣēv , 'ăśôt, 'aś<br>3 - am , îm , îm<br>3 - bĕqeren, ben-šāmen, bĕ'ušîm |

[1] Author's transl.

In the opening of Isaiah 5, it is impossible *not* to see the triplet sound pattern; it is tight and pervasive and a significant contrast to the previous Isaianic oracles' doublet sound pattern. That a lyricist can render such repetition with so many triplets of sound in just two verses is extraordinary.[41] Is this new pattern attributed to the singer of a different genre? To a woman prophet? Whether the triplet pattern belongs to a different genre or to a woman prophet matters not at this point, since the triplet suggests women's utterances.[42] Sympathetic listeners are drawn in to a beautiful and endearing serenade, then surprised with the bad outcome. While it is not clear where such an originating oral performance happened or if it was only imagined and composed in writing, now her beloved responds to her lyrics about his vineyard. Yet he directs his speech not back to her (as the male beloved occasionally does in the Song of Songs) but *to the male listeners* (5:3–6):

41. Muilenburg noted triplet repetitions in Second Isaiah that he called "triads'; *Isaiah 40–66,* 390.

42. A woman prophet, with double entendre, sings for her beloved (for Isaiah and for YHWH).

| *(male voice)*<br>*SO NOW*, resident of Jerusalem<br>and man of Judah,[1]<br>Discern justice[2] now between me<br>and my *VINEYARD*. (3)<br>What **more** is there to *PUT FORTH*[3]<br>for my *VINEYARD*<br>that I have *NOT* *PUT* into it?<br>Why when I hoped for (it)<br>to *PUT* out **grapes**,<br>it *PUT* out stinking **grapes**?[4] (4)<br>*SO NOW*, let me **tell**<br>**you what** *I* am *PUTTING FORTH*<br>for my *VINEYARD*—<br>**removing** its *HEDGE AND IT WILL BE*<br>**devoured**, breaking down[5] its wall<br>and *IT WILL BE*<br>*TRAMPLED*! (5)<br>And I will *MAKE* it a waste, empty,<br>*NOT* pruned<br>and *NOT* hoed. (6a) | *WĚ'ATTÂ YÔŠĒV YĚRÛŠ*ālaîm<br>**wě'îš** yěh**û**d**â**<br>šiphṭû-**nā'** **bên*î***<br>ûvên *KARMÎ*<br>**ma**h-*LA'ĂŚÔT* **'ôd** *LĚKARMÎ*<br>wě*LÔ' 'ĀŚÎTÎ* **bô**<br><br>**maddû'a** *QIWWÊTÎ*<br>*LA'ĂŚÔT* **ă'nāvîm**<br>wayya*'AŚ* **bě'ūšîm**<br>*WĚ'ATTÂ* **'ôdî'â-nā'**<br>**'et***KEM*<br>**'ēt 'ăšer-'ănî** *'ŌŚEH LĚKARMÎ*<br>h**ā**s**ē**r *MĚŚÛKĀTÔ WĚHĀYÂ*<br>**lěvā'ēr** pār**ō**ṣ gě*DĒRÔ WĚHĀYÂ*<br>**lě***MIRMĀS*<br>wa*'ĂŠÎT*ēhû vātâ<br>*LÔ'* **yi**zzā*MĒR*<br>wě*LÔ'* **yē**ʿā*DĒR* | (favors sound *doublets*)<br>**2 wě'attâ , wě'attâ**<br>**2 yôšēv , yěrûš 2 yě , yě**<br>**2 'îš , ši 2 ûdâ, ddû'a**<br>**2 nā', nā' 2 bên , vên**<br>**2 bê , bě 4 lě , lě , lě , lě**<br>**3 karmî , karmî , karmî**<br>**2 mah , ma 2 'ôd , 'ôd**<br>**2 qiwwêtî , kātô 2 îtî, êtî**<br>**4 la'ăśôt, la'ăśôt, 'āśîtî, 'aś**<br>**2 lô', bô 2 ă'nāvîm, 'â-nā'**<br>**2 îm , îm 2 'et, 'ēt**<br>**2 kem , karmî 2 měś, mās**<br>**2 'ăšer, hāsēr 2 vā'ēr, gědēr**<br>**2 wěhāyâ, wěhāyâ**<br>**2 měś , mās 2 hās , mās**<br>**2 'ōśeh , ōṣ 2 'ăšer , 'ăšî**<br>**2 mir , mēr**<br>**2 lô' yizzāmēr, lô' yēʿādēr**<br>**2 dēr , dēr** |
|---|---|---|

[1] Author's transl.
[2] 'Discern justice," a peculiar legal dispute that needs settling between a man and his vines!
[3] Author's transl. to capture repetition of the root's nuances (*'āśâ*).
[4] Author's transl.
[5] IQIsa[a] has *'āsîr* instead of *hāsēr*, same root; both preserve doublet sounds. Tull notes in Isa 3:14 leaders "devour' the vineyard and steal from the poor; *mirmās* in Isa. 7:25 refers to the trampling of sheep, in Isa 10:6 of invading foes; *Isaiah 1-39*, 122.

Not only with the apparent male prophetic voice in vv. 3–6 is there a major *shift* back to heavy repetition of *doublet sounds* in just four verses (about 32 doublets or 64 syllables), but his questions to the listeners echo the same words of the opening voice above—four times he repeats forms of *ʿāśâ* ('to put forth' or '*do*')—that would evoke a sympathetic response from the hearts and minds of the listeners: 'there was nothing more you could have *done*!' (Whether the *doublet* sound pattern belongs to the male prophet, or to the owner of the vineyard singing in response matters not. They are both male.) He next exploits the syllable sounds of this same verb, *ʿăśâ*, fourteen times rendering his destroying actions against the vineyard.

Only with line 6c might the impact of this dialogic parable dawn on the hearer, when God is suddenly given voice, saying, "And unto the clouds I will command no drop of rain upon it!" The triplet sound pattern suggests *the woman's voice* speaking for God (6b–7a), as she resumes describing the vineyard owner to the audience. The hearers might expect her to say *the vineyard owner is God*, but instead she says, "the vineyard is . . . *Israel*" [presumably now destroyed in the political context, as the hearers would be well aware]. But . . . "*you*, Judah," she says, "are the seedling of his delight" (*šaʿăšûʿāw*) (v. 7b), endearing language, keeping their attention, as she draws her *šîrâ* to an end by an inclusio repeating the same poetic sounds and words she stressed at the very beginning of the song (*š*, *y*, *ṣe*, *ke*).

| *(female voice resumes)* | | *(pulls lyrics back to **triplets**)* |
|---|---|---|
| And will *COME UP* **thorns**<br>and **thistles**<br>and *UNTO* the clouds I will **order**:<br>*NO **DROP***<br>*UPON IT* ***OF RAIN***.[1]<br>(6bc) | *WE'ĀLÂ* **šāmîr**<br>**wāśā**yit<br>*WE'AL* he'āvîm **'ăṣawwe**<br>**mēhamṭîr**<br>*'ĀLĀYW* **māṭār** | **3 we'ālâ , we'al , 'ālāyw**<br>**3 we**'ālâ **šā,** wā**śā**, **'ăṣawwe**<br>**3** šā**mîr**, ham**ṭîr** , **māṭār** |
| For (the) ***VINEYARD*** of **YH**WH of **hosts**<br>(is the) **house**<br>of **Israel**!<br>but (the) **man** of **Judah**, **seedling**<br>of his **delight.** (7a)<br>He ***HOPED***<br>***FOR*** *JUSTICE* — ***BUT LOOK!***<br>*BLOODSHED*<br>***FOR*** *RIGHTEOUSNESS*—***BUT LOOK!***<br>*A SHRIEK*![2] (7b) | **kî *KEREM* YHWH ṣ**ĕvā'**ôt**<br>**bêt**<br>**yi**śrā'ēl<br>**wĕ'îš yĕhûdâ** **nĕ**ṭa'<br>**ša'ăšû'āw**<br>***WAYQAW***<br>**lĕ***MIŠPĀṬ* ***WĔHINNĒH***<br>*MIŚPĀḤ*<br>**li***ṢĔDĀQÂ* ***WĔHINNĒH***<br>*ṢĔ'ĀQÂ* | *(triplets around doublets)*<br>**1 kerem** (completes triplet w/**kem** , **karmî** above)<br>**3 ôt , êt , ĕṭ 3 YH, yi , yĕ**<br>**3 'îš , ša'ăšû**<br>**3 wĕ, wĕ , wĕ**<br>**3** wĕ'**iš** , lĕ**mišpāṭ** , **miśpāḥ**<br>**2 lĕ, li**<br>**2 wĕhinnēh , wĕhinnēh**<br>**2 mišpāṭ , miśpāḥ**<br>**2 ṣĕ**dā**qâ , ṣĕ'āqâ**<br>**3 qaw , qâ , qâ** |

[1] Author's transl. for triplet soundplay: "*thorns* … *thistles* … I will *order*…'
[2] Author's transl. for staccato alliteration.

The stinging indictment comes—it is not clear whether the voice using triplets, or Isaiah is suggested to utter this part, with repetition of *wayqaw*—"and he hoped for" (part of a triplet soundplay with *qâ* and *qâ*) "*mišpāṭ*, 'justice' but look! bloodshed (*miśpāḥ*)!"[43] The obvious doublet soundplays are embedded in a larger triplet pattern from the verse just before (for example, *yĕhûdâ, wĕhinnēh, wĕhinnēh:* Judah, look, look). We should not forget that the apparent female voice's opening lines ended with a surprising twist of the grapes gone bad. If the woman's voice is sustained in describing the vineyard owner's disappointment, then this would contribute to the surprise element of the parable's indictment. For it is often the case that a poet with a consistent style and sound pattern will purposefully alter it for dramatic effect.[44] Perhaps it is 'just right' that we cannot know which of these voices dropped the hammer on the gavel, for the Hebrew of the text suggests a joining together in partnership, I would argue, of an extraordinary interplay of prophetic singing. While most commentators note the sharp wordplay with *mišpāṭ* and *miśpāḥ*, they usually miss the long, cascading *string* of sibilant sounds

43. *Miśpāḥ* probably derives from an agricultural term, *sāpîaḥ* (spilled, wasted grain that produced haphazard vegetation; BDB: 705), also suggestive of spilling of blood.

44. Gitay, "Reflections on the Study of the Prophetic Discourse," 213.

that these two voices bring/sing to a climactic crescendo here. Their joint performance strengthens the prophetic message, gives greater impact than if Isaiah alone simply 'imitated' an anonymous song and uttered a judgment oracle, like a lone individual crying out in the wilderness. Instead, two prophets may imaginatively weave familiar genres to construct, maybe in the public square or town gate, the world of the song, with people gathered round. The Hebrew of Isa 5:1–7 appears to suggest a prophetic *dialogical oracle*, and the Hebrew doublet and triplet sound patterns *alternating voices*.

But now it is important to say that the one place in the Bible representing male and female voices expressing love songs is of course the Song of Songs. And there, especially with gendered grammatical forms, it is possible to distinguish between the woman's and the man's speech. Most important, in Song 1 the *woman's lyrics bear the triplet sound* repetition pattern, and *the male voice uses the doublet* sound pattern. Apparently this is how Hebraic men and women differed in their singing traditions.

## Isaiah 9

Let us move to Isaiah 9, which features genres typically sung by women; the genres are a victory song (as salvation oracle) and a birth song for the royal child.[45] The singer in vv. 1–2 (English) below is suggestive of Isaiah as he favors the *doublet* sound pattern. Of approximately 49 syllables, 32 are composed of doublets sounds.

<table>
<tr>
<td>(male)<br>**But** there is no **gloom**<br>for her *WHO* had **distress**,<br>**as** at the time<br>he *FORMERLY* *ABASED*[1]<br>(the) ***LAND*** of Zebulun<br>and (the) ***LAND*** of Naphtali,<br>for *AFTERWARD*<br>he made *HONORABLE*<br>(the) **way** of *THE SEA*,<br>over *THE JORDAN*,<br>Galilee of *THE NATIONS*. (1)</td>
<td>**kî** **lō'** **mû'āph**<br>**la** *'ĂŠER* **mûṣāq lāh**<br>**kā**'ēt<br>*HĀRI'ŠÔN* *HĒQ***al**<br>***'ARṢÂ*** zě**vulû**n<br>**wě** ***'ARṢÂ*** n**aph**t**ālî**<br>**wě***HĀ'AḤĂRÔN*<br>*HIK*bîd<br>**derek** *HAYY***ām**<br>'ēver *HAYYAR***dēn**<br>**gělîl** *HAGGÔY***im**</td>
<td>**2 kî , kā 2 la , lāh**<br>**2 mû'āph , mûṣāq**<br>**2 'āph ,** n**aph**<br>**2 'ăšer , hāri'š**<br>**2 hāri'**_š_**ôn , ḥărôn**<br>**2 'arṣâ , 'arṣâ**<br>**4 āq , hēq , hik , ek**<br>**2 al , al**<br>**2 wě , wě 2 lî , lîl**<br>**2 hā'aḥăr , hayyar**<br>**2 de , dē 2 gě , gôy**<br>**2 hayyām , haggôyim**</td>
</tr>
<tr>
<td colspan="3">1 Abased and honorable, *NJPS*.</td>
</tr>
</table>

45. On the text as birth announcement, not enthronement song, see Wegner, "Reexamination of Isaiah IX 1–6"; Seitz, *Isaiah 1–39*, 86–87; Brueggemann, *Isaiah 1–39*, 83; Blenkinsopp, *Isaiah 1–39*, 250.

Moving to vv. 3–7, below, as the lyrics shift to *a victory song*, the *triplet* sound pattern emerges clearly and pervasively. Is this a woman prophet ('Hannĕvî'â') singing here? Let us proceed assuming it is; she addresses God as 'you' who brought this reversal to good fortune.[46] The victory is the end of war: Judah's escape either from Israel or from Assyria. If the sound pattern is correct, precisely in the middle of 6a with the announcement of the birth of a royal child, two voices participate, each with a line:

| *(female)* | | *(triplets)* |
|---|---|---|
| **You** *MAGNIFIED THE NATION*; | *HIRBÎTĀ HAGGÔY* | **3 hirbîtā, ḥittōtā, hāyĕtâ** |
| **you** *INCREASED* its ***JOY***; | *LÔ HIGDALTĀ* ha*ŚŚIMḤÂ* | **3 haggôy, lô hig**daltā, **yāgîlû** |
| they ***REJOICE*** | *ŚĀMĔḤÛ* | |
| before you as with ***JOY*** | lĕphān**êkā** | *KĔŚIMḤAT* | **3 śimḥâ, śāmĕḥû, śimḥat** |
| at the *HARVEST*, | ba*QQĀṢÎR* | **3 û, û, û** |
| *JUST AS THEY EXULT* | *KA'ĂŠER YĀGÎLÛ* | **6 êkā, kĕśi, aqqāṣîr, ka'ăšer , āg , ĕqā** |
| when **di***VIDING* | bĕḥ**allĕ***QĀM* | |
| **plunder** (3) | **šālāl** | **3 kĕ , qāṣ, ka'ăš** |
| ***FOR*** *THE YOKE* of **his burden**, | ***KÎ 'ET***-*'ŌL* sub**bălû** | **3 bĕḥal, šālāl,** sub**băl** |
| and the bar across **his** *SHOULDERS* | wĕ***'ĒT*** **ma**ṭṭēh **ši***KMÔ* | **3 qām, kmô, kĕyôm** |
| the rod of the **opp**ressor on **him**, | **ševeṭ** hannō**gēš** **bô** | **3 kî, kî, kî** |
| *YOU HAVE BROKEN* as *DAY* of **Midian**. | ha*ḤITTŌTĀ* *KĔYÔM* **mi**dyān | **3 'et, 'ēt, eṭ** |
| ***FOR*** *ALL* the ***TRAMPING BOOTS*** | ***KÎ*** *KOL* - ***SĔ'ŌN SŌ'ĒN*** | **3 'kî 'et-'ōl, kî kol, 'ăkōlet** |
| of (the) warri**or**, and *GARMENTS* | **bĕra'aš** wĕ*ŚIM***lâ** | **3 ši**kmô **ševeṭ** hannō**gēš** |
| **rolled** | **mĕ**gô**lālā** | **3 śim** (+**2 śim** above) |
| in **blood** | vĕ**dāmîm** | **3 â, ā, â** |
| *SHALL BE* **burned** | wĕ*HĀYĔTÂ* **liś**rēph**â** | **3 lâ , lālā** |
| *AS FUEL* (for) **fire**. (4-5) | **ma** *'ĂKŌLET* **'ēš** | **3 gēš, 'aš, 'ēš** |
| ***FOR*** a ***CHILD***[1] | ***KÎ - YELED*** | **2 sĕ'ōn, sō'ēn** |
| ***IS BORN*** | ***YULLAD*** | **3 mi, im, mîm** |
| ***TO US,*** (6a) | ***- LĀNÛ*** | **3 ma, mĕ, ma** |
| | | **3 yeled yullad lā**nû |
| [1] The root *yld* appears in Isa 7:14, 8:18 and here with regard to the royal birth; in the former, the mother, her pregnancy and the child are the sign from God, implying that in 8:18 it is not Isaiah who speaks, but *Hannĕvî'â*: "See! I and the *children* (*haylādîm*) the Lord has given me are signs and portents in Israel. . . .' | | |

| *(male)* | | *(doublets)* |
|---|---|---|
| a **son** is **given** | **bēn nittan** | **2 lānû** (with **lānû** above) |
| ***TO US;*** (6a') | ***- LĀNÛ*** | **2 itta, attĕ** |
| and there **shall** be ***AUTHORITY*** | **wattĕ**hî ***HAMMIŚRÂ*** | **1 hammiśrâ** (+ 1 below) |
| upon *HIS SHOULDERS*— | 'al-*ŠIKMÔ* | **2 šikmô , šĕmô** |
| and *HE IS NAMED*: (6b) | **way**yiqrā' *ŠĔMÔ* | **2 ele', 'ēl** |
| Won**derful** Coun**selor,** | **pele'** yô'**ēṣ** | **2 'ēṣ, iś** |
| Mighty **God**, | **'ēl** gibbôr | **1 gibbôr** |
| Eternal Father— | 'ăvî'ad | **1 'ăvî'ad** |
| *(female)* | | *(interjects triplet)* |
| *PEACEFUL PRINCE*— (6c) | śar-*ŠĀLÔM* | **3 šālôm (+ šikmô, šĕmô)** |

46. Brueggemann, *Isaiah 1–39*, 83, notes the poet emphasizes "the newness is the work of Yahweh" (a frequent motif in women's victory songs).

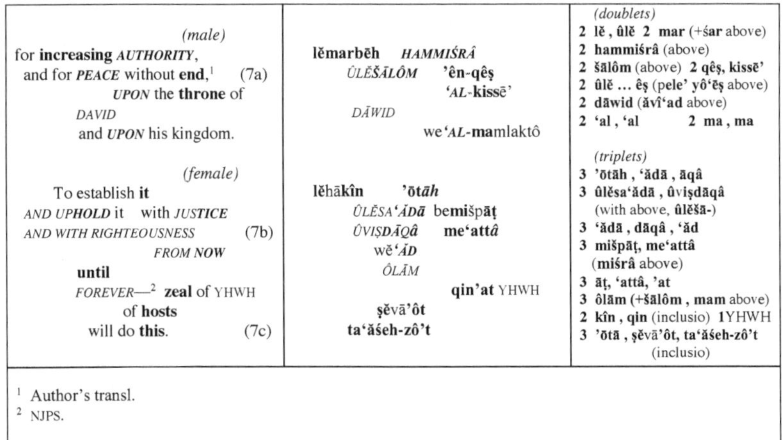

| | | |
|---|---|---|
| *(male)*<br>for **increasing** ***AUTHORITY***,<br>and for ***PEACE*** without **end**,[1] (7a)<br>***UPON*** the **throne** of<br>*DAVID*<br>and ***UPON*** his kingdom. | **lĕmarbēh** ***HAMMIŚRÂ***<br>*ÛLĔŠĀLÔM* **’ên-qêṣ**<br>**‘*AL*-kiss**ē’<br>*DĀWID*<br>we **‘*AL*-ma**mlaktô | *(doublets)*<br>2 **lĕ , ûlĕ** 2 **mar** (+**śar** above)<br>2 **hammiśrâ** (above)<br>2 **šālôm** (above) 2 **qêṣ, kissē’**<br>2 **ûlĕ … êṣ** (pele’ **yô‘ēṣ** above)<br>2 **dāwid** (**ăvî‘ad** above)<br>2 **‘al , ‘al** 2 **ma , ma** |
| *(female)*<br>To establish **it**<br>*AND UP**HOLD*** it with ***JUSTICE***<br>*AND WITH RIGHTEOUSNESS* (7b)<br>*FROM **NOW***<br>**until**<br>*FOREVER*—[2] **zeal** of YHWH<br>of **hosts**<br>will do **this**. (7c) | **lĕ**hā**kîn** **’ōt*āh***<br>*ÛLĔSA**‘ĂDā*** be**mi**šp**āṭ**<br>*ÛVIṢDĀQâ* **me‘att*â***<br>wĕ***‘ĂD***<br>*ÔLĀM*<br>**qin’at** YHWH<br>**ṣ**ĕvā**’ôt**<br>**ta‘ăśeh-zô’t** | *(triplets)*<br>3 **’ōtāh , ‘ădā , āqâ**<br>3 **ûlĕsa‘ădā , û**v**iṣdāqâ**<br>(with above, **ûlĕšā-**)<br>3 **‘ădā , dāqâ , ‘ăd**<br>3 **mišpāṭ, me‘attâ**<br>(**miśrâ** above)<br>3 **āṭ, ‘attâ, ’at**<br>3 **ôlām (+šālôm , mam** above)<br>2 **kîn , qin** (inclusio) **1**YHWH<br>3 **’ōtā , ṣĕvā’ôt, ta‘ăśeh-zô’t**<br>(inclusio) |

[1] Author’s transl.
[2] NJPS.

In the bestowing of names on the royal child, Isaiah gives three, and the sound pattern suggests Hannĕvî’â interjects in 6c a fourth—‘Peaceful Prince’—indicated just there by a triplet soundplay across three words (*šikmô, šĕmô,* and *šālôm*). Male and female prophet together announce the ‘birth’ with alternating voices.[47] Isaiah resumes right after her interjection with his lyrics of doublet sounds. The reappearance of the triplet pattern here in Isaiah 9 again suggests that a *signature* feature of a *women’s lyrical tradition* in ancient Israel is asserting itself. The woman’s voice expresses joy at the victory, as women typically sang victory songs and witnessed the sharing of spoils (recall the lines in Deborah’s song). Her lyrics also convey the dispensing of warrior’s blood-soaked clothing. With v. 7a, it appears that Isaiah’s voice moves the lyrics forward, shifting the focus to the king’s leadership—a male-dominated sphere in the culture—with hopeful, authoritative titles. Yet at v. 7b—note the return to sound *triplets*—Hannĕvî’â takes up the song again with important stress on the king ruling with ‘justice’ and ‘righteousness’ (cf. Isa 5:7).[48] Notable in Hannĕvî’â’s words at the end is emphasis on *what God has done* to bring victory and this turn of events (as in Miriam’s and Hannah’s lyrics). While two primary genres are at work across the text, these are not likely originally separate, but the prophetic voices compose and weave them

47. Some commentators regard the birth motif not as literal but a metaphor for royal accession; Clements, *Isaiah 1–39*, 107–8.

48. Brueggemann, *Isaiah 1–39*, 84, suggests, “The prophetic tradition dares to claim that it is justice and righteousness, that is, properly deployed social power, and not arms, that will make the nation secure.”

into a unified performance marked by strong threads, such as the triple use of *kî* over vv. 3–6, each of which also forms a triplet 'sound-phrase.' Here again we have two voices in dialog, I propose a male prophet and a female prophet.

## Excursus: The Song of Hannah

Isaiah 9:1–7, with its song of victory to YHWH and a birth song, shows similarity to the Song of Hannah in 1 Sam 2:1–10. It is a case study in itself to observe scholarly attempts to understand this 'female gendered' text; most regard the song as simply a redacted piece of formulaic fragments, yet others raise the possibility of a woman's composition (Brueggemann and Hackett).[49] Let us focus on the lyrical artistry of 'the song of Hannah' itself (1 Sam 2:1–10). Because this text is important for the argument here, I include its entirety.

| *(female)* | | *(triplets)* |
|---|---|---|
| **My** heart *EXULTS* *IN YHWH*!<br>**My** strength **arches high** *IN YHWH*!<br>**My** speech **is amplified**[1]<br>*ABOVE* my enemies.<br><br>***INDEED!***<br>**I rejoice** *IN YOUR SALVATION*. (1)<br>***NO*** **holy one** **like** *YHWH*,<br>***INDEED!***<br>***NO ONE*** *BESIDES YOU*!<br>and ***NO*** rock *LIKE* our ***GOD***.(2) | **'ālaṣ** li**bbî** **ba***YHWH*<br>**rāmâ** **qarnî** **ba***YHWH*<br>**raḥ**av **pî**<br>**'al-'**ôyĕvay<br>***KÎ***<br>**śāmaḥtî** *BÎŠÛ 'ĀTEKĀ*<br>***'ÊN*-qā**dôš **ka***YHWH*<br>***KÎ***<br>***'ÊN*** *BILTEKĀ*<br>wĕ ***'ÊN*** ṣûr ***KĒ'LŌH***ênû | 3 **libbî , qarnî , pî**<br>3 **rāmâ , raḥav , śāmaḥtî**<br>3 **ba**YHWH **, ba**YHWH **,**<br>**ka** YHWH<br>3 **'āl , 'al , 'al**<br>3 **bî , bî , bi**<br>3 **kā , qā , ka**<br>3 **kî , kî , kî**<br>3 **'ên , 'ên , 'ên**<br><br>3 **bîšû'ātekā, biltekā, ātāq** |
| *DO NOT ANY MORE*<br>*TALK* ***PROUDLY***,<br>***PROUDLY***,[2]<br>or *ARROGANCE* come from your **mouth**.<br>***INDEED!***<br>a ***GOD*** of *KNOWLEDGE*<br>is ***YHWH***<br>and *BY HIM*[3] are **weighed**<br>*ACTIONS*. (3) | **'al** - *TARBÛ*<br>*TĔDABBĔRÛ* ***GĔVŌHÂ***<br>***GĔVŌHÂ***<br>yēṣē' *'ĀTĀQ* mipp**îke**m<br>***KÎ*** ***'ĒL*** dē**'ôt**<br>***YHWH***<br>w*ĔLÔ*<br>**nitkĕ**nû<br>*'ĂLILÔT* | 3 **gĕvō , gĕvō** (+**gibbō**<br>below)<br>3 **kē'lō , kî 'ēl , ĕlō'**<br>3 **arbû , tĕdabbĕrû , ibbōr**<br>3 **îke, nitkĕ +nik** (v. 4 below)<br>1 **YHWH** [7 total]<br><br>3 **'ēl** dē**'ôt, wĕlô, 'ălilôt** |

[1] Literally, 'the mouth opens wide' suggestive of her proud speech that she has been vindicated by God.
[2] Author's transl.
[3] *Qere:* 'by him' (*lô*), not 'not' (*lō'*).

49. Childs, *Introduction to the Old Testament*, 272–73; Freedman, *Pottery, Poetry, and Prophecy*, 93–94; 243–61; Brueggemann, *First and Second Samuel*, 16–17; Balentine, *Prayer in the Hebrew Bible*, 218–20; Noll, *Faces of David*, 76–78; Hackett, "First and Second Samuel" in Newsom and Ringe, *Women's Bible Commentary* (1998), 91–101; see also the revised (3rd) edition from 2012, pp. 150–63.

The representation of this singer’s use of a triplet sound pattern is obvious. She begins her song with the triple emphasis of “*my* heart exults,” “*my* strength arches high (*rāmâ*),” “*my* speech is amplified.” The verb ‘arches high’ (*rāmâ*) is the same verb that Miriam is represented as singing in the famous lyric in the Song of the Sea: “horse and rider YHWH has *thrown* into the Sea” (or literally, shot them like an arrow). Jo Anne Hackett has suggested generally that this singer’s occasional use of martial terminology should not avert the possibility of a woman composing since women sang (military) victory songs.[50] Hannah is represented as repeating YHWH three times in the first part of the song, then as emphasizing YHWH once (v. 2) and then *three more times* in the last section (vv. 5–8). She repeats the emphatic *kî* three times in the first part of the song, and three times later in a sound wordplay with *kissē’* (v. 7, emphasizing the ‘throne’ God gives the needy). The first *kî* emphatically gives the reason for her triple empowerment—‘because I rejoice in your [God’s] salvation.’ The triplet sound pattern continues in the next six lines of the song.

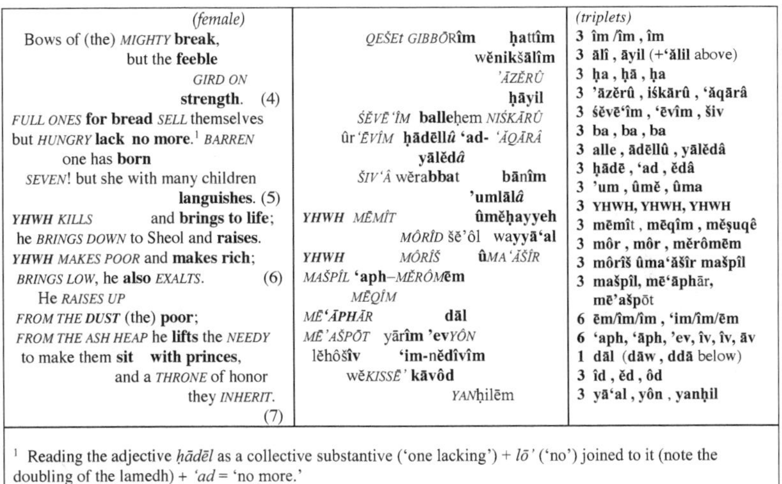

| *(female)* | | *(triplets)* |
|---|---|---|
| Bows of (the) *MIGHTY* **break**, | *QEŠEt GIBBŌR***îm** **ḥattîm** | 3 îm /îm , îm |
| but the **feeble** | **wĕnikšālîm** | 3 ālî , āyil (+‘ălil above) |
| *GIRD ON* | *’ĀZĔRÛ* | 3 ḥa , ḥā , ḥa |
| **strength**. (4) | **ḥāyil** | 3 ’āzĕrû , iśkārû , ‘ăqārâ |
| *FULL ONES* **for bread** *SELL* themselves | *ŚĔVĒ‘ÎM* **balle**ḥem *NIŚKĀRÛ* | 3 śĕvē‘îm , ‘ēvîm , šiv |
| but *HUNGRY* **lack no more**.[1] *BARREN* | ûr*‘ĒVÎM* **ḥādēllû ‘ad-** *‘ĂQĀRÂ* | 3 ba , ba , ba |
| one has **born** | **yālĕdâ** | 3 alle , ādēllû , yālĕdâ |
| *SEVEN*! but she with many children | *ŠIV‘Â* wĕra**bba**t **bānîm** | 3 ḥādē , ‘ad , ĕdâ |
| **languishes**. (5) | **’umlālâ** | 3 ’um , ûmĕ , ûma |
| *YHWH KILLS* and **brings to life**; | *YHWH MĒMÎT* **ûmĕḥayyeh** | 3 YHWH, YHWH, YHWH |
| he *BRINGS DOWN* to Sheol and **raises**. | *MÔRÎD* šĕ’ôl **wayyā‘al** | 3 mēmît , mēqîm , mĕṣuqê |
| *YHWH MAKES POOR* and **makes rich**; | *YHWH MÔRÎŠ* **û***MA‘ĂŠÎR* | 3 môr , môr , mĕrômēm |
| *BRINGS LOW*, he **also** *EXALTS*. (6) | *MAŠPÎL* **‘aph**–*MĔRÔM***ēm** | 3 môrîš ûma‘ăšîr mašpîl |
| He *RAISES UP* | *MĒQÎM* | 3 mašpîl, mē‘āphār, mē’ašpōt |
| *FROM THE DUST* (the) **poor**; | *MĒ‘ĀPHĀR* **dāl** | 6 ēm/îm/îm , ‘im/îm/ēm |
| *FROM THE ASH HEAP* he **lifts** the *NEEDY* | *MĒ’AŠPŌT* yā**rîm ’ev***YÔN* | 6 ‘aph, ‘āph, ’ev, îv, îv, āv |
| to make them **sit with princes**, | lĕhôš**îv** **‘im-nĕdîvîm** | 1 dāl (dāw , ddā below) |
| and a *THRONE* of honor | wĕ*KISSĒ’* **kāvôd** | 3 îd , ĕd , ôd |
| they *INHERIT*. | *YAN*ḥilēm | 3 yā‘al , yôn , yanḥil |
| (7) | | |

[1] Reading the adjective *ḥādēl* as a collective substantive (‘one lacking’) + *lō’* (‘no’) joined to it (note the doubling of the lamedh) + *‘ad* = ‘no more.’

Hannah’s represented lyrics (across a total of *nine* verses) alternate between what YHWH has powerfully done for her (divine incomparability, also found in the Song of the Sea) and YHWH’s empowering others who are disempowered. Notable is the composer’s extraordinary proclivity, about ten times in the song, of a play of three or four of the same consonants

50 Hackett (1998), “First and Second Samuel,” 96.

across three words clustered in proximity (e.g., *mēmît, mēqîm, mĕṣuqê / ʾăzĕrû, iśkārû, ʿăqārâ / môrîš ûmaʿăšîr mašpîl / yāʿal, yôn, yanḥil / ṣuqê, ḥōšek, kōaḥ / yāšet, yišmōr, ûrĕšāʿîm.*[51]

After the triplet soundplays end in vv. 8–9 (below), a new doublet sound pattern suddenly emerges in v. 10. Indeed suggestive of another voice, v. 10 has long been regarded as a later addition—*a male,* suggested by the doublet pattern. He repeats YHWH twice, emphasizing power, and how God will destroy his enemies and exalt his king.[52]

| | | |
|---|---|---|
| (female) | | (triplets) |
| INDEED! | KÎ | 3 kî, ĕṣuqê (+ ĕkissē' above) |
| to YHWH belong PILLARS of EARTH; | laYHWH MĔṢUQÊ 'EREṢ | 1 'ereṣ |
| he has set upon them | wayYĀŠet 'ălêhem | 3 kî , kî (+kissē' above) |
| the world. (8c) | tēvēl | 3 wĕkissē', mĕṣuqê, ḥōšek |
| The feet of his FAITHFUL | raglê ḤĂSîdāw | 3 ḥăs , ḥōšek , kōaḥ |
| he will guard, | YIŠmōr | 3 yāš , yiš , yigbar-'îš |
| but the wicked | ûrĕšā'îm | 3 yāšet , yišmōr , ûrĕšā'îm |
| in DARKNESS perish;[1] | baḤŌŠEK YIDDāmû | 3 'ălêhem tēvēl raglê |
| BECAUSE not | KÎ-lō' | 3 îdāw , iddā (dāl above) |
| by MIGHT | vĕKŌAḤ | 3 yi , yi , yi 3 ba, vĕ, ba |
| does one prevail.[2] (9) | YIgbar- 'ÎŠ | |
| (male voice) | | (favors doublet repetitions) |
| YHWH! | YHWH | 2 YHWH, YHWH |
| SHATTERED will be his adversaries;[3] | YĒḤATTû mĕrîvāw | 2 yēḥatt , wĕyitt 2 āw,'ālāw |
| against them | 'ālāw | 3 ar'ē , 'āre , ārē |
| in the HEAVENS HE WILL THUNDER.[4] | baŠĀMayim YAR'ĒM | 2 yādîn (+yiddā above) |
| YHWH will JUDGE | YHWH YĀDîn | 2 'aphsê - 'āreṣ |
| the ends of EARTH;[5] | 'aphsê – 'ĀREṢ | 2 'āreṣ (+ 'ereṣ above) |
| and GIVE strength[6] to HIS KING, | wĕYITTen-'ōz lĕMALKÔ | 2 malkô , mĕšîḥô 2 en , en |
| AND EXALT | wĕYĀRĒM | 2 yar'ēm, yārēm |
| the power of HIS ANOINTED.'[7] (10) | qeren MĔŠÎḤÔ | (yārîm above) |

1 NJPS.
2 NRSV.
3 NRSV.
4 Author's transl.
5 NRSV.
6 In a number of victory songs a woman sings of my 'strength' ( *'ōz*) from God. Here an apparent male voice uses this term for the strength of the king, parallel to his power (*qeren*), echoing the woman referring to her power (*qeren*) in v. 1.
7 NRSV.

Walter Brueggemann moves further than most commentators on this text with his sociorhetorical reading that opens a door at least to a tradition of women's composing.[53]

> Hannah sings of my heart, my horn, my mouth, my enemies (v. 1), but these are placed in stark contrast to *your* deliverance. It

51. In vv. 6–7, a myriad of terms begin with an *m* sound.

52. This is an interesting twist by the insertion of a *human* king at the end of the song, because the Song of the Sea closes by naming YHWH as king.

53. Brueggemann, *First and Second Samuel*, 16–17.

> is Hannah's joy but Yahweh's power. Verse 2 complements verse 1 by *a powerful triad of 'none, none, none,'* asserting there is no other like Yahweh . . . This is hope beyond the defined boundaries of current social reality, a hope most urgent for those excluded by present boundaries . . . Hannah/Israel asserts that Yahweh is the creator who has established the world on pillars . . . The hope of the poor and weak is rooted in the foundational *power of the creator* . . . Yahweh is free to *reorder the earth* and will do so on behalf of the marginal. The poem thus links . . . Yahweh's sovereignty over creation *with the hope of the marginal* . . . No wonder Hannah sings![54]

In Isaiah 5 and 9, Hannĕvî'â's lyrics parallel key emphases here—not only the removal of power from those practicing injustice, but the empowering of the downtrodden by the power of YHWH as Creator.

So let us give some fuller credence to the contribution of this composer with her socially subversive Yahwistic faith.[55] Why not? The tradition did its best to attribute *a great deal* to a woman's voice here.[56] These lyrics, likely rooted with a historical person, represent a women's lyrical tradition. The song shows many parallels to Deborah's story and song that also express *YHWH's outworking power in partnership with women.* It is fair to say that a redaction-critical approach that deems the song merely an editorial collection of formulaic pieces—thus diverting attention from a woman's compositional role—bears an androcentric bias that *erases the voice of a women's lyrical tradition* that the biblical canon *aimed to preserve*. It may *not* be that those hypothesized to have reconstructed a fictive Hannah (ancient editors or contemporary critics) have simply put words in her mouth, but it is just as likely that it was *a women's lyrical tradition* about Hannah that *influenced the editors.* It is a different thing to say that these lyrics (as any lyrics in the Bible attributed to, say, David or Isaiah) likely are not *exactly* as a creative singer composed them[57] (no doubt) than it is to say in a gender-discriminating way that 'she' or the women *cannot* have composed them. Balancing a hermeneutic of suspicion and of trust, we need a fuller understanding and *acceptance* of the power of lyricizing women in ancient Israel.

54. Ibid., 17–20 (italics original).

55. Ibid. Hannah's song resembles Psalm 113, which also has triplet soundplays.

56. Noll, *Faces of David*, 76–77, refreshingly suggests that Hannah "perceives herself to be an anointed vessel of God," referring to her own 'power' (*qeren*) in v. 2.

57. Or later composers whose work is attributed under their authoritative name.

Most important, the represented Song of Hannah is another strong piece of evidence—especially since it presents a woman's *solo voice*, not a dialog—that women's lyrical tradition followed a way of composing/performing that employed a *triplet sound pattern*.[58] One need only examine closely the victory/thanksgiving song attributed to *David* in 2 Samuel 22 (also Psalm 18) to see that it is *permeated* with *a doublet sound pattern*.[59]

## Isaiah 11

Returning to Isaiah chapter 11 (also *nine* lines) shows a dialogical structure.[60] The male prophet (using doublet soundplays) appears to begin with the famous cultivation metaphor for the emerging king and is answered by a female prophet (using triplet soundplays) referring to the Spirit of YHWH that will rest upon him. [61]

| | | |
|---|---|---|
| *(male)* | | *(doublets)* |
| And a shoot shall *COME OUT* | **wĕ***YĀṢĀ'* **ḥōṭer** | **2 wĕ , wĕ 2 yāṣā , yišāy** |
| **from** the tr**unk** of *JESSE*, | **miggēza'** *YIŠĀY* | **2 āṣ , 'ēṣ 2 ēza' , ēṣer** |
| and a bra**nch** | **wĕnēṣer** | **2 ṭer , ṣer 2 āy , eh** |
| **from** his roots shall grow.[1] (1) | **mišārāšāw yiphreh** | **2 miggēza' , mišārāšāw** |
| | | **2 yi , yi 2 šārāšā** |
| *(female)* | | *(triplets)* |
| And resting | | |
| upon him (the) | **wĕnāḥâ** | **3 wĕnāḥâ** (+**wĕyāṣā'**, **wĕnēṣer** above) |
| ***SPIRIT***[2] of ***YHWH***: | **'ālāyw** | **3 āḥâ , 'ālāyw , aḥ Y(a)h** |
| ***A SPIRIT*** of wisdom and | ***RÛAḤ YHWH*** | **3 rûaḥ , rûaḥ , rûaḥ** |
| *UNDERSTANDING* | ***RÛAḤ*** **ḥokmâ** *ÛVÎNÂ* | **3 'ēṣâ** (+ **ēzar , ēṣer** above) |
| ***A SPIRIT*** of **counsel** and *MIGHT*... (2ab) | ***RÛAḤ*** **'ēṣâ** *ÛGĔVÛRÂ* | **2 ûvînâ, ûgĕvûrâ 1 YHWH** |

[1] Blenkinsopp reads (foll. Clements, *Isaiah 1-39*, 122) *yiphraḥ* ('shall spring'; with TG, LXX) for MT's *yiphre*; yet all three textual traditions affirm the wordplay; *Isaiah 1*-39, 263.
[2] NJPS.

58. With regard to the metaphor, *ṣûr*, used for God (dated late by Freedman)—perhaps a women's lyrical tradition, reflected in Hannah's song, *influenced David and the psalmists.*

59. Ironically, many scholars regard this song as authentic to David.

60. Scholars have debated whether Isa 11:1–9 is a unified song or two compositions (vv.1–5 and 6–9); viewed as a unity by Kaiser, *Isaiah 1–39*, 152–55; Blenkinsopp, *Isaiah 1–39*, 263; and Seitz, *Isaiah*, 106–7; here, oral-poetic analysis recognizes dialogical performance of a song by two voices with different perspectives.

61. While quickly alternating voices pose difficulty in discerning who is speaking (as sound patterns overlap and as one voice may complete another's pattern), one must look for shifts in content focus, or for one voice picking up where the previous left off, or for the restoring of their own pattern.

The male voice then responds (below), giving four verses, picking up the theme of the Spirit, and adding (twice) an emphasis on the king's 'reverence' (or 'fear') of YHWH, even his delight in it. He goes on to describe the king's way of administering justice (a male sphere) and uses martial imagery to describe how the king will kill the wicked, closing with emphasis on righteousness; this echoes his vision about the king in Isaiah 9.

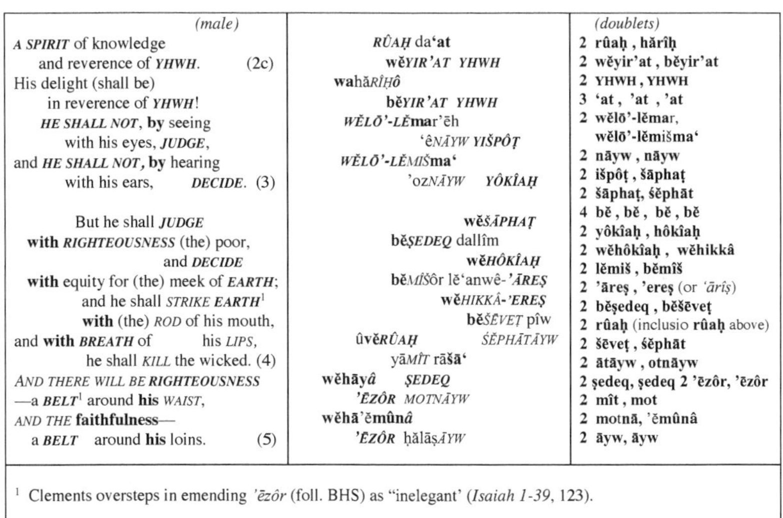

| *(male)* | | *(doublets)* |
|---|---|---|
| ***A SPIRIT*** of knowledge<br>and reverence of ***YHWH***. (2c)<br>His delight (shall be)<br>in reverence of ***YHWH***!<br>***HE SHALL NOT***, **by** seeing<br>with his eyes, ***JUDGE***,<br>and ***HE SHALL NOT***, **by** hearing<br>with his ears, ***DECIDE***. (3)<br><br>But he shall ***JUDGE***<br>**with** ***RIGHTEOUSNESS*** (the) poor,<br>and ***DECIDE***<br>**with** equity for (the) meek of ***EARTH***;<br>and he shall *STRIKE* ***EARTH***[1]<br>**with** (the) *ROD* of his mouth,<br>and **with** ***BREATH*** of his *LIPS*,<br>he shall *KILL* the wicked. (4)<br>*AND THERE WILL BE* ***RIGHTEOUSNESS***<br>—a ***BELT***[1] around **his** *WAIST*,<br>*AND THE* **faithfulness**—<br>a ***BELT*** around **his** loins. (5) | ***RÛAḤ*** da**'at**<br>**wĕ*YIR'AT YHWH***<br>**wa**hă*RÎḤÔ*<br>**bĕ*YIR'AT YHWH***<br>***WĔLŌ'-LĔ*****ma**r'ēh<br>'ê*NĀYW* ***YIŠPÔṬ***<br>***WĔLŌ'-LĔ****MIŠ***ma'**<br>'oz*NĀYW* ***YÔKÎAḤ***<br><br>**wĕ*ŠĀPHAṬ***<br>**bĕ*ṢEDEQ*** dallîm<br>**wĕ*HÔKÎAḤ***<br>**bĕ***MÎŠ*ôr lĕ'anwê-***'ĀREṢ***<br>**wĕ***HIKKÂ*-***'EREṢ***<br>**bĕ***ŠĒVEṬ* pîw<br>ûvĕ***RÛAḤ*** *ŚĔPHĀTĀYW*<br>yā*MÎT* rā**šā'**<br>**wĕhāy*â*** ***ṢEDEQ***<br>***'ĒZÔR*** *MOTNĀYW*<br>**wĕhā**'ĕ**mûn*â***<br>***'ĒZÔR*** ḥălāṣ*ĀYW* | 2 **rûaḥ , hărîḥ**<br>2 **wĕyir'at , bĕyir'at**<br>2 **YHWH , YHWH**<br>3 **'at , 'at , 'at**<br>2 **wĕlō'-lĕmar**,<br>**wĕlō'-lĕmišma'**<br>2 **nāyw , nāyw**<br>2 **išpôṭ , šāphaṭ**<br>2 **šāphaṭ, śĕphāt**<br>4 **bĕ , bĕ , bĕ , bĕ**<br>2 **yôkîaḥ , hôkîaḥ**<br>2 **wĕhôkîaḥ , wĕhikkâ**<br>2 **lĕmiš , bĕmîš**<br>2 **'āreṣ , 'ereṣ** (or *'ārîṣ*)<br>2 **bĕṣedeq , bĕšēveṭ**<br>2 **rûaḥ** (inclusio **rûaḥ** above)<br>2 **šēveṭ , śĕphāt**<br>2 **ātāyw , otnāyw**<br>2 **ṣedeq, ṣedeq 2 'ēzôr, 'ēzôr**<br>2 **mît , mot**<br>2 **motnā, 'ĕmûnâ**<br>2 **āyw, āyw** |

[1] Clements oversteps in emending *'ēzôr* (foll. BHS) as "inelegant' (*Isaiah 1-39*, 123).

Each voice renders their different perspectives. An implied call and response allows their beautiful back-and-forth description of the personal qualities of the future king.

However, it may be that the male voice's emphasis on the violence of the king evokes from the female voice four lyrics of her own (vv. 6–9) about a *peaceful* kingdom, and vision of a child playing among nature's (non)violent creatures. The woman voice's emphasis on *peace* and children contrasts with Isaiah's previous lyric about the king *killing* by the words of his mouth.

| (female) | | (triplets) |
|---|---|---|
| **And sojourns** WOLF | WĔGār ZĔ'ĒV | 3 wĕgā , gĕ , wĕ''ēgĕ (+ ēg) |
| WITH LAMB, | 'IM - keVEŚ | 3 'im , 'im , ûm |
| **and** LEOPARD WITH | WĔNĀMĒR 'IM- | 3 'im-keveś, 'im… yirbāṣ yirbĕṣû |
| **kid** LIE DOWN, | gĕdî YIRBĀṢ | |
| **and calf and** LION | WĔ'ĒGel ÛKĔPHÎR | 3 ûkĕphîr , ûmĕrî' , ûphār |
| **and** FATLING[1] TOGETHER; | ÛMĔRÎ' YAḤDĀW | 3 nāmēr, na'ar, nōhēg |
| **and** a little CHILD | WĔNA'AR qāṭōn | 4 wĕ , wĕ , wĕ , wĕ |
| is **leading** them. (6) | nōhēg bām | |
| COW **and bear** shall graze, | ÛPHĀRâ wādōv tir'ênâ | 3 yaḥdāw, wādōv, yaḥdāw, (+ yaldêhen) |
| TOGETHER | YAḤDĀW | |
| THEY LIE DOWN- | YIRBĔṢû | 3 na'ar, ûphār, 'aryē |
| **their** YOUNG; | YALDÊhen | |
| **and** LION LIKE THE OX | wĕ'ARYĒ KABBĀQār | 3 yē ka , yō'kal, yônēq 'al |
| EATS **straw**. (7) | YŌ'KAL - teven | 3 en , en, en |
| **And** plays A BABE OVER **viper's** hole | wĕši'ăša' YÔNĒQ 'al-hur pāten | 3 al, 'al, 'al |
| **and** OVER the adder's den | wĕ'al mĕ'ûrat | 3 kabbāqār, kal , bĕkol-har |
| a WEANED CHILD shall **put** | ṣiph'ônî | 3 ĕši'ăša' , ašḥî , qodšî |
| his **hand**.[2] (8) | GĀMÛL yādô | 3 gāmûl , kî-māl , kammayim la |
| | hādâ | 3 ādô, ād, od 3 yā, yā, ya |
| They will NOT **hurt**, | LÔ '-yārē'û | 3 hā , har , hā'ār |
| **and** they will NOT **destroy** | wĕLÔ'-yašḥîtû | 3 lô'-yā , lô'-yā , layyām |
| ON ALL my **holy** MOUNTAIN. | BĔKOL-HAR qodšî | 1 'āreṣ (plus 2 above=3) |
| | | 7 ya (total +1 YHWH) |
| INDEED! FILLED (will be) the EARTH | KÎ-MĀLĕ'â HĀ'ĀREṢ dē'â | 3 im, ām, îm |
| with knowledge— YHWH's — | 'et-YHWH | 2 YH , yām |
| LIKE WATERS | KAMMAYIM LAYYĀM | 3 kî-mā , kammayim , mĕkassîm |
| SPREADING OVER TO THE SEA.[3] (9) | MĔKASSÎM | |

[1] Blenkinsopp (*Isaiah 1-39*, 263) proposes deleting the third animal in this line (though two Qumran texts support it) apparently because it breaks a pattern of *two paired* animals previously; yet this misses the important *triplet* soundplay of three animals here and above.
[2] Foll. NJPS for the most part.
[3] Author's transl.

Above, the woman prophet's triplet soundplays especially *join realities and images that don't usually go together* to poignantly imagine a world of peace: "the wolf with the kid and the calf" (*wĕgār 'im-gĕdî wĕ'ēgel*); or, "the lion and the fatling and the cow" (*ûkĕphîr ûmĕrî' ûphārâ*); or, "together, together, their young" (*yahdāw, yahdāw, yaldêhen*). Her prophetic vision overcomes, as it were, binary opposites. Much more may be said here about Hannĕvî'â's theological vision, but it is important to note that she speaks for God in these lines, who says of "my holy mountain" that there be no "hurt" or destruction there (and she does not refer to the mountain, as male prophets usually do, as 'Daughter Zion'). In none of the texts considered thus far does a proposed woman prophet's voice make the city female. Further, Hannĕvî'â's vision stretches to include the entire earth and created order, wherein humanity's knowledge of YHWH and expected way of living—with justice and righteousness, and protection of the vulnerable—will fill the earth as waters are naturally drawn to fill the sea. Here may very well be a development of Miriam's lyrical tradition with the sea.

## Isaiah 12

Isaiah 12 is regarded by many commentators as a close to the first section of Isaiah. It is a song of thanksgiving with more than one voice.[62] Numerous feminine grammatical markers indicate that one is a woman's voice. Further, the sound patterns suggest an overall call-and-response structure, including a woman speaking in two lines of vv. 1–3, and a male voice speaking in two lines of vv. 4–6, the two sections each opened by the refrain "you will say on that day."

| *(A voice says:)*<br>***AND YOU*** [ms] ***WILL SAY ON THAT DAY*** | ***WĔ'ĀMARTĀ BAYYÔM HAHÛ'*** | Addresses audience |
|---|---|---|
| *(male)*<br>"I will give thanks to **you**, ***YHWH***,<br>***FOR*** you were **angry with me**,<br>(but) it *TURNED* away,[1]<br>**your** anger, and you **comforted me**." (1) | **'Ô***DĔ***kā** ***YHWH***<br>***KÎ*** **'ān***APHTĀ* bî<br>*YĀŠŌV*<br>**'appĕkā** ûtĕ**na**ḥămē**nî** | *(doublets)*<br>**2 kā, kā**<br>**2 'ānaphtā** bî<br>ûtĕ**naḥă**mē**nî** |
| *(female)*<br>**See**!<br>**God** of my ***SALVATION***![2]<br>I will **trust**<br>and I will **not** be **afraid**;<br>***FOR*** my **strength**— | hin**nēh**<br>**'ēl** ***YĔŠÛ'Ā***tî<br>*'EVṬAḤ*<br>**wĕlō'** *'EPHḤĀD*<br>***KÎ*** **'ozzî** | *(triplets )*<br>**3** hin**nēh** (+**na, na** above)<br>**3 'evṭaḥ, 'ephḥā**d<br>(+'ān**aphtā** above) |
| *(A voice rejoins)*<br>and you **sing** [woman][3]<br>"***YAH***"! | wĕ**zi***MMĀRT*<br>***YĀH*** | *(doublets)*<br>**2** wĕ**zi** (+ **'ozzî** above)<br>**2 Yāh (+ YHWH** above) |
| *(female)*<br>—***YHWH***!<br>and [*YHWH*] ***IS*** my ***SALVATION***!<br>And you [m.pl.] will **draw**<br>*WATER* with joy<br>*FROM WELLS* of ***SALVATION***!<br>(2-3) | ***YHWH***<br>***WAYĔHÎ-LÎ*** **lî***ŠÛ'Â*<br>ûšĕ**'avtem-**<br>*MAYIM* bĕśāśôn<br>*MIMMA'AY*nê ha***YŠÛ'Â*** | *(triplets)*<br>**3 YHWH, yĕhî**<br>(+**Yāh** above)<br>**3 lîšû'â, hayšû'â**<br>(+**yĕšû'ātî** above)<br>**3 mayim, mimma'ay**<br>(+zi**mmā**rt above) |

[1] NRSV foll. LXX, SYR, instead of MT's jussive (Blenkinsopp, *Isaiah 1-39*, 269).
[2] Seitz links, as others, 'salvation' here 3x to Isaiah's name in Hebrew (*yĕša'yāhû*; 'the Lord is salvation') as "an unmistakable signature of the [male] prophet' (*Isaiah 1-39*, 112-13). However, the triplet sound pattern is more likely the 'signature' of *hannĕvî'â*, partner of *yĕša'yāhû.*
[3] My translation renders the verb a lyrical rejoinder, not an imperative. Today's translations often don't follow the difficult MT consonantal text, but follow a variant (in 1QIsa[a], Mss, Sam., Vulg.) regarding this term as either a 1cs perfect verb, or fs noun with suffix: thus, 'so I sing' or 'and my song'. Might this form be an archaic *feminine* perfect? With the allusion to a female addressee later in the song, here I follow this latter that would be equivalent to the MT consonantal text, yet repointing MT as *wĕzimmārt* (2fs pi. perfect), not *wĕzimrāt* (fs noun) (the MT has the *same form* also in Exod 15:2). This is supported by reading the consonantal text of 1QIsa[a] with its *yod*-ending as an *archaic 2nd feminine perfect* (such are found in the proto-Sinaitic inscriptions, in Ugaritic, and in Judg 5:7 referring to the prophet Deborah; also in Jer 2:33); on archaic forms, see Sáenz-Badillos, *History of Hebrew Language*, 31, 35, 57, and Smith, "Why Was "Old Poetry" Used in Hebrew Narrative," in Lundberg, *et al.*, *Puzzling Out the Past*, 201-203.

62. Brueggemann, *Isaiah 1–39*, 111, notes, "Israel's final word [of Isaiah 1–12] is praise and thanks . . . because Yahweh's final act is *not wrath but comfort'* and anticipates Isaiah 40."

| | | |
|---|---|---|
| *(male)*<br>*AND YOU* [mpl] *WILL SAY* on that day:<br><br>*GIVE THANKS* to *YHWH*;<br>call on *HIS NAME*.<br>*MAKE (IT) KNOWN* among<br>the peoples. His deeds<br>remember [m.pl.] | *WA'ĂMARTem BAYYÔM HAHÛ'*<br><br>*HÔDû* la*YHWH*<br>*QIR'û* vi*ŠMÔ*<br>*HÔDÎ'û* vā'ammîm 'ălîlōtāyw<br>haz*KÎRû* | *(doublets)*<br>2 'ămartem bayyôm hahû' ('āmartā bayyôm hahû' above)<br>2 hôdû , hôdî'û<br>2 qir'û , kîrû |
| *(female)*<br>*FOR* exalted is *HIS NAME*! (4)<br>*SING* [m.pl.]<br>*YHWH*,<br>*FOR* triumphantly<br>he has done! | *KÎ* niśgāv *ŠĔMÔ*<br>*ZAMMĔRû*<br>*YHWH*<br>*KÎ* gē'ût<br>'āśâ | *(triplets)*<br>3 kî , kî (+kî above)<br>3 zammĕr (+zimmār, 'ozzî)<br>2 višmô, šĕmô<br>3 YHWH (YHWH, yĕhî above)<br>3 niśgāv , gē'ût 'āśâ |
| *(male)*<br>She is *MAKING IT KNOWN*[1]<br>in all the earth! (5)<br>Shout aloud and sing for joy![2]<br>O woman seated in Zion,<br>*FOR* great [magnified]<br>within you is the Holy One of Israel!(6) | mĕ*YADD*e'et zô't<br>bĕkol-hā'āreṣ<br>ṣahălî wārōnnî<br>yôševet ṣîyyôn<br>*KÎ* – gādôl<br>bĕqirbēk qĕdôš Yiśrā'ēl | *(doublets)*<br>2 mĕyadde'et<br>(+ hôdî'û above)<br>2 'et , et 2 ṣa, ṣî 2 î, î<br>2 add, ād 2 'ār, wār<br>2 hā, hăl 2 ol, ôl<br>2 ōn , ôn 2 ôš, ôš<br>2 kî (inclusio with v. 1)<br>3 gā (gā, gē above)<br>3 bĕk , bĕqirbēk |

[1] The verb root *yādâ* (doubly weak) is difficult, with a *khetib* (some read pu.) and *qere* (some read ho.), *both* fem. participles with passive sense, 'this [f.s.] is made known'. I propose instead translating the *khetib* as a pi. intensive causative (*she* is causing 'this' to be known; in the pattern of a lamedh-aleph verb in which the fem. sing. participle adds a final taw following silent aleph (e.g., mĕmaṣē't); here, *mĕyaddē't* or *mĕyadde'et,* the final ayin silent. Note the pi. imperative verb at the beginning of v.5, 'Sing!' forming a 'gender-matched' parallelism with this pi. fem. participle in v. 5b: 'she is making this known.' Kaiser (*Isaiah 1-39*, 167; foll. *qere* and Q, *mūda'at*) and Blenkinsopp have 'let this be known' (*Isaiah 1-39*, 269).
[2] Imperatives are fem. sing.

The most important parts of this text for identifying a female prophet's voice are the use of the Miriam tradition and lyrics remembered from the Song of the Sea (v. 2 and 4 above). Isaiah 12:2 is likely a verbatim formula passed down from Exod 15:2. I translate, 'and you sing!' (*wĕzimmārt*), as one voice giving a rejoinder to a female singer.[63] A comparison to Deborah's song also has strong emphasis (Judg. 5:3) on *zāmar*: 'I (*'ānōkî*), to the Lord, I (*'ānōkî*), I will sing (*'āšîrâ*), I will sing (*'ăzāmmēr*) to the Lord, God of Israel!'

The voice singing of 'my salvation' in Isa 12:2 echoes the voice of Miriam in Exod 15:2, I will argue later, and here also uses the same terms, 'strength' and 'sing.'[64] "You will draw water with joy from the wells of

63. Some translations of *zmr* render 'protection' (LXX) or 'fortress' from a different nuance of the root; recently, 'my might' (NJPS, NRSV) or 'power' (e.g., Blenkinsopp, *Isaiah 1–39*, 269; from NW Semitic and Arabic, *dimr*). Tull, *Isaiah 1–39*, 246, suggests, in light of possible meanings of the term, that we need not choose, but perhaps both meanings reverberate in the lyric. (Propp, *Exodus 1–18*, 513, proposed this for the term in Exod 15:2.) However, reading a noun *does not allow* for a *feminine verbal form*.

64. Song of the Sea in Exodus 15 likewise shows these two sound patterns

salvation!" (12:3) combines the motifs of women's typical activity with the traditions of Miriam's joyful singing, of 'Miriam's well' and her prophetic gift of finding water in the desert.[65] Notably, in Isa 12:4, the term for 'triumphantly' (*gē'ût*) is from the same verb root as in Miriam's line from Exod 15:21, "Sing to the Lord, for he has *triumphed triumphantly*."

Moreover, vv. 5–6 use three feminine verbs suggestive of a woman prophet: 'she is making it known' followed by two feminine imperatives ('shout aloud', 'sing'). I translate the term *yōševet* describing 'her' differently than most: 'O woman *seated* in Zion.' The NRSV translates this term as 'royal', a metaphor of a queen enthroned, or the *female city* personified. Indeed, nearly all commentators so interpret, without justification by argument.[66] Yet, there is no reason why the female referent must be objectified into a metaphor as elsewhere. [67] Neither does 'Daughter' in construct with Zion appear here.

Rather, the feminine participle *yōševet* I interpret as a real woman 'seated' in the city. This *exact* feminine term (rare) is used to describe *the prophet, Deborah,* the one who 'was seated' as a judge under the palm of Deborah (Judg. 5:4), *and the exact term* is used *for Huldah*, the prophetess (2 Kgs 22:14; 2 Chr 34:22)—'she (*hî'*) was seated' (*yōševet*; perhaps as a judge also, but certainly a prophet and authority figure) in Jerusalem.

Further, of the woman seated in Zion here, she is described (Isa 12:6): *kî-gādôl bĕqirbēk qĕdôš Yiśrā'ēl.* Typically this is interpreted, 'great within your midst is the Holy One of Israel' (i.e., God within female Zion personified). Yet this Hebrew construction is unprecedented elsewhere; the only other instance of the 'Holy One' in proximity to Zion appears to be in Isa 60:14: 'the descendents of those who oppress you [Zion] will call you "city of YHWH, Zion of the Holy One of Israel."' That text does not say the Holy One will be *inside* the city. But he term *qerev* is used in the sense of 'within' *a person* in Isa 19:1, 3, 14; 26:9; and 63:11: "where is the One who put *within* him [Moses] his holy spirit?" That a manifestation of YHWH can be *within* a prophet, see also Mic 3:8.[68] So Isa 12:6, I propose, describes a woman prophet, affirmed either by Isaiah or perhaps by her

suggestive of alternating male and female voices.

65. See Ginzberg, *Legends of the Jews*, 369–71; Gafney, *Daughters of Miriam*, 143. Blenkinsopp, *Isaiah 1–39*, 270, notes allusion at v. 3 to *śimḥat bēt ha-shō'evâ* ('the rejoicing of the place of water-drawing').

66. See Gruber's justified critique, "Women's Voices in the Book of Micah," n.p., of "the tendency to ignore female voices by turning them into personifications."

67. *yōševet* personifies a city of Moab in Jer 48:18 but *with the term* 'daughter.'

68. A parallel to Isa 12:6 is Mary's song/Magnificat (Luke 1:46–47): 'My soul magnifies [μεγαλύνει; 'makes great/extols'] the Lord' (NRSV).

women followers: "O woman seated in Zion, indeed great (magnified) *within you* is the Holy One of Israel!"

So what might this proposal of *Hannĕvîʾâ* as a singer mean for this Isaiah text (12:1–6)? I would suggest that in a large crisis for Judah, she has a prophetic vision that God will rescue Jerusalem ('on that day'), that they will sing praise for this 'triumph' of God's rescue. The first three verses serve as an 'oracle of salvation,' and the second three as songs of praise for God's victory, with an 'answering' voice to hers, as we've seen earlier in the dialogical prophetic lyrics in First Isaiah. Perhaps she is *Hannĕvîʾâ* associated with Isaiah, but no matter who she is, in this text, hers is the central voice, and the male prophet's voice extols her utterance.[69] Once again, in time of national crisis, not only were there male prophets called by God to serve ancient Israel, but there were always women prophets (Miriam, Deborah, Hannĕvîʾâ, Huldah, Noadiah).

## Isaiah 15–16

Isaiah 15–16 falls within a section of the book of Isaiah including oracles about other nations and the general context of the domination of Assyria over the region. While some nations (such as Judah, until Hezekiah) were vassals to Assyria, others rebelled against it. Just how these prophetic speeches that concern Moab fit into this picture is not entirely clear, though Moab paid tribute, like Judah, to Assyria.[70] A biblical tradition of Israel's negative views of and animosity toward Moab is well known.[71]

Isaiah 15–16 is important for this analysis, as it is a lament genre (concerning death) often associated with women, though here modified to describe communal destruction. While the Hebrew text has some difficulties of translation, the extraordinary thing about the song is its very *compassionate attitude toward Moab*, toward its suffering,[72] and toward

69. Commentators suggest the difficulty of finding the male prophet Isaiah's voice in this text!

70 Moabite kings paid tribute to Assyria, supplied troops to Ashurbanipal, initially submitted to the Babylonians, but were defeated by them; Kaiser, *Isaiah 13–39*, 63–64; Miller and Hayes, *History of Ancient Israel and Judah*, 352–63.

71. E.g., Gen 19:37; Deut 23:3; 1 Kgs 11:7, 33; 2 Kgs 3; Isa 11:14; 25:10; Jer 9:26; 25:21; 48; Neh 3:23 and 13:1; Deut 34:5–6. Yet, David visited Moab and appealed to the Moabite king to take in his parents for their safety during David's dangerous rise to kingship (1 Sam 22:3–4). Judean exiles fleeing to Moab after the Babylonian destruction of Jerusalem return to Judah from there (Jer 40:11).

72. Kaiser, *Isaiah 13–39*, 63–64, suggests that in the last part of the eighth century, Assyria called upon Moab to support its attack on Egypt (and its Arab allies). The

Moabite women. As in the book of Ruth, so here the term "Moab" is also heavily used (ten times). Across this song is a *triplet* pattern, yet the lament does not start with it, but with a voice in vv. 1–4 using a *doublet* pattern, presumably Isaiah or a male prophet. The second voice, let us suggest Hannĕvî'â, utters most of this long song, using triplet soundplays in composing; perhaps due to the lament genre, the triplet pattern is less thorough than in previous genres. Expressing compassion for the suffering Moabites, Hannĕvî'â is interrupted at vv. 6–7 by a voice (using doublets) who in what sounds to be a sarcastic tone says, "Let the Moabites lament for Moab." Yet the dominant woman's voice returns and insists continuing lamenting for Moab. At 16:1, the lyrics portray *a Moabite woman appealing* for help to Jerusalem. Nearly all commentators believe the appeal is to the *female persona* of Zion; yet, in light of the patterns illuminated here in First Isaiah, I believe the Moabite appeal for empathy and help is more than likely to a well-known *woman prophet* in Jerusalem. Isaiah 15 is below:

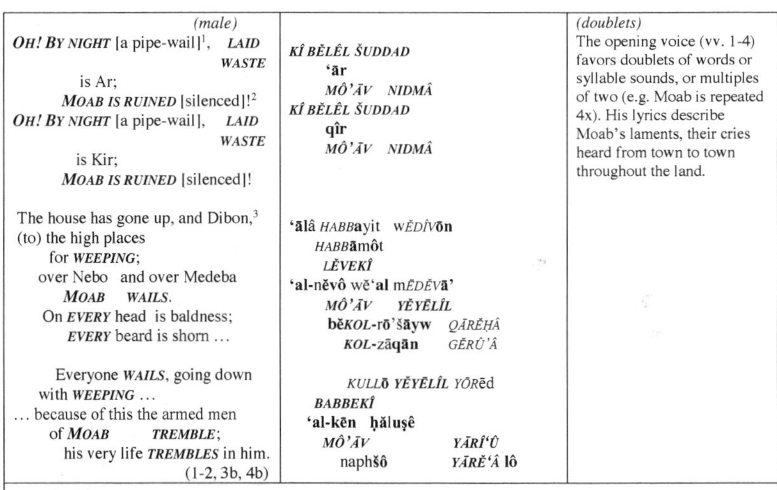

| *(male)* | | *(doublets)* |
|---|---|---|
| ***OH! BY NIGHT*** [a pipe-wail][1], ***LAID WASTE***<br>is Ar;<br>***MOAB IS RUINED*** [silenced]![2]<br>***OH! BY NIGHT*** [a pipe-wail], ***LAID WASTE***<br>is Kir;<br>***MOAB IS RUINED*** [silenced]! | ***KÎ BĔLÊL ŠUDDAD***<br>**'ār**<br>***MÔ'ĀV NIDMÂ***<br>***KÎ BĔLÊL ŠUDDAD***<br>**qîr**<br>***MÔ'ĀV NIDMÂ*** | The opening voice (vv. 1-4) favors doublets of words or syllable sounds, or multiples of two (e.g. Moab is repeated 4x). His lyrics describe Moab's laments, their cries heard from town to town throughout the land. |
| The house has gone up, and Dibon,[3]<br>(to) the high places<br>for ***WEEPING***;<br>over Nebo and over Medeba<br>***MOAB WAILS***.<br>On ***EVERY*** head is baldness;<br>***EVERY*** beard is shorn … | **'ā**lâ *HABB***a**yit w*ĔDÎV***ō**n**<br>*HABB***ā**môt<br>***LĔVEKÎ***<br>**'al**-nĕvô wĕ**'al** m*ĒDĔV***ā'**<br>***MÔ'ĀV YĔYĒLÎL***<br>**bĕ***KOL*-rō'š**ā**yw *QĀRĔḤÂ*<br>***KOL***-zā**q**ā**n** *GĔRÛ'Â* | |
| Everyone ***WAILS***, going down<br>with ***WEEPING*** …<br>… because of this the armed men<br>of ***MOAB TREMBLE***;<br>his very life ***TREMBLES*** in him.<br>(1-2, 3b, 4b) | *KULL***ō** ***YĔYĒLÎL*** *YŌR*ēd<br>***BABBEKÎ***<br>**'al-kēn ḥăluṣê**<br>***MÔ'ĀV YĀRÎ'Û***<br>naph**š**ô ***YĀRĔ'Â* lô** | |

[1] NRSV translates *bĕlêl* 'in the night," a short form of *layil* or *laylâ*; this term in 15:1 sounds like the verb in vv. 2 and 3 (*yĕyēlîl* from *yālal*; to wail; see also in 13:6; 14:31; 15:8; 16:7); its noun form can be masculine (yĕlēl) or feminine (yilālâ). A similar term is the word for the pipe (*ḥālîl*) that wails (Isa 5:12; 30:29). Wordplays are likely intentional by an improvising singer; the term in v. 1 may have sounded like all three meanings at once: in the night (*bĕlêl*), with wailing (*bîlêl*), the pipe-wail (*bĕḥālîl*).
[2] Verb from *dāmâ*, to cut off, destroy, silence (the city), in the form *nidmâ*, likely a wordplay with the term *dim'â,* 'tears," as crying is referred to in the very next verse (15:2), and 'tears' in 16:9.
[3] Author's transl., retaining MT's *bayit* ('house'), following Sweeney's view (*Isaiah 1-39*, 243) possibly alluding to survivors of the royal house. Contra *bat* ('daughter'), not in the text.

Next, a voice with triplet soundplays takes up the lament across vv. 5–9.

Moabite king, Kamashaltā, was killed and may have brought an invasion of Moab producing devastation and fleeing refugees, as suggested by Isaiah 15–16.

| *(female)* | | *(triplets)* |
|---|---|---|
| My heart for MOAB<br>CRIES OUT;<br>her fugitives flee to Zoar,<br>to Eglath-shelishiyah.<br>OH! (at) the ascent of<br>the Luhith<br>with WEEPING he goes up on it. | libbî lēMÔ'ĀV<br>YIZ'ĀQ<br>bĕrîḥehâ 'ad-ṣō'ar<br>'eglat šĕlišîyâ<br>KÎ ma'ălē<br>hallûḥît<br>BIVKÎ ya'ăle-bô | 3 bî , bĕ , bibĕ<br>3 z'āq , za'ăq , hazz'āqâ<br>3 'ălē , all , 'ăle 3 ḥehâ, ha<br>1 bivkî (compl tripl above)<br><br>3 bĕrîḥehâ, šĕlišîyâ, šeber |
| OH! (on) way to Horonaim A CRY of<br>destruction they rouse up;[1]<br>OH! waters of Nimrim<br>a desolation they are;<br>OH! the grass is withered, | KÎ derek ḥôronayim ZA'ĂQAT-<br>šever YĔ'O'ĒRÛ<br>KÎ - mê nimrîm<br>mĕšammôt yihyû<br>KÎ- yāvēš ḥāṣîr | 6 bivkî + 5 kî<br>1 yĕ'o'ērû<br>(completes triplet with above)<br>3 kî , kî , kî<br>3 kî …im, kî-mê nimrîm,<br>mĕšamm |
| FAILS the new sprouts,<br>the lush green is no more.<br>THEREfore the abundance made<br>and what they LAID UP<br>OVER the Wadi of the Willows<br>they carry away.<br>OH! IT GOES,<br>THE CRY of distress<br>around the border of MOAB;[2]<br>(5-8a) | KĀLâ deše'<br>yereq lō' hāyâ<br>'AL-KĒN yitrâ 'ĀŚÂ<br>ûPHĔQUddātām<br>'AL naḥal HĀ'arāvîm<br>yiŚĀ'ûm<br><br>KÎ - HIQQIPHÂ<br>HAZZ'ĀQÂ<br>'et-gĕvûl MÔ'ĀV | 3 ĕš , ēš , eš<br>3 kāl , 'al-kēn, 'al naḥal<br>3 yihyû, hāyâ, yitrâ<br>3 'āśâ , yiśā', hazz'ā<br>3 ām, îm, ûm<br><br>3 ûphĕquddā, hiqqiphâ,<br>hazz'āqâ<br>2 mô'āv (inclusio) |

[1] This is the verb, *'ûr*, appearing in a number of songs, usually translated "wake up" or "arouse yourself" as in the Song of Deborah, also in songs of Second Isaiah.
[2] Author's transl.

A voice with doublet soundplays interjects in v. 8b; the female voice resumes in v. 9.

| *(male)* | | *(doublets)* |
|---|---|---|
| The WAILING reaches to Eglaim,<br>the WAILING reaches to Beer-elim.(8b) | 'ad-'eglayim YILLĀTĀ<br>ûvĕ'ēr 'êlîm YILLĀTĀ | 2 yillātā, yillātā<br>2 'eglayim, 'êlîm |
| *(female)*<br>Oh! waters of DIMON<br>are full of BLOOD,<br>but I WILL offer for DIMON more—<br>for the woman survivor of MOAB<br>I WILL drench[1] (with tears);<br>and for the last one remaining,[2]<br>I WILL LAMENT.[3] (9) | kî mê DÎMÔN<br>mālĕ'û DĀM<br>kî-'āšît 'AL - DÎMÔN nôsāphôt<br>liphlêṭat MÔ'ĀV<br>'aryē<br>wĕliš'ērît<br>'ĂDĀMÂ | *(triplets)*<br>3 kî, kî (+ 1 kî above)<br>3 dîmôn, dām, dîmôn<br>(+'ădāmâ)<br>3 'āšît, ôsāphôt, iš'ērît<br>3 'āšît, 'aryē, 'ădāmâ<br>3 'al (+ 2 above)<br>3 mô'āv (+2 above)<br>3 li , liphlê (+ libbî above,<br>inclusio) |

[1] From *râwa* (to drench; cf. Isa 16:9); thus also NJPS.
[2] The term is feminine singular.
[3] From *dâmam* (another term for 'wail'; cohortative), or perhaps from *dâma'* (to 'weep," with final *'ayin* dropped off); see also 16:9, where the voice says "I will weep with the weeping (from *bâkah*) of Jazer…I will drench (from *râwa*) you with my tears (dim'âtî from *dâma'*)." Note the wordplay with 'Let me lament' (*'adâmâ*) with 'ground' (*'ădâmâ*), related to people lamenting, sitting on the ground.

The above tracking suggests again the interplay of voices. The woman's voice genuinely laments for the women of Moab; this is evident from the poignant lyrics of v. 9 (above).

In Isaiah 16, below, it appears a Moabite woman is rendered by the female prophetic voice as appealing for help to the mountain of daughter Zion (note triplet sounds in her line as well: *šil, šēl, sel*). The woman of Moab expresses an urgent need: water-jars for scattered refugees at the fords of the Arnon River;[73] in a time of oppressive heat, they also need shade, literally and metaphorically. In v. 2, doublet sounds suggest that a male prophet describes the women refugees; then he appeals to the woman prophet (indicated, in my translation, by his use of the feminine imperative verb, 'prophesy'), and he next appeals to a group to intervene with prayer mercifully to help the refugees (v. 3a). The male prophet's words are followed in v. 3b–c by a woman's voice: the woman prophet with an oracle, appealing to Zion to take in the refugees:

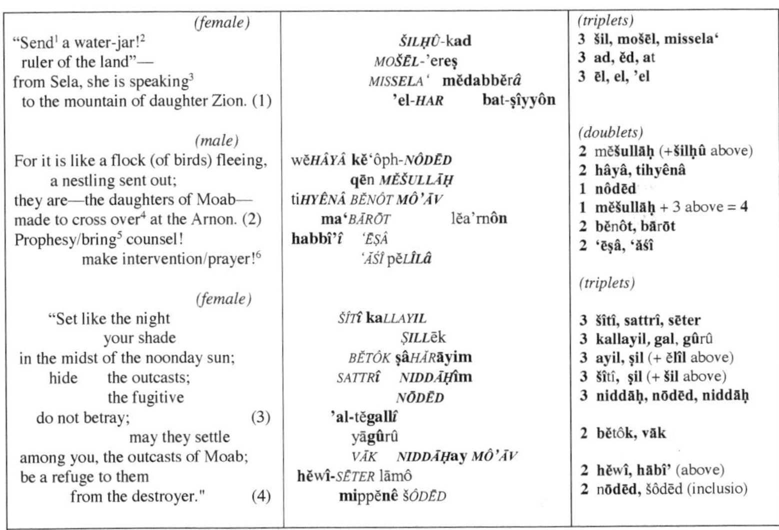

| | | |
|---|---|---|
| *(female)*<br>"Send[1] a water-jar![2]<br>ruler of the land"—<br>from Sela, she is speaking[3]<br>to the mountain of daughter Zion. (1) | ŠILḤÛ-kad<br>MOŠĒL-'ereṣ<br>MISSELA' mĕdabbĕrâ<br>'el-HAR bat-ṣîyyôn | *(triplets)*<br>3 šil, mošēl, missela'<br>3 ad, ĕd, at<br>3 ēl, el, 'el |
| *(male)*<br>For it is like a flock (of birds) fleeing,<br>a nestling sent out;<br>they are—the daughters of Moab—<br>made to cross over[4] at the Arnon. (2)<br>Prophesy/bring[5] counsel!<br>make intervention/prayer![6] | wĕHÂYÂ kĕ'ôph-NÔDĒD<br>qēn MĔŠULLĀḤ<br>tiHYÊNÂ BĔNÔT MÔ'ĀV<br>ma'BĀRŌT lĕa'rnôn<br>habbî'î 'ĒṢÂ<br>'ĂŚÎ pĕLÎLâ | *(doublets)*<br>2 mĕšullāḥ (+šilḥû above)<br>2 hâyâ, tihyênâ<br>1 nôdēd<br>1 mĕšullāḥ + 3 above = 4<br>2 bĕnôt, bārōt<br>2 'ēṣâ, 'ăśî |
| *(female)*<br>"Set like the night<br>your shade<br>in the midst of the noonday sun;<br>hide the outcasts;<br>the fugitive<br>do not betray; (3)<br>may they settle<br>among you, the outcasts of Moab;<br>be a refuge to them<br>from the destroyer." (4) | ŠÎTÎ kaLLAYIL<br>ṢILLēk<br>BĔTÔK ṣâHĂRāyim<br>SATTRÎ NIDDĀḤîm<br>NŌDĒD<br>'al-tĕgallî<br>yāgûrû<br>VĀK NIDDĀḤay MÔ'ĀV<br>hĕwî-SĒTER lāmô<br>mippĕnê ŠÔDĒD | *(triplets)*<br>3 šîtî, sattrî, sēter<br>3 kallayil, gal, gûrû<br>3 ayil, ṣil (+ ĕlîl above)<br>3 šîtî, ṣil (+ šil above)<br>3 niddāḥ, nōdēd, niddāḥ<br><br>2 bĕtôk, vāk<br><br>2 hĕwî, hābî' (above)<br>2 nōdēd, šôdēd (inclusio) |

[1] The following several verses have posed difficulties for translation/interpretation; BHS has the first verb, *šālaḥ*, as qal mpl imper. ('send'), and 'lambs' (for the singular *kar* in Hebrew); the appeal for help to Jerusalem as the dominant power in the region makes sense of the verb 'stretch out' or 'extend'; one expects 'hand' to follow in the proverbial symbol of power, though the appeal is to collective Israel.
[2] Reading the object not as *kar* (lamb), which makes little sense in the passage, but *kad* (water-jar), as the *rêš* and *dālet* can be indistinguishable in IQIsa[a]. Thus, send something to collect water in for refugees bereft of means of collecting water.
[3] Instead of NRSV, "from Sela, by way of the desert," re-point "from Sela *she is speaking*" (*piel* fem. sing. participle from *dābar*), referring to the one who just asked for help, a woman Moabite refugee.
[4] *Hophal* fpl participle.
[5] There is a *kĕtîb/qĕrê* for the first verb; *kĕtîb* suggests 3mpl; *qĕrê* suggests 2fs; following the *qĕrê* 2fs and pointing *not* primarily for the verb, *bô'* (*hiphil* 2fs imperative; 'bring'). Reading instead the verb *nābā'* (*hiphil* 2fs imper., thus 'prophesy'; the *nûn* drops out)—this verb can have an object (e.g., Jer 23:26, 32).
[6] Though *pĕlîlâ* is a fs noun and has the connotations both of one who judges or intervenes as well as the arbitration of justice itself, it is from the verb *pālal* (to pray, intervene). All fit the role of the prophet.

The woman prophet continues (triplet pattern) with an oracle of comfort/salvation, extraordinarily, *for Moab*, and with imagery similar to the

73. Refugees fleeing from Moab toward Judah might appear small at a distance, from a watchman's elevated height, like a flock of birds being scattered.

end of war rendered in Isa 9:5 (‘boots of tramping warriors’), and similar to Isaiah 11 in reference to the good qualities of the king.

| *(female)* | | *(triplets)* |
|---|---|---|
| Indeed, vanished[1] is violence,<br>ceased is destruction,<br>finished is trampling[2]<br>on the land. (4cd) | **kî-**’āphēs **hammēṣ**<br>**kālâ** *ŠŌD*<br>**tammû**<br>**rōmēs**<br>min-hā’āreṣ | 3 **ēs, hammēṣ, hā**’āreṣ<br>3 **hammēṣ,** tammû, rōmēs<br>3 **ālâ, ‘ālāyw,** ’ōhel<br><br>3 **šōd, ḥesed, ṣedeq** |
| And (there is) established a throne,<br>in covenantal kindness<br>and he sits on it in faithfulness<br>in the tent of David,<br>one judging<br>and seeking justice<br>and is swift (with) righteousness. (5) | **wĕ**hûkan **ba***ḤESED* **kissē’**<br>**wĕ**yāšav **‘ālāyw** **be** *’ĔMET*<br>**bĕ’ōhel Dāwid**<br>*ŠŌPHĒṬ*<br>**wĕdōrēš** *MIŠPĀṬ*<br>**ûmĕhir** *ṢEDEQ* | 3 **ba, be, bĕ**<br>3 **wĕ, wĕ, wĕ**<br>3 **Dāwid, dō**<br>3 **’ĕmet, šōphēṭ, mišpāṭ**<br><br>3 **hammēṣ, min-hā’āreṣ,**<br>**ûmĕhir** |

[1] Perfect suggests completed action, not future (contra NRSV). NJPS suggests “violence’ (thus *ḥâmmes*, perhaps infin. abs., instead of MT’s *hammēṣ* or IQIsa[a] *hamûṣ*).
[2] The term is *rāmas* (to trample, as a warrior or by horses’ hooves); cf. Isa 9:4 (Heb), *rā‘aš* (boots causing quaking or vibration).

An apparently new male voice (below) interjects with a very different tone than the woman prophet’s comfort speech and different than the previous male prophet who was sympathetic to the Moabite refugees. This voice’s words ring with sarcasm and implicit judgment of Moabite religion, ridiculing the loss of ‘raisin-cakes.’ [74] His triple mention of Moab seems to ridicule the previous voice, as does his fourfold repetition of the *g* sound to describe Moab’s pride and insolence, which he tops off with a final *g* sound to say, “*groan,* how they [the raisin-cakes] are struck down!”

| *(male)* | | *(doublets)* |
|---|---|---|
| We have heard of the pride of Moab<br>—very proud!—<br>of his arrogance,<br>and his pride,<br>and his insolence—<br>his boasts are not true! | šāma‘nû *GĔ’ÔN-MÔ’ĀV*<br>**gē’** **mĕ**’ōd<br>**ga**’ăw**ātô**<br>û*GĔ’ÔNÔ*<br>wĕ‘evr**ātô**<br>**lō’-kēn** bāddāyw | 2 **gĕ’ôn, gĕ’ôn**<br>2 **gē’, ga**<br>1 **gû**<br>1 **mô’āv** (+2 below)= **3**<br>2 **ātô, ātô**<br><br>2 **lō’-kēn, lākēn** |
| *Therefore let Moab wail*<br>for Moab;<br>(let) everyone wail<br>for the raisin cakes of Kir-hareseth!<br>Groan, how they are struck down! (6-7) | **lākēn** *YĔYĒLÎL* *MÔ’ĀV*<br>**lĕ***MÔ’ĀV*<br>**kullō** *YĔYĒLÎL*<br>**la’ăšîšê qîr-**ḥăreśet<br>teh**gû** **’ak** nĕkā’îm | 2 **yĕyēlîl, yĕyēlîl**<br>2 **mô’āv, mô’āv**<br>2 **lĕ, la**<br>2 **šîšê**<br>2 **’ak** nĕkā’îm |

74. A common food, only in Hosea (3:1) is there reference to another people’s ritual fare: “the LORD loves the people of Israel, though they turn to other gods and love raisin cakes (*ăšîšê ʿănābîm*).”

In spite of this interjection, the woman prophet resumes her lament, now more extensively for the natural environment—the vines, grain, and tragic loss of agrarian life—ending the Moabite people's fullness of life and festive occasions. She too (!) employs a fourfold use of the *g* sound (plus one more) to retort about the vines (*gephen*) that the leaders of nations (*gôyim*) cut down—that they struck *(nāgā'û)*, destroying the fruitful land (v. 8).[75] She persists in saying 'I will weep' for the vines (*gephen*) and locales of Moab, and the loss of gladness *(wāgîl)*, in v. 9 below:

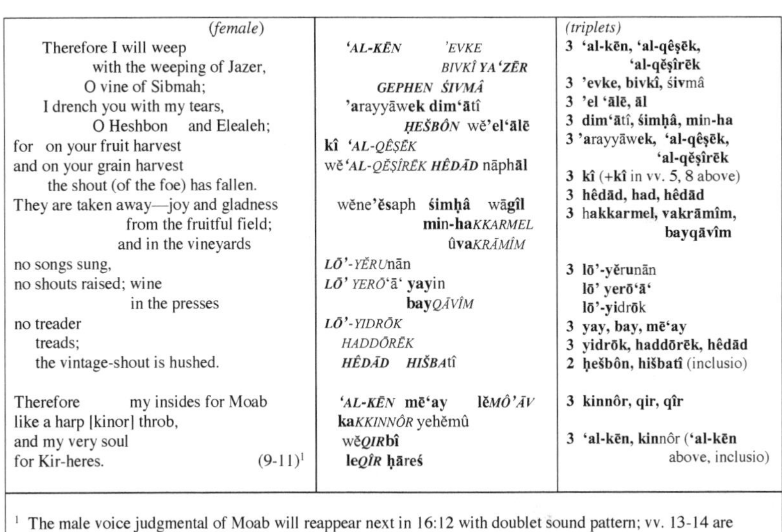

| *(female)* | | *(triplets)* |
|---|---|---|
| Therefore I will weep<br>with the weeping of Jazer,<br>O vine of Sibmah;<br>I drench you with my tears,<br>O Heshbon and Elealeh;<br>for on your fruit harvest<br>and on your grain harvest<br>the shout (of the foe) has fallen.<br>They are taken away—joy and gladness<br>from the fruitful field;<br>and in the vineyards | 'AL-KĒN 'EVKE<br>BIVKÎ YA'ZĒR<br>GEPHEN ŚIVMÂ<br>'arayyāwek dim'ātî<br>ḤEŠBÔN wĕ'el'ālē<br>kî 'AL-QÊṢĒK<br>wĕ'AL-QĔṢÎRĒK HÊDĀD nāphāl<br>wĕne'ĕsaph śimḥâ wāgîl<br>min-haKKARMEL<br>ûvaKRĀMÎM | 3 'al-kēn, 'al-qêṣēk,<br>'al-qĕṣîrēk<br>3 'evke, bivkî, śivmâ<br>3 'el 'ālē, āl<br>3 dim'ātî, śimḥâ, min-ha<br>3 'arayyāwek, 'al-qêṣēk,<br>'al-qĕṣîrēk<br>3 kî (+kî in vv. 5, 8 above)<br>3 hêdād, had, hêdād<br>3 hakkarmel, vakrāmîm,<br>bayqāvîm |
| no songs sung,<br>no shouts raised; wine<br>in the presses<br>no treader<br>treads;<br>the vintage-shout is hushed. | LŌ'-YĔRUnān<br>LŌ' YERŌ'ā' yayin<br>bayQĀVÎM<br>LŌ'-YIDRŌK<br>HADDŌRĒK<br>HÊDĀD HIŠBAtî | 3 lō'-yĕrunān<br>lō' yerō'ā'<br>lō'-yidrōk<br>3 yay, bay, mē'ay<br>3 yidrōk, haddōrēk, hêdād<br>2 ḥešbôn, hišbatî (inclusio) |
| Therefore my insides for Moab<br>like a harp [kinor] throb,<br>and my very soul<br>for Kir-heres. (9-11)[1] | 'AL-KĒN mē'ay lĕMÔ'ĀV<br>kaKKINNÔR yehĕmû<br>wĕQIRbî<br>leQÎR ḥāreś | 3 kinnôr, qir, qîr<br>3 'al-kēn, kinnôr ('al-kēn<br>above, inclusio) |

[1] The male voice judgmental of Moab will reappear next in 16:12 with doublet sound pattern; vv. 13-14 are regarded as a later addition about the dire future fate of Moab.

The woman prophet's voice, along with a sympathetic male voice, in the largely unified text of laments in Isaiah 15–16 reveals especially her compassion for a suffering people beyond Israel, the Moabites, thereby showing some affinity to the countercultural story of Ruth. Here is an extraordinary text, embedded in the book of Isaiah, of a woman prophet's lament, perhaps alongside Isaiah in dialog, that counters the dominant ideology in Israel and Judah against the Moabites, in spite of an interjecting condemnatory voice. While male prophets typically modified the dirge for woe oracles to condemn other nations, here a woman prophet, it is suggested, modified the dirge, a woman's genre, to show compassion and to lament for a foreign people suffering tragedy.

75. This term used by the poet in Isa 5:2.

## Conclusion

By examining a number of passages in First Isaiah (Isaiah 1; 5; 9; 11; 12; 15; and 16) and considering Isaiah's represented style of lyricizing in comparison to texts that contain songs of particular genres associated with women, this study has found that a woman's prophetic voice (here called 'Hannĕvî'â') can be discerned among these texts beyond Isaiah 1. She utilized a *triplet syllable sound repetition* pattern suggested to be a *signature* of biblical women's lyrical tradition, at times in dialog with a male prophet using a doublet sound pattern. Finding the same triplet soundplay technique in biblical texts clearly attributed to women (Hannah's song and the female voice in the Song of Songs) provides textual evidence across genres and books that there were different lyrical composing traditions by women and men in the culture of ancient Israel. They pursued their activities and callings in gender-based groups and yet could pursue collegial interaction within the larger society. Of course, once composed, oral lyrics could be utilized in retellings or liturgies by the community, and anyone, male or female, might benefit from them.

## CHAPTER 2

# A Woman Prophet in the Book of Micah?

THE HISTORICAL PROPHET CALLED Micah was active also during the reigns of Jotham, Ahaz, and Hezekiah, along with Isaiah, who probably preceded him slightly. Thus Micah lived and worked before, during, and after the collapse of the northern kingdom and also dealt with the threats and problems of Judah. Recent studies of Micah,[1] as with other prophetic books, have focused on both the diachronic (historically contextual and redactional) as well as the synchronic aspects (final form and shared themes). Noting alternating use of judgment and salvation in the prophetic messages, and in light of the key historical contexts of the demise of Israel (and then Judah), commentators have nevertheless focused on Micah's possible intended unity or coherence.[2] There is some consensus among commentators that the book of Micah has at least two sections: chapters 1–3 (some include 4–5), suggestive of the preexilic context of Micah's time (the latter eighth century), and chapters 6 and 7, which some suggest are added from the later Judean postexilic context. However, some scholars see close connection between the first part of the book and the last two chapters, even with some differences in lyrical style. While questions of the book's redaction are important and

1. For a detailed review of scholarship on the book of Micah, see Jacobs, "Bridging the Times." On rhetoric, see Dempsey, "Literary Artistry, Ethical Message"; Shaw, "Micah 1:10–16 Reconsidered"; Shaw, *Speeches of Micah*; for emphasis on Micah as a written work, see Ben Zvi, *Micah*. For a recent reader-response and postcolonial study of Micah, including on issues of gender, ambiguity, and justice, see Runions, *Changing Subjects*; she critiques the tendency to homogenize the image of women as oppressed victims in the Bible and oversimplification of the texts (190–94).

2. Jacobs, *Conceptual Coherence of the Book of Micah*.

have a bearing on our understanding, my aim here is not to conjecture what were original settings of the utterances, or of the redactors, but to analyze the poetic patterns and voices, in order to discern, as I did in Isaiah, whether there appears to be a woman prophet's voice, or women's prophets' voices, embedded in the book. It will be interesting to see if the practice of a dialogical dynamic of prophets' voices is represented in Micah as I propose it is in Isaiah, since Micah and Isaiah were active during the same historical time.[3] It will also be interesting to discern not only whether there *are* utterances suggested to be by a woman prophet or women prophets, but whether women's prophetic voices will be found to use the traditional *judgment speech* genre usually associated with men.

Apparently diverging from all commentators, Mayer Gruber[4] has recently drawn attention to chapters 6 and 7 of the book of Micah regarding women's voices there and has proposed the presence of two women prophets in conflict, in addition to the male prophet Micah's[5] utterances earlier in the book.[6] His was a brave proposal, and an extremely important step and open door in the reevaluation of the question at hand with regard to the book of Micah. A close examination of the rhetoric there (see below) does reveal several feminine grammatical forms suggestive of women's voices apart from references only to a personified city, even though nearly all commentators (including women) attribute every instance of women's voices to personified cities of Jerusalem or Samaria.[7] So I will draw together analysis of that element, along with another unnoticed important textual feature in Micah 7, as well as application of the theory of women's triplet-sound lyrical style for an initial assessment of

3. An implied general question is whether the redaction of the book of Micah, like the book of Isaiah, included multiple prophetic voices.

4. Gruber, "Women's Voices in the Book of Micah."

5. Note that in Jer 26:18–19, in the story about threats against Jeremiah's life, the elders intercede on his behalf, remembering Micah of Moresheth, the male prophet, and his dire words for Jerusalem.

6. Quoting Fiorenza, Gruber calls to task both "malestream," and he suggests "femalestream" scholarship, for refusing to explore realistically the possibility of a woman prophet's voice embedded in the book; Gruber, "Women's Voices, " n.p. So often it appears that modern scholars, while eschewing the reliability of authorship from attribution or headings of a male authority figure over a biblical book, at the same time are logically inconsistent in dismissing any possible women's prophetic voices by a *literalism* that, not seeing a woman's name attached, means they were absent from the arena.

7. *The Women's Bible Commentary* neglects to consider the matter; Sanderson, "Micah" in Newsom and Ringe (1998), 229–31; or Fentress-Williams (2012), 326–28.

the presence within the book of Micah of the voices of a woman prophet or women prophets.

## Micah 1

The study turns to an examination of the lyrics and style of the prophetic voice that opens the book in Micah 1.[8] Apart from the heading of the book, a male prophetic voice is indicated by a doublet sound pattern in the first seven verses, uttering a judgment oracle.[9]

| *(male)* | šimʿû ʿammîm KULLām | *(doublets)* |
|---|---|---|
| Hear, peoples, all of you; | haqšîvî *ʾEREṢ* ûmĕlōʾāh | 2 ši , šî 2 kullām ûmĕlōʾ |
| listen, O earth, and (all) who fill her; | wîhî *ʾĂDŌNĀY YHWH* | 2 kul, kal 2 ădōnāy, ădōnāy |
| and let the Lord YHWH | *BĀK*em lĕʿēd | 2 imʿû ʿammîm ām |
| against you be a witness, | *ʾĂDŌNĀY MĒHÊKAL* | 2 bāk, baq (below) |
| the Lord from his temple | *QOD*šô | 2 ʾereṣ , ʾāreṣ 2 wîhî , kî-hi |
| holy. (2) | | |
| For look! YHWH is coming forth | kî-hinnē *YHWH* yōṣēʾ | 2 YHWH , YHWH |
| from his dwelling place, | *MIMMĔQ*ômô | 2 qod, kad (below) |
| and will come down | wĕyā*RAD* | 2 qad, rād 2 kî , kî (below) |
| and stride | wĕ*DĀR*ak | 4 mēhêkal, mimmĕqôm, hehārîm , hāʿămāqîm |
| on the heights of earth.[1] (3) | ʿal-*BĀMÔ*tê *ʾĀREṢ* | 2 wĕyārad wĕdārak |
| Then the mountains will melt | wĕnāmassû *HEHĀRÎM* taḥtāyw | 4 ār , ār , ʾār , ār |
| under him | wĕ*HĀʿĂMĀQÎM* | 2 bāmô , bĕmô |
| and the valleys | yit*BAQQ*āʿû *KADD*ônag mippĕnê hāʾēš | |
| will burst open like wax before fire, | | |
| like water | kĕmayim | 2 wĕyārad bĕmôrād |
| cascading | muggārîm | 2 ka, kĕ 2 ag, gā |
| down a slope.[2] (4) | *BĔMÔRĀD* | 4 îm , îm , im, îm |

[1] NJPS.
[2] V. 4b: NJPS.

8. The context is likely ca. 701 BCE, when Assyria invaded Judah; Mays, *Micah*, 21, 53.

9. See Dempsey for the notable use of repetition of words, roots, and wordplay in Micah; "Literary Artistry, Ethical Message," 119.

| *(male)* | | *(doublets)* |
|---|---|---|
| Because of the transgression of Jacob | BĚPHEŠA ʿ YA ʿĂQŌV | 2 bě , bě |
| —all this— | | |
| and for the sins of the house of Israel. | KOL-zōʾt | 2 phešaʿ yaʿăqōv , phešaʿ ... |
| What[1] is the transgression of Jacob? | ûvěḥaṭṭôʾt bêt yiśrāʾēl | 4 ōʾt , ôʾt , bêt , bāmôt |
| Is it not Samaria? | mā-PHEŠA YA ʿĂQŌV HĂLÔ ʾ ŠŌMĔRÔN | 2 mā, mā 2 hălôʾ , hălôʾ |
| And what is the high place[2] of Judah | ûmā bāmôt yěhûdâ HĂLÔ ʾ yěRÛŠĀLĀIM | 2 šōměrôn , šōměrôn + |
| Is it not Jerusalem? (5) | | yěrûšālāim |
| And I will make Samaria | wěśamtî ŠŌMĔRÔN | |
| into a heap in the field,[3] | lěʿî HAŚŚĀDEH | 2 bām , śam 2 śāde , sōdê |
| for planting vineyards. | | 4 tî , ṭāʿê , tî + tû |
| | lěmaṭṭāʿê KĀRem | 2 lěʿî , lě 4 kār, gar, ga , ga |
| I will tumble | wěhiGGARtî | 2 laggay , ʾăgalle |
| into the valley | LAGGAY | |
| her stones and her foundations | ʾĂVĀNÊHĀ wîSŌDÊHĀ | 2 nêhā , dêhā |
| lay bare.[4] (6) | | 2 ʾăvānêhā, ʿăṣabbêhā |
| | ʾĂGALLEH | 4 wěkol, wěkol, wěkol+ kol |
| And all her images will be smashed[5] | WĔKOL- pěsîLÊHĀ yukkattû | 4 hā, hā, hā, hā (9 total) |
| and all her wages shall be burned | WĔKOL-ʾETNANNÊHĀ YIŚŚĀRPHÛ VĀ ʾĒŠ | 3 ʾetnannêhā + 2 ʾetnan |
| with fire, | | |
| and all her idols I will make a waste; | WĔKOL- ʿĂṢABBÊHĀ ʾāŚÎM | 2 ʾetnan zônâ , ʾetnan zônâ |
| | ŠĔMāmâ | 2 śîm šěm 2 śîm +śam |
| for from the wages of a prostitute | kî mēʾETNAN ZÔNÂ | (above, inclusio) |
| they were gathered,[6] | | |
| and to the wages of a prostitute | qiBBĀṢÂ | 2 kî , qi 2 ʿăṣabbê , bbāṣâ |
| they shall return. (7) | wěʿad-ʾETNAN ZÔNÂ YĀŠÛVÛ | 2 yiśśārphû , yāšûvû |

1 Q has ‘what’ rather than ‘who’.
2 Lxx, Syriac, and Targum have “sin”, not “high place.”
3 Author’s translation; the simplicity of the term ‘field’ suggests the diminishing of Samaria.
4 NJPS.
5 NJPS.
6 NJPS.

The dispute or covenant lawsuit between God and the people is against both Israel and Judah. Typical is the invocation of nature as witness and a theophany of God in relation to the forces of nature. The prophet uses both genders to critique: male Jacob (Israel) and female Samaria. Also not surprising is his personifying the city of Samaria as a prostitute for non-Yahwistic practices. However, the punishment of ‘laying bare’ her foundations echoes and embeds, as elsewhere, misogynist lyrics. However, it is important to remember that this metaphor is aimed primarily at the *male leaders* of Samaria, whose lack of loyalty to YHWH is suggested, and whose grave social injustices against the people (women and men) brought the demise of northern Israel.

The next lines have been analyzed by nearly all commentators as though they render the same male prophet’s lament. James Luther Mays calls it a “skilled adaptation of the mourning song used in the lament for the dead,”[10] which is a widely recognized feature of prophetic rhetoric adapted for judgment speeches. Yet, the lyrical artistry shows a tight triplet sound pattern in this Micah passage of the lament genre most prac-

10. Mays, *Micah*, 54.

ticed by women. The question immediately arises as to whether a male prophet proceeds to imitate a woman's dirge lament, or whether this is a woman's composing voice. A critical approach cannot simply assume that only men speak in the Bible.[11]

Let us consider the text below, with its triplet pattern, then move on to consider whether, in the larger context of the book's oracles, the voice may be that of a woman prophet embedded in the book. In the lament, reference to "her wound" refers to female Samaria, in answer to the prophet's lyric of judgment above. The voice below, after lamenting the suffering and destruction of Samaria, begins turning the focus south, rendering the devastation, one by one, of the towns along the Assyrian military's path as it marches on toward Jerusalem; poignantly, this voice also utilizes and adapts for the present context that specific lament motif of *wordplays with towns* (associated with women lamenters, who lament national defeat in 'David's' lament): "Tell it not in Gath!" (Mic 1:10; cf. 2 Sam 1:20).

The Micah text opens with a suggestive variant. The MT has, "I will lament and wail." The LXX has, "she will lament and wail." [12] In spite of the tendency for interpreters to see every female voice in biblical lyric as a personification, it is just as possible that the allusion in LXX is to an actual woman lamenting. Indeed, this lament serves a different purpose than the oft-seen laments in oracles against the nations as judgment speeches. Perhaps this is a genuine lament for Samaria and a warning of the approaching danger to Judah.

11. I have proposed that in David's represented lament (dirge) in 2 Sam 1:17–27 there are triplet and doublet soundplays embedded suggesting a performative call and response of male and female voices, though David's voice uses doublet soundplays to lament, *until* he imitates (better put, 'answers') the woman's triplet soundplay *technique* rendering Jonathan's name. For an analysis of the soundplay in David's' lament, see Lee, *Hebrew Sound Patterns and Women's Biblical Composing* (Kindle Books, 2014).

12. Noted by Beal, "System and the Speaking Subject," 181, and that the Syriac has 2nd f.s. imperatives. It is possible the Syriac suggests a tradition in which the male prophet exhorts a woman (prophet?) to lament.

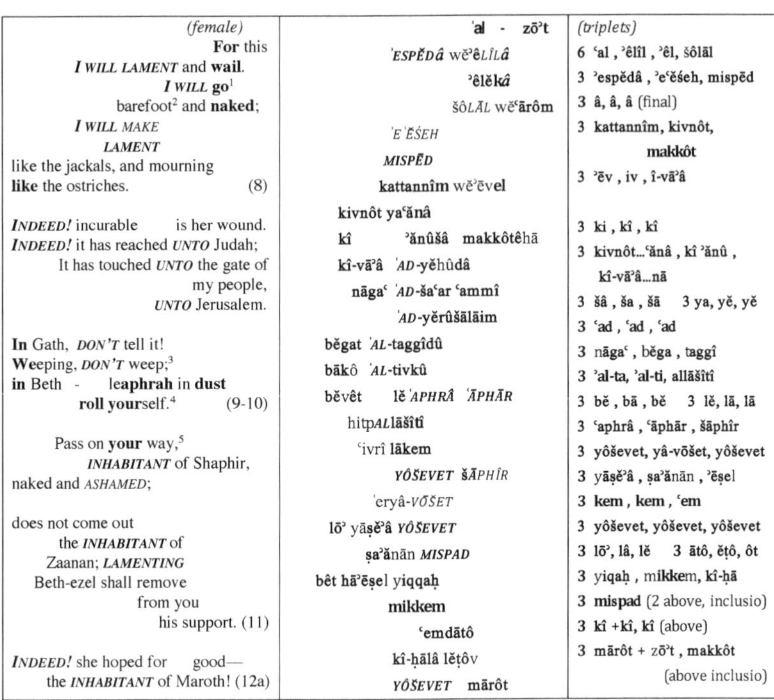

| *(female)* | ʽal - zōʼt | *(triplets)* |
|---|---|---|
| For this<br>I WILL LAMENT and wail.<br>I WILL go[1]<br>barefoot[2] and naked;<br>I WILL MAKE<br>LAMENT<br>like the jackals, and mourning<br>like the ostriches. (8) | ʼESPĔDâ wĕʼêLÎLâ<br>ʼêlĕkâ<br>šôLĀL wĕʽārôm<br>ʼEʽĔŚEH<br>MISPĒD<br>kattannîm wĕʼēvel | 6 ʽal , ʼêlîl , ʼêl, šôlāl<br>3 ʼespĕdâ , ʼeʽĕśeh, mispēd<br>3 â, â, â (final)<br>3 kattannîm, kivnôt, makkôt<br>3 ʼēv , iv , î-vāʼâ |
| INDEED! incurable is her wound.<br>INDEED! it has reached UNTO Judah;<br>It has touched UNTO the gate of my people,<br>UNTO Jerusalem. | kivnôt yaʽănâ<br>kî ʼănûšâ makkôtêhā<br>kî-vāʼâ ʽAD-yĕhûdâ<br>nāgaʽ ʽAD-šaʽar ʽammî<br>ʽAD-yĕrûšālāim | 3 ki , kî , kî<br>3 kivnôt...ʽănâ , kî ʼănû , kî-vāʼâ...nā<br>3 šâ , ša , šā 3 ya, yĕ, yĕ<br>3 ʽad , ʽad , ʽad |
| In Gath, DON'T tell it!<br>Weeping, DON'T weep;[3]<br>in Beth - leaphrah in dust<br>roll yourself.[4] (9-10) | bĕgat ʼAL-taggîdû<br>bākô ʼAL-tivkû<br>bĕvêt lĕʽAPHRÂ ʽĀPHĀR<br>hitpALlāšîtî | 3 nāgaʽ , bĕga , taggî<br>3 ʼal-ta, ʼal-ti, allāšîtî<br>3 bĕ , bā , bĕ 3 lĕ, lā, lā<br>3 ʽaphrâ , ʽāphār , šāphîr |
| Pass on your way,[5]<br>INHABITANT of Shaphir,<br>naked and ASHAMED; | ʽivrî lākem<br>YÔŠEVET ŠĀPHÎR<br>ʽeryâ-VŌŠET | 3 yôševet, yâ-vōšet, yôševet<br>3 yāṣĕʼâ , ṣaʼănān , ʼēṣel<br>3 kem , kem , ʽem |
| does not come out<br>the INHABITANT of<br>Zaanan; LAMENTING<br>Beth-ezel shall remove<br>from you<br>his support. (11) | lōʼ yāṣĕʼâ YÔŠEVET<br>ṣaʼănān MISPAD<br>bêt hāʼēṣel yiqqaḥ<br>mikkem<br>ʽemdātô | 3 yôševet, yôševet, yôševet<br>3 lōʼ, lâ, lĕ 3 ātô, ĕṭô, ôt<br>3 yiqaḥ , mikkem, kî-ḥā<br>3 mispad (2 above, inclusio)<br>3 kî +kî, kî (above) |
| INDEED! she hoped for good—<br>the INHABITANT of Maroth! (12a) | kî-ḥālâ lĕṭôv<br>YÔŠEVET mārôt | 3 mārôt + zōʼt , makkôt (above inclusio) |

[1] Multiple Mss have "let me go" (cohortative form).
[2] Qere.
[3] The admonition not to weep seems incongruous; Mays follows Schwantes in reading a likely original emphatic *lamed* rather than the particle for "not"; *Micah*, 48.
[4] Qere, appears to be an old feminine ending.
[5] There is an odd mixing of the number of the verb (singular feminine), the object 'you' (masculine plural), and the participial noun (feminine singular); the lyricist apparently refers to a single woman inhabitant who represents the plurality of people.

Here is obvious the lyricist's sophisticated artistry with pervasive triplet soundplays. This is a significant contrast to the previous prophetic speech with doublet soundplays in 1:2–7. Just a few examples will suffice, which again are suggestive of a women's lyrical tradition. The triple repetition of the particle *kî* is linked to the threefold emphasis of 'unto' *(*ʽ*ad,* ʽ*ad,* ʽ*ad*), as the Assyrians enter Judah and attack and ransack Judean towns, closer coming to "the gate of my people, *unto* Jerusalem." With the triple sound of *ga* ʽ, *ga, aggî*, the lyricist (prophet) emphasizes "in *Gath*, don't tell of it (*taggîdû*). This is not an "unoriginal" lyric[13] but is a signal of a song tradition in which the composer draws on a popular lyric and employs it anew in this context.[14] The composer's imperatives in the lament include

13. Mays, *Micah*, 56.

14. On this and the eleven wordplays here with names of towns, see Mays, *Micah*,

a mix of masculine and feminine forms, addressing men and women, but female inhabitants of towns (which need not be personified!) *three times* (*yôševet*)—of Shaphir, Zaanan, and Marot. The threefold sound repetition with *al, al, al* emphasizes "don't tell it," "don't cry," but "roll yourself" in dust, thus echoing her line above with sound emphasis (*êlîlâ, ʾêlĕkâ, šôlāl*): "I will lament and wail, barefoot . . ."

Most commentators interpret this text as a lament by the male prophet, in contrast to YHWH's voice and tone in vv. 1–7 in a different genre (though the male prophet renders YHWH's voice there). Alternatively, Timothy Beal suggestively reads Mic 1:8–9 as God's empathetic lament. He suggests it is "a biblical instance of divine abjection," and he challenges the notion that the Bible renders only a "monolithic Father, Author, and Guarantor of the Western patriarchal and hierarchical symbolic order."[15] Beal suggests that "the speaking subject of any piece of biblical discourse, divine or otherwise, can never be entirely univocal or monological."[16] Yet ironically, in interpreting the *same voice* speaking from v. 5 to v. 16 in order to show that the deity is capable of abjection and of ambiguity (both judgmental and grieving), this approach itself may impose the implied 'subject-voice' of a *male* prophet as dominant composer over this long piece. It may miss contrasting prophetic composing voices, I would suggest, of a male prophet and a female prophet, where, not surprisingly, *she renders for God* the divine lament, and together they (male and female prophet) render God's complex character. While intertextuality, multiple meanings, and the dialogical are at play, and there is "no univocal subject" in the Bible, it is also the case that the biblical traditions, in all their complexities, do convey human subjects who had an embodied voice from an indigenous culture. Whether assuming/accepting a master male narrative, or challenging the claim of that, such premises lack full recognition of women's composing voices *as speaking subjects* in this indigenous culture, and thus may erase their lyrics. This is ironic when today's sympathetic interpreters, along with some ancient biblical men, and even an assumed Deity beyond the texts—affirm(ed) Israelite women singers and prophets! Here I would invoke Musa Dube's general suggestion that the colonizing perspective that deems indigenous

---

52, 57. 'Inhabitant' in each case is the feminine form, woman inhabitant.

15. Beal, "System and the Speaking Subject," 172.

16. Ibid., 173, refers to Julia Kristeva to note that "intertextuality leads to a transgression of *monologism* . . . The Hebrew Bible has no univocal subject . . . and its divine subject is, as are all subjects of intertextual discourses, fundamentally ambivalent."

women absent or silent is not necessarily or always the case.[17] Not only is Jer 48:30–33[18] an intertextual link for YHWH lamenting, but more relevant to Micah's context, so is Isaiah 15–16, in which, it has been suggested, a woman prophet (or at the least, a woman lamenter) laments with "I" language—is it possible?—inspired by YHWH. Beal's comment about Micah 1 might be more prophetic than he imagines: "one finds traces of anxiety concerning who the 'I' of this text might be."[19] Beal does importantly push the limit of possibility in interpreting the text, as he suggests that the (male) prophet can have the male God lament like an 'abject female'; but the possibility that *an indigenous woman prophet could have lamented God's lament* has been, apparently, beyond the imagination of those of us in modern/postmodern cultures.

The last section of Micah 1 continues with the male prophetic voice's summative statements (12b, and 13b), bearing the doublet sound pattern, then a quick call and response of the two voices, as outlined below. At times, it is difficult to know who is speaking, yet the sound pattern is a consistent signal, joined usually to a shift in genre, focus, or perspective within the general rhetorical context. It should not be surprising that with v. 13a apparently the woman prophet says, "Harness the horses (*lārekeš*) to the chariot, inhabitant of Lachish," as she resumes her previous litany with wordplay on the towns (also in v. 14a), and this is also reminiscent of Miriam's and Deborah's lyrics on horses and chariots.[20] Also not surprisingly, the male voice begins personifying sinful female Daughter Zion (v. 13b) yet echoes the female voice's reference to Moresheth-gath, with Mareshah, thus suggesting the text preserved a call-and-response dynamic. Not only does each speaker prefer their own doublet or triplet soundplay, but as seen in other texts, they also pick up on their own previous syllable soundplay in creating their next line. For example, the female speaker utters *lākēn* in v. 14, which completes a triplet soundplay with her *lārekeš* and *lākîš* in her v. 13a.

17. Dube, *Postcolonial Feminist Interpretation*, 20–21.

18. Ibid., 181.

19. Ibid.

20. Mays recalls the prophetic critique of too much reliance on horses and chariots (Hos 10:13; 14:3; Isa 2:7; 30:16; 31:1; and Deut 17:16); *Micah*, 58.

<table>
<tr><td>(male)<br>Indeed has come down<br>evil from YHWH<br>to the gate of<br>Jerusalem. (12b)</td><td>kî-YĀRad<br>rāʿ mēʾēt YHWH<br>lĕšaʿar<br>YĔRûšālāim</td><td>(doublets)<br>2 ra, rāʿ 2 ār, ʿar 2 yār, yĕr<br>2 mēʾēt (compl doublet with mārôt above)<br>2 lĕ, lāim 2 ša, šā</td></tr>
<tr><td>(female)<br>Harness<br>the chariot<br>to the horses!<br>inhabitant of<br>Lachish! (13a)</td><td>RĔTŌM<br>hammERKĀvâ<br>LĀREKEŠ<br>yôševet<br>LĀKÎŠ</td><td>(triplets)<br>1 rĕtōm, et (+rāʿ mēʾēt above)<br>3 merkā , lārek , lāk<br>3 lārekeš, lākîš<br>(+ lĕšaʿar above)<br>3 eš , še , îš 2 āvâ, eve</td></tr>
<tr><td>(male)<br>The beginning of sin<br>it was to Daughter Zion;<br>indeed, in you were found<br>the transgressions of<br>Israel. (13b)</td><td>rēʾšît ḥaṭṭāʾt<br>hî' lĕvat - ṣiyyôn<br>kî - vāk nimṣĕʾû<br>pišʿê<br>yiśrāʾēl</td><td>(doublets)<br>2 rēʾšît (comp doubl w/rekeš)<br>2 ḥaṭṭāʾt hî' lĕvat<br>2 kî + kî (above) 2 ĕva , vā<br>2 ṣiyyô , ṣĕʾû 2 pišʿê , yiś</td></tr>
<tr><td>(female)<br>Therefore<br>you shall give parting gifts<br>unto Moresheth-<br>gath;<br>houses of Achzib<br>shall be a deception<br>to the kings of Israel.<br>(14)</td><td>LĀKēn<br>tittĕnî šillûḥîm<br>ʿal môrešet<br>gat<br>bāttê ʾAKZÎV<br>lĕ ʾAKZĀV<br>lĕmalkê yiśrāʾēl</td><td>(triplets)<br>3 lākēn (+ lārek , lāk above)<br>3 lākēn , lĕʾak , lĕmalkê<br>3 tit , rešet + rēʾšît (above)<br>3 gat , bāttê + ṭāʾt (above)<br>3 tê ʾakzîv, lĕʾakzāv,<br>lĕmalkê yiś<br>2 yiśrāʾēl + yiśrāʾēl (above)</td></tr>
</table>

In vv. 15–16, the male prophet utters an imperative to a female inhabitant of Mareshah to carry out the practices of grieving.[21] While his triplet repetition of the *g* sound there seems irregular in comparison to his doublet sound pattern, perhaps he uses it precisely because he is calling for female speech. Thus while the genders favor their patterns, they each may also include an occasional lyric with the other pattern for emphasis; they worked within tradition yet had freedom of expression and could innovate forms.

## Micah 2

The following text in Mic 2:1–5 again returns to a dominant *triplet sound pattern.* While the earlier lament in triplet soundplays was left open as to whether this was a woman lamenter imitated by the male prophet, or a woman prophet herself, the next text is highly suggestive, since it is a woe oracle of judgment *with a triplet sound pattern.* This is further suggestion in the Hebrew that embedded in the book of Micah may be the voice and utterances of a woman prophet, in addition to a prophetic

21. It is not necessary to read these as female personifications of the towns.

lament in 1:8–12a. Here, she condemns the exploitation of the people by the powerful ones who take their land; the oppressors will be punished when God takes away their land in return.[22] This text is significant, for perhaps the first time, at least in this study, there appears textual support for a woman prophet uttering a lyrical *judgment speech*,[23] as follows.

| *(female)* | hôy | *(triplets)* |
|---|---|---|
| Alas! | ḤŌŠĔVÊ-ʾāwen | 3 hô , ḥō , pḥō (12 h sounds) |
| for devisers of wickedness | ûphōʿălê RĀʿ | 3 ḥōšĕv +ḥōšēv, šôvēv (below) |
| and deeds of evil | ʿAL - MIŠkĕVÔ TĀM | 3 rāʿ + rāʿâ , rāʿâ (below) |
| on their beds! | bĕʾôr | 3 ʿal-miškĕ + yeš-lĕʾēl |
| At the light of | | ʿal-hammiš |
| the morning, they do it, | habbōqer yaʿĂŚÛhā | 2 bĕʾôr, bōqer |
| because | kî | 3 kĕ , qer , kî (+ 1 kî below) |
| there is power in their hands. (1) | yeš-lĕʾēl yĀDĀM | 3 ha , hā , ḥā 3 ya , ye, yā |
| They covet | wĕḥĀMĔDû | 3 tām , dām , ḥām |
| fields and seize, | śĀDÔt wĕgāzālû | 3 yādām , ḥāmĕdû , śādôt |
| and houses, and bear them away; | ûVĀTTÎM wĕnĀŚĀʾû | 3 vôtām , vāttîm , vêtô |
| they oppress | wĕʿāšĕqû | 3 yaʿăśû , śā , nāśāʾû |
| a strong man | gever ûVÊTÔ wĕʾîš | 6 yaʿăśû , śā , wĕgāzālû, |
| and his house, and a man | wĕnaḥălātô | wĕnāśāʾû, wĕʿāšĕqû , wĕʾîš |
| and his inheritance. (2) | | 3 YHWH, yihye, YHWH (below) |
| Therefore thus says YHWH: | lākēn kōh ʾĀMAR YHWH | 3 wĕn, lākēn, hin 3 ô, ô, ō |
| Look! | hinnî | 3 wĕʿāš , wĕʾîš , ʾăšer |
| A devising | ḤŌŠĒV | 3 ʾāmar, ʾāmar, yāmîr(below) |
| against this family | ʿAL-HAMMIŠpāḥâ hazzōʾt | 3 hammiš , tāmîš , mišš |
| —evil! from which | RĀʿÂ ʾăšer | 3 lōʾ , lōʾ (+lōʾ below) |
| you cannot remove | LŌʾ-tĀMÎŠû | 3 tāmîšû, têkem, tēlĕkû |
| from there your necks; | MIŠŠām ṣawwĕʾrōtêkem | 3 ām, kem, ôm |
| and you shall not walk haughtily, | wĕLŌʾ tēlĕkû rômâ | 3 rōtêkem, rômâ, ʿălêkem (below) |
| for an evil time it will be. (3) | kî ʿēt RĀʿÂ hîʾ | 3 rāʿâ , rāʿâ + rāʿ (above) |

22. See Nasuti, "Once and Future Lament."

23. However, see below, in Micah 6, for the woman prophet's similar judgment speech.

| *(female)* | | *(triplets)* |
|---|---|---|
| On that day they[1] shall raise | **bayyôm hahû᾽** yiśśā᾽ **ʿă***LÊK***em** | 3 **ba** (+ **bě, bi** below) |
| a taunt song against you, | *MĀŠĀL* | 6 **ʿălêk , ḥēleq , ḥallēq, lākēn , lěkā ,** mašlîk |
| and wail | wě**nāhâ** | |
| with bitter | **něhî** | 3 **māšāl , yāmîš lî , mašlîk** |
| lamentation, and say, | **nihyâ** *ʾĀMAR* | 3 **nāhâ , něhî , nihyâ** |
| | ***ŠĀDÔD*** | 3 **šādôd , něšaddunû , śādênû** |
| "Utterly ruined! | | |
| We are ruined— the inheritance of | **ně***ŠADD***unû** *ḤĒLEQ* | |
| my people | **ʿammî** | |
| is changed! | *YĀMÎR* | 3 **ʿammî , yāmîr, yāmîš** |
| How he removes it from me! | **ʾêk** *YĀMÎŠ LÎ* | 6 **yā, yā, yě, yihyeh,** YH |
| To our captors | **lě***ŠÔVĒV* | 1 **ʾêk** |
| our fields he divides up!"(4) | *ŚĀD***ênû** *YĚḤALLĒQ* | 2 **lākēn** (+**lākēn** above, inclusio) |
| Therefore | ***LĀKĒN*** | 3 **ḥevel , gôrāl , qhal** |
| there will not be for you | ***LŌ*** ʾ - *YIHYEH LĚK*ā | 2 **běgôrāl , biqhal** |
| one casting | *MAŠLÎk* | (+ **běʾôr, bōqer** , v. 1, inclusio) |
| the line | **ḥevel** | |
| by lot | *BĚGÔRĀL* | 2 YHWH, YHWH (v. 3, inclusio) |
| in the assembly of YHWH. (5) | *BIQHAL* ***YHWH*** | |

[1] The verb is actually singular.

In light of the previously cited evidence for a triplet soundplay in lyric to be a signature feature of women's composing, this analysis interprets that a woman prophet uttered the above lines. While the raw data above discloses a myriad of triplet soundplays for effect and enhancement of meaning, just a few examples begin to show the extraordinary lyrical artistry of her composing pattern that emphatically drives home the specifics of why God is angry over injustice and bears compassion for its victims. Not only the judgment speech, but the taunt song embedded in it, contain her threefold use of stinging verbs[24]—"they seize, they take, they oppress" (*wěgāzālû, wěnāśāû, wěāšqû*) describes the powerful ones' exploitation of the people. The devising of those same ones (*ḥōšěvê*) who take people's land will be met with God's devising (*ḥōšēv*), of taking 'their' land and doling it out to their captors (*šôvēv*). For those same ones who devise evil (*rā*), God will devise evil (*rāâ*) against them for an evil time (*rāâ*). Against those whose *hands coveted fields* (*yādām wěḥāmdû śādôt,* another stinging triple soundplay), God will intervene, stop them, and bring *them* to say, now "we are utterly ruined! (*šādôd něšaddunû*)—he (God) has taken away *our* fields (*śādênû*)!"

While it is beyond the scope of this study to analyze the entirety of the book of Micah (the remainder of chapter 2 and 3 through 5) for

24. See Dempsey's observation of the particularly heavy use of vivid verbs in Micah; "Literary Artistry, Ethical Message," 119.

the sound patterns suggestive of different prophetic voices, chapters 6 and 7 will be considered next since they have been interpreted by some scholars possibly to include a woman's prophetic voice or women's prophetic voices.

## Micah 6 and 7

Scholars are divided as to whether Micah 6[25] and at least part of Micah 7 include the prophet Micah's oracles or another's.[26] Here I will assess the lyrical sound patterns and the presence of multiple voices represented in these texts. Nearly all commentators regard the women's voices in these chapters as personifications of cities (Jerusalem and Samaria).[27]

Important for our focus on women prophets, Mic 6:4 includes an affirmation of Miriam along with Moses and Aaron, all early prophetic leaders. Judith E. Sanderson makes an important observation about the Micah 6 reference to Miriam: not only *that* she is included, but that as a woman she is "named the equal of two men." Moreover, since neither Moses' nor Aaron's nor Miriam's roles are explained in this reference (while Balak and Balaam *are* in the following verse), the three must have been well known at the time this text was created (whether in the eighth century BCE or later).[28] Mayer Gruber goes farther and suggests the strong likelihood that it was *a woman prophet* in Micah's time period who created this lyric of Miriam's remembrance.[29] This is not at all a far-fetched possibility when we consider that we have reference to a woman prophet (Hannĕvîʾâ) active during Isaiah's, and Micah's, timeframe.

25. Author's translation in Mic 6:1–2 in chart below.

26. For example, Mays, *Micah*, 9, 13, 31–32, views Micah's utterances as coming only in the first three chapters; he notes there are antiphonal voices in Micah 6–7, yet he concludes that the female voice is always a personified city.

27. Gruber's critique is applied directly to this text, of "the tendency to ignore female voices by turning them into personifications"; see Gruber, "Women's Voices. in the Book of Micah."

28. Sanderson, "Micah," in Newsom and Ringe, *Women's Bible Commentary* (1998), 230.

29. Gruber, "Women's Voices in the Book of Micah."

## Micah 6

Indeed, a consistent triplet sound pattern that opens Micah 6 is suggestive of a woman's voice. Her lyrics begin with the striking threefold repetition of "hear" (*šmʿ*), the threefold repetition of the word "dispute" (*rîv*), and threefold repetition of the name YHWH: "*Hear* now what the Lord says: Raise a dispute before the mountains and let the hills *hear* your voice. *Hear*, mountains!" While it would have been convenient if the pattern with her voice maintained itself through v. 4 that mentions Miriam, I do not find this to be the case. Instead, the doublet sound pattern picks up at v. 3 below, suggesting a male voice, that begins invoking the exodus tradition that should be remembered, by repeating 'my people, my people' (*ʿammî, ʿammî*). Here is an interesting possibility: that *a male prophet*, in dialog with a woman prophet, is about to affirm Miriam's role in his lyrics, speaking on behalf of YHWH.[30] He next emphasizes the *three* leaders with *doublet* soundplays rendering God speaking: "I brought you up from the land of Egypt. From the house of slavery I *bought you (pĕdîtîkā)*, and I sent *before your face* (*pānêkā*) Moses, Aaron, and Miriam (*ʿet-mōše ʿahărōn ûmiryām*)." This said, the prophet has created a *doublet* soundplay with Miriam's name, joined to 'Egypt' above (*miṣrayim, miryām;* see below). Thus, the opening five verses of Micah 6 suggest a female then a male prophet in dialog, and both speak YHWH's words. This suggested woman prophet, here and also further in Micah 6 below, and in Micah 7, as will be seen, certainly is, as Mayer Gruber suggests, "a highly gifted and original poet."[31] A question remains as to whether she is the same woman prophet suggested in Micah 1.

30. We should allow the possibility that the male prophet Micah might have been sympathetic to Miriam's role, particularly if he had a woman prophet as a dialogical partner as Micah 1, and other Micah texts, suggest. In any case, the vast simplification that *all* male prophets were misogynist because of negative examples of female personification of cities in some of their rhetoric, or that all men of ancient Israel oppressed or disregarded women, is an extreme modern projection beyond all the biblical evidence, and ethnocentrically dismisses an indigenous culture as not capable of any respect of women or real allowance of their leadership roles.

31. Gruber, "Women's Voices," n.p.

| *(female)* | | *(triplets)* |
|---|---|---|
| Hear now! what YHWH says: | ŠIMʿÛ-NĀʾ ʾĒT ʾăšer-YHWH ʾōmēr | 3 šimʿû-nāʾ, tišmaʿnâ, šimʿû |
| Raise a dispute | qûm RÎV | 3 ʾēt , ʾet , ʾet (+hāʾētānîm) |
| before the mountains | ʾET-HEHĀRÎM | 3 YHWH, YHWH, YHWH |
| and let hear the hills your voice. (1) | wĕTIŠMAʿNÂ haggĕvāʿôt qôlekā | 12 mʿû, ʾōm, ûm, ma, mʿû, mō, mô +5 îm |
| Hear, mountains![1] | ŠIMʿÛ HĀRÎM | |
| the dispute of YHWH, | ʾET-RÎV YHWH | 3 rîv , rîv , rîv |
| and enduring foundations of earth! | wĕHĀʾĒTĀNÎM mōsĕdê ʾāreṣ | 3 hehārîm, hārîm, hāʾētānîm |
| Indeed a dispute YHWH has | kî RÎV laYHWH | 1 kî |
| with his people, | ʿim-ʿammô | 3 qôlekā , kî , akkāḥ |
| and with Israel | wĕ ʿim- yiśrāʾēl | 2 yiśrāʾēl , yitwakkāḥ |
| he will contend. (2) | yitwakkāḥ | |
| [1] The Hebrew does not have "you." | | |

Her call to hear God's dispute is followed by the male prophet's unfolding of the dispute by YHWH's hearkening back to the exodus.

| *(male)* | | *(doublets)* |
|---|---|---|
| "My people[1]! What did I do to you? | ʿAMMÎ ME-ʿĀŚîtî lĕkā | 2 ʿammî , ʿammî |
| In what have I wearied you? | ûMÂ HELʾĒTÎKĀ | 2 me , ûmâ |
| Answer me! (3) | ʿĂNĒH vî | 2 helʾētîkā , heʿĕlitîkā |
| Indeed! I brought you up | kî HEʿĔLITÎKĀ | 2 miṣrayim , miryām |
| from the land of Egypt, | mēʾereṣ MIṢRAYIM | 2 ešlaḥ , mōše |
| and from a slave-house I bought you; | ûmibbêt ʿăvādîm PĔDÎTÎKĀ | 2 mē , ûmi |
| and I sent before your face | wāʾešlaḥ lĕPHĀNÊKĀ | 2 pĕdîtîkā , phānêkā |
| Moses, Aaron, and Miriam! (4) | ʾet-mōše ʾahărōn ûMIRYĀM | 1 ʾet-mōše ʾahărōn ûmiryām |
| My people, remember now | ʿAMMÎ zĕkār-nāʾ | 2 me-ʿāśîtî, ma-yyāʿaṣ |
| what he devised, | ma-yyāʿAṢ | 2 ma , ûme ('what?'4x total) |
| Balaq, king of Moab, | BĀLāq melek môʾāv | 2 ʿănēh , ʿānâ |
| what he answered him— | ûme-ʿĀNÂ ʾōtô | 2 môʾāv + mibbêt ʿăv(above) |
| Balaam | BILʿām | 2 bāl , bil |
| son of Beor— | ben-bĕʿôr | 2 be , bĕ |
| from Shittim to Gilgal | min-haššiṭṭîm ʿad-haggilgāl | 4 ʿad, daʿat, id |
| so that you may know | lĕmaʿan daʿat | 1 YHWH |
| the saving acts of YHWH." (5) | ṣidqôt YHWH | |
| [1] Foll. NJPS. | | |

Next in Micah 6 comes a quoted male voice (note the doublet pattern) asking the infamous, likely sarcastic[32] question about what God expects in the way of a sacrifice. Interestingly, just following this quoted voice, in this analysis it is the woman prophet who answers him, indicated by the triplet sound pattern. An occasional doublet appears for emphasis, like "what, what?"

32. For this interpretation, see Scoggin, "Expository Exegesis."

| *(a quoted male)* | | *(doublets)* |
|---|---|---|
| "With what shall I come before YHWH, | **bammâ** *ʾĂQADDĒM YHWH* | 2 YHWH , YHWH |
| and bow before God | **ʾikkaph lĕʾlōhê** | 2 ba , ba 4 bĕ bĕ bĕ bĕ |
| on high? | **mārôm** | 2 mâ, mā 2 men, men |
| Shall I come before him | ha*ʾĂQADDĔM*ennû | 2 ʾăqaddēm , ʾăqaddēm |
| with burnt offerings, | **vĕʿôlôt** | 6 lĕʾlōhê , vĕʿôlôt, gālîm, |
| with calves, offspring a year old? (6) | **baʿăgālîm bĕnê šānâ** | ʾalphê ʾêlîm, naḥălê |
| Or will be pleased YHWH | hăyirṣeh *YHWH* | 5 ha, hă, ḥă, ha, ḥa |
| with thousands of rams? | **bĕʾalphê ʾêlîm** | 2 šānâ , šāmen 8 'n' |
| with ten thousands of rivers of oil? | *BĔRIVVÔT* naḥălê-šāmen | 2 bĕrivvôt , pĕrî viṭnî |
| Shall I give my firstborn[1] | | 6 haʾettēn + 4 î (final), |
| (for) my transgression? | *HAʾETT*ēn **bĕkôrî pišʿî** | ḥaṭṭaʾt + 1 î 2 pišʿî , pĕrî |
| my fruit of my body | *PĔRÎ VIṬNÎ* | 3 kaph, ʾalphê, naphšî |
| (for) the sin of my soul?" (7) | *ḤAṬṬAʾT* **naphšî** | 2 šʿî, šî |
| *(female)* | | *(triplets)* |
| He has told (to) you, | higgîd *LĔKĀ* | 3 higgîd , ʾādām , dôrēš |
| 'adam', | **ʾādām** | 3 ma , ûmâ, mimmĕ |
| what is good; | *MA-ṬÔV* | 3 maṭôv, mišpāṭ, ʾahăvat |
| and what YHWH is seeking | û*MÂ-YHWH* dôrēš | 1 YHWH |
| from you: | **mimmĕkā** | 3 ʿăś , ḥes, haṣ |
| But to do justice, | **kî** *ʾIM*-**ʿăśôt miš***PĀṬ* | 3 mim, ʾim, ʿim 8 'm' |
| and to love | **wĕʾahă***VAT* | 3 wĕʾahăvat, ḥesed, wĕhaṣnēaʿ |
| kindness, | *ḤES***ed** | 2 ḥesed, higgîd (inclusio) |
| and humbly to walk | **wĕ***HAṢ*nēaʿ *LEKET* | 3 lĕkā, leket, ʾĕlōhêkā |
| with your God. (8) | *ʿIM - ʾĔLŌHÊKĀ* | 3 ĕkā, ĕkā, êkā |

[1] Hebrew does not have "for" (ie, in exchange for); the father lays his transgression onto his firstborn.

The woman prophet's response above to the question of what is expected of humans uses *four* primary triplet soundplays in a stinging retort of truth; "he has *told* you (*higgîd*), *human* (*ʾādām*) what the Lord is *seeking* (*dōrēš*) from you. Then comes not just one thing, not just three things, but a threefold list, also in triplets(!): *tōv, mišpāṭ, ahăvat* (*good, justice, love*); and *ʾahăvat, ḥesed,* and *haṣnēa* (*love, kindness, and humility*). Moreover, *you* (*lĕkā*) then are *to walk* (*leket*) with *your God* (*ʾĕlōhêkā*). What appears in translation as a famous threefold ethical statement has multiple layers of soundplay emphasis in the lyrics and, I would suggest, was created and given its very shape *by the women's lyrical tradition.*

In the very next line (v. 9), a voice with a doublet pattern rejoinder—the male prophet, I would suggest—affirms the woman prophet's voice.

| *(male)* | | *(doublets)* |
|---|---|---|
| The voice of YHWH to the city cries.<br>Yah's wisdom–she fears[1] your name.<br>Hear, O tribe!<br>for who has appointed her?[2]<br>(9) | **qôl** ***YHWH*** **lāʿîr** *YIQRĀʾ*<br>wĕtûši**yyâ** *YĀRĔʾÂ* ***ŠĔM*****ekā**<br>***ŠIMʿ*****û** **maṭṭeh**<br>**ûmî yĕʿādāh** | **2 YH , yâ**<br>**2 yiqrāʾ , yārĕʾâ**<br>**2 šĕm , šim 2 ʿû ma, ûmî**<br>**1 ʿādāh + ʾādā**m (above, inclusio) |

[1] The ancient witnesses and current translations range widely on the Hebrew of this apparent interjection that comments on what came before and calls people to listen to the judgment speech to follow. Here I translate the MT term *yr'h* (pointed as Qal imperf., 3ms, from *r'h*, 'to see," which makes little sense), instead as the verb 'to fear' (thus NRSV, but it has 'to fear' as an infinitive but there is no *lamed*). I point it as 3fs Qal perf.: "she has feared" (*yārĕʾâ*), i.e., her prophetic speech shows she reveres the name of YHWH.
[2] LXX has 'who has appointed *the city*,' another female personification of the city.

In a text that has been difficult to make sense of, the line falls into place when the rhetorical context of multiple prophetic voices is allowed, including a woman, who here, I suggest, is referred to as 'the voice of YHWH to the city':

> The voice of YHWH to the city cries—
> Yah's wisdom (she fears your name!)
> *Hear*, O tribe! for who has appointed her? (9)

'Yah's wisdom'[33] translates *tûšiyyâ,* a feminine noun, which has the connotation of 'sound' wisdom or advice,[34] suggestive of what has just been heard. (It is what Lady Wisdom referred to in Prov 8:14: "I have good advice and sound wisdom.") In what appears to be an 'aside', the male prophet suggests the female prophet (she) reveres 'your' (YHWH's) name. Therefore, he calls for the 'tribe' being addressed to listen (masculine imperative). "For who has appointed her?" The implied answer is, YHWH has appointed her to speak.

It is not possible to identify historically who was this woman prophet represented by the text, though the woman prophet with Isaiah lived during Micah's context. Because this woman prophet is included in the book of Micah, one might assume that it is a different woman prophet associated with him. In any event, I will create an appellative for the purposes of referring to her. While the book represents Micah as uttering the term *šimʿû* to open Micah 1, Mic 6:1 opens with the proposed woman prophet's emphatic term, *šimʿû-nā* ("Hear now!"). Let it be, perhaps, her appeal and her appellative, for now, "Šimuna."

33. NRSV and NJPS both translate 'wisdom'; I have simply added the soundplay embedded in the Hebrew term with the name Yah.

34. BDB, 444.

The judgment oracle in Micah 6 announced by the woman prophet, then begun to be rendered by the male prophet, followed by the above exchanges, now continues; vv. 10–16 below are entirely in the triplet sound pattern. 'Šimuna' continues with the judgment oracle and brings it to its conclusion in the following seven verses.

| *(female)* | | *(triplets)* |
|---|---|---|
| Still can I forget in the wicked house | ʿôd *HAʾIŠ* **bêt** ***RĀŠĀʿ*** | 3 **ʿôd, ʾōṣĕrôt, rāzôn** |
| treasures of wickedness | ʾōṣĕrôt ***REŠAʿ*** | 3 **rāšāʿ , rešaʿ , rešaʿ** |
| and the cursed cheating measure? (10) | wĕʾêphat rā*ZÔN* **zĕʿûmâ** | 3 **zôn zĕʿûmâ , ʾezke ,** |
| | | **mōʾzĕnê** |
| Can I tolerate | **haʾezke** | 3 **ʾezke , zĕnê ,** ʾ**avnê** |
| scales wicked | **bĕmōʾ***ZĔN***ê** ***REŠAʿ*** | 3 **mâ, mō, mâ (20 'm')** |
| and a bag of dishonest weights!? (11) | **ûvĕkîs ʾavnê mirmâ** | 3 **ʾăšer ʿăšîrê , šāqer** |
| That | *ʾĂŠER* | 3 **haʾiš , hāmās , hašmēm** |
| her wealthy | *ʿĂŠÎR*êhā | 6 **bê , bĕ , bā, bĕ , be, bĕ** |
| are full of violence? | **mālĕʾû** *ḤĀMĀS* | 3 **ālĕʾû , ûlĕ , ĕlê** |
| Her inhabitants speak lies, | wĕyōšĕvêhā dibbĕrû - *ŠĀQER* | 3 **šĕ, šā, šô** |
| with their tongues of deceit | **ûlĕšônām rĕmiyyâ** | |
| in their mouths. (12) | **bĕ**phî*HEM* | |
| | | 3 **hām, hem, hašmēm** |
| And I have even struck you weak, | **wĕ**gam- **ʾănî heḥĕlêtî** *HAKKÔTEKĀ* | 3 **hakkôtekā ,** |
| stunned you[1] for your sins— (13) | *HAŠMĒM* *ʿAL-ḤAṬṬŌʾTEKĀ* | **ʿal-ḥaṭṭōʾtekā , ʾattâ tōʾkal** |
| (but now) you[2] go on eating! | *ʾATTÂ TŌʾKAL* | 2 šḥă**kā , qir**be**kā** |
| with no satisfaction | ***WĔLŌʾ*** *TIŚBĀʿ* | 3 **lōʾ ti**śbāʿ, **lōʾ taphlîṭ ,** |
| and your bottomless pit | **wĕ**yešḥă**kā** | **tĕphallēṭ** |
| within you.[3] | **bĕ**qir**bekā** | |
| You are hoarding, but *not* safeguarding, | **wĕtass**ēg ***WĔLŌʾ TAPHLÎṬ*** | 3 ʾ**ett**ē**n** (+ **a**ṭṭō, ʾ**attâ** above) |
| and what you safeguard, | **waʾăše**r ***TĔPHALLĒṬ*** | 1 ʾ**ett**ē**n** (+2 ʾ**attâ , ʾattâ** |
| to the sword I will hand it over. (14) | la**ḥ**erev *ʾETTĒ*n | below) |

[1] NJPS's word.
[2] Possibly a wordplay is at work here with "you" and "now!" to capture the ironic audacity.
[3] Not "a gnawing hunger" (NRSV, NJPS similarly)—the verses describe not hunger but insatiable *greed*; the rare noun *yšḥ* (perhaps 'emptiness'; BDB, 445) likely related to the noun *šḥt* ("pit'; BDB, 1001).

In her judgment speech the woman prophet critiques the abusive practices of the powerful in society, and in the "wicked house." Is this a house of a merchant? The king's house? In either case, she refers to 'her' wealthy and 'her' inhabitants, suggestive of the female persona of the city of Jerusalem. The woman prophet expresses God's scathing critique using the lyrical artistry passed down by the women of ancient Israel: "Can I forget in the *wicked* (*rāšā)* house the treasures of *wickedness* (*rešaʿ*) . . . can I tolerate *wicked* (rešaʿ) scales? Can I tolerate . . . *that* her *wealthy* (*ʾăšer ʿăšîrêhā*) are full of violence? . . . and *lies* (*šāqer*)" they speak. Through most of these lyrics, the object of the verbs is addressed to a singular masculine 'you' (except in v. 16). "I have *struck you* (*hakkôtekā*) for *your sins* (*ḥaṭṭōtekā*)—(but now) *you go on eating* (*ʾattâtōkal*)!" (vv.13–14a).

But for all you hoard, she says with more triplet soundplays, there is "no satisfaction" (*lōʾ tiśbāʿ*), "no safeguarding" (*lō taphlît*), and what you "safeguard" (*tĕphallēṭ*), "I" (God) will give to the sword of the enemy. She continues below, not only linking God's "giving away" (*ʾettēn*) their spoil to God's now emphatic "you" (*ʾattâ, ʾattâ*), but her lyrics exponentially increase from three to *six* soundplays, and even to *nine*.

| *(female)* | | *(triplets)* |
|---|---|---|
| *You* shall sow, but *not* reap;<br>*you* shall tread olives, but *not* anoint with oil,<br>and juice of grapes<br>but *not* drink wine. (15) | *ʾATTÂ TIZRAʿ* **WĔLŌʾ** *TIQṢÔR*<br>*ʾATTÂ TIDRŌKĔ*-zayit **WĔLŌʾ**- *TĀSÛK*<br>**šemen**<br>**wĕ***TÎRÔŠ* **WĔLŌʾ** *TIŠ***teh**-yāy**in** | 3 **ʾattâ , ʾattâ** (+ ʾettēn above)<br>6 **tizraʿ / tiqṣôr**<br>**tidrōkĕ-za / tāsûk**<br>**tîrôš / tišteh**<br>3 **wĕlōʾ , wĕlōʾ , wĕlōʾ** |
| For you are keeping the laws of Omri<br>and all the practices of Ahab's house;<br>and you have walked in their ways.<br><br>Therefore, I will make you<br>a desolation, and her inhabitants<br>an object of hissing;<br>and the scorn of my people<br>you shall bear. (16) | **wĕy***IŠTAMM***ēr ḥuqqôt ʿomrî**<br>**wĕkōl ma***ʿĂŚĒ* **vêt-ʾaḥʾāv**<br>**wa**ttē**lĕkû** bĕ**mō** *ʿĂṢÔTĀM*<br>**lĕmaʿan tittî ʾōtĕkā**<br>**lĕ***ŠAMM***â wĕyōšĕvêhā lišrēqâ**<br>**wĕ**ḥerpat **ʿammî** *TIŚŚĀʾ*û | 6 **štam , ʿām , ṣôtām,**<br>**maʿan , šam , ʿam**<br>9 **wĕ (8) + wa (1)**<br>3 **qôt, kōl, kû** 3 **lĕ, lĕ, lĕ**<br>3 **tittî ʾōtĕkā** 3 **ēqâ, êhā, ēqâ**<br>3 **lĕša, šĕ , liš**<br>3 **maʿăśē , mōʿăṣôtām ,**<br>**ʿammî tiśśāʾû** |

The prophet renders a triple denial from the deity: "You shall sow, but *not* (*wĕlōʾ*) *reap;* you shall tread olives, but *not* (*wĕlōʾ*) *anoint* yourselves with oil, and juice of grapes but *not* (*wĕlōʾ*) *drink* wine." Alliteration of *ten* Hebrew syllables beginning with the *t* sound are embedded in this verse to emphasize YHWH's rejection of those enjoying the fullness of life while abusing others.

## Micah 7

The voice of the woman prophet continues in Micah 7 (below) with triple soundplays, now with a personal lament. "Woe is me! For I am like the gatherer of summer fruit (*qayiṣ*) . . . (but) there is no cluster to eat!" This recalls God's question of Amos, "What do you see?" He answered, "*qayiṣ*"—a basket of summer fruit. In a wordplay, God responded, "the *qēṣ* ('end') has come upon my people Israel" (Amos 8:1–2). If the woman prophet here, after Amos' time, is symbolically a gatherer of the *qayiṣ*, then perhaps she is present to see the devastated 'orchard' of Judah when there is nothing left. In lamenting, she also speaks God's pathos, who like a woman gleaner disappointingly sees no fruit that one would expect. Sociologically, she/God may be like the vineyard owner, or like the poor one who comes with expectation to be satisfied, only to be disappointed, thus echoing Hannĕvîʾâ's and Isaiah's poetic vision in Isaiah 5. As before, she describes the rampant violence and corruption and now warns of the violation of trust in all human relationships.[35] Triplet soundplays permeate these lines.

| *(female)* | ʾallay lî | *(triplets)* |
|---|---|---|
| Woe is me! | kî hāyîtî | 3 ʾallay lî, kî āyîtî , qayiṣ |
| Indeed I am | kĕʾospê-qayiṣ | |
| like the gatherer[1] of summer fruit,[2] | KĔʿŌLĕlōt bāṣîr | 3 kî , kĕ , kĕ |
| like the gleaners[3] of grapes— | ʾên-ʾešKÔL | 3 ʾos, ayiṣ , āṣîr |
| no cluster | leʾĕKÔL | 3 kĕʿōlĕlōt, kôl , leʾĕkôl |
| to eat! | bikkûrâ ʾiWWĔTâ NAPHŠÎ | 3 ʾallay, ʿōlĕle, leʾĕ |
| or first-ripe fig my soul[4] could desire.[5] (1) | ʾāvad | 3 ʾên + min , ʾāyin |
| Perished are the faithful from the land, | ḥāsîd min-hāʾāreṣ | 5 ʾāvad ḥāsîd , bāʾādām , lĕdāmîm, yāṣûd |
| and upright among 'adam'—none! | wĕYĀŠĀR bāʾĀDĀM ʾāyin | 18 'h' sounds |
| They all, for blood, lie in wait— | KULLām lĕDĀMÎM yeʾĕrōvû | 2 yāšār, yāšār (below) |
| a man for his brother, they hunt to destroy. (2) | ʾîš ʾet-ʾāḥîhû yāṣûdû ḥērem | 6 ḥāsîd, hāʾāreṣ, ʾāḥîhû, ḥērem , hāraʿ, haśśar |
| With evil their hands are adept— | ʿal-hāraʿ kappayim lĕhêṭîv | 3 hāʾāreṣ, hāraʿ, haśśar |
| the official asks, | haśśar ŠŌʾEL | |
| and the judge is bribed, | wĕhAŠŠŌPHEṭ bAŠŠILLÛm | 3 šōʾēl , haššō , baššill |
| and the powerful is speaking; | wĕHAGGĀDÔL DŌVēr | 3 ʾiwwĕtâ naphšî (above), wĕhaššōphēṭ, hawwat naphšô |
| the desire of his soul it is— | haWWAT NAPHŠÔ hûʾ | |
| so they have contrived. (3) | wayĕʿabbĕtûhā | |

1 Reading with LXX, fs participle, but reading an asseverative kaf, not 'like.'
2 In Isa 16:9, the woman lamenting also used this term alliteratively.
3 This appears to be a fpl participle in construct (following the mpl participle before it, thus a gender-matched parallelism), with male 'gatherers' and female 'gleaners.' Unfortunately modern translations remove the active sense of the verbs and their gendered subjects to focus simply on the end of the harvest season rather than the "I" prophetic speaker's pointed simile implying familiarity with this experience.
4 "Soul" is not the best translation for *nepheš*, but "life" or "being" or "I" doesn't quite capture it either.
5 "Desire," foll. NJPS.

After lamenting the unethical practices of leaders and family members against each other, the woman prophet in v. 4 below says, "the day of your *sentinels* . . . has come." In numerous biblical texts, the term "sentinel" (*mĕṣappeh,* from the verb 'to watch,' *ṣāpāh*) is used as a metaphor for a prophet (Hos 9:8; Isa 21:6; 52:8; Jer 6:17; Ezek 3:17; 33:1–6; Hab 2:1).[36] The regular sentinel would hold a post or stand watch over the city

35. Gruber, "Women's Voices in the Book of Micah" notes her "gender-matched synonymous parallelism" across vv. 5–6.

36. Usually in the *piel* form. Gafney, *Daughters of Miriam*, 145n2, 203, notes the Babylonian Talmud refers to prophets at the end of the first temple period as "watchers," and the term is found in Isaiah, Jeremiah, Nahum, Habakkuk, Zechariah, and

and announce when danger (or a messenger) was approaching. Likewise, the prophet was God's metaphorical sentinel for a city or nation, often bringing dire news to warn the people. It will be highly significant, then, that the woman prophet in v. 7 below will use this verb to refer to herself.

| *(female)* | | *(triplets)* |
|---|---|---|
| The best of them<br>is like a brier,<br>the upright worse than[1] a thornhedge<br>–the day of your sentinels,<br>of your punishment, has<br>come–<br>now will be<br>their confusion. (4) | ṬÔVām<br>KĔḤĒDEQ<br>YĀŠĀR MIMMĔSÛKÂ<br>yôm MĔṢAPPÊKĀ<br>PĔQUDDĀTKĀ vā'â<br>'ATTÂ TIHyeh mĕvûkātām | 3 ṭôvām kĕḥēdeq ,<br>pĕquddātkā vā'â<br>(+haggādôl dōvēr above)<br>3 kâ , kā , kā<br>3 mimmĕsûkâ , mĕṣappêkā,<br>mĕvûkātām<br>3 'attâ tih , 'al-ta'ămînû,<br>'al-tivṭĕḥû |
| Put no faith in a friend,<br>do not trust<br>in a loved one;<br>from her lying in your embrace,<br>guard the doors of your mouth. (5) | 'AL-TA'ămînû vĕrēa'<br>'AL-TIVṭĕḥû<br>bĕ'allûph<br>MIŠŠŌKevet ḥêqekā<br>ŠĔMŌr pitḥê-PHÎKĀ | 3 vā'â , vû, vĕrēa'<br>3 'al , 'al , 'all<br>3 pêkā, pĕq (above) + phîka<br>3 mĕsûkâ (above) +<br>miššōke , šĕmō |
| Indeed! a son disrespects<br>a father, a daughter rises up<br>against her mother, a daughter-in-law<br>against her mother-in-law;<br>a man's enemies are men of<br>his own house! (6) | kî-vēn mĕnABBĒL<br>'āv bat qāmâ<br>vĕ'immāh kallâ baḥămōtāh<br>'ōyĕvê 'îš 'anšê<br>vêtô | 2 ḥêqekā , ḥê-phîkā ,<br>ḥămōtāh (below)<br>4 vām, tām, qām, ḥăm<br>9 vām, vā'â, vû, vĕ, vet,<br>vēn, vĕ, vê, vê (total) |

1 Foll. NJPS.

In the next verses (7:7–8, 10), the prophetic speaker makes a first-person self-reference, in connection with her vocation, but also her own hardship, in relation to her faith in God. She says, "But I, for the Lord, I will *watch* (as a sentinel; *'ăṣappeh).* That this is a woman speaker is further corroborated by the feminine grammar in the lines, where she quotes her enemy as speaking against 'her' in v. 10. Mayer Gruber's assessment of a persecuted woman prophet here is on target,[37] in contrast to many commentators who regard the woman's voice as the persona of the city. However, I would disagree that we can know who her female enemy is. It need not necessarily be another female prophet, as Gruber claims, since the prophets could evoke enemies from all social quarters.

Daniel.

37. Gruber, "Women's Voices in the Book of Micah."

| | | |
|---|---|---|
| *(female)*<br>But I, for YHWH, I will watch,<br>I will wait<br>for the God of my salvation;<br>my God will hear me. (7)<br>Do not rejoice, O my enemy;<br>when I fall,<br>I rise;<br>when I sit in darkness,<br>YHWH is my light.(8) | waʾănî baYHWH ʾăṣappeh<br>ʾÔḤÎLÂ<br>LĔʾLŌHÊ YIŠʿÎ<br>YIŠMĀʿĒNÎ<br>ʾĔLŌHĀY ʾal-TIŚMĔḤÎ ʾōyavtî lî<br>KÎ nāphaltî<br>qāmtî<br>KÎ -ʾēšēv baḥōšek YHWH ʾôr lî | *(triplets)*<br>3 YHWH , ya , YHWH<br>3 waʾănî , māʿēnî , mĕḥî<br>3 ʾôḥîlâ , lĕʾlōhê , ʾĕlōhāy<br>3 lē , lî , lî 3 ʾĕl , ʾal , al<br>3 yišʿî , yišmāʿēnî , tiśmĕḥî<br>2 kî , kî 3 ʾal-ti, altî, āmtî<br>2 kî-ʾēšēv baḥōšek<br>6 ti , tî , tî , tî , tî , tî |
| *(male)*<br>Indignation of<br>YHWH I must bear,<br>because I have sinned against him,<br>until he disputes<br>my dispute and settles<br>my justice.<br>He will bring me out to the light;<br>I shall see<br>his righteousness. (9) | zaʿaph<br>YHWH ʾEŚŚĀʾ<br>KÎ ḥāṭāʾtî lô<br>ʿad ʾăšer yāRÎV<br>RÎVÎ wĕʿĀŚÂ<br>mišpāṭî yôṣîʾēnî lāʾôr ʾerʾeh<br>bĕṣidqātô | *(doublets)*<br>2 zaʿaph (compl w/ʾăṣappeh)<br>2 ʾeśśāʾ , ʿāśâ 2 ʾăš , iš<br>1 YHWH 2 rîv rîvî 1 kî<br>3 ṭāʾtî, pāṭî, qātô<br>2 lāʾôr (ʾôr lî above) 2 ṣîʾ, ṣi |
| *(female)*<br>Then my enemy will see,<br>and shame will cover<br>the (woman) who said to me,<br>"Where is YHWH<br>your God?"<br>My eyes<br>will look against her;<br>now she will be trodden down<br>like the mire of the streets. (10) | wĕTĒREʾ ʾōyavtî<br>ûtĕkassehā vûšâ<br>hāʾōmĕrâ ʾĒLAY ʾayyô YHWH<br>ʾĔLŌHĀYIK<br>ʿÊNAY<br>TIRʾÊNNÂ bāh<br>ʿattâ tihye lĕmirmās<br>kĕṭîṭ ḥûṣôt | *(triplets)*<br>3 tēreʾ, mĕr, tirʾênnâ<br>3 ʾōyavtî + ʾayyô, ye (below)<br>3 hā, hā, ḥû<br>1 YHWH +2 above = 3<br>3 ʾēlay , ʿênay ,ʾênnâ<br>3 ʾēlay , ʾĕlōhāyik , ʿênay<br>3 mĕr, mirmās 3 ti , ti , ṭî<br>1 ʿattâ tihye (inclusio with<br>ʿattâ tihye v. 4 above) |

V. 9 appears to be an interjecting voice in the flow of these lines. I will disagree with those who interpret that v. 9 is the same "I" voice of the woman prophet who has been speaking, suggesting she admits sinning against God. While it is not impossible for a prophet to 'confess,' it is highly unusual. A close look at the poetry further reveals a disjuncture between her words about her enemy from v. 8 to v. 10. Verse 9 is a non sequitur; it bears a doublet sound pattern suggestive of an interjecting male voice. Just why it is heard here or is put here is unclear. However, a clue to the dynamic may be seen in the intention by the voice of v. 9, or a redactor, to match the woman prophet's previous line, *waʾănî bayhwh ʾăṣappeh* ("But I, for the Lord, *I will watch,*" *as a sentinel/prophet*), with 'his' words, put into her mouth: *zaʿap* YHWH *eśśaʾ* ("The Lord's indignation I must bear," because I have sinned against him.) While the woman prophet lamented being in the darkness, suggestive of the suffering of persecution, this voice seems to impute her darkness is of her own cause, and God needs to bring her to the light! (In my view, it is more likely that a later redactor is trying to 'put her in her place.')

Micah 7:11–15 closes with poetry marked by a doublet sound pattern in lyrics that express oracles of comfort for a future time. The poetry of vv. 16–20, however, shows minimal doublet sound patterns and diverges markedly from the lyrics of the book's other chapters.

## Conclusion

This partial treatment of the sound patterns embedded in the Hebrew of the book of Micah has shown that there appear to be at least two different, composing prophetic voices represented by the lyrics. Therefore, it follows the same design as First Isaiah, suggestive of a male and female prophet in partnership, including dialogical performance.

# PART 2

# Named Women Prophets in Premonarchic Israel: Seers and Singers

# CHAPTER 3

## Miriam and the Song of the Sea[1]

WE HAVE SEEN IN the book of Micah (6:4) the invoking of three prophetic leaders from the exodus liberation tradition—Moses, Aaron, and Miriam—esteemed as God's servants in the rescue of an enslaved and suffering Hebrew people.[2] It is also proposed in the book of Micah alternating prophetic voices using doublet and triplet sound patterns, most notably the triplet pattern by a woman's voice in Micah 6 and 7.

Within Exodus, Miriam is called a 'prophet' (Exod 15:20).[3] Miriam appears in the books of Exodus and Numbers,[4] but through much of the

1. See early studies, e.g., by Cross and Freedman, *Studies in Early Yahwistic Poetry*, 31–45; Cohen, "Miriam's Song"; Brenner, *Israelite Woman*, 46–56; Burns, *Has the Lord Indeed Spoken*; Anderson, "Song of Miriam Poetically"; Brueggemann, "Response to 'The Song of Miriam'"; Trible, "Bringing Miriam out of the Shadows"; Janzen, "Song of Moses, Song of Miriam"; Bach, "With a Song in Her Heart"; Graetz, "Did Miriam Talk Too Much?"; Meyers, "Miriam the Musician"; and van Dijk-Hemmes, Some Recent Views"; and Ackerman, "Why Is Miriam Also among the Prophets?"

2. Miriam is said to be the oldest sibling by Ibn Ezra; *Exodus*, 30–32.

3. Moses is not called a prophet in Exodus. The first person called 'prophet' (*nābî'*) in the Bible is Abraham in Gen 20:7. The Hebrew term for Miriam in Exod 15:20 is *nĕbî'ā* (fem. noun + 'the'-*ha*). Biblical texts referring to an earlier historical period often use the term *rō'eh* ('seer'; cf. 1 Sam 9:9) for prophetic figures. Moses (though not by his name) is alluded to as a 'prophet' in Hos 12:13 and in Deuteronomy (8th to 6th c.). Recent research found an Old Babylonian term for prophets at Mari (*nabûm*), similar to the Hebrew *nābî'*; thus the Hebrew term is older than once thought; Gafney, *Daughters of Miriam*, 66–68; Huffmon, "Company of Prophets"; Grabbe, *Priests, Prophets*, 89–90; Petersen, "Defining Prophecy," 37–38.

4. Miriam is mentioned by name in seven different texts in the Hebrew Bible (Exod 15:20–21; Num 12:1–15; Num 20:1; Num 26:59; Deut 24:9; 1 Chr 5:29; and Mic 6:4),

history of interpretation, biblical commentators gave little attention to her. If she were mentioned at all, it was less with an affirmation of women biblical prophets, or that women prophets were common in ancient Near Eastern cultures, than to raise a problem: *how* can *Miriam* be a *prophet*? Yet this way of approaching Miriam may be prompted more by a common default assumption that biblical 'prophets' were male, characterized by their delivery of judgment or salvation oracles, and by views of Miriam perhaps influenced by Num 12 that casts her in a bad light compared to Moses. More recent studies have emphasized Miriam's importance in the canon.[5] Here, we will focus on the Song of the Sea in order to assess whether the Hebrew lyrics themselves bear traces of a woman's compositional contribution.

## Exodus 14–15

As the exodus narrative drama heightens, the Hebrews pull free from the grip of Egyptian slavery, break away en masse but are halted in the night at the imposing impasse of the Sea. The Egyptian forces make pursuit bearing down upon them (Exod 9:14–23). The narrative intends no purely natural explanation of what happened next, but tells of an incredible path sweeping through the sea (*yām*), nothing less than the wind (*rûaḥ*) of YHWH. The Creator directs and sustains the forces of nature all night, and whisks the people away from the reach of death on the arm of life, like a mother rushing away, protectively carrying her young.[6]

Exodus 15 represents the singing of victory and thanks by the Hebrew people for YHWH's unimaginable rescue. Most modern scholars affirm the antiquity of the song,[7] passed down through the generations,

more often than any other woman, notes Meyers, "*B'shalach*,"392.

5. Butting's groundbreaking book, *Prophetinnen gefragt* (2001), was the first, to my knowledge, dedicated to the larger topic of women prophets in the Bible; she focused on biblical narratives with Miriam, Deborah, Huldah, and Noadiah; see as well, Irmtraud Fischer's book, *Gotteskünderinnen* (2002) on women prophets in narratives, though she also treated themes of Deborah's song. See more recently, Gafney, *Daughters of Miriam*, 75–85.

6. Or, in the imagery of Exod 19:4, as if carried on eagle's wings, gliding to safety.

7. There seems to be a consensus that the Song did not originate with the J or E or P sources but was an independent tradition showing some congruities with them having influenced them; Childs, *Exodus*, 245.

that it retains archaic elements[8] and may be the oldest literature in the Hebrew Bible.[9] There also would have been multiple versions of the song as it was resung from earliest times, as well as possibly different songs about the event. A recent discovery among the Dead Sea Scrolls has found a similar song about the rescue, also attributed to Miriam.[10] With that text, then, there are *three* ancient references to Miriam as singer/performer with regard to a song at the Sea (also in Exod 15:20 and in v. 21), while for Moses, we have only the heading in Exod 15:1a.[11] It is not my intent to prove Miriam composed these lyrics or can be identified as the/a historical voice in Exodus 15, any more than we can prove, say, that David composed lyrics and thus identify his voicing lyrics in various songs. That Miriam was a historical person about which traditions developed, and from whom a lyrical tradition was inspired, seems beyond question.

However, let us preface the analysis by some discussion of how scholars and interpreters have dealt with the gender issues and contribution of Miriam or women regarding this song.[12] Meyers notes that because

8. Following Cross, *Canaanite Myth*, 112–44; Cross and Freedman, *Studies in Ancient Yahwistic Poetry*, 3. Archaic elements include features also found in Ugaritic poetry, including incremental repetition, the prefixed *yqtl* verbal form, the absence of definite articles, and the pronominal suffix *–mo;* Sarna, *Exodus*, 76; M. Brenner, *Song of the Sea*, 19, on the other hand proposes the Song of the Sea, including its introduction and closing, was composed entirely by "Levitical cult personnel of the second temple," teachers and singers (men and women?) who understood they carried on the work of the prophets.

9. Meyers, "Miriam, Music, and Miracles," 27–48. The present analysis does not pursue matters of poetic metrics coming from non-Hebraic cultural perspectives; Durham's, *Exodus,* 204–5, comment is apropos: "The application of the quantitative meters of classical poetry and the qualitative meters of English and European poetry to the poetry of the OT has created more problems than it has solved . . . Too much attempted systematization has blunted, rather than sensitized, our feel for the poetry of the OT . . . a brilliant commingling of sense and sound."

10. Importance of this text (fragment 6, a–c, of 4Q365) is additional evidence of recognition of Miriam as a singer about this deliverance (it is included within the canonical lines of Exodus 15 in the Dead Sea Scrolls), and it offers seven 'lines' of a slightly different lyrical version of God's rescue at the crossing of the sea, yet using some of the same terms; see Crawford White, "4Q364 & 365," in Barrera and Montaner, *Madrid Qumran Congress*, 1:217–28; also Brooke, "Long-Lost Song of Miriam," 62–65; more recently, Tervanotko,"'Hope of the Enemy has Perished.'"

11. While there are texts representing Moses' admitted difficulty in expressing himself in Exod 3:10 and 6:12, in principle a speech impediment may not preclude gifted singing. In this analysis, I will be concerned to track gendered singing, based on Hebrew sound patterns, and not the identity of singers.

12. For questions about this in Exodus 15, see Brenner, "Women Poets and

this song is "one of the most important passages of Hebrew Scripture . . . it thus seemed inconceivable to generations of (male) biblical scholars that the poem could have originated with women."[13] She credits, however, Cross and Freedman for making "a crack in this androcentric reading" and labeling the whole song as 'the Song of Miriam,'" since ironically it is more difficult to explain the tradition associating it to her than to Moses, and because the text as a victory song resembles the Song of Deborah.[14] It is important to emphasize that Israelite women not only sang victory songs for returning warriors, but with more than a little irony, prophetic and other women *modified the victory song* genre to give praise *to God as their heroic victor*.[15] This understanding would illuminate the representation of Miriam singing, not to honor Moses,[16] but to praise YHWH. In the victory song for male warriors, only women typically sang;[17] however, in modified victory songs/praise/thanks to YHWH, it is likely that not just women sang, but the entire community. However, some recent commentators with a concern for women's contributions believe that Miriam must have originally composed the entire Song of the Sea in Exodus 15,[18] and

Authors," *Feminist Companion to the Song of Songs*, 1993.

13. Meyers, "Miriam, Music, and Miracles." For example, Ibn Ezra, (trans. Strickman and Silver) *Exodus*, 291, says "Moses composed the song by himself. He then taught it to all of Israel"; Ibn Ezra simply skips any comment on the verses referring to Miriam, the prophet, singing.

14. Ibid., 29. Cross and Freedman, *Studies in Ancient Yahwistic Poetry*, 31, also call the text "the Song of Miriam," to distinguish it from "the Song of Moses" in Deut 32, and they saw Exod 15:1b–18 as a unified poem by a single author. Admirable as the suggestion is that Miriam composed the whole song, the Hebrew lyrics rather suggest evidence for multiple singer-composers of the lyrics in antiphony. However, neither is the opposite extreme likely the case, that Miriam has been largely silenced.

15. E.g., in Hannah's, Miriam's and Deborah's lyrics; see also Meyers, *Exodus*, 116–17. See Westermann, *Praise and Lament in the Psalms*, 81–93, for discussion of 'victory songs' and 'declarative psalms of praise' [for God], that Exodus 15 is of both genres.

16. A few scholars highlight the importance of Moses *not being the subject* of the Song in any way (Childs, *Exodus*, 249; Sarna, *Exodus*, 75; Meyers, "*B'shalach*," 386.

17. Meyers, *Exodus*, 117.

18. See especially Trible, "Bringing Miriam out of the Shadows," 19; Trible suggests the androcentric redactors took the words out of her mouth and gave them to Moses. Brueggemann suggests that "Moses," as the official leader, has "taken over and preempted the singing first done by the women," that their song was independent and older (Brueggemann, *Exodus*, 799). More recently, Kessler, "Miriam and the Prophecy," 77–86, suggests "the pushing aside of Miriam and her song to the second place (vv. 20–21) and the colonization and expansion of the song by 'Moses and the people of Israel' (v 1)."

that the attribution to Moses and the Israelites in the heading was secondary.[19] On the other hand, in spite of (or because of) limited attribution to Miriam in Exod 15:20–21, other commentators suggest Miriam (with the women) likely composed additional lyrics about the event, that is, a fuller or different song than that preserved in Exodus 15.[20] A crux for scholars has been the text's representation of who is singing (implying composing), with allusions to specific persons in vv. 1 and 20–21. Verse 1a is a heading or introduction, and the song's refrain follows:[21]

> Then Moses sang—and the people of Israel—this song to the LORD, and they said:[22] "I will sing to the LORD,[23]
> for he has triumphed gloriously;
> horse and rider he has thrown into the sea." (NRSV)

The heading, by naming Moses, *implies* he was the lead composer/singer; on the other hand, the heading may simply suggest that Moses, along with everyone else, participated in singing the refrain, and perhaps the

19. While the heading emphasized Moses' authority in the tradition, it also imposed one might be called a *hierarchy of authorship* on the song. Yet, claiming the *whole* song for Miriam may continue a hierarchical, modern Western model of 'authorship,' or miss an oral culture's likelihood of multiple singers and its more communal, even 'democratic," composing/performing process. Bach's caveat is helpful: "Instead of a song that is attributed either to Moses or to Miriam, I hear one that is contrapuntal" (Bach, *Women in the Hebrew Bible*, 420–21). See below for my recognition of yet another woman singer rendered in Exod 15:20. A first-century-CE Jewish contrapuntal singing tradition of the Therapeutrides and Therapeutae (women and men in Alexandria) took on Moses' and Miriam's singing roles, reenacting the Song of the Sea. See page 87 below, fn 88.

20. E.g., Cohen, "Miriam's Song," 182, 190; Goldin, *Song of the Sea*, 54; Anderson, "Song of Miriam," 290–91, had aimed to focus on Miriam's neglected lyric in Exod 15:21 and suggested this was Miriam's and her companions' original song, independent from the lyrics now preceding it; they took the lead in celebrating the event and this inaugurates subsequent liturgical tradition of poets and singers. Similarly, van Dijk-Hemmes, "Some Recent Views," suggested that the refrain of v. 21 is likely Miriam's older actual composition; lyrics in the previous verses were added later; thus her full song is 'drowned' by the redactors favoring Moses.

21. The first words of a Hebrew book or composition often form the title; this is noted by Cross and Freedman, *Studies in Ancient Yahwistic Poetry*, 31, and they suggested that vv. 1 and 20–21 do not indicate that we have two songs, but are indications of the song title.

22. The heading has a m.s. verb for Moses and a m.pl. verb for the group, which could include women.

23. The name YHWH appears more than any other word in the lyrics, 10 times (if 'adōnāy is included in v. 17); Propp, *Exodus 1–18*, 509.

following lyrics of the song.[24] Headings are considered later additions by scholars and not reliable indicators of who was or were the composing voice or voices of the text. At the end of the passage, v. 20 is usually set forth as a prose statement similar to v. 1a, naming Miriam as singing, followed by the refrain (v. 21) with a different form of the same verb as in v. 1, suggestive of a call-and-response performance:

> Then the prophet Miriam, Aaron's sister, took a drum in her hand;[25] and all the women went out after her with hand-drums and with dancing (v. 20). And Miriam sang to [or 'answered'] them [m.pl.]:
>
> Sing [m.pl.][26] to the LORD,
> for he has triumphed gloriously;
> horse and rider he has thrown into the sea! (v. 21)

Traditional interpreters regarded that Miriam and the women simply sang the refrain as an echo or repetition of Moses' or the men's previous lyrics, thus a secondary role.[27] Others suggest that Miriam actually *started* the song, a type of women's victory song, calling on others to sing in v. 21.[28] I follow this premise, based not only on the imperative verb, but on the full evidence of the Hebrew lyrics to be analyzed here. The male or group voice in v. 1b thus answers Miriam: "I will sing," yet is credited with the full song only by the heading. Feminist interpreters posit either the implied, nearly complete exclusion of Miriam's voice and song, or, the question of who should get credit for 'authorship' of 'the' song as we have it.

A way out of this modern quagmire is an oral-poetic approach integrated with feminist postcolonial concerns, which sets aside for the moment Western scholarly questions of authorship, redaction, and meter. How might the song lyrics be analyzed as indigenous Hebrew lyrical oral composition? Of the three criteria previously utilized in search of women prophets' voices—grammatical references to women's participation; the genre practice that women typically took the lead in singing

24. Propp notes that the "I" in v. 1 is not necessarily Moses, and several versions render the verb as collective: 'Let us sing'; ibid., 509. However, a lead singer likely composed this line.

25. Technically, a 'hand-drum,' thus Meyers, "Of Drums and Damsels."

26. MT; but LXX and Targum of Jonathan have "I sing."

27. Those trying to discern Miriam's role ask whether she sang to the men, the women, or the whole group.

28. Janzen, "Song of Moses, Song of Miriam"; Janzen, *Exodus*, 108–11.

victory songs, including adapting them for praise of YHWH; and lyrical patterns in the Hebrew suggestive of gendered voices—the first two can be met. Below I will focus on the third criterion as previously, along with attention to dialogical performance often found in indigenous oral cultures.[29] In this old song, is there precedence for a triplet sound pattern of a woman's voice as in Hannah's song, Song of Songs, and parts of First Isaiah and Micah? Let us turn now to the song:

29. We cannot know, as Muilenburg suggests, that the Song of the Sea as it stands is a composition *designed for use in the cult*, but his recognizing varying types of speech in the Song of several participants is also suggestive of lyrics from oral-poetic performance soon after the event; Muilenburg, "Liturgy on the Triumphs of Yahweh," 237. Blenkinsopp, "Ballad Style and Psalm style," 62–63, recognized antiphonal structure; also Sarna, *Exodus*, 76, and Cross and Freedman, *Studies in Ancient Yahwistic Poetry*, 3, though they did not pursue the compositional elements of different voices; see Kugel, *Idea of Biblical Poetry*, 116–27, for historical forms of Jewish *antiphonal* singing of this and other biblical songs, as well as scribes' writing practices to format this and other poetry in the Dead Sea Scrolls and later (e.g., brick over log pattern, etc); versification of lyrics did not happen until c. 1200 CE in the Latin Bible by Christians, adopted with variation by Jews; Propp, *Isaiah*, 39; see Jaffee, *Torah in the Mouth*, 31–38, for some scribes' understanding themselves also, at Qumran, as communing with the ancient prophets in their work.

| *(male/people's voice echoes Miriam)*<br>I will sing to *YHWH*<br>for he has ***TRIUMPHED***<br>***TRIUMPHANTLY***!<br>horse and his charioteer[1]<br>he has **thrown** into **the sea**! (1) | 'āšîr*ā* la*YHWH*<br>kî-*GĀ'Ō*<br>*GĀ'Â*<br>sûs wĕ**rōkĕv*ô* rām*â***<br>vayy**ām** | *(doublets)*<br>**2 Yah , yām 2 kî , kĕ**<br>**2 gā'ō , gā'â**<br>**2 rō , rā**<br>**2 vô , va**<br>**2** rā**mâ , yām** |
|---|---|---|
| *(female)*<br>**My strength**!<br>*(exhorter)*<br>"You **sing** [f.s.]![2] *YAH*!"<br>*(female)*<br>He *IS* for me salvation!<br>**This** is my ***GOD* and I will** praise **him**<br>***GOD*** of my father<br>**and I will** exalt **him**!<br>(2) | 'oz**zî**<br><br>wĕ**zimmā**rt *YĀH*<br><br>wa***YĔHÎ*-lî lîšû**'â<br>**ze *'ĒLÎ*** wĕ'anw**ēhû**<br>***'ĔLŌHĒ*** 'āvî<br>wa**'ărōmmenhû** | *(triplets)*<br>**3 'ozzî (+ zi ) + ze**<br>**1 yĕhî** (completes triplet with YHWH & **Yāh** above)<br>**3 lî , lî , lî 3 û , û , û**<br>**3 yĕhî-lî , 'ēlî , 'ĕlōhē**<br>**1 rōm** (completes triplet with **rām , yām** above)<br>**2 wēhû , enhû** (see v. 13) |
| *(male)*<br>***YHWH*** is a warrior;<br>***YHWH*** is his name! (3) | *YHWH* **'îš milḥām*â***<br>*YHWH* **šĕm*ô*** | *(doublets)*<br>**2** YHWH, YHWH<br>**2 milḥāmâ** (compl. doublets with **menhû** & **rāmâ** above)<br>**1 'îš** (compl dbl w/ **lîš** above)<br>**2 'îš , šĕmô 2 mâ , mô** |
| *(female)*<br>The ***CHARIOTS***<br>of **Phar**aoh<br>and his **forces**[3]<br>he **cast** ***INTO THE SEA***!<br>His **chosen officers**,<br>**sunk** ***IN THE SEA*** of '**reeds**'!<br>The **deeps**[4]<br>*COVERED* them;<br>they *WENT DOWN*<br>**into** (the) **depths**<br>**like** a stone. (4-5) | ***MARKĔVŌT***<br>**par'*ō***<br>wĕ**ḥêl*ô***<br>*YĀRÂ VAYYĀM*<br>**ûmivḥar šālišā**w<br>**ṭubb'û *VĔYAM*-sûph**<br>**tĕhōmōt**<br>**yĕkas*YUMû***<br>*YĀRĕdû*<br>**vimṣôlōt**<br>**kĕmô-'āv**en | *(triplets)*<br>**3 markĕvōt** (+ **rōkĕvô** , zim**mārt** above)<br>**3** m**ar** , p**ar** (+**'ăr** above)<br>**3 ḥ**êl, **ḥ**ar, h**ō**m **3 ō , 'ō , ô**<br>**3** ḥêlô (+**ēlî** , **'ĕlōhē** above)<br>**3 yār , ḥar , yār** (2nd triplet)<br>**1 šālišā** (+**'îš , šĕ**mô above= **3**)<br>**3 vayyām , vĕyam , yumû**<br>**3 sû , syu , ṣô 3 û , û , û**<br>**3** mark**ĕvōt, tĕhōmōt ,** vimṣôlōt **3 mōt, mû, mô**<br>**2** mar**kĕvōt, kĕmô-'āv**en (inclusio) |

[1] Author's translation. 'Charioteer' captures the singer alluding to military hardware overthrown. Later in the poem the singers emphasize the human enemy.
[2] This alternative translation (see my note on identical text in Isa 12:2 in chapter 1) is supported by repointing the MT as *wĕzimmārtt* (2nd f.s. piel perfect), not *wĕzimrāt*, as well as by the consonantal text of this in 1QIsa[a] with its *yod*-ending as an archaic 2nd feminine perfect. The term was often translated traditionally as 'my song' (supported by 1QIsa[a]). Nachmanides and Ibn-Ezra translated 'my song'; *Commentary on Torah, Exodus*, 193.
[3] Author's translation to capture the double meaning of collective term, *ḥêlô* (his strength/his army).
[4] NJPS.

As seen above, doublet and triplet sound patterns,[30] and different perspectives, suggest alternating voices. While both singers offer praise speech to YHWH, the female voice focuses on the sea and the forces of creation that YHWH uses to foil the enemy, while the male voice focuses on YHWH as holy warrior against the enemy.[31] A 'call and response' in the first thirteen

30. A few scholars point to the poetic use of sound—alliteration or assonance; e.g., Muilenburg, "Liturgy on the Triumphs of Yahweh," 246, 250; Cross, *Canaanite Myth*, 121; Freedman, *Pottery, Poetry and Prophecy*, 206–10; Brenner, *Song of the Sea*, 28–32; Propp, *Exodus*, 505–40; however, sound repetition is common in biblical poetry, so the question at hand is *how* do the composers *use* sound repetition? To my knowledge no one has linked consistent use of particular sound patterns to different singers in call and response, or to their gender.

31. Miller, *Divine Warrior in Early Israel*, 113–17.

verses will be seen to be embedded in the Hebrew of the text.[32] If the pattern reflects gendered composition and performance, as I suggest it does, then these traditions of lyricizing by women and men may be of greater antiquity than the lyrics in the above books (e.g., Samuel, Isaiah, and Micah). Here is an outline tracking the voices:

## Exodus 15:1–21 (outline of singers/voices, with doublet or triplet sound patterns)

| | | |
|---|---|---|
| 1 | Prose voice (later) | [heading] |
| | Refrain: group/male | [victory/thanksgiving; (divine warrior and sea motif)] |
| 2 | *Female* singer | ["I" lyrics of victory/praise refers to YHWH in 3rd person][33] |
| 3 | Male singer | [praise of YHWH, referred to in 3rd person; word doublet] |
| 4–5 | *Female* singer | [narrates ('sea' motif); 4a modifies *refrain;* YHWH in 3rd person] |
| 6–7 | Male singer | [addresses YHWH in 2nd person ('right hand'/word doublet)] |
| 8 | *Female* singer | [renarrates specifics ('sea' motif); YHWH addressed in 2nd person][34] |
| 9 | Male singer | [renarrates with specifics and I-speech of enemy] |
| 10–11 | *Female* singer | [renarration completed ('sea' motif); praises YHWH in 2nd person] |

32. There is little agreement among scholars as to the poem's structure. Here, I follow proposed alternating voices to mark off short lyrical sections.

33. The rabbis traditionally regard this line also as Moses' utterance; e.g., Nachmanides (trans. Chavel), *Commentary, Exodus,* 194.

34. This tendency of the Song to double-back and repeat or renarrate the specifics of the sea event was noted in Childs, *Exodus,* 251, and Propp, *Exodus,* 505; Halpern, *Emergence of Israel,* 38–39N, sees a repeating of the victory three times in vv. 1–12.

| | | |
|---|---|---|
| 12 | Male singer | [addresses YHWH in 2nd person ('right hand' motif)] |
| 13 | *Female* singer | [summarizes YHWH's actions; YHWH addressed in 2nd person] |
| 14–15 | Male singer (later) | [narrates people's movement through Transjordan] |
| 16–18 | Male singer (later) | [further narrates people's movement to land, sanctuary] |
| 19 | Prose voice (added) | [summarizes sea event] |
| 20 | *Female* singer (later?) | [narrates *Miriam's* drumming/ dancing] |
| 21 | Prose voice (added) | [attributes *Miriam* calling on group to sing *refrain*] |
| | *Female* singer | [creates lyric for the men/group; double use of root, 'sea' motif] |

The victory song proper is vv. 2 through 13[35] (the triplet sound pattern does not appear again in the remaining lyrics, except in v. 20—see below). As numerous scholars note, v. 1 as a heading essentially gives what became the title of the song, identified by its refrain. Where this refrain was originally placed and sung in the song is impossible to determine (now at vv. 1, a version in 4, and 21). It is possible the refrain either was composed by a male voice (indicated by the lyric's doublet sound pattern) or was a lyric *composed by Miriam / a woman for the men or the group to sing* (as she calls them to sing it in v. 21; they do so, as the heading says, in v. 1). The song of vv. 2–13 is broken into two sections. After crafting the opening refrain (in v. 21), the woman *takes the lead* (first in offering a lengthy first-person thanksgiving/praise (v. 2); second, in beginning narration of the event (v. 4–5); third, in beginning a *reiteration* of the event (v. 8). After each of these expressions by her, the male

35. While a few scholars consider whether v. 13 concludes the first section or is a transitional verse, a majority mark the end of the first section at v. 12. This analysis finds a triplet soundplay extending into v. 13 with a poetic image of the people's arrival in a safe encampment and long-awaited place of rest. Sarna, *Exodus*, 76, regards the first section as ending with v. 13.

singer follows her lead with his own response to the lyrical content. The second section (at v. 8) 'starts over' and narrates the event again, each voice taking two turns. The female singer closes the song with a summary of YHWH's actions.[36] It is the evidence of the Hebrew lyrics, it is argued here, that actually conveys the woman's leading role, likely representing a tradition from Miriam.

Verse 1 bears a doublet sound pattern suggestive of a male voice: "I will sing to the Lord for he has triumphed triumphantly! Horse and chariot he has thrown into the sea!" This lyric crafted for the male voice makes sense as he alludes to YHWH as divine warrior.[37] The doublet sounds are *gāʾō, gāʾâ / vô, va / rāmâ, yām / Yah, yā* . In a moment we will see how the woman's voice, using triplet sounds, composes *a complex version of this refrain* in v. 4. There her virtuosity takes the simple refrain to another level (see below).

With v. 2 above, a woman's voice (suggested by a triplet sound pattern) sings "my Strength!" (*ozzî*)[38], which it becomes apparent refers to the deity, as she praises YHWH for their rescue. Lest we think it more likely Moses or a man sang this line about one's 'strength,' this term suggests close parallels with other victory songs by women, and Hebraic tradition did not limit such a line to men only. For example, Hannah is represented as opening her victory song about her 'strength' (*qeren*), followed by "I rejoice in your [i.e., God's] salvation." The term appears in Deborah's song (Judg 5:21): "March on, my soul, with *might/strength (ʿōz)*." David, in his song of praise in 2 Sam 22:3, opens his song by praising God as "the horn (strength/power) of my salvation." Jeremiah opens a song of God's rescue—YHWH, "my Strength" (*ozzî*; in 16:19). "My Strength" is clearly a reference to YHWH by the composing voice raising a song of praise and thanks for the deity's rescue/help in answer to lament; it is also found this way in Ps 28:7; 59:17; 62:7 (rock of my strength); and 118:14.[39] Clearly,

36. Muilenburg, "Liturgy on the Triumphs, of Yahweh" 237, noted in the Song some alternation of "confessional speech of praise, on the one hand, and the narrative concerning the enemy, on the other," and a similar alternating style in Pss 68, 118, and 135.

37. On this root for "throw" also associated with shooting an arrow (Ps 78:9), see Ibn Ezra (trans. Strickman and Silver), *Exodus*, 292.

38. Hannah is rendered speaking of her power (*qeren*) that God has given her in 1 Sam 2:1, and strength (*ʿōz*) and power (*qeren*) from God are also received by the king at the end of Hannah's song; YHWH is 'my strength' (*ʿōz*), uttered in Isa 12:2, I suggest, by *Hannĕvîʾâh*.

39. Propp, *Exodus*, 512, finds further linkage of the term *ʿōz* to praise singing itself,

either a man or a woman can sing this specific line. It is worth noting that 'my' and 'I' lyrics—"I" songs—are not what modern cultures might think of as 'individualistic' songs. "I" songs in communal cultures meant the whole community was singing, but through lead singers' voices, yet also involving group response.

Returning to the song, the voice raising the lyric, 'my Strength,' in Exod 15:2 appears to be interrupted by another voice affirming/exhorting her (as we noted earlier in Isa 12:2): "You sing [woman] Yah'!"[40] The exhorter addresses her after she has sung.[41] This interprets that the text is representing Miriam as a lead singer, who elicits an exhortation by another. Miriam goes on to complete her lyrical sentence, [Yah] "has become / is for me, salvation!" A slight difference from Hannĕvî'âh's lyric in Isa 12:2 is that there she restated YHWH with a wordplay with the verb 'to be' or 'is'; here, Miriam follows what appears to be the exhorting voice's mention of Yah directly with *wayĕhî-lî*, without restating YHWH. (Hannĕvî'âh of Isaiah 12 likely knew the tradition of Miriam's lyric, yet made YHWH emphatic in her own lyric.) It appears that *only in* Exod 15:2, Isa 12:2, and Ps 118:14 is the singer's use of the term *ozzî* (my Strength) matched with a lyric of *a wordplay of YHWH's name* with the verb 'to be': *wayĕhî-lî.*[42] Most important for this analysis, *all four songs* (these three and Hannah's), are marked by these singers' use of the *triplet sound pat-*

e.g., in Ps 68:33–36 "when worshippers give Yahweh the *ʿōz* he inherently possesses, he returns *ʿōz* to them."

40. The abbreviated 'Yah' for YHWH appears in lyics, in this early poem, in a lyric fragment in Exod 17:16; in Isa 12:2; 26:4; 38:11; particularly in Psalms (68:5, 19; 77:12; 89:9; 94:7, 12; 102:19; 104:35; 105:45; 106:1, 48; 111:1; 112:1; 122:4; 130:3; 135:1, 3, 4, and 21; 146:1, 10; 147:1, 20; 148:1, 14; 149:1, 9; 150:1, 6), and especially in the Hallel songs associated with the Passover celebration (Pss 113:1, 9; 115:17, 18; 116:19; 117:2; 118:5a, 5b,14, 17, 18, and 19). Thus we may say that 'Yah' was an early lyrical term of exuberant tribute by a singer commemorating the crossing of the sea, and became a term handed down through the generations by singer-composers of Israel.

41. Loewenstamm, "Lord is My Strength," 464–70, has called into question the tendency of translating here (implicitly for parallelism) not 'song' but alternatively 'protection' or the like (from proto-Semitic *d_mr*). He notes: "The use of the verb זמר 'to sing' is restricted in the Bible to hymns; it occurs forty-two times and always denotes 'to praise the Lord in song and the playing of instruments' (which is identical with meaning of the Ugaritic term)" in a hymn to El. Loewenstamm suggests the noun had a *yôd* suffix that suffered haplography due to the following *yôd* of YHWH's name (470). However, this relates to *writing* but not to the *sound* of the two terms juxtaposed (*t* or *tî* and *yāh*) that would not have been confused.

42. Called a 'formula' in hymns in Loewenstamm, "Lord is My Strength," 464, rooted in the Exodus 15 lyric.

*tern* in the Hebrew lyrics, suggestive of women composing/singing (see further below).

We may posit, therefore, that Miriam the prophet was remembered as coining this victory/praise lyric with YHWH's name. Therefore, Miriam is singing affectionate praise of the name of the One who has rescued the people. This would be extraordinary in light of the tradition that Moses received the revelation of the name of YHWH earlier in the exodus drama at the burning bush. But it would be just as extraordinary when we remember the haggadic tradition that it was to Miriam in a dream that YHWH revealed the coming drama of rescue for the people through Moses.[43] The Song of the Sea lyrics are a tribute to YHWH, who has been true to the revelation and promise, who has truly rescued, but who has also been true to her, just as she has been true to YHWH. The song she is implied to lead is an ironic *transformation of the victory song* women in the larger culture normally sang for heroic warriors (in this case, Moses her brother also rose to victory with Aaron's help, but not as warrior, and only due to God's empowerment).[44] Moses is not the subject of the song, but a redactor made sure to mention him participating in the song.

The text of vv. 1–2, if it accurately reflects two (or three) singers uttering expressions one after another, then shows Miriam *completing* a triplet sound pattern: the first singer mentions *YHWH*, the exhorter mentions *Yah*, and Miriam lyricizes *yĕhî*.[45] She follows with *wĕ'anwēhû* ('I will praise him,' or *raise* him!) in which the syllable *wēh* completes the second half of Yahweh's name. While commentators ponder this unusual verb and how it should be translated,[46] it is likely chosen precisely for its sound wordplay. Moreover, Miriam's word *ărōmmenhû* ('I will exalt him' or 'lift him up') completes an ironic triplet sound repetition (by *rōm*) with the male or group singers' doublet sounds above: *rāmâ vayyām* ('thrown [down] into the sea'). This triplet would suggest that v. 1b did precede her utterance.

43. See Cohen, "Miriam's Song," 183; Kramer, "Miriam," 104–33; Ginzberg, *Legends of the Jews*, 277–93; Gafney, *Daughters of Miriam*, 144; this view of Miriam is found in *Megillah* 14a and reiterated in the *gemara* on *Sotah* 12b (Gafney, *Daughters of Miriam*, 202fn46); also in *Pseudo-Philo*.

44. Because the song is *not* a song about victorious warriors, Alice Bach, *Women in the Hebrew Bible*, 422, has suggested it may even have an embedded critique of war or pacifist leaning that the women extolled.

45. Brueggemann, *Exodus*, 799, notes a triple use of YHWH's full name over vv. 1–3.

46. Propp, *Exodus*, 514, discusses its likely cognate in Arabic ("to raise, elevate, acclaim, mention"), in parallel meaning with *'ărōmmenhû*.

With the second part of Miriam's line (v. 2) there is a triplet sound (*lî*), that YHWH is to 'me' salvation (*wayĕhî-lî lîšû'â*), overlapping with the word for 'my' God (*'ēlî*):

*wayĕhî-lî lîšû'â* — *ze 'ēlî wĕ'anwēhû*
*'ĕlōhē 'āvî wa'ărōmmenhû*

["This is my God and I will (p)raise him,
the God of my father and I will exalt him."]

At the same time, Miriam completes another triplet sound—after having said *'ozzî* ('my strength!'), and the exhorter says *wĕzimmārt* ('you sing!'), Miriam then answers *ze* ('this is my God!').[47] In English or other translation, the above looks like a simple parallelism of two lines; in Hebrew, it is a series of *triplet sounds* and with wordplay, next with the terms for "God" (*'ēl* and *ĕlōhîm*). While *'ēlî* and *'ĕlōhē* rhyme somewhat with *wayĕhî*, they also appear to leave a doublet repetition only with *el*, as a male voice interjects next with doublet sound repetitions: "The Lord is a warrior, the Lord is his name!" (v. 3). Yet Miriam *completes* a triplet sound with her *'ēlî* and *'ĕlōhē* (above) next in v. 4 (see chart) by saying *wĕḥêlô'* (and his army) and continues through v. 5 with multiple other triplets.

Note that the male voice in his lyric affirmed the 'name' of the Lord (*YHWH*), as though hearing her wordplay. We have seen how singers take turns, respond to one another (sometimes completing another's sound pattern or simply rendering their own doublet or triplet sound using several lines). If they are resuming their singing, they may pick up not only their thematic focus but also their previous sound pattern and complete it, as Miriam does above, yet propel the movement of imagery, thought, or narrative flow. This call-and-response dynamic at times can become a sort of 'contest' of rhetoric to demonstrate not just a faithful tribute to God but also an exuberant virtuoso of lyrical ability.[48]

So the male singer emphasizes YHWH's power and military skill with "The Lord is a warrior [literally, 'man of war']; the Lord is his name!" (*YHWH 'îš milḥāmâ YHWH šĕmô*). Here he offers more doublet sounds

47. Also noted by Propp, *Exodus*, 513.

48. For example as today in oral cultures, informal performance can involve multiple voices taking turns in a contest of lyric. In informal rap, singers take turns in call and response.

(YHWH twice; *ʾîš* and *šĕ*) that also continue the sound pattern with his lyric above (*ḥāmâ* with *rāmâ*—'he threw' into the sea).

In v. 4, the woman's voice resumes with lyrics on the fate of the enemy, whom she doesn't hesitate to identify, but with focus on the sea: "The chariots *of Pharaoh* and his army he *cast* into the sea!" (v. 4). While some might prefer that her line here is the 'origin' of the refrain in v. 1, the rhetorical context rather suggests here she creatively responds with a 'riff' on the refrain. She sings 'he [YHWH] *cast* into the sea!' (*yārâ vayyām*—note the wordplay in this with Yah *rāmâ*!) instead of *rāmâ vayyām*; but she keeps moving on to elaborate on the sea with more lyrics. As nothing stays constant for long in this oral performance, she takes the word *yām* now and varies it two more times (thus three sound repetitions) across her lyrics in vv. 4 and 5, adding: "his chosen officers sank in the *Sea of reeds*' (*ṭubbʿû vĕyam-sûph*); the deeps covered them (*tĕhōmōt yĕkasyumû*); they went down into the depths[49] like a stone." The third term, *yĕkasyumû* ('covered them') is unparalleled and bears three incongruities[50]: it should not have *either* of the *y* sounds embedded in the form of the verb, or *mû* ending for *'them'*, but *mô*, and it should be a *feminine* plural verb (*tiksenatmô*) to go with feminine noun 'deeps'; that form would have been a good soundplay with *tĕhōmōt*. Yet *precisely because* the singer 'sounds' those three syllables (*yĕ, syu*, and *mû*) in a masculine verb, this creates and completes the triplet soundplay with *yām* and *vĕyam-sûph* in v. 4! In this analysis then, a female singer appears to bend the rules of grammar away from a feminine form[51] in order to serve her triplet sound pattern with a particular emphasis on the Sea! Further, with *sûph* she echoes horse (*sûs*) earlier, and conjures two more meanings—sea of the 'end' [*sôph*] and sea of 'rushing wind' [*sûphâ*]![52] Moreover, Miriam's threefold sound repetition with *ṭubbʿû* / *tĕhōmōt* / *vimṣôlōt* emphasizes 'sunk' / 'the deeps'/ 'into the depths.'[53] These are just a few examples thus far of Miriam's use of triplets of sounds for emphasis (refer to the chart for a full list), in contrast to the male singer's use of *doublet* sound repetitions.

49. The root for 'depths' (*meṣôlōt*) is the same as for 'they sank' (*ṣālălû*) in v. 10, also interpreted as Miriam's lyric; Ibn Ezra (trans. Strickman and Silver), *Exodus*, 300.

50. Propp, *Exodus*, 517.

51. This unmatched gender between verb and subject is not all that unusual.

52. BDB, 692–93.

53. From Gen 1:2: the 'deep' (*tĕhōm*). Scholars link defeat of the historical enemy with defeat of the Babylonian sea dragon, 'Tiamat' (possibly etymologically related with *tĕhōm*).

There are traditions in Ugarit, and across the ancient Near East, of the mythical 'sea' deity (Yam) defeated in cosmic battles by superior deities.[54] Here in Miriam's lyrics, she renders the sea as nearly a powerful creature, yet still merely a natural force controlled by YHWH. As the song is likely older than texts regarded as the P source, it may be proposed that *Miriam has influenced the P tradition*, perhaps even the P tradition's referring to 'the deeps' in Gen 1:2 (to this matter we will return). On the other hand, some lyrics in the song also show similarity to lines in the previous narrative that scholars identify as the J-source (e.g., Exod 14:27 where YHWH 'hurls' the Egyptians into the sea). Thus Miriam's lyrics, if older, may also influence that source.

Next, in the verses below, the male singer, using doublet soundplays utters another refrain, again speaking YHWH's name twice, as he did in v. 3, and then goes on to describe YHWH as warrior defeating the enemy. The woman singer returns to her focus on the sea's role in YHWH's victory.

| *(male)* | | *(doublets)* |
|---|---|---|
| **Your** *RIGHT HAND, YHWH*, | *YĚMÎNĚKĀ YHWH* | **2 yěmîněkā , yěmîněkā** |
| **awesome**[1] in **power**— | ne'**dārî bakkōaḥ** | **2** YHWH, YHWH |
| **your** *RIGHT HAND, YHWH*, | *YĚMÎNĚKĀ YHWH* | **2 dārî** (completes doublet w/ **yārdû** above) **2 aḥ, aḥ** |
| **decimated**[2] the foe. (6) | *TIR'AṢ* **'ôyēv** | **2 tir'aṣ , taḥărōs + těšallaḥ** |
| **In** (the) greatness of **your** *TRIUMPH*[3] | **ûvěrōv** *GĚ'ÔNĚKĀ* | **2 gě'ôněkā , qāmêkā** |
| **you destroyed your** opponents; | *TAHĂRŌS QĀMÊKĀ* | **2 ḥărō , ḥărō 2 ěš , aš** |
| **your fury you sent forth**, | **těšallaḥ** *ḤĂR*ōně***kā*** | **2 allaḥ , ělē 7 kā** (w/ **2 qa**) |
| it **consumed** them **like straw**. (7) | **yō'kělē**mô **kaqqaš** | |
| *(female)* | | *(triplets)* |
| **At** the **blast** of **your nostrils** | *ÛVĚRÛAḤ* **'appêk*ā*** | **1 ûvěrûaḥ** 'appê**kā** (completes triplet w/**ûvěrōv** gě'ôně**kā** , qāmê**kā** above) **3 kā, kě, qā** |
| the **waters piled up**; | **ne**'erm***û*** **mayim** | **3 ûvěrû , vû , phě'û** |
| they **stood up** | **niṣṣv*û*** | **3 ne , ni , nēd 3 û , û , û** |
| in a **heap**—the **floods**— | **kěmô-nē**d **nōzělîm** | **3 mû…im, mô…îm, mō…ām 2 'appê, āphě'** |
| they congeal**ed** | **qāphě'*û*** | **1 těhōmōt** (+1 in v. 5 inclusio) |
| ***THE DEEPS*** in the heart of ***THE SEA***. (8) | ***TĚHŌMŌT bělev-YĀM*** | **1 yām** (+ **2** above, v. 4= **3**) |

[1] Author's translation (likewise of the root *'dr* also in vv. 10 and 11 below).
[2] Using two different verbs in vv. 6 and 7 yet rendering the alliteration.
[3] Translating the root that is the same as in v. 1.

54. Fox, *Now These Are the Names*, 3, reminds us that the Nile was also regarded as divine by Egyptians.

The male singer's lyrics above also address the deity directly—*your* 'right hand'[55] decimated[56] and destroyed (*tirʿaṣ* and *taḥărōs*) the enemy. His doublet sound emphasizes "your fury" (*ḥărōnkā*) that "destroyed" (*taḥărōs*). In elaborating on YHWH's hand, he furthers Miriam's image of 'casting' into the sea. While the singers have a different though related focus, and different lyrical styles, they are yet in dialog; note how the male singer picks up on the sound of Miriam's use of the verb, *yārdû* ('they went down') and sings *neʾdārî* ('awesome' the power of your hand). She will complete a triplet soundplay with variations of *neʾdārî* in vv. 10 and 11 below. This beautiful ability of two singers to listen to one another and craft responses while conveying the dramatic content and passion of the song is extraordinary. Whether this was improvised or crafted in partnership and then performed (or both!) matters not for the text's representation of the dynamic.

In v. 8 above, Miriam continues the direct (second-person) address of YHWH (which goes on through v. 11); yet she shifts from the male singer's focus on YHWH's 'hand' to return to envision the sight and sound of the 'waters' (*mayim*) of the moving sea, of YHWH's breath that blows a powerful wind (*rûaḥ*, as in Genesis 1) to direct the waters. Her threefold *û, û, û* sound is formed by three verbs describing how YHWH causes the waters to 'pile up,' 'stand up,' and 'congeal.' Also, two of the verbs join with the sound of the word for 'wind' to create a triplet sound onomotopoeia: *ûvĕrû, vû, phĕʾû*. Her lyrical artistry uses three internal *mû, mô, mō* sounds, and three final *im, îm, ām* sounds to convey YHWH's invisible harnessing of the straining, moaning movements of sea and wind. She repeats as in v. 5 the notable term for the deeps, *tĕhōmōt*, which must be a wordplay with *môt* (death).

55. Sarna, *Exodus*, 75–76, notes how the Song emphasizes YHWH's 'hand' causing things to happen, while the narrative in Exod 14:16 and 21 emphasizes Moses lifting his hand to activate *YHWH*'s power; Moses is absent from the Song of the Sea, as are any intermediaries of God's presence (the cloud, angel); the Song "celebrates God's direct, unmediated, personal incursion into the world of humankind"; the Song is also distinguished by its focus on YHWH from similar accounts of Egyptian battles, in which the exploits of the Pharaohs are highlighted. Nachmanides (trans. Chavel) *Commentary, Exodus*, 196, noted that the singer in v. 6 uses both the masculine and feminine forms to modify the term for 'right hand.'

56. The rare term (*râʿaṣ*) might be translated "crushed"; it is similar to the term (*râṣaṣ*) in Ps 74:14 where God "crushed the heads of Leviathan" in the sea, paralleling the enemy with the mythic sea monster.

Miriam's lyrics are thus focused on the sea, YHWH's power in the forces of nature, and the fate of the enemy caught up in it, while the male lyrics are focused on God's power as victorious warrior and the destruction of the enemy.[57] While the death of the enemy is gruesome, the situation described is by those who had been sorely oppressed by the enemy for decades and felt great relief and joy that God had finally freed them, vanquishing the oppressor.[58] Other texts suggest that Moses and Aaron were in their eighties, making Miriam at least ninety years old.[59]

With v. 9 below and the rendering of the enemy's speech, it is difficult to discern which speaker (male or female) composes/utters the lyrics, as the composition includes both triplets and doublets; nor is it simple to separate the line into two singers. If Miriam, the triplet sound pattern is evident in the enemy's threatening speech soon to be silenced (*aśśîg, ăhallēq, ʾārîq*)—"I will overtake, I will divide, I will draw my sword!"[60] The enemy boasts three times of "*my* desire, *my* sword, *my* hand" (all ending in *î*). However, two sets of doublet sounds to close this verse suggest the male singer rejoins with the enemy's arrogant claims: *timlāēmô, tôrîšēmô* (my soul "will have its fill,"[61] my hand "destroy"), and *ʾăḥallēq šālāl* ("I will divide the spoil").

57. For this motif in Exodus 15 and in the Bible, see Cross, *Canaanite Myth*, 91–111; and Miller, *Divine Warrior in Early Israel.* More broadly, see Niditch, *War in the Hebrew Bible.*

58. Later Jewish commemoration of the event in Passover tempers its celebration. For example, "it is customary to spill a drop of wine for each of the ten plagues and catastrophes that struck the Egyptians. The reason for this is that although the Egyptians oppressed our people cruelly, our cup of joy cannot be complete because the freeing of the Israelites entailed suffering for the enemy . . . The Rabbinic tradition on the Red Sea episode is singularly unvindictive. God Himself is seen as reproaching the angels for singing hymns of glory upon the miraculous overthrow of the Egyptians: 'The works of My hands are drowning in the sea, and you offer songs of praise!' Accordingly, during the last days of Passover, commemorating the miracle at the Red Sea, the synagogue liturgy calls for a recitation of half-*Hallel* (part of the Hymns of Praise) rather than the complete service" (Goldberg, *Passover Haggadah,* 16n5 and 17n6).

59. Exod 7:7

60. Cassuto, *Exodus*, 175, notes the alliteration of five consecutive words beginning with *ʿaleph* in v. 9.

61. The archaic plural suffixes, *timlāʾēmô* and *tôrîšēmô*, also serve the singer's doublet soundplay.

| *(mixed sound pattern; likely male)* | | *(doublets & triplets)* |
|---|---|---|
| The enemy said, | ʾāmar ʾôyēv | **2 ōph , aph 2 dō,** dî |
| "**I** will pursue, | ʾ**erdōph** | **3** ʾ**aśśîg** , ʾ**ăḥ**allē**q** , ʾ**ārîq**+ |
| **I** will **overtake**, | *ʾAŚŚÎG* | (4 "I" verbs) ʾ**erdōph** |
| **I** will **divide** the **spoil**, | *ʾĂḤALLĒQ* ***ŠĀLĀL*** | **3 al , ālāl 3 šā , šî , šē** |
| **my** desire *SHALL HAVE ITS FILL OF THEM.* | *TIMLĀʾĒMÔ* ***NAPHŠÎ*** | **2 ti**mlāʾ**ēmô , tôrîšēmô** |
| **I** will **draw my** sword, | *ʾĀRÎQ* ḥ**arbî** | **2** ʾ**ārî , arbî** |
| **my** ***HAND*** | *TÔRÎŠĒMÔ* **yādî** | **3** naphšî **,** ḥarbî **,** yādî |
| *SHALL DESTROY THEM."* (9) | | |
| *(female)* | | *(triplets)* |
| You **blew** | ***NĀŠAPHTĀ*** | **1 nāšaph** (compl doublet with **naphšî** above) |
| with your ***WIND***; | *vĕ**RÛḤĂ***kā | **3** nā**šaphtā** , **ʿôpheret** , **phel** |
| ***SEA*** *COVERED* them; | *KISSĀMÔ* ***YĀM*** | **3 vĕrûḥă** (+**ûvrûaḥ** , **ûvrōv** in vv. 7-8 above) |
| they **sank like lead** | *ŠĀLĂL*û **kaʿôph**eret | |
| *IN WATERS* ***AWESOME.***[1] (10) | *BĔMAYIM* ***ʾADDÎR**î**m*** | **1** YHWH **2 bĕmayim, bāʾēlim** (**+mayim**, v. 8) |
| ***WHO IS LIKE YOU***! | ***MÎ-KĀMŌKÂ*** | **3 kissāmô** yām**, mî-kāmō, mî-kāmō 3 im, îm, im** |
| *AMONG THE GODS,* ***YHWH***? | *BĀʾĒLIM* ***YHWH*** | |
| ***WHO IS LIKE YOU,*** | ***MÎ KĀMŌKÂ*** | **3 ʿaddîr, neʾdār , ōdeš nôrāʾ** |
| ***AWESOME*** | ***NEʾDĀR*** | **3 bĕ, bā, ba** |
| **in** holiness, *INSPIRING FEARFUL* | **baqqōd**eš *NÔR*āʾ | |
| praises,[2] doing **wonders**!? (11) | tĕhill**ō**t ʿōśēh **pheleʾ** | |

[1] Translating 'awesome' (inspiring awe) here and for the same root used for YHWH in v. 11 below.
[2] This nuance suggested by Rashi, and Nachmanides, *Commentary, Exodus*, 202.

The woman's voice takes up the lyric in v. 10 above: "You (YHWH) blew" (nāšaphtā)[62] (completing the male voice's doublet lyric with naphšî [my soul/self] above), but she goes on with a triplet of descriptive effects of YHWH's mighty wind. "You blew *with your wind* (*nāšaphtā vĕrûḥăkā*) . . . they sank like lead (*kaʿôpheret*)"—which parallels and completes a triplet she began with her line above (v. 8), "at the *blast* of *your nostrils*" (*ûvĕrûaḥ ʾappêkā qāphĕʾû*), *congealed* the waters. Then she shifts with v. 11 with an implied "therefore," "Who is like you (*mî-kāmōkâ*)[63] among the gods, YHWH?" Again, "Who is like you (*mî-kāmōkâ*) majestic in holiness, awesome in splendor, doing wonders?" She creates a triplet sound here by joining the double question to her lyric just uttered, *kissāmô yām* ("Sea covered them").[64] Yet *only once* in this section does she utter the

62. Nachmanides (trans. Chavel), *Commentary, Exodus*, 198–99, noted a variation elsewhere on this verb (*nāšaphtā*) with *bêt*, "*nashavta*" with same meaning (the only other instance of *nāšaphtā* appears to be in Isa 40:24, but *nashav* appears in 40:7); he gives examples of sound interchanges also with *gîmel* and *kāp*.

63. This is the basis for the name Micah.

64. This ancient lyric coined here, 'Who is like You!' becomes an important rhetorical question/affirmation passed down through the generations by Jewish tradition, and today in daily Jewish liturgy is called *Mi Chamochah* (Meyers, "*B'shalach*," 388); the entire song became part of Sabbath liturgy in the Second Temple period (Meyers,

name of YHWH, to emphasize the deity's singular reality. But three times here she utters a *d* sound: first with the 'awesome' waters (*ʾaddîrîm*) in which the enemy sank, linked to YHWH, 'awesome in holiness' (*neʾdār baqqōdeš*). This echoes her earlier line (v. 5) that the enemy 'went down' (*yārdû*), and forms an ironic image of the enemy going down in the sea while YHWH is raised majestically.

The male singer interjects below with doublet soundplay in v. 12 (as he did in v. 3), elaborating with the same term he used of YHWH in v. 6 (*yĕmînĕkā*): "You stretched out *your right hand* (*yĕmînĕkā*) . . . ." Even in this short line, his lyrical skill is most evident as he manages *four* different doublet sound repetitions (*nā /nĕ, ṭî/ti, ĕmî/ʿēmô,* and final *ā/ā*). Moreover, he extends the doublet in his line above (v. 9) describing the enemy who aimed to have his fill of them (timlāʾēmô) and *his hand* that would destroy them (tôrîšēmô), here no match, he sings, for YHWH's right hand that causes the earth to swallow (tivlāʿēmô) *them* (the enemy), thus making an unexpected triplet.

| | | |
|---|---|---|
| *(male)*<br>*YOU STRETCHED out*<br>***YOUR RIGHT HAND***<br>earth swallowed **them**. (12) | *NĀṬÎT***ā** **YĔMÎNĔKĀ**<br>***ti****vlāʿ***ēm***ô ʾāreṣ* | *(doublets)*<br>2 **nā , nĕ** 2 **ā , ā** (final)<br>2 **ṭî, ti** 2 **ĕm, ʿēm**<br>1 **ti**vlāʿ**ēm**ô (echoes **ti**mlāʾ**ēmô** above)<br>1 **yĕmînĕkā** (**2** in v. 6 above) |
| *(female)*<br>*YOU LED* **in** *YOUR STEADFAST LOVE*<br>the **people** whom<br>*YOU REDEEMED*;<br>*YOU GUIDED* **by** *YOUR STRENGTH*<br>to *YOUR HOLY*<br>**encamp**ment. (13) | *NĀḤÎTĀ VĔḤASDĔKĀ*<br>*ʿ***am***-zû*<br>*GĀʾĀLTĀ*<br>*NĔHALTĀ VĔʿOZZĔKĀ*<br>*ʾ***el-nĕ***wē QODŠEKĀ* | *(triplets)*<br>3 **nāḥîtā , nēhaltā** (compl triplet w/**nāṭîtā** above)<br>3 **nāḥîtā** , gā**ʾāltā , nēhaltā**<br>3 **ʾāl, al, ʾel** 3 **ḥî , ḥa , ha**<br>3 **vĕḥasdĕkā , vĕʿozzĕkā , qodšekā** 3 **nā, nē, nĕ**<br>1 ʿ**āz** (inclusio w/ʿ**oz** in v. 2) |

With v. 13, the poem shifts with Miriam's voice still addressing YHWH: "you led the people whom you redeemed." The emphasis in her lyric is not on 'our people' or 'your people.' Her lyric limits reference to the people God has just redeemed, as if to focus first solely on God's rescue on their behalf. She completes a doublet with the male singer's word, *nātîtā* (you *stretched*) above, with *nāḥîtā vĕhasdĕkā,* still addressing YHWH ("You *led* in your steadfast love . . . "); she forms a new triplet-sound of verbs by adding two more, "the people whom you *redeemed*, you *guided*" (*gāʾāltā nĕhaltā*). As above, where Miriam only mentioned

*Exodus*, 120).

YHWH one time, here she only mentions the people one time (*'am*), as if to emphasize their singular status, though bedraggled survivors of trauma and rescue. They are the recipients, she sings, not only of YHWH's *three actions* on their behalf, but they are now surrounded beautifully, as it were, by a blanket of *three divine comforts*: "your steadfast love" (*ḥasdĕkā*) "your strength" (*ʿāzzĕkā*), and "your holy encampment" (*nĕwē qādšekā*) [literally, 'holy pasture'].[65] Indeed, she began her song singing 'my strength' is YHWH, and closes her song here with an inclusio, pointing back to YHWH, addressing YHWH directly: '(it is) *your strength*', the end of her powerful tribute. Miriam's lyrics paint an emerging picture of an intimate relationship between this people and this God moving forward. With this line the oldest passage of the Song of the Sea comes to an end.

Next in the text, a male singer (perhaps different than the previous one, though not necessarily) in vv. 14–18 lyricizes about the people's later passage through the lands to the southeast of their destination.[66] A doublet sound pattern (twenty different doublets!) is pervasive across his lyrics, while the previous antiphonal singing with a female voice disappears. However, two exceptions are that YHWH occurs three times, and the *ka* sound seven times (emphasizing of God, '*your* arm,' '*your* people,' 'you *redeemed*,' '*your* possession,' '*you* made,' '*your* hands', etc).[67]

Now after these verses, the poem oddly returns in vv. 19–21 to the earlier song and topic. Most Bibles print vv. 19–20 as prose. While v. 19 has some repetition, a comparison of the lyrical artistry by the woman's voice in vv. 10–11 shows there *seven* triplet sound repetitions, three wordplays, onomatopoeia, irony, imagery, and multiple rhyming elements. In contrast, v. 19 bears two doublet sounds and only three main triplet sounds, two of which are simply repetitions of the same syllables. Several elements also suggest a later composition: the mention of 'Israel'

65. Following Hyatt, *Exodus*, 166. Cross translates 'tent-shrine' (*Canaanite Myth*, 243); however, this term displaces the lyricist's term, which encompasses all the people's place of rest (pasture), not just the religious space. Most scholars separate v. 13 from 1–12 (see footnote 35 above), presuming this term *nĕwē* refers to the sacred space of Mount Sinai, a temporary or later local sanctuary, the land of Canaan, even the Temple; however, all these leap forward too quickly esp. to v. 17 (and the later context); a mountain is not mentioned here; I interpret the singer referring to the first place of safety (encampment) to which the Hebrews are led by the Deity.

66. His lyrics cover five verses; in the older part of the song (above) each singer sang no more than two verses. This suggests perhaps that his song is not dialogical.

67. Childs, *Exodus*, 252, suggests the tone of these lyrics is like the celebratory parts of the Joshua narrative.

for the first time in Exodus 15 (other than in the heading); the use of the Hebrew term indicating direct objects (*ʾet*), not usually found in early poetry; and the use of the term 'dry land,' found also in what is usually regarded as later Priestly narrative or material, in Exod 14:21 and 29 and in Gen 1:9–10.[68] In fact, v. 19 includes a verbatim quote of 14:22a and 29a (or vice versa), and includes a variation of 14:23 and 26b. Exod 15:19 therefore is a *prose* summary statement, even with some lyrical repetitions (as in Exodus 14). It appears to serve as a reason for v. 20, the following verse, with its description of Miriam and the women's celebration.

V. 20, on the other hand, bears a skilled, lyrical *triplet sound* pattern; it is less than half the length of the previous verse, yet has *four* triplet repetitions. Of twelve words, nearly all of them bear either a '*ha*' or an '*ah*' sound. Thus even though the line refers to Miriam in third person, it is a lyric; thus we may suggest another woman sang/composed it. It is impossible to know whether she sang at an originating setting, or later. But her affinity to Miriam is strong; she sings the term, *hannĕvîʾâ* (the woman prophet) in sound parallel with *kol-hannāšîm* (all the women); both Miriam and all the women have drums in their hands; perhaps the women are prophets too.

| *(woman singer)* | | *(triplets)* |
|---|---|---|
| *AND SHE* **took**—Miri**am** *THE PROPHET*,<br>*SISTER*<br>of *AARON* — a ***DRUM***<br>**in** her **hand**;<br>*AND THEY* **went out**—all *THE WOMEN*<br>*AFTER HER* **with *DRUMS***<br>and **with** *DANCING*. (20) | **watti**qqa**ḥ** mir***YĀM*** *HANNĔ*vîʾâ<br>*ʾĂḤÔT*<br>*ʾAHĂRŌN* **ʾet**-ha***TTŌPH***<br>**bĕyād***āh*<br>**wattē**ṣeʾ**nā** kol-*HANNĀŠ***îm**<br>*ʾAḤĂRÊHĀ* **bĕ*TUPP*îm**<br>û**vim***ḤŌLŌT* | 1 **miryām** (**yām** above)<br>3 **hannĕ**vîʾâ, **ṣeʾnā, hannā**šîm<br>3 ʾ**ăḥô**t , ʾ**ahă**rō**n** , ʾ**aḥărêhā**<br>3 **îm, îm, im** 2 **tōph , tupp**<br>3 **watt, hatt , watt**<br>3 **bĕ , bĕ , vi**<br>3 ʾ**ăḥôt, hattō, ḥōlōt** |

And so we come full circle to v. 21 where, by its placement by a later redactor, Miriam is portrayed as singing the refrain already uttered *by a male singer* at the song's beginning—yet we now can see that her own lyric in v. 4 had amplified the refrain in triplet form, but the shorter version everyone now sings, perhaps including herself. Yet here we must employ a hermeneutic of suspicion further: this analysis of the sound pattern has also found that *another woman singer* in v. 20, in lyric (not prose), identified Miriam as 'prophet' and portrayed her as taking up drumming and dancing followed by the women; but a voice then adds in prose (v. 21) a line implying that Miriam only sang the refrain *with the women*! It now

68. Ibid., 248.

becomes even clearer—by the way a scribe or redactor arranged the order of the canonical text in placing Miriam at the end—that he subordinated Miriam in importance and *in the way* she contributes. Yet v. 21 *still attributed singing to Miriam*, likely because she could not be completely erased in the attribution or the record. As Phyllis Trible most aptly put it, "Miriam is both diminished and included."[69] However, the oral-poetic, feminist analysis here has exposed that this portrayal of Miriam in v. 21 *only comes after much lyricizing*, the Hebrew language reveals, by a female singer in the body of the song, implied to be Miriam. The evidence is *in the indigenous Hebrew lyrics* that cannot be suppressed, and her voice is borne up and borne out by a distinctive women's lyrical tradition, with its signature triplet sound pattern, including the woman singer of v. 20. (She herself must have been overlooked in the history of transmission of the song, as unimportant.)

While interpreters may disagree about the import for Miriam of the refrain of vv. 1b and 21, here I conclude, based on the Hebrew lyrical evidence across 15:1–21, that Miriam is represented in v. 21 as coining a refrain and throwing it to the men, or people, to sing—Sing to YHWH! V. 21 is not her independent, older song separate from 1b–13. Instead, much of the Song of the Sea, as evidenced by a triplet sound pattern in the Hebrew lyrics, was composed by a woman, implied to be Miriam, yet along with a male singer. The canonical text both implies—yet while it hides!—this reality. It is fair to say that each singer *is embodied in their lyrics* in the Song of the Sea, and they weave them together in beautiful fashion in call and response. If Miriam were the lead singer of this victory song in the group of rescued Hebrews, her role is no less noteworthy than if she sang the entire song for everyone.

Walter Brueggemann describes Miriam's contribution in crafting this lyric and calling everyone to sing:

> the poetic articulation is at the heart of the liberation . . . presumably it was not visibly evident to anyone that Yahweh had

69. Fox, *These are the Names*, 86, notes the structural feature that the whole deliverance is framed by Miriam, as a girl at the river Nile and as a prophetess at the Sea; Phyllis Trible, "Bringing Miriam Out of the Shadows," 18, 20, suggests that the overall story begins with women, the midwives and others, and ends with women led by Miriam performing at the end of chapter 15, suggesting that women played important roles in the exodus event from beginning to end; Brueggemann, *Exodus*, 803, notes that the Song of the Sea by Miriam and the women "stands as a massive, lyrical resolution to the grief and cry of 2:23–25. Israel's initial cry . . . and concluding shout stand in an arc of faith."

> pushed the horse and the rider into the sea . . . . One might conjecture many different readings of the event . . . But this particular reading, which is now normative, depends on the poet to create an event which did not happen until she uttered it so. Thus, the *liberation of politics* depends on the *liberation of imagination* . . . The hymn wrought by the poet makes the world. Had there been no poet, the world offered would not have been this particular world . . . And one may well wonder why these world-creating poems that run from Miriam to Mary are preserved in the tradition as the speech of women, who then are the 'world-makers' in Israel. Perhaps in that society they are the only ones free enough from the 'known world' to have the capacity to speak an alternative world.[70]

The above analysis yet leads to an inevitable question: apart from the late heading in v. 1a, who was the implied male singer/composer in dialog with Miriam in the Song of the Sea? Was it Moses, attributed at the opening? Was it an unknown singer? Was it *Aaron*, obliquely attributed at the end by being paired with Miriam? The proposed woman singer/composer in v. 20 mentions Aaron, almost as an interrupting interjection, while introducing Miriam's singing. Commentators have noted how odd it is that Miriam is called Aaron's sister, not Moses' sister.[71] It may be that this woman's lyric intended to highlight not different *parents* (!) for Miriam and Aaron, but their different *parts* in *partnership* as sibling leaders, which may not have existed between Miriam and Moses; could her mention of Aaron even have been an indirect nod to his singing role in this Song?[72] If so, the attribution of the whole Song to Moses is a travesty not only against Miriam but also against Aaron. Apart from this conjecture, the Hebrew lyrics of the Song of the Sea strongly suggest Miriam is being represented as composer/lead singer, illuminated and amplified by the *signature triplet sound* feature of the women's lyrical tradition.

In the end, the Song text reflects a *community practice*, process, and performance, with such call and response that the song is composed line by line by different lead singers; so no one produced the whole—but all sang in tribute to YHWH; nor would the singers think in terms of "my song," as we might today. While this may be something of a disappointment to

70. Brueggemann, "Response to 'the Song of Miriam,'" 299.

71. She is also not linked to a husband here.

72. Cohen, "Miriam's Song," 184, notes it is not surprising the older siblings, Miriam and Aaron, are paired in Exodus 15, since both are "singers of 'the song of redemption,'" Miriam at the Sea and Aaron in the cult.

us feminists—that Miriam appears to have composed *most* of the song, *not the whole* song—it is important to respect the indigenous culture and oral lyrical practice from which this comes, which in the end did preserve a version of Miriam's voice and faithfully pass down the tradition of her leadership role. While the rescued community would recognize and appreciate their leaders and singers, the community would likely regard 'the' Song of the Sea as '*our song*,' even in its variations, proclaiming God's victory, to which all contributed, sang and danced, as they celebrated.

Nevertheless, those who lyricized about YHWH's great deeds and faithfulness in the Bible—who regularly used sound repetition, wordplay and imagery—are often referred to as 'prophets.' In light of her portrayed lyrical artistry, inspired skill, and faithfulness through this exodus drama of redemption, it is not an overstatement to suggest that Miriam became *an early precedent* for what a prophet was to be in Israel. Is it any wonder that Miriam was called a prophet? Modern Western interpreters are surprised, but ancient Hebraic traditionists were not, however much a few androcentric Israelite male leaders might have looked askance at Miriam's role. No doubt the women, but also the text of Exodus 15 (through scribes, compilers, and redactors), in the end *all made sure to remember and include Miriam* at this auspicious occasion. Not only Miriam, but *the women's lyrical tradition was preserved* in this important song.

In conclusion, Miriam's involvement in God's rescues from the waters (two of them!), and singing of the latter in Exodus 15, suggests a larger role for her as a prophetic lyricist than the narrative portrays or than has been recognized through the generations. Miriam's appearance at the beginning and end of the exodus narrative suggests she was a leader all along.[73]

## What about the Narrative of Exodus 1 as a Women's Tradition?

If Miriam had an obvious gift for rendering the dramatic event in song, it is possible she also played a behind-the-scenes role *in the oral composing of the exodus narrative*. In ancient times, bards chanted or sang epic tales lyrically.[74] We may ask who contributed to the early reciting of the

73. Trible, "Bringing Miriam out of the Shadows," 18.

74. Cassuto, *Exodus*, 2, has suggested that the narrative of the exodus story is less likely composed of the usual pentateuchal 'sources' than it is from a *lyrical* epic

liberation account, though we can never know for sure. It is at least fair to suggest the possibility, as Miriam disappears as a player in the story, that her presence may be embodied instead in telling/singing the story that gets passed down through the generations. Would a comparison of the exodus *narrative* (likely from oral tradition) and Miriam's lyrics in the Song of the Sea suggest a larger expressive contribution from Miriam than she has been given credit for, or at least a Miriamic women's narrative tradition? Does the narrative at the beginning of Exodus, dominated by women figures, bear a triplet sound pattern?

Indeed, yes! The opening of Exodus—with its emphasis on fruitfulness, the many Hebrew offspring, and the unusual featuring of the contributions of women—*bears a triplet sound pattern* in the Hebrew of its storytelling.[75] Elements of this part of the narrative have long been attributed to a 'priestly' source/tradition;[76] yet, is it possible that such rhetoric might have been composed by a women's tradition, influenced perhaps by Miriam and/or the women who told/composed this part of the story, which in turn *influenced* Gen 1:27–28? This part of the Exodus story gives details to which women would have been especially privy and likely would have told one another as a matter of women's solidarity, eventually worked into an oral tradition. Especially the account of their resistance to Pharaoh would have been treasured and passed down by women.[77] Brueggemann notes that the narrative of Exodus is a voice of "revolutionary criticism, which mounts a vigorous assault on every (Pharaonic) establishment of abusive power . . . to assert that other social possibilities are available, if enacted with freedom, courage, and faith."[78] If this voice opening the narrative is largely that of an indigenous, Hebraic women's tradition, then they were not only the subject matter here but also the *composers* of part of the story of the oppressed, which shaped subsequent history. This recognition could mean, therefore, a 'decolonization' and liberation finally not only of the text but also of those contributing women composers.

---

tradition.

75. For the sound patterns in Exodus 1, see Lee, *Hebrew Sound Patterns and Women's Biblical Composing.*

76. E.g., Childs, *Exodus*, 2.

77. Brueggemann, *Exodus*, 695–96, notes that the storyteller renders the Egyptian king as speaking *three times* in relation to the midwives—in Exod 1:16, 18, 22.

78. Ibid., 682.

Scholars note that Exod 1:1–4 and its listing of the sons of Jacob has intertextual links with Gen 46:26–27, and with Gen 35:23–26. But several scholars' comments are suggestive: Childs noted that "the actual order of the names follows the older tradition of Genesis 35 which organized the names according to *the eponymic wives* of Jacob."[79] Cassuto noted that "the names of the tribes are arranged symmetrically, in *three* series": the first four sons of Leah, the last two sons of Leah and second son of Rachel, and two pairs of the handmaids' sons.[80] Sarna commented, "The sons/tribes are listed matrilineally, with those of the two wives mentioned first in order of seniority, followed by those of the two handmaids in reverse order to form a chiasm."[81] Reuben is listed first even though, as Sarna reminds us, he was no longer the firstborn after Jacob deprived him of that status! Moreover, Jacob preferred Rachel to Leah. Could the canonical order have something to do with *a women's rhetorical tradition of telling the genealogy*? (perhaps one upholding Leah foremost?)

Most commentators also note the obvious intertextual link between lines in Exodus 1 with the 'prolific' terminology of Genesis 1 and assume it must mean this is a Priestly redaction or emphasis in the early part of Exodus.[82] However, my analysis finds evidence of a triplet sound pattern *in the second half of Genesis 1*, where *these very words and themes* are emphasized.[83] Could a woman composer or women's tradition have been responsible for portions of the second half of Genesis 1, particularly as it renders 'be fruitful and multiply' rhetoric, as well as the famous egalitarian statement on gender in v. 27? If so, this evidence suggests more largely, not only that a women's oral tradition (in poetry and narrative) persisted on in the period of the exile, but may have been included to *give shape to very important parts of Genesis and Exodus*. In this regard, the 'final form' of the biblical canon has just as much to do with the *originating creators* of lyrics and stories and other genres, than with the decisions of redactors. Along these lines, however, we must ask whether women who inherited and passed on oral traditions, and women prophets, also

79. Childs, *Exodus*, 2 (italics added).

80. Cassuto, *Exodus*, 8–9 (italics added).

81. Sarna, *Exodus*, 3.

82. E.g., Ibn Ezra (trans. Strickman and Silver), *Exodus*, 9, noted the same root for the verb 'swarm' in Gen 1:20 is used for 'increased abundantly' in Exod 1:7 (*šrṣ*; NRSV: 'prolific').

83. For the sound patterns across Genesis 1, see Lee, *Hebrew Sound Patterns and Women's Biblical Composing*.

had a hand in the scribal/redacting activity during the crisis of the exile that helped shape the biblical canon, besides the usually recognized male priestly and deuteronomic circles. Moreover, should this be the case, it is possible that the aforementioned circles may have been *somewhat* open to women's influence in this important activity, which has not been considered possible. Should it be the case, on the other hand, it would not be surprising, since the Israelite/Judean written canon, while both circumscribing and including women's contributions, nevertheless came out of a longstanding oral culture never fully controlled by its own religious or political establishment.

Apropos to my proposal of women composers responsible for the opening narrative of Exodus, Brueggemann notes that the exodus narrative overall (as was true about the Song of the Sea) "is not fundamentally interested in the person of Moses. It is not a 'hero story.' The story, however, cannot manage without Moses."[84] Yet we must say as well that the story cannot manage without Miriam and the women.[85] Brueggemann seems to come to a razor's edge of recognizing women composers of this text when he says, "The narrator has wrought a powerful interface between the hiddenness of God and the daring visibility of the women. One might conclude . . . closer to the voice of the text itself, the women have displaced the providence of God and are the ones who assure the baby's future . . . Israel's liberated future." [86]

In Exodus, the prophetic roles are represented as both action and speech. Moses' calling was to receive divine guidance and speech, with Aaron's help, to lead the people's rescue, and to receive the initial revelation of Torah and convey its teaching. Extrabiblical Jewish traditions suggest Miriam's prophetic calling was to receive divine guidance to help effect the infant Moses' rescue (and thus the whole people), and implicitly, *to communicate* this to her parents and more largely—perhaps by crafting the tale—but certainly to lead the lyricizing announcing YHWH's rescue through song. Of course, early oral accounts were by multiple voices and overlaid through the generations with re-telling, additions, and reinterpreting. As the Hebrew people journeyed on through the desert, an oral tradition also developed of 'Miriam's well', of Miriam's shamanic/diviner

84. Brueggemann, *Exodus*, 699.

85. Cf. Propp, *Isaiah*, 32–33, who posits three heroes in the narrative—Moses, Israel, and Yahweh, but leaves out Miriam and the women, further suggesting that the midwives' story is "extraneous."

86. Brueggemann, *Exodus*, 701.

gift of finding water for the people; so her association with water continued.[87] In sum, in action and speech suggested by biblical and postbiblical traditions, Miriam and Moses, as well as Aaron, made indispensable contributions during the liberation event, and, on the other side of the sea.

In the end, the Exodus, Numbers, and postbiblical traditions are all pushed and pulled both by voices supportive of Miriam's prophetic role and by voices against it who would squelch it. For the gifted singer and prophet called Miriam, whose voice is given a small space in the biblical text, it is with great irony, some would say with greater providence, that her story and her voice survive and continue to speak to us today.

## More Postbiblical Traditions

That postbiblical Jewish traditions kept Miriam the prophet alive in memory for centuries has been noted above, in Talmudic and other midrashic references. This is also seen in the practice of the Therapeutrides (women) and Therapeutai (men) who lived in a Jewish spiritual community in Alexandria (20 BCE to 40 CE, according to Philo). They had a custom of closing their Sabbath observance by antiphonally singing the Exodus Song of the Sea, the women led by a singer representing Miriam the prophet, and the men by a singer for Moses.[88] Importantly, women prophets in the second century CE Montanist movement "cited Miriam the prophet and the four daughters of Philip as precedent for women clergy, making a linkage between prophecy and other Christian offices."[89]

87. Ginzberg, *Legends of the Jews, 369–71.*

88. Taylor, *Jewish Women Philosophers of First-Century Alexandria*, 311–34.

89. Kraemer, *Her Share of the Blessings*, 157–58; 185–86

# CHAPTER 4

# Deborah and Judges 5

THE PROPHET DEBORAH IS portrayed as the central figure in Judges 4 and 5. The song of victory[1] genre adapted for praise of YHWH in Judges 5 is a lyrical account of an event narrated in Judges 4, which itself has oral traditional qualities.[2] Judges 5 is often called 'the Song of Deborah' and thus is a key text in the present study for analysis of a women's lyrical tradition, which women prophets may have employed. However, the heading of the song also attributes Baraq, leader of the Israelite warriors, as singer with Deborah. This lyrical text has long been considered one of the oldest texts in the Hebrew Bible.[3] This analysis will not aim to date the written text or its parts, but as before, will examine sound patterns in the Hebrew (*based on the consonantal texts* of MT and variants, while including MT vowel pointing, and pertinent variant readings); the aim is to assess the lyrical artistry and proposal of gendered composing voices in the text as it has been passed down.[4] This analysis recognizes that the canonical lyrics are a snapshot from a particular time and that there could have been other song versions not preserved. An assumption

1. Poethig, "Victory Song Tradition"; for cross-cultural examples in Egypt and Assyria, see Boling, *Judges*, 117; Globe, "Literary Structure and Unity," 496–99; for recent discussion of the genre, see Echols, *"Tell Me, O Muse,"* 175–83.

2. Niditch, *Judges*, 17–18; 59–67; Kugel, *Idea of Biblical Poetry*, 76–95.

3. For a review of the earlier scholarship and recent treatments, see Brettler, *Book of Judges*, 62–66.

4. While this is a focus and may not attend to every aspect of the poetry, it nevertheless broadens the usual scholarly attention to syllable counts, strophic structure, unity, or the poetic use of sound repetition simply for effect or wordplay reinforcing parallelism; cf. Coogan, "Structural and Literary Analysis," 159.

of a literary approach of 'the author' or 'the poet' distanced a long time after the originating context is not a premise, since Israelite culture likely handed down this song through oral tradition, even though a scribe or scribes at some stage recorded the text. Neither will a *single* composing poet or singer from an early context simply be assumed,[5] even though some commentators regard the entire song to be Deborah's composition. As will be seen, the flow of the whole, including third-person references to key players, and shifting first-, second-, and third-person expressions and perspectives, make more sense when multiple, antiphonal voices are recognized, a complexity that tradition preserved. Nevertheless, the Hebrew sound-pattern analysis will suggest that a female voice, i.e., Deborah as implied composing prophetic singer, is the most prevalent.[6] But as I mentioned earlier, the historical identification of the singer is not possible to prove or necessary to pursue, but rather, whether the song's artistry suggests originating composing from a women's *tradition*, which was probably rooted with a historical figure, Deborah. Finally, the pursuit by some commentators to find a 'unified' poem is not required, other than a unity found in an antiphonal song rendering aspects and perspectives of a single event, with an overall aim to give praise to YHWH.[7]

## Judges 5

The heading in v. 1 gives Deborah as subject of the feminine singular verb, "sing," and Baraq is added as subject, but without a separate or plural verb.[8] After the heading, the opening lyric in v. 2 (with triplet

5. Contra Globe, "Literary Structure and Unity," 508.

6. Hackett, "In the Days of Jael," 15–38, suggested that some of the stories in Judges in which women's lives and issues are central may "derive from women's literature . . . composed by and/or preserved in women's circles . . . Judges 5 . . . describes the battle with the Canaanites precisely from the perspectives of the women in the story" (32). The present study provides a key to discerning *a signature* of women's composing. While men may have imitated this pattern, evidence thus far suggests male composers consistently preferred a doublet sound pattern across genres, even when composing a genre typically sung by women.

7. Cf. Blenkinsopp, "Ballad Style and Psalm Style," 62, 74.

8. There are other cases where multiple subjects are attached to a singular verb; Sasson, *Judges*, 283. On matters of gender roles, ideology, and differences in Judges 4 and 5, see Bal, *Murder and Difference*, 56–59; 66–75. Bal, *Death and Dissymmetry*, 211, 241, suggests that Judges 4, as an epic genre, is a male text, and the song of Judges 5 a women's text as "Deborah's poetic work"; this conclusion seems to be based only

soundplay) sets the stage and appears to initiate or repeat a refrain; it reappears varied each time in vv. 9, 11 and 13 (in doublet soundplay) but all containing the two terms *ʿām* and *YHWH*. The final words of v. 2, "*bārăkû* ('bless') YHWH," may also be a soundplay alluding to 'Baraq,' yet it is a phrase typically found in (likely later) psalms.[9]

While commentators debate the translation of the first line (see below), as long hair was a ritual practice of male warriors in this early period,[10] a new translation here suggests the double root is a wordplay with the second term a concrete feminine *subject*, perhaps the singer's (Deborah's) ironic humor to allude also, if not first, to the women who led the men.[11] As the first lines (vv. 2–3) bear triplet soundplays, Deborah is represented beginning the song and making immediate yet subtle allusions in soundplay to herself, Jael, the people (or warriors), and Baraq in v. 2, all of whom will be unfolded dramatically in the ensuing lyrics—by Deborah's renderings, or by their own words.[12]

on presumed genres the genders used; similarly, see Brenner, *Judges*, 98–109. For the sound patterns in Judges 4 and its composing related to gender, see Lee, *Hebrew Sound Patterns and Women's Biblical Composing.*

9. The exhortation for people to "bless the Lord" is found in songs of praise, e.g., Ps 68:26; 96:2; 103:20–22; 115:18; 134:1–2; 135:19–20.

10. Ackerman, *Warrior, Dancer*, 32–34.

11. See Hackett's argument ("In the Days of Jael," 15–38) that prior to the monarchy and centralization of government, women could more easily rise to positions of leadership, especially in crisis situations.

12. Sasson, *Judges 1–12*, 285, notes that the Targum inserts for v. 3, "Deborah said in prophecy before YHWH." Niditch, *Judges*, 76, suggests "the author" of the song, "whether male or female, assumes the voice and the perspective of a woman"; this analysis suggests, rather than a literary model with one author, several alternating singers (and sound patterns): an individual female singer, an individual male singer, and another male singer who describes the tribes and refers to Deborah and Baraq in third person.

| | | |
|---|---|---|
| Then Deborah sang, and Baraq,<br>son of Abinoam, on that day, saying:<br>(1) | wattāšar dĕvôrâ ûvārāq<br>ben-ʾăvînōʿam bayyôm hahûʾ lēʾmōr | |
| *(female)*<br>“**When** (warrior) locks were *LONG*<br>/ (women) restraint *UNLOOSED*[1]<br>**in** ***ISRAEL***,<br>**when** the **people**<br>freely offered themselves,<br>**bless** *YHWH*!” (2) | **biphrōaʿ**<br>**pōr**ʿôt<br>**bĕ*YIŚRĀʾĒL***<br>**bĕ**hitnaddēv **ʿām**<br>**bārāk*û*** ***YHWH*** | *(triplets)*<br>**3 bi, bĕ, bĕ**<br>**3 phrōaʿ, pōr**ʿôt, **bārā̆**<br><br>**3** YHWH<br>**1 bā**răk (ironic soundplay) |
| **Hear**,<br>O **kings**;<br>**give** *EAR*,<br>O *PRINCES*; | **šim*ʿû***<br>**mĕlākîm**<br>ha*ʾĂZÎN**Û***<br>*rŌZĒN***îm** | **3 û, û, û**<br><br>**3** mĕl, ʾ**ĕl, ʾēl**<br>**3** šim, **îm, îm** |
| ***I***, ***TO YHWH***,<br>***I***,<br>**I** will sing! **I** will *MAKE MELODY*<br><br>***TO YHWH***,<br>***GOD*** of<br>***ISRAEL***.” (3) | ***ʾĀNŌKÎ*** ***LAYHWH***<br>***ʾĀNŌKÎ***<br>**ʾā**šîrâ *ʾĂZA***mmē**r<br>***LAYHWH***<br>***ʾĔL***ōhê<br>***YIŚRĀʾĒL*** | **3 ăzîn, ōzĕn, ʾăzam**<br>**3 ʾānōkî, ʾānōki** +ʾ**ā**šîrâ<br>**3 ʾā, ʾā, ʾā (+ 1)**<br>**3 ʿām, mĕ**lā**kîm,** ʾă**zam**<br>**1** ʾ**ĕ**lōhê<br>**2 yiśrāʾēl** (+yiśrāʾēl inclusio) |

[1] There is no consensus for the translation of the double root (*pr*ʿ); the rendering here affirms the two main meanings in what likely was an intentional wordplay: the root *pr*ʿ (qal infinitive construct as verb here, lacks number and gender), elsewhere in the Bible, for men or women, means to ‘let loose,’ ‘let grow’ the hair (Nu 6:5), associated with Nazirites or warriors (Deut 32:25); further, a more symbolic, poetic meaning of this root could be to ‘remove restraint,” in this context perhaps implying *to resist oppression*, and hesitant restraint of warriors, yet with a feminine subject; see Janzen, “Root *pr'* in Judges V 2,” 403; yet reading the second term as a qal *feminine* participial noun (simply repointed as *pōrʿôt,* instead of MT’s *pĕrāʿôt*) and *as subject*, in parallel with *ʿām*, suggests both nuances of women *loosing* the social restraint imposed on them, as well as long-haired warriors, taking the lead to free the people from oppression. Given the content of the song, let the translation be unloosed (!) to consider a female plural subject here; Craigie, “Note on Judg 5:2,” 397-99, translated the infinitive, drawing on an Arabic cognate, as “wholly dedicated themselves”, thus a parallel to “freely offered themselves.”

As Susan Niditch and others note, v. 3 contains formulaic pairs of terms typically found in songs of victory and praise (e.g., ‘hear’/ ‘give ear’ as well as ‘I will sing to YHWH’).[13] As an early song, these lyrics may have helped solidify such formulas for later generations,[14] while ‘sing to YHWH’ appeared already in Exod 15:1 and 21. Blenkinsopp’s analysis of Judges 5 suggested a blending of a ‘war ballad’ (e.g., v. 2) to psalm elements (v. 3) *at a later stage* to form the present song in Judges 5.[15] However, ‘bless YHWH’ in v. 2 certainly is a psalmic element. The present analysis suggests

13. Niditch, *Judges*, 71; Hauser, “Judges 5” 28–29, suggests the singer is calling on the defeated Canaanite kings to listen to this song in praise of YHWH by the victors.

14. Coogan, “Structural and Literary Analysis, 155–56. Blenkinsopp, “Ballad and Psalm Style,” 67, notes the climactic pattern of Judg 5:3b is similarly found in Ps 29.

15. Blenkinsopp, “Ballad Style and Psalm Style,” 63–64; similarly Echols, *“Tell Me, O Muse,”* 90–92; Frolov, *Judges*, 132–33, suggests at best Judg 5:2–31a is a “rudimentary . . . hymn of praise” expanded from a “profane composition,” in light of the deity’s “inconspicuousness” through much of it; however, ‘YHWH’ appears 14 times in Judges 5, and the indigenous worldview implies the divine working through nature (vv. 4–5; 20–22).

that together these verses (2–3) reflect an indigenous worldview that did not separate the sacred and the secular,[16] that the two verses were already intimately joined by the singer's (Deborah or a women's tradition) lyrical artistry, and drawn tight by three distinct *triplet soundplays*, including *three* imperative plural verbs (*bārăkû, šimʿû, haʾăzînû*), and *three* repetitions of YHWH across them. That is, Deborah's (represented) sophisticated lyrics had *already infused* the traditional battle victory song, which the culture(s) *expected* women typically to sing for male warriors, with praise of YHWH; as such, and as will be seen, she is an exemplar of a women's prophetic lyrical tradition, in the footsteps of Miriam, both of whom, it might be proposed, are shown to have *innovated this genre* for Israel. Both Miriam and Deborah, moreover, are suggested to have infused and innovated indigenous theophanies with nature into their lyrics, helpfully found in the traditions of their neighbors.[17]

At first glance, the *double* use in v. 3 of the first-person independent pronoun "I" (*ʾānōki*) seems to suggest a male compositional pattern. But in fact this doublet is part of a triplet with the verb *ʾāšîrâ* ("I will sing"), which is then quickly followed by *ʾăzammēr* ("I will make melody" or "make music"), which forms the third of a triplet soundplay with the *z* sound in *haʾăzînû* and *rōzĕnîm* just uttered. As will also be seen below, this voice typically uses a *doubled word joined* to another *syllable* for *triplet* soundplay (as above: *phrōaʿ*, *pĕrāʿ*ôt + *bār* and *ʾānōkî, ʾānōki* + *ʾāšîrâ*).[18]

After her opening lines, the song continues with Deborah's extended lyrics in v. 4–6 calling to mind the earlier theophany of YHWH's presence dramatically departing from Sinai[19] accompanying Israel; the imagery is much like that used by poets to describe the Canaanite storm

16. Thus also Globe, "Literary Structure and Unity," 494.

17. While readers may find it troubling to find women's voices, especially composing voices, responding to or involved with conflict or war, unfortunately this was what the culture—and every culture of the ancient Near East—was embroiled with. While the questions that Exum raises in her treatment of Judges, "Feminist Criticism: Whose Interests are Being Served?" 65–90, are helpful in assessing the interests and ideologies of the texts, I do not regard the composer or master 'narrator' of Judges 5 to be male, who simply co-opts women's voices and roles to serve male ideology; this analysis finds embedded in Judges 5, if not driving the whole, a women's lyrical tradition diverging from male warrior ideology.

18. The heavy use of repeated words in the song has been identified as a feature of early Hebrew composition similar to Ugaritic texts; see Globe, "Literary Structure and Unity," 509 (following Albright).

19. Freedman, *Pottery, Poetry, and Prophecy*, 158.

deity, Baal.[20] Deborah's lyrics are notable, since in the Judges 4 narrative, YHWH is simply alluded to behind the event.[21] Judges 5:4 and 5:31a–b are the only places in the song where a singer *addresses* YHWH *directly*. This is suggestive of Deborah's role as intermediary for the people with YHWH, thus the shift from theophany to rendering the people's plight. Once again, while doublets of words and phrases appear in her lyrics, she consistently adds a *third* syllable or word for triplet soundplay (*mippĕnê* YHWH */ ze sînay / mippĕnê* YHWH, and, *bĕṣēʾtĕkā miśśēʿî / bĕṣaʿdĕkā miśśĕdē / ʾĕdôm*). Her lyrics in v. 5 closely parallel her lyrics in v. 3.[22] She continues in v. 6, with the compassion of a prophet, contrasting YHWH's cosmic going forth, surging like stormwater, as though coming to the rescue of the people—whose mundane hardship is rendered by their inability simply to walk or travel the roads freely without danger.[23] (Scholars have been perplexed by how to translate v. 6; yet *five* tight *triplet* soundplays (fifteen syllables in one verse!) by the singer, topped off with the singular *ʿăqalqallôt*, are stunning lyrical artistry (below).

20. Blenkinsopp, "Ballad Style and Psalm Style," 67–68; Cross, *Canaanite Myth*, 147–77.

21. This does not suggest a disagreeing perspective, simply different, likely due to the storytelling genre.

22. Globe, "Literary Structure and Unity," 502.

23. Niditch, *Judges*, 78.

| *(female)* | *YHWH* | *(triplets)* |
|---|---|---|
| "*YHWH*,<br>*WHEN YOU WENT FORTH* **from** *SEIR*,<br>*WHEN YOU MARCHED* **from** *FIELDS*<br>of *EDOM*,<br><br>**Earth** trembled,<br>*ALSO* the *SKIES DROPPED*,<br>*ALSO* **clouds** *DROPPED*<br>*WATER*! (4)<br>Moun**tains,** *CASCADES*![1]<br><br>*BECAUSE OF YHWH'S PRESENCE*,[2]<br>(the) One of **Sinai**,<br>*BECAUSE OF YHWH'S PRESENCE*,<br>*GOD* of<br>*ISRAEL*! (5)<br>"*IN DAYS* of Shamgar,[3]<br>**son** of Anath,<br>*IN DAYS* of Jael,<br><br>*CEASED*[4] *ROAD-TRAVEL*<br>and those *WALKING* on path**ways**<br>*WALKED* by *ROADS*<br>*ROUNDABOUT*."[5] (6) | *BĔṢĒ'TĔKĀ MIŚŚĒ*ʿîr<br>*BĔṢA'DĔKĀ MIŚŚĔ***dēh**<br>**ʾĕd**ôm<br><br>ʾereṣ rāʿ**āšâ**<br>*GAM-ŠĀMAYIM NĀṬĀPHÛ*<br>*GAM* - ʿāv*ÎM NĀṬĔPHÛ*<br>*MĀYIM*<br>hār**îm** *NĀZĔLÛ*<br>*MIPPĔNÊ YHWH*<br>ze s**înay**<br>*MIPPĔNÊ YHWH*<br>**ʾĕ**lōhê<br>*YIŚRĀ'ĒL*<br>**bî**mê *ŠAMGA*r<br>**be**n- ʿănāt<br>**bî**mê yāʿēl<br>*ḤĀ*dĕ*LÛ* *'ŎRĀḤÔT*<br>wĕ*HŌLĔK*ê nĕtîv**ôt**<br>yē*LĔKÛ* *'ŎRĀḤÔT*<br>ʿă*QALQALL***ôt** | 3 **YHWH, YHWH, YHWH**<br>3 **bĕṣē,** miśśē, **bĕṣa**<br>3 **bĕṣēʾtĕkā miśśē**ʿîr<br>**bĕṣaʿdĕkā miśśĕ**dēh, ʾ**ĕd**ôm<br>3 ʾereṣ + **bĕṣ, bĕṣ**<br>3 **gam-šām, gam**<br>3 **gam** šām**ayim nāṭāphû**<br>**gam ʿāvîm nāṭĕphû**<br>hār**îm nāzĕl**û<br>3 **šāmayim,** ʿā**vîm, māyim**<br>3 **mippĕnê YHWH,** ze s**î**nay,<br>**mippĕnê YHWH**<br>2 ʾ**ĕ**lōhê **yiśrāʾēl** (+ 1 above)<br>3 **bîmê šamgar** (+ above:<br>**gam šāmayim, gam ʿāvîm**)<br>3 **bîmê,** ben, **bîmê**<br>3 **ḥôt, hō, ḥôt**<br>3 **ʾŏrāḥôt,** nĕtîv**ôt, ʾŏrāḥôt**<br>(+ʿăqalqall**ôt** = 4)<br>3 **ḥā**dĕ**lû, hōlĕk**ê, yē**lĕkû**<br>3 **ōlĕkê, ēlĕkû, alqa**<br>2 **ʿăqalqallô**t |

[1] Translating a noun for the verb to express the 'flowing' (*nzl*) of water from the mountains as an effect of rainfall. Frolov, *Judges*, 130, citing M. Vincent (2000), notes that vv. 4-5 form a chiasm. While three sets of repeated doublet phrases are most apparent, in fact, the *center* of the chiasm is formed by a *triplet* soundplay with three parallel subjects and verbs, reversed order for emphasis (*šāmayim nāṭāphû / 'āvîm nāṭĕphû / hārîm nāzĕlû*), and preceded and followed by overlapping triplet soundplays.
[2] Lit. 'before the face of YHWH.'
[3] V. 6a suggests that both Shamgar (depicted as a mighty warrior in Judg 3:31) and Jael (likely for her actions here) had become well-known figures by the people; Hackett, "Days of Jael," 15-38.
[4] Freedman, *Pottery, Poetry & Prophecy*, 150, translates the root *ḥdl* in each occurrence in vv. 6-7 from the meaning 'to enrich.'
[5] Scholars have noted the chiasm in v. 6cb, however this is embedded within a larger pattern of four to five different *triplet* sound plays.

Just after the female voice mentions the people's movements "ceased," a male voice (implying Baraq) interjects (v. 7) and employs four *doublet soundplays* to say, "deliverance" had also "ceased," "until you arose Deborah, arose a mother in Israel!"[24] Commentators have regarded vv. 6–8 as a non sequitur with the theophany in vv. 4–5. However, the link is a triplet soundplay between v. 4 and v. 6: *bîmê šamgar* ('days of Shamgar'; v. 6) + above, *gam šāmayim, gam 'āvîm* ('also the skies, also the clouds'; v. 4). A call and response between Baraq and Deborah appears to ensue from v. 7 until v. 12.

24. This is a symbolic title for a prophet; Boling, *Judges*, 257; Hackett, "In the Days of Jael," 28. The title may also suggest Deborah's role in uniting tribes as 'sons' in a common effort.

| | | |
|---|---|---|
| *(male)*<br><br>"*CEASED*—deliverance[1]<br>*IN ISRAEL*!<br>*CEASED* until<br>*YOU AROSE*, Deborah![2]<br>*YOU AROSE*, a mother,<br>*IN ISRAEL!*" (7) | *ḤĀDĔLÛ* phĕrāzôn<br>*BĔYIŚRĀʾĒL*<br>*ḤĀDĒLLÛ* ʿ**ad**<br>*ŠAQQAMTÎ* dĕvôrâ<br>*ŠAQQAMTÎ* ʾēm<br>*BĔYIŚRĀʾĒL* | *(doublets)*<br>2 **ḥādĕlû, ḥādēllû** (+**ḥādlû** above)<br>2 **ḥād**, ʿ**ad**<br>2 **bĕyiśrāʾēl, bĕyiśrāʾēl**<br>2 **šaqqamtî, šaqqamtî** |
| *(female)*<br>"*GOD* **choosing**<br>**new ones** (leaders),[3]<br>then *WAR* (at the) **gates**.<br><br>A shield, **was it seen**?<br>or **spear**?<br>**among forty**<br>**thousand** *IN ISRAEL*?!" (8) | **yi**vḥ**ar**<br>ʾ**ĕ***LŌHÎM* ḥ**ădāšîm**<br>ʾāz *LĀḤEM* šĕʿ**ārîm**<br>**mā**gēn ʿ**im-yērāʾeh**<br>wārōma**ḥ**<br>**bĕʾarbāʿîm**<br>ʾ**el**eph *BĔYIŚRĀʾĒL* | *(triplets)*<br>3 **yi + yi, yi** (above)<br>3 **yivḥar, ʾim-yērāʾeh**, **yiśrā**ʾēl<br>3 **ʾĕlōhîm, lāḥem, ʾele**<br>3 **ʿārîm, ārōm,ʾar**bāʿ**îm**<br>6 **îm, îm, em, îm, ʾim, îm**<br>3 **bĕ**ʾarbāʿîm, **bĕ** 2 **mā, ma**<br>3 **bĕyiśrāʾēl** (+ 2 above) |

[1] NJPS; cf. Hab 3:14.

[2] The use of *ša* before the verb, *šaqqamtî*, may be for sound effect. Translating the verb "arose" (*qamtî* in MT) not as a 1st person sing., "I arose" but as an archaic 2nd fem. sing. qal perfect ("you arose"); this archaic form (for 'sing') is also found in variant MSS of Exod 15:2, where Miriam is a lead singer, and in Isa 12:2 (1QIsa[a]). The song genre in all cases primarily praises YHWH for bringing victory, and though much of Judg 5 is suggested to be in Deborah's composing voice, it is not for her self-acclamation; Baraq is suggested as extolling Deborah as God's deliverer and 'mother," prophetically leading the tribes. Webb, *Judges*, 203, notes that mention of Deborah's activity in the song is 'muted' compared to the narrative, but this might be explained because she is a primary singer of the lyrics. Schneider, "Who is Interpreting the Text?" in McCabe, *Women in the Biblical World*, 10-23, reminds that the Deborah texts are regularly read in the synagogue *parashah* (weekly portion) each year as a prophetic *haftarah* along with the Torah reading of the crossing of the Red Sea and Song of the Sea (*Beshallach*); Fischer cites Butting's observation (*Prophetinnen gefragt*, 100) that after Moses and Miriam in the Torah the first prophet to appear in the Prophets section of the Bible *was a woman*, Deborah, also a judge; thus Fischer suggests the biblical canon here intends to present Deborah as both *the successor to Moses* and to carry on Miriam's prophetic role; *Gotteskünderinnen*, 123-24.

[3] Foll. Sasson, *Judges 1-12*, 291.

V. 8, above, poses difficulties of translation; it is usually rendered 'new gods were chosen,' perhaps suggestive of Israel's following other gods, yet this does not fit the context here. This translation has Deborah's voice render that God was choosing who would lead in the effort (she had used the plural construct of *ʾĕlōhîm* in v. 3, above). There is a subtle point in her line, that God chose (and Jael should be kept in mind); Deborah did not, so Baraq should not look to her for accolades or affirmation. In sharp contrast to the 'holy war' rhetoric in Joshua in which he and the Israelites are said to defeat many Canaanite peoples and places, including the king of Hazor (Jabin), "by the edge of the sword" (e.g., Josh 11:1–14), here Deborah ironically comments by a lyrical question that the forty thousand of Israel in this situation were *virtually weaponless* and without resources, further setting the stage for her to show how YHWH *alone* made possible their *rescue*, *not* their conquests.

A doublet sound pattern (male voices) next continues the song from v. 9 through 19, with one interjection by Deborah. Verse 9, below, is suggested by the content to be Baraq, as he expresses gratitude for those who volunteered to fight, repeating *ʿām* and YHWH from v. 2. His words are ironic and rather sanguine, since we know from the narrative of Judges 4 that *he* did not initially willingly go to battle! Yet, he describes voices now round about recounting the victory (vv. 10–11), and affirms those who 'marched down' toward the battle front. He interrupts himself to appeal to Deborah to 'awake' and 'sing', presumably to join in the retelling of his/their victory (v. 12).[25]

| *(male)* | **libbî** | *(doublets)* |
|---|---|---|
| "My **heart** belongs | **lĕ**ḥôqqê | 2 **li, lĕ** 1 **bî** (+**bĕ** above) |
| **to** the commanders of ***ISRAEL,*** | *IŚRĀʾĒL* hammitnaddĕ**vîm** | 2 mitnadd**ĕv**...**bāʿām bārăkû** |
| the ones freely offering themselves | | YHWH (+ in v. 2 above) |
| **for** the people. | **bā** *ʿĀM* | |
| *BLESS YHWH*! (9) | ***BĀRĂKÛ YHWH*** | 2 **yiśrāʾēl** (below) 2 **bā, bā** |
| "Those **riding tawny** | | 2 rō**kĕvê, yō**š**ĕvê** |
| *DONKEYS*, | rō**kĕvê** ʾ**ătōnôt** | |
| those **sitting** | *ṢĔḤ***ōrôt** | 2 ʾ**ătōnôt, ṣĕḥōrôt** |
| *ON* **saddle** rugs,[1] | yō**šĕvê** *ʿAL*-midd**în** | 2 **ṣĕḥō, śîḥû** 2 **ōl, ôl** 2 **ʿal, ʿal** |
| and those **walking** | | 2 **wĕhōlĕkê** (**wĕhōlĕkê,** v. 6) |
| *ON* the **way** | *WĔHŌLĔKÊ* ***ʿAL*** - **de**rek | 2 **mĕḥaṣṣîm, maš**ʾabb**îm** |
| —*TELL* (of it)![2] (10) | *ŚÎḤ***Û** | 2 **ĕtan** (+ ʾ**ătōn** above) |
| | miqq**ôl mĕḥaṣṣîm** | 2 **ṣidqôt, ṣidqôt** (chiasm |
| By voices of those **going out**[3] | **bê**n **maš**ʾabb**îm** | with ôt, ôt above) |
| **among watering places**, | šām **yĕtannû** | 2 **pirzōnô** (+ **phĕrāzôn** in v. |
| there let them *RECOUNT* | | 7 above; inclusio) |
| (the) ***RIGHTEOUS ACTS*** of ***YHWH***! | ***ṢIDQÔT*** ***YHWH*** | **4 yārĕdû** (below) |
| ***RIGHTEOUS ACTS*** of his deliverance | ***ṢIDQŌT*** pirzōnô | 1 ʿ**am** (+2 above, 1 below=**4**) |
| **in** ***ISRAEL***! | **bĕ***YIŚRĀʾĒL* | 4 **ʿûrî ʿûrî , ʿûrî ʿûrî** |
| ***THEN DOWN MARCHED,*** to the gates, | *ʾĀZ YĀRĔD*û laššĕʿārîm *ʿAM - YHWH* | 2 **dĕvôrâ, dabbĕrî** |
| the ***PEOPLE*** of ***YHWH***! (11) | *ʿÛRÎ ʿÛRÎ DĔVÔR*â | |
| | *ʿÛRÎ ʿÛRÎ DABBĔR*î - **šîr** | |
| ***AWAKE, AWAKE, DEBORAH***! | | |
| ***AWAKE, AWAKE, UTTER***[4] **song**!" (12a) | | |

[1] NJPS.
[2] Transl. of this Hebrew term is uncertain, though it participates in the doublet sound pattern.
[3] Transl. of people "going out" (*mĕḥaṣṣîm*) to a certain place, parallels above images of people moving along telling what happened (perhaps this is a rare verbal form of *ḥûṣ*, a noun meaning 'outside,' chosen for soundplay with *maš'abbîm*); since women customarily collected water, the masc. plural participle should include them among those recounting victory, perhaps with hand-drums. On *hapax legomena* and rare grammatical forms, see Baruch Margalit's evidence, "Alliteration in Ugaritic Poetry," 538, that a poet may choose them purposefully instead of an expected term of a word-pair *to serve an alliterative sound function*. Coogan's claim ("Structural and Literary Analysis," 160, fn 83) that "word pairs are, of course, the building blocks of West Semitic verse," is not entirely accurate; word pairs may be a building block; this study suggests that sound *syllables* are basic.
[4] The doublet sound plays on the name Deborah and the same root, *dbr*, to speak.

25. The line is unlikely a "call to arms" simply because the verb *ʿûr* elsewhere may be used to rouse YHWH to military action (Ackerman, *Warrior, Dancer,* 44); Miller, *Divine Warrior,* 93–95; if the admonition were Deborah as prophet speaking to the warriors or to YHWH, it could easily be interpreted as her calling them to arms, but *she* is addressed, asked to utter a song (also Boling, *Judges,* 117); the double use of this verb also appears as 'awake, my soul' to sing praise and thanks (as in Ps 57:9; 108:3); in Isa 52:1, the double use of the term calls for Zion to awake or arise from her captivity.

Deborah responds (with triplet soundplays), ironically, with a brief response to Baraq, not by recounting the warrior's battle or victory, but by calling him to 'get up' and take his captives away! (v. 12b).[26] This is doubly ironic, if not sardonic and humorous, since in the narrative account, Deborah repeatedly called Baraq to 'get up' and go to battle.

| | | |
|---|---|---|
| *(female)*<br>"Get up, **Baraq**, **lead** away<br>your **captives**,<br>O **son** of **Abi**noam." (12b) | qûm **bārāq ûšăvēh**<br>**ševyĕkā**<br>**ben** - ʾăvînōʿ**am** | *(triplets)*<br>**3 bār** (+ **vôr, bĕr** above)<br>**2 bā, be**<br>**3 šă, še** (+**šîr**, above)<br>**3 ăvēh, evyĕ, ʾăvî** |
| *(male)*<br>"Then ***DOWN MARCHED***<br>a **remnant**<br>**of** the **nobles**;<br>the ***PEOPLE*** of ***YHWH***<br>***MARCHED DOWN*** **for me**<br>against the **mighty**!"[1] (13) | ***ʾĀZ YĔRAD***<br>**śārîd**<br>**lĕʾaddîrîm** *ʿĀM YHWH*<br>***YĔRAD*-lî**<br>baggibb**ôrîm** | *(doublets)*<br>**2 yĕrad, yĕrad**<br>**2 ārîd, ʾaddîr**<br>**2 ʿām , ʿam** (+2 in vv. 9, 11)<br>**2 lĕ, lî** **2 rîm, rîm**<br>**2 YHWH** (+1 above) |

[1] Coogan notes the syntactic chiasm in v. 13 (verb-subject:subject-verb); "Structural and Literary Analysis," 160; not only does this disruption of normal word order highlight Baraq's emphasis on "the people of YHWH" who marched down, *for me*, but when his doublet soundplays are lined up (4 sets of them!), what appears is that *only* "the people of YHWH" are without a paired sound—he *breaks* the doublet pattern for 'singular' effect. On the meaning of the term 'people' here as warriors, see Miller, (foll. von Rad), *Divine Warrior*, 92.

Here in the song there sounds to be a subtle tension in the two singers' call and response, and further irony in light of the tension between them in the prose account.[27] All the voices here are participating, in different ways, in a victory song, but *who is praised, and how*, is dramatically unfolding. Deborah does not immediately raise a song after her retort. Nonetheless, Baraq resumes his singing in v. 13 (doublet soundplays), now *recounting for himself* those who marched down 'for me' (or ironically, who didn't) against the enemy warriors. This analysis interprets that Baraq is preoccupied more with *the genre of a victory song for male warriors* (albeit with God's help), while Deborah, who knows how the victory was really won, dispenses with that in order to render (in coming verses) YHWH's theophany, and a different, hidden front, where Jael took matters into her own hands to bring the final victory. Given the custom of women singing victory songs for male warriors, these lines are highly ironic, as

26. Schneider, *Judges*, 90, notes the further wry irony implicit in the comment to Baraq that he did not get the one captive he wanted—Sisera.

27. Commentators disagree on whether Deborah's call for him here to 'get up' is anticipatory, recounting her calling him to battle, or subsequent to it and part of the victory song. Ackerman, *Warrior, Dancer*, 34–35, reads v. 12b as part of Deborah's rousing Baraq to battle; yet, Deborah is hardly "ordered to sing."

the chosen *male warrior asks* the woman prophet to join him in singing about a victory *which he did not bring.*[28] The voices are at odds due to their different roles and different gendered concerns. One might even say the song is a satire on Baraq.[29] In this regard, I propose that here we have a song mostly composed by a woman, or conveying a women's tradition, and which *does not* essentially serve a male worldview.[30]

A different male singer[31] appears to step up, using pervasive doublet soundplays and carries Baraq's song forward from v. 14 through 18, describing the clans of the different tribes.[32] This voice refers to both Baraq and Deborah in third person. The irony is heightened here because a male singer rather than the expected female now sings of the tribes' and Baraq's victory. Yet, the poem and the prose agree overall in giving less importance to this.

After the catalog of tribes by this other male voice, Baraq apparently returns to take up the song of the battle in v. 19 (below); the voice employs

28. As Pressler notes, *Joshua, Judges,* 166, the song does not allude to Baraq's hesitation to fight or "his failure to achieve glory," as happened in Judges 4; yet this analysis still finds some tension between the song's voices. Baraq's voice is preoccupied with what Exum, "Feminist Criticism," 71, suggests was typical of men's ideology of warfare: glory, acclaim, and "to have their valor praised."

29. Butler, *Judges,* 158, calls Judges 4 a 'parody on holy war' and Judges 5 contains satirical elements. He further asks an incisive question about the point of the texts: "Are women really praised in their own right? Or are they part of a battle parody showing how far men have sunk? Is this a call to liberate women or a call to revitalize the masculine element of society?" (175).

30 Cf. Exum, "Feminist Criticism," 67, who suggests though women may have composed some of the stories or songs in the Bible, "even if the Bible's authors were not all male, it is the male worldview that finds expression in the biblical literature, for, as the dominant worldview of the time, it was shared by men and women alike." While the Bible is overall androcentric, the present study finds cautionary evidence against generalizations that may stereotype all ancient women to think the same, or all men, in a given culture; certainly some women adopted male dominant cultural views, but some would have not; generalizations may oversimplify ancient Hebraic culture and shortchange the independence, callings, and capabilities indigenous women actually had and expressed; on these issues, see also Meyers, "Miriam, Music, and Miracles," in Good, *Mariam, Magdalen, Mother,* 27–48.

31. Contra Frolov, *Judges,* 134. Klein, *Triumph of Irony,* 44, also notes there are multiple voices in the overall song: vv. 13–18 'a song of the people'; Webb, *Judges,* 210. While a doublet sound pattern is often used by a male composer/singer, it is possible it is also used for communal singing; i.e., the refrain of 15:1b.

32. Niditch, *Judges,* 68–80, suggests not reading these tribes in a negative light, but this is a "traditional catalogue formula" (74), following Frank Moore Cross, *Canaanite Myth and Hebrew Epic,* 235n74.

pervasive *doublet* sound repetitions referring to the Canaanite kings arriving to fight, yet this will be his last utterance in Judges 5.[33] Because the prophet Deborah takes up the song and quickly shifts the focus to the cosmic realm (v. 20), yet also zooms in to focus on Sisera down near the Kishon, who suddenly appears small indeed! While Deborah's lines include doublet sounds (and thus may appear to belong to Baraq), her poetic device is just as before; in this case she answers/repeats his precise word doublet[34] but adds to it *a third* syllable or word for *triplet* soundplay: *nilḥāmû, nilḥāmû* + . . . *naḥal* ("they fought, they fought") plus a wordplay—*naḥal* means not only 'torrent', but '*took possession*'—Kishon 'took down' Sisera! Precisely as Baraq appeared to begin to describe the battle, Deborah takes over the 'narrative' and renders how the victory was accomplished.[35] "From the sky, the stars fought" of course suggests the intervention of the divine realm; in earlier lines Deborah described YHWH's manifestation through nature's forces.[36]

| *(male)* | | *(doublets)* |
|---|---|---|
| "The *KINGS* came, *THEY FOUGHT*; | bāʾû *MĔLĀK*îm *NILḤĀMÛ* | 2 nilḥāmû, nilḥāmû |
| then *FOUGHT* | *ʾĀZ* *NILḤĂMÛ* | 2 mĕlāk, malk |
| the *KINGS* of **Canaan**, | *MALK*ê kĕnaʿan | 4 kĕ, kĕ, ke, qā |
| **at Taanach**, | bĕtaʿnak | 2 kĕnaʿan, aʿnak 2 beṣ, kes |
| **by waters** of **Me**giddo; **extorted** | ʿal-mê mĕgiddô beṣaʿ | 2 bĕta, beṣaʿ 2 nāk, lāq |
| **silver**, they did **not take**!" | keseph lōʾ lāqāḥû | 3 ʿal mĕ, ʿal mê (+wĕʿal mi) |
| (19) | | 2 āḥû, ḥămû 2 lōʾ lā |
| *(female)* | | *(triplets)* |
| "**From** (the) sky the stars *FOUGHT*, | min - šāmayim *NILḤĀMÛ* hakkôkāvîm | 1 min +2 mini v. 14(inclusio) |
| **from** their **courses** they *FOUGHT* | mimmĕsillôtām *NILḤĂMÛ* | 3 min, mim, ʿim |
| **against** *SISERA*. *TORRENT* | ʿim - sîsĕrāʾ *NAḤAL* | 3 hakkôkā + 2 nāk, lāqa |
| *KISHON* (took posession) | qîšôn | 3 nilḥāmû, nilḥāmû, naḥal |
| swept **them** (away)." | gĕrāphām | 3 sillô, sîsĕrāʾ, qîšôn |
| (20-21a) | | 3 ḥāmû, ḥāmû, phām |

The term *naḥal* is also a Janus parallelism, not only facing and completing the previous soundplay, but spinning as though in the midst of battle

33. Blenkinsopp,"Ballad Style and Psalm Style," 73, notes v. 19, includes stairstep parallelism and chiasm.

34. As Hauser, "Judges 5," 33, notes, nowhere to be found here are the Israelite warriors; the battle is between the stars (embodying divinity) that 'fight, fight,' against Canaanite kings that 'fight, fight.'

35. An Israelite tradition also suggested victory may come from *non*fighting, joined with God's miraculous intervention, as in the exodus liberation.

36. For the role of stars as deities at Ugarit, see Miller, *Divine Warrior in Israel*, 21–23. For similar ancient Near Eastern victory songs joining deities and nature, see Globe, "Literary Structure and Unity," 497–501.

to start a new triplet of Kishon's next actions. With a striking *series* of triplet soundplays, Deborah sings of the sky and stars supplying a downpour of water[37] and the hurried motion of the "torrent Kishon" racing, *with her striding beside*, virtually addressing Kishon like a warrior doing its part on the front line of attack, and Kishon *caused* to surge (*qal* passive) by a force beyond itself.[38] (A modern Western view calls this personification, but for an indigenous culture where spiritual energy and forces permeate nature, the singer renders the ancient worldview and participates in it.) Deborah sings of their empowered partnership, she with YHWH and nature, accomplishing *what no man had been able to do*.[39]

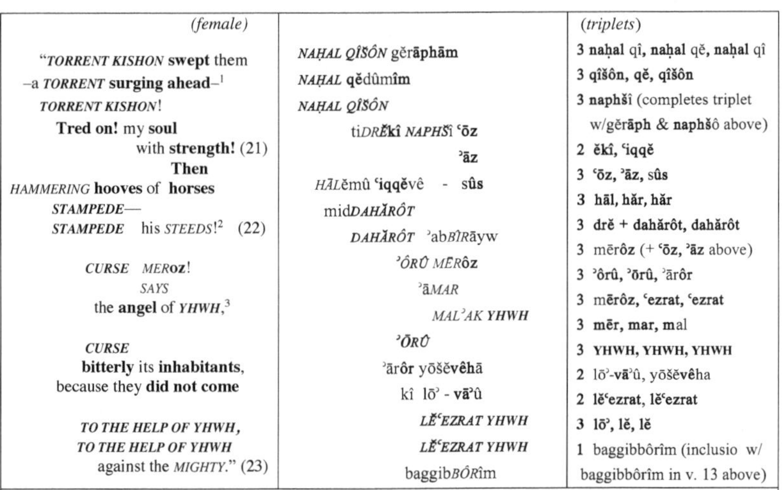

| *(female)* | | *(triplets)* |
|---|---|---|
| "*TORRENT KISHON* **swept** them | *NAḤAL QÎŠÔN* gĕr**āphām** | 3 **naḥal** qî, **naḥal** qĕ, **naḥal** qî |
| –a *TORRENT* **surging ahead**–[1] | *NAḤAL* **qĕ**dûm**îm** | 3 **qîšôn, qĕ, qîšôn** |
| *TORRENT KISHON*! | *NAḤAL QÎŠÔN* | 3 **naphšî** (completes triplet w/gĕr**āph** & **naphš**ô above) |
| **Tred on!** my **soul** | ti*DRĔ***kî** *NAPHŠ*î **ʿōz** | 2 **ĕkî, ʿiqqĕ** |
| with **strength!** (21) | **ʾāz** | 3 **ʿōz, ʾāz, sûs** |
| **Then** | *HĀL*ĕmû **ʿiqqĕ**vê - **sûs** | 3 **hāl, hăr, hăr** |
| *HAMMERING* **hooves** of **horses** | mid*DAHĂRÔT* | 3 **drĕ + dahărôt, dahărôt** |
| *STAMPEDE*— | *DAHĂRÔT* ʾab*BÎR*āyw | 3 mērôz (+ **ʿōz, ʾāz** above) |
| *STAMPEDE* his *STEEDS*![2] (22) | *ʾÔRÛ MĒR***ôz** | 3 **ʾôrû, ʾōrû,** ʾārôr |
| *CURSE MER***oz**! | ʾā*MAR* | 3 mērôz, **ʿezrat, ʿezrat** |
| *SAYS* | *MALʾAK YHWH* | 3 **mēr, mar, m**al |
| the **angel** of *YHWH*,[3] | *ʾŌRÛ* | 3 **YHWH, YHWH, YHWH** |
| *CURSE* | ʾā**rôr** yōšĕ**vêhā** | 2 lōʾ-**vā**ʾû, yōšĕ**vê**ha |
| **bitterly** its **inhabitants**, | kî lōʾ - **vā**ʾû | 2 **lĕʿezrat, lĕʿezrat** |
| because they **did not come** | *LĔʿEZRAT YHWH* | 3 **lōʾ, lĕ, lĕ** |
| *TO THE HELP OF YHWH*, | *LĔʿEZRAT YHWH* | 1 baggibbôrîm (inclusio w/ baggibbôrîm in v. 13 above) |
| *TO THE HELP OF YHWH* | baggib*BÔR*îm | |
| against the *MIGHTY*." (23) | | |

[1] Translating *qdm*, a qal passive participle, as something that 'precedes' or 'goes before' (its other terms are 'the sunrise,' 'the east,' 'olden times before'; *BDB:* 869-70). The MT form also serves soundplay.
[2] Author's translation, foll. Niditch, 'stampeding," *Judges*, 69. See Coogan, "Structural and Literary Analysis," 150, for 'hammering'.
[3] *malʾak* (NRSV: 'angel') is not out of bounds given the cosmic dimension (cf. Ps 18:10), but the term may also refer to Deborah as YHWH's 'messenger'; if the latter, she may refer to herself.

Here are rendered two themes already important, I have suggested, in a Hebraic women's lyrical tradition: a focus on the role of water (seas,

37. Pressler, *Joshua, Judges*, 164, notes that in nearby Ugarit it was believed the stars caused rain.

38. Niditch, *Judges*, 80, suggests the Kishon that helped water the fertile Esdraelon Plain may have been regarded as "the power of the deity in the water." A number of commentators note that the wadi Kishon does not flood and could not of its own accord (size!) take down Sisera's chariot army.

39. Klein, *Triumph of Irony*, 47, observes that no divine intervention helping the enemy kings is described.

rivers, a wady!) through which YHWH manifests power, and the description of horses and chariots of battle. Both are important in the triplet sound lyrics of the Miriamic tradition in the 'Song of the Sea.'[40] While the horses in Judges 5 obviously suggest, on the mundane level, Sisera's warriors fleeing, it is possible that there are two levels of meaning going on. As the poetry is so cosmically charged, with the Kishon surging, the prophet striding, and the horses racing—each and all conveyed along by their own triplet soundplays—these may also be *the deity's* steeds racing, doing their part to defeat Sisera's chariots. Deborah's lyrics seem to suggest that YHWH, as invisible divine warrior, unleashes the heavenly host or multitude to participate in the thwarting of Sisera. The term translated 'steed' or 'stallion' (*ʾabbîr*), as Sasson reminds, can refer to a mighty person or warrior, or to a mighty animal.[41] It can also refer to an angel (Ps 78:25) or to God, the 'Mighty One' (Gen 49:24). (This joining together in one word a powerful, present entity—as incarnating an angel, perhaps an ancestor, an animal, or a deity—is suggestive of a worldview shared by many indigenous peoples.) YHWH's theophanic horses or chariots are described in numerous biblical texts often associated with prophets, e.g., with Elijah and Elisha (2 Kgs 2:11–12; 6:15–16), in Zechariah's visions (Zech 1:9–11; 6:1–8), in Habakkuk's vision (Hab 3:8, 15), and in Ezekiel's vision (Ezekiel 1). YHWH as the 'Rider in the sky' [42]also appears in Deut 33:26 and Ps 68:18, depicted as coming from Sinai with thousands of chariots. W. F. Albright noted that Anat and her sister, Astarte, were depicted with horses in a Ugaritic text, and Astarte rides a horse (in Egyptian traditions).[43]

A number of scholars have rightfully suggested that Deborah is likened to the Canaanite war goddess Anat, who fights to bring victory for her brother, Baal (a god analogous to YHWH).[44] As Susan Ackerman

40. Hauser, "Judges 5," 30–31, notes the importance of the theme of water throughout Judges 5 by the poet he refers to as male; however, the two male singers that I identify by using doublet sound patterns refer in an everyday fashion to bodies of water, yet it is by the singer using triplet soundplays—I propose the represented female prophet—that water is rendered most powerfully as participating in YHWH's intervention.

41. Sasson, *Judges 1–12*, 303.

42. Cross, *Canaanite Myth*, 157.

43. Astarte was also associated with the evening star (Albright, *Yahweh and the Gods*, 133fn60).

44. Dempster, "Mythology and History," 33–53; Craigie, "Deborah and Anat," 374–81; Rasmussen, "Deborah, the Woman Warrior," 79–93; and Ackerman, *Warrior,*

notes, in the Bible the goddesses are demythologized in favor of YHWH, and their traits here are made human in Deborah and Jael.[45] However, it is possible the woman prophet regards YHWH as encompassing the ancient feminine divine force, reaching earth; and the 'cosmic/earthly' and 'divine/human' dichotomies in the song, besides demythologizing for a historical presentation,[46] may be attributed also to a dichotomy *in gendered perspectives*: in this song, the female voice mostly renders the cosmic/divine, the male voices the earthly/human, due to their roles. A similar female/male difference of focus is found in the Song of the Sea.

However, Deborah is not herself, like Anat, described as doing the fighting, though in Judg 4:7 she intended to take troops to a location to draw Sisera out for Baraq's attack, and she goes to the battle scene (4:9); her fighting was not necessary, both because the victory was assured by YHWH and by the male warriors' willingness to go forth and put pressure on Sisera. While it was not unusual for prophets (male and female) in the ancient Near East to advise on military strategy, there does not appear to be significant evidence that they were also warriors.[47] Deborah's major role here as prophet after the battle is in rendering lyrics that create the world of the event *and* the changed world in which Israel now finds itself.

Yet, Deborah lyricizes drawing from Canaanite and ancient Near East mythology in expressing a Yahwistic song; is it possible that Deborah affirmed some elements of the old worldview, much as peoples the world over have often retained their ancient indigenous traditions along with adopting newer religious ideas? More to the point of this study is the importance of examining whether the Ugaritic texts about Anat, particularly those in her voice, might bear a triplet syllable sound pattern

---

*Dancer*, 51–73, suggests Israel was familiar with Anat, as indicated by personal and place-names in Israel (51–52), and it "adopts and adapts" (66) the Anat-Baal tradition where these deities are 'two sides of the same coin' (67). Sasson, *Judges*, 304, cites Kogan's study (2005) noting an Akkadian text in which Sargon of Agade was also battled by the stars.

45. Ackermann, *Warrior, Dancer*, 66.

46. Ibid.

47. Contra Frolov, *Judges*, 146–47, reading through a 'competitive' lens, he suggests Deborah failed both in picking the wrong commander—Baraq—and in not leading the fighting herself (she lost the glory to Jael). *Neither* is Deborah portrayed in Judges 4 as 'only' Baraq's 'advisor' (Ackerman, *Warrior, Dancer*, 63–64, 71), as this misses her significant role as YHWH's prophet, the highest authority, given by the narrative, and the song; also Hackett, "In the Days of Jael," 22, who attributes not her prophetic role, but her judging role, to convincing Baraq to go out.

suggestive of a wider indigenous women's lyrical tradition also, or whether this is a signature feature only of Hebraic women's tradition.

While the female voice (Deborah) has extolled the forces of nature in defeating Sisera, she moves next to lyricize an extended section praising Jael and her actions (v. 24–31), permeated by the triplet syllable sound pattern. That Jael is called 'blessed' implies that Deborah regards divine power also working through her (not stressed in the prose account), regardless of the reader's ethical quandary about Jael's gruesome actions. Deborah's triplet pattern serves a narrative-like flow in vv. 24–25, and then shifts to a rapid staccato effect with onomotopoeia in v. 26 to render Jael's attack on Sisera.[48] Triplet repetitions of numerous, entire words emphasize Sisera's collapse in v. 27, with sexual undertones and his overturn.[49] As many commentators note, Sisera, the victimizer of women and oppressor of Israel for many years, becomes the victim of a woman whose hand brings an end to his violence with surprising dispatch.

48. Blenkinsopp, "Ballad Style and Psalm Style," 74, notes importance of sound repetition in this section.

49. It is not necessary to imagine that Jael killed Sisera while he was standing up (cf. Sasson, *Judges 1–12*, 317), though the text is ambiguous. For an analysis, see Niditch, *Judges*, 81, and idem, "Eroticism and Death in the Tale of Jael," 43–57. Ackerman, *Warrior, Dancer*, 60–61, suggests the recounting of Jael's actions may also be influenced by the Canaanite Anat traditions, particularly by the goddess Anat (also an "erotic assassin") sending a messenger to strike Aqhat in the head while he is inside a tent; the scene of Judith with Holofernes also has parallels; see also Skehan, "Hand of Judith," 94–110.

| | | |
|---|---|---|
| *(female)* | | *(triplets)* |
| "*MOST BLESSED* of *WOMEN*, **Jael**! | *TĚVŌRAK* *MINNĀŠÎM* yāʿēl | 1 yāʿēl 3 ʿēl, el, el |
| **wife**[1] of | ʾēšet | 3 sîsěrāʾ, sîsěrāʾ, sîsěrāʾ |
| *HEBER* the **Kenite**, | | |
| of *WOMEN* | ḥ*EVER* haqqênî *MINNĀŠÎM* | 3 těvōrak, ḥever, těvōrāk |
| *AMONG THE TENTS* | bāʾōhel | 3 āšî, ʾēše, āšî 3 rak, haq, rāk |
| *MOST BLESSED*! (24) | *TĚVŌRĀK* mayim šāʾal | 3 minnāšîm, minnāšîm + mayim |
| '*WATER*' he **asked for**; | ḥālāv nātānâ běsēphel | |
| *MILK* she gave *IN A BOWL* | | 3 bāʾōhel, šāʾal, běsēphel |
| (for) **lords**, | ʾaddîrîm | 3 ḥever, ḥālāv, hiqrîv |
| she *PRESENTED* **curds**.[2] (25) | hiqrîvâ ḥemʾâ | 4 îm, îm, im, îm |
| Her *HAND*, | yādāh | 3 nâ, vâ, mʾâ |
| **for the** *TENT PEG* | layyātēd | 3 yādāh, yātēd (+ ʾad above) |
| she **stretched it,** | tišlaḥnâ | 3 āh, nâ, nāh 3 la, laḥ, lěh |
| and **her right** (hand) | wîmînāh | 3 lěhalm, ʿămēl, wěhālěm |
| **for** the *HAMMER* of | lě*HALM*ût | 3 sîsěrāʾ, rōʾšô, raqqātô |
| *WORK* (trouble)— | ʿămēlîm | 7 āh, nâ, nāh, mâ, qâ, ṣâ, phâ |
| and she *HAMMERED* *SISERA*! | wě*HĀLĚM*â *SÎSĚRĀ*ʾ | 3 wîmînāh, wěhālěmâ, wěḥālěphâ |
| *CRUSHED* **his head**; | *MĀḤĂ*qâ *RŌʾŠÔ* | |
| and *SHATTERED* | û*MĀḤĂ*ṣâ | 3 māḥăqâ, māḥăṣâ, wěḥālěphâ |
| and *PIERCED* **his temple**. (26) | wě*ḤĀLĚ*phâ raqqātô | |
| ***BETWEEN HER LEGS HE BENT;***[3] | ***BÊN RAGLÊHĀ KĀRA***ʿ | 3 raqqāt (above) + 2 raglêhā kāraʿ, raglêhā kāraʿ |
| ***HE FELL,*** **laid** out; | ***NĀPHAL*** šākāv | |
| ***BETWEEN HER LEGS HE BENT,*** | ***BÊN RAGLÊHĀ KĀRA***ʿ | 3 bê, bê, ba |
| ***HE FELL***; | ***NĀPHAL*** | 3 kāraʿ, kāraʿ, kāraʿ |
| **Just** where ***HE BENT,*** **there** | baʾăšer *KĀRA*ʿ šām | 3 nāphal, nāphal, nāphal |
| ***HE FELL,*** **ravaged**. (27) | ***NĀPHAL*** šādûd | 3 šākāv, šām, šādûd |

[1] In Hebrew, literally, 'woman of.' Some translators wish to delete Heber, the Kenite because it doesn't work with the perceived doublet repetitions; however, both terms serve multiple *triplet* soundplays.
[2] Sasson notes the verb switches from Jael simply 'giving' Sisera milk, to ceremonially 'presenting' him curds in a lordly bowl; *Judges 1-12*, 307; Niditch dubs the interaction as between "seductive assassin and assassinated dupe," and Jael represents a folk motif of "the iron fist in the velvet glove"; *Judges*, 75, fn eee, 81.
[3] The singer conjures sexual imagery (he repeatedly bent and fell between her legs), and ironic with Sisera still as subject of verbs (possibly who takes or rapes women after battle), but here acted upon; *rglym* ('feet' in NRSV and NJPS) is a euphemism, translated 'legs' by commentators; *kr*ʿ means 'bent/arched' and also 'leg' (BDB: 502).

An analysis of these lines cannot stop with the lyrical sound artistry only but must pause to consider an ideological criticism, as do Fewell and Gunn: the realist ramification of the woman's voice glorifying Jael for her act of violence.[50] Fewell and Gunn note that Deborah is portrayed as opting in to a dominant (male) ideology of war and violence; she "endorses the very patriarchal values that her 'motherhood' might seem to challenge."[51] With the singing of both Deborah and Baraq, they suggest, "in celebration the violence is legitimated."[52] However, the above analysis suggested that the voiced lyrics of Deborah and Baraq, while participants in this version of a holy war against the enemy, are more *divergent* in their

50. Fewell and Gunn, "Controlling Perspectives," 389–411.
51. Ibid., 397.
52. Ibid., 406.

expressed interests than similar.[53] It should be said as a sociological caveat, about women being co-opted to the ideology of war, rarely do individuals (male or female) all at once overturn any society's entire culture or system of political ideology, but rather history shows that they must chip away at its structure, challenging its premises over time through group effort. The above analysis suggests that Deborah, once in the 'system' and empowered, does not simply promote it; her voice, above, may disdain Baraq's preoccupation with a song to glorify his human fighters' actions and victory. A closer reading discerning who is speaking and when, while open to interpretation, is nevertheless crucial for the analysis of the figures involved. In the song, Deborah's and Baraq's are not collapsed into one voice.[54] Nor does Deborah promote herself; her focus previously was on how YHWH brought promised relief from human oppression through nature's forces.

Yet Gunn and Fewell ask an important question about Deborah's lyrics at the end of the song in Judges 5: "Why savor so the death of Sisera? The problem for the singers is that they are themselves badly compromised by violence."[55] No doubt the people of Israel as a whole was caught up in the terrible ideology of holy war and conquest; yet it was indigenous through the ancient Near East. In light of this, why are these women subjected to such judgment about their participation, but so often male biblical figures are not judged similarly by most biblical commentators? This verges on a double standard, especially when at the same time interpreters of biblical texts expect to find individual men portrayed in *various lights—good and bad*, with complexity.

While feminist and ideological critics (the present author included) surely do not expect to find a sanguine woman's (motherly) prophetic

53. The present analysis, while affirming the importance of the questions raised by Fewell and Gunn, disagrees somewhat with their premise that "the voices seem not to distinguish between male or female values. It is as though gender is of no concern. Even when the song alludes to specific characters, poetic parallelism balances male and female: 'In the days of Shamgar . . . , in the days of Jael;' 'Awake, Deborah! . . . ; Arise, Barak!' ("Controlling Perspectives," 400). Focus only on poetic parallelism of lyrics (especially of content/theme apparent in translation) has missed the women's tradition's contributions through lyric.

54. Cf. Fewell and Gunn, "Controlling Perspectives." In their disagreement with Mieke Bal's reading that wants to remove Baraq's voice from the lyrics, they yet collapse Deborah and Baraq's voice into a monolithic, ideological message, thus erasing any *difference* between them: "The song is sung by combined voices. Deborah and Barak, despite earlier tensions, unite to tell the story" (399).

55. Ibid., 408.

voice of peace in this particular context, for the good of all people, is complete dismissal of the women in Judges 4–5 as totally co-opted warranted? Need the female 'hero' or 'heroes' suggested to be sanctioned by God, be perfect? Passivist? Passive with Sisera? Psychologically, years of abuse, powerlessness, and pent-up rage often cause persons finally to do horrible things. Should the women refrain from ironic rejoicing in song over Sisera's defeat and death, precisely in the terms with which he oppressed? (He was the 'head' of the forces of oppression.) Should they not be happy or relieved about the end of the man who had likely brutalized dozens or hundreds of women, some of whom they might have personally known? For women caught in the violent culture, it is perhaps unrealistic to expect a kind of morally 'pure' response. This is a 'text of terror' also, but the victim was guilty of traumatizing others, unlike the infamous innocent women victims in texts of terror later in the book of Judges.[56] Fewell and Gunn rightly challenge interpretations that simply extol Deborah's and Jael's roles without critique. Yet, blaming the women (and Baraq) alone for an ideology of violence, or for not rising above it, may be 'overkill.' Yet, would that interpreters more often challenge the simple extolling of so many male heroes in the Bible for their victories wrought through violence, while simply looking past or accepting the violence as a necessary evil against the enemy. More important, would that interpreters might consider how we ourselves rarely critique our *own* historical and contemporary cultures and interests, which underlie our nation's political, ideologically driven violence and glorification of it—while innocent people (including women, and children) suffer as a consequence at home and abroad.

In Judg 5:24, below, Deborah's lyrics shift scene from the demise of Sisera to portray his mother awaiting his return, which she 'narrates' with triplet soundplays.[57] In what many label a 'taunt,' Deborah ironically has her ask about the delay of his chariot.[58] Globe suggests these lyrics mock the scene involving the victory song when women await the arrival of

56. For this phrase and focus, see Trible, *Texts of Terror.*

57. Van Dijk-Hemmes, "Mothers and a Mediator," 110–14, proposed identifying female (F) and male (M) texts in part based on whether they reflect women in 'competition' or a 'cooperation' paradigm (the latter exemplified by the book of Ruth); she found Judges 5 to have cooperation by Deborah and Jael, yet the final lines about Sisera's mother reflect a competition paradigm.

58. Leuchter, "'Why Tarry the Wheels?,'" 256–68, sees a link between the waning of Egypt's control of Palestine in this time and the failure of Sisera's *chariot*, and suggests the song is not about just one decisive victory but represents the collective memory of numerous clashes between Israel's tribes situated in the highlands and others in the lowland plains for control in the region.

returning, victorious warriors in order to sing for them.[59] That Deborah waits until the end of her song lyrics to mention Sisera's mighty *chariot or chariots* is highly ironic, and that she renders it or them *missing* even moreso! (This echoes her earlier lyric that among the Israelites no shield or spear was to be found.) The hearer of the song may sympathize with this mother's lament unawares, but then her greedy and horrifying speech that Deborah renders, of brutal, sexual capture of Israelite women, darkens humanitarian regard.[60] While doublet soundplays in v. 30 next appear to mark the return of a male singer, Deborah is more likely ironically rendering the speech of Sisera's mother singing what sounds like a *male warrior's* (her son's?) *victory chant* of his sexual conquest over women and gain of spoil. As Bal observes, the speech content gives "expression to the fate of captive women in the rude language that suits *gibborim* (male warriors) rather than fellow women."[61] Deborah's precise use of doublet sounds and words convey a male tone. Yet, it is possible to hear in Deborah's lyric not only a judgment of the enemy's practice, but also a condemnation of *any such treatment of women.*[62] The song proper closes in v. 31a–b with another cosmic allusion, to the rising sun, by the female singer, suggested to be Deborah, who has narrated this portion entirely. An apparent male voice closes the passage with a summative remark in v. 31c.[63]

59. Globe, "Literary Structure and Unity," 498.

60. A number of commentators note these lines suggest a contrast between the mother of Sisera and the 'mother' Deborah. Fewell and Gunn, "Controlling Perspectives," suggest that Deborah's last lines leave her "trapped in the very value system which we imagine her to be subverting" (397); because she renders the 'hardness' of Sisera's mother and the Canaanite women, it allows her ["the victorious singers"] to "revel in irony . . . But why use his women as the vehicle for this mockery?" they ask. They suggest, the singers "are themselves badly compromised by violence," and Deborah leaves it to the listener's imagination to realize that the hoofbeats coming toward Sisera's mother are the Israelite hoofbeats come to vanquish the Canaanite women (ibid., 408).

61. Bal, *Death and Dissymmetry*, 30.

62. Contra Exum, "Feminist Criticism," 74, who posits a male narrator using women's voices in service of male ideology of warfare. As Matthews, *Judges and Ruth*, 76, notes, Baraq's and Sisera's mothers are paralleled in that *both* fail or are thwarted in receiving the expected spoils and booty of war. Having Deborah and Jael as heroic figures "allows for a form of comedic satire in which male characters are superseded or humiliated." (ibid., 78).

63. Many commentators highlight Deborah's bringing a long peace of forty years, yet Sasson, *Judges 1–12*, 311, reminds that there was the same also with Othniel and Gideon, and longer for Samson's days and for 'minor' leaders.

| | | |
|---|---|---|
| *(female)*<br>"*OUT OF* **the** window she<br>**looked down**,<br>and **shrilled out**, mother of *SISERA*,<br>*OUT OF* **the** lattice:<br><br>'*WHY* delayed, for **shame,**<br>*HIS CHARIOT*<br>in **coming**?!<br>*WHY* tarry the hoofbeats of<br>*HIS CHARIOTS*?' (28) | *BĔʿAD* **haḥa**llôn ni**š**qĕphâ<br>wattĕyab**bēv** ʾēm *SÎSĔRĀʾ*<br>*BĔʿAD* **hā**ʾeš**nāv**<br>**madd**ûaʿ **bōšēš**<br>rik**bô**<br>**lāv*ôʾ***<br>**madd**ûaʿ ʾeḥĕrû paʿămê<br>**markĕvôtāyw**<br>**ḥ**akm**ôt**<br>**śārôtêh*āh*** | *(triplets)*<br>3 **bĕʿad, bēv, bĕʿad** (2+1)<br>4 **ʿad, ʿad, maddûaʿ, maddûaʿ**<br>3 **madd**ûaʿ, **madd**ûaʿ + **mar**<br>3 **haḥallôn, hā**ʾeš**nāv**<br>3 **haḥallôn** (+**ḥ**akm**ôt**, **hălōʾ**<br>below)<br>3 niš**qĕphâ, sîsĕrāʾ, śārôtêhāh**<br>3 **bō, bô, vôʾ**<br>3 ri**kbô, lāvôʾ**, mar**kĕvô**<br>3 **ôt, ôt, ôt**<br>3 **tĕ**ya, **taʿănênnāh,**<br>**tāšîv ʾămārêhā** |
| **Her wise**<br>**noble-women**<br>**answer her**; also, **she**<br>**replies**, **saying** to **herself**: (29)<br><br>'**Are they not**<br>**finding,**<br>**dividing**<br><br>*SPOIL*? | **taʿănênn*āh*** ʾaph-**hîʾ**<br>tāšîv **ʾămārêhā l*āh***<br>**hăl*ōʾ***<br>**yimṣĕʾ*û***<br>**yĕḥallĕq*û*** | 3 **markĕvôtā, śārôtêhāh,**<br>ʾă**mārêhā**<br>3 **hā lāh, hălōʾ, ḥall**<br>2 **yimṣĕʾû, yĕḥallĕqû**<br>3 **hăl, ḥal, šālāl** (also below) |
| *(citing a male)*<br>'A *WOMB* or<br>two *WOMBS* *FOR* the head warrior!<br>*SPOIL* of *DYED CLOTHS FOR SISERA*<br>*SPOIL* of *DYED CLOTHS*<br>*EMBROIDERED CLOTH*,<br>*EMBROIDERED* *FROM NECKS* of<br>*SPOIL*!'[1] (30) | *ŠĀLĀL*<br>*RAḤAM*<br>*RAḤĂM*ātay**im** **lĕrōʾš** gever<br>*ŠĔLAL ṢĔVĀ* **ʿîm** **lĕ***SÎSĔRĀʾ*<br>*ŠĔLAL ṢĔVĀ* **ʿîm**<br>*RIQMÂ ṢEVAʿ*<br>*RIQMĀ*tay**im** **lĕṣawwĕʾrê**<br>*ŠĀLĀL* | *(doublets)*<br>2 **raḥam, raḥăm**<br>2 **šĕlal ṣĕvāʿîm, šĕlal ṣĕvāʿîm**<br>4 **lĕrōʾš, lĕsîsĕrāʾ, lĕṣa**wwĕʾ**rê**<br>4 **ṣĕvā, ṣĕvā, ṣevaʿ, ṣa**wwĕ<br>2 **riqmâ, riqmā** 3 **lĕ, lĕ, lĕ**<br>4 **im, ʿîm, ʿîm, im**<br>4 **šālāl, šĕlal, šĕlal, šālāl** |
| *(female)*<br>**So** *PERISH*<br>**all** *YOUR ENEMIES*, *YHWH*!<br>But may *YOUR FRIENDS* (be)[2]<br>**as the rising sun in** its **might**." (31a) | **kēn** *YŌʾVĔ*d*û*<br>**kol** -*ʾÔYĔVÊKĀ* *YHWH*<br>wĕ *ʾŌHĂVÊKĀ*<br>**kĕṣēʾt ha**ššemeš **bigvur**āt*ô* | *(triplets)*<br>3 **kē**n, **kol**, **kĕ**<br>1 YHWH (inclusio with v. 2)<br>3 **yōʾvĕ, ʾôyĕvêkā, ʾōhăvêkā**<br>1 **bigvur**ātô (**baggibbôr**îm in<br>v. 13, 23 = **3**) |

[1] Foll. Sasson's option; *Judges 1-12*, 310.

[2] Reading *ʾōhăvêkā* with two MSS and Syriac; Webb, *Book of Judges*, 199; this is a better triplet soundplay and parallel of possessive pronouns than MT's *ʾōhăvāyw*.

## Conclusion

In summary, the outline of singing voices in Judges 5, based on analyzed sound patterns, coinciding with their focus of content, is as follows:

| **female** (*triplet pattern*) | **male** (*doublet pattern*) |
|---|---|
| :2–6 | |
| | :7 |
| :8 | |
| | :9–12a |
| :12b | |
| | :13–19 |
| :20–31a–b | (23 cited) |
| | :31c |
| appr. 18 verses | appr. 13 verses |

The sound patterns of the overall song in Judges 5 suggest a female composing/singing voice employing a triplet sound pattern, which is the central voice, as indicated by the total verses in the table above; nevertheless, there is also something of a balance. In spite of the fact that Deborah is the primary figure, followed by Jael, the song of Judges 5 still affirms, albeit with much irony, that both women and men were needed to accomplish the victory.[64] However, it appears that a different male voice than Baraq's is responsible for most of the male part of the song. We can assume that the female part is meant to be understood as Deborah's voice, since she is identified as a prophet in the accompanying narrative, and her lines in the song coincide with biblical prophets' emphasis on the deity's saving actions that elicit praise.

To conclude, the lyrics of Judges 5 represent Deborah's voice as indicated by a triplet syllable sound repetition pattern found elsewhere to suggest a women's lyrical tradition. In this case, the singer often composes with a doubled word joined to a third like-sounding syllable or term. While Deborah's voice is presented in dialog with Baraq's represented voice, she performs in her lyrics a victory song *innovated* for praise of

64. As Brenner, *Feminist Companion to Judges*, 105, 108, notes, "a certain cooperation between the male and female social spheres is required."

YHWH, utilizing *both narrative and praise* elements, while the content of her lyrics includes the following: narrative elements setting the scene (v. 2); praise of YHWH (v. 3); a theophany of YHWH, including second-person address of YHWH (vv. 4–5); description of the people's distress (v. 6); description of YHWH choosing those who would facilitate the people's rescue (v. 8); an aside/response to Baraq to get up and lead away his captives (v. 12b); an account of nature's forces joining in the battle against Sisera (vv. 20–22); extolling and narrating Jael's role, calling her blessed, in bringing Sisera to an end (vv. 24–27); an ironic rendering of Sisera's mother waiting, who will not see his return or enjoy the spoils of war (vv. 28–30); and Deborah's direct address of YHWH, closing with a wish for death upon YHWH's enemies and good for those who love YHWH (v. 31a–b).

As Fewell and Gunn grimly note about this last line, "the singers . . . dispose of others without conscience because there is no middle ground."[65] Thus the theology is an exclusive one at this time, as in the Song of Moses and Miriam, that rejoices in the defeat of Israel's and YHWH's enemies, even through violence and death. Fewell and Gunn go on to suggest that "in the face of [the] authority [of violence], the woman, Deborah, has offered no real alternative."[66] This study offers a tempered and more nuanced conclusion. It is that Deborah's role explicitly and her lyrics implicitly ironically critique a 'holy war' rhetoric and ideology as found in the book of Joshua, which *collapses male warriors'* (and priests' and Moses') words and actions *as equal to* YHWH's, thus beginning to separate the authority (and reality) of YHWH from male domination and male construals.

As with Miriam's lyrics presumably earlier,[67] also with Deborah's, they do not praise the male warrior or warriors as was expected from women singers, but *primarily* praise YHWH as the cause and reason for rescue from an oppressor; these lyrics by *prophets* with compassion for their people, they recount and rejoice over YHWH's intervention to end the injustice of their suffering. The imagining of a complete alternative to war, of overcoming the binary opposite with 'enemies', will have to wait till Hannĕvî'â's and Isaiah's peace lyrics in their time, and even there it will only be possible because *YHWH's* 'kingdom' is not the same as those of 'men.'

65. Fewell and Gunn, "Controlling Perspectives," 409.

66. Ibid., 408.

67. Freedman, *Pottery, Poetry, and Prophecy*, 131.

Finally, as with the association of a woman prophet's lyrics of victory/praise for YHWH linked with a narrative account of the event (as in Exodus with Miriam), so too here we must ask whether Deborah or a women's tradition was also responsible for composing Judges 4? Does Judges 4 reflect a triplet sound repetition pattern? Pursuit of this question must await a subsequent study.[68]

68. For an analysis of the sound patterns in the narrative of Judges 4, see Lee, *Hebrew Sound Patterns and Women's Biblical Composing*. Joseph Blenkinsopp alludes to two triplet repetitions of phrases in Judges 4; "Ballad Style and Psalm Style," 64fn3.

# PART 3

# Named and Unnamed Women Prophets from the Seventh Century through the Exilic and Postexilic Periods

# CHAPTER 5

# Huldah and 2 Kings 22

## Huldah the Prophet

THE WOMAN PROPHET HULDAH, appears in the narrative of 2 Kgs 22:3–20,[1] a setting from the late seventh century, where she is consulted by Josiah, king of Judah, after the high priest, Hilkiyah, says he found a 'writing' or scroll of Torah in the temple (literally, 'house of YHWH'). In this passage, the king sends his officials to 'inquire' about the words of the book and God's anger against Judah. While one may not expect to find a sound pattern suggestive of a woman's speech distinctive from the Deuteronomistic style of recounting, it is necessary to investigate, since a prophet's oracle may be distinctive from the surrounding narration.

## 2 Kings 22:3–20

Interestingly, the narrative of 2 Kings 22:3–20 does not say the king sent the officials *to Huldah* specifically, but her first reply to the officials once they have arrived from the king is, ironically, "tell the man who sent you to me . . ." (15b)—not Josiah, not 'the king', but 'the man.' Later in the passage she will refer to 'the king' (used 10x in vv. 8–20), but never by name. YHWH is referred to also 10x across these same verses (14x if the preliminary vv. 3–7 are included). Up through v. 14 there is a great deal

1. Also in 2 Chr 34:8–28. The main difference between the accounts is that in 2 Chr Josiah has destroyed non-Yahwistic worship sites before the finding of the book or scroll, in 2 Kings afterward.

of repetition of words in the recounting of the finding and dealing with the scroll (*sēpher*; repeated 6x; *hattôrâ* 2x), the names of figures involved (*šāphān* 9x and *sōphēr* 3x; *ḥilqiyyâ* 5x). In the larger passage, the only significant triplet soundplays I find before v. 15 when Huldah speaks include in vv. 8–9, with a word repeated: *vabbayit, bêt YHWH, bĕvêt YHWH* (the term 'house' appears a total of 3x in the passage from vv. 8–20; it already appeared 5x in vv. 3–7, for a total of 8). The second triplet soundplay occurs after the king orders his officials to inquire (of a prophet) 'on behalf of me . . . the people . . . all Judah' (*baʿădî, ûbĕʿad, ûbĕʿad* said three times). Perhaps this is formulaic for requesting a prophetic oracle, or perhaps it is simply used for emphasis, given the larger text's predominance of doublet soundplays. So in the narrative preceding Huldah's response, repetitions of words and syllables are in multiples of two primarily.

Huldah's speech (vv. 15b–20c) is not normally printed in Bibles as lyric, but in the table here below it is lined up to find any represented oral sound patterns. Her very first 'verse' of utterance is marked by *four* overlapping triplet soundplays, the signature, I argue, of women's composing voices. The second verse (16) also has four triplets.

| *(female)* | | *(triplets)* |
|---|---|---|
| "THUS SAYS YHWH, | KŌ-ʾĀMAR YHWH | 6 YHWH (total) |
| GOD of Israel: | ʾĔLŌHÊ yiśrāʾēl | 3 kō-ʾāmar, ʾimrû, kō ʾāmar |
| 'TELL THE MAN | ʾIMRÛ lāʾîš | 3 lāʾîš, ʾăšer-šālaḥ |
| WHO | ʾĂŠER- | 3 ʾĕlōhê, ʾet, ʾēlāy |
| SENT **you** | šālaḥ ʾ**et**kem | 3 ʾăšer-šālaḥ, rāʿâ, ʾăšer qārāʾ |
| **to me**,' (15) | ʾēlāy | 3 kō-ʾāmar, kō-ʾāmar, |
| THUS SAYS YHWH: | KŌ ʾĀMAR YHWH | kol-divrê |
| | hinnî mēvîʾ rāʿâ | 3 mēvîʾ, māqôm, melek |
| 'Look! I will **bring** disas**ter** | ʾ**el** -HAMMĀQÔM | 3 rāʿâ, divrê, qārāʾ |
| **to** THIS | HAZZEH | 3 hammā, hazzeh, hassē |
| VERY PLACE | | |
| and **on** its inhabitants— | wĕʿ**al**-yōšĕvāyw | 3 ʾel, ʿal, kol |
| **all** the **words** of | ʾēt KOL- divrê | 1 divrê (+divrê sēpher, v. |
| THE writing THAT | HASSĒpher ʾĂŠER | 11 + dĕbārîm, v. 18 = 3) |
| the **king** of JUDAH | qārāʾ | 2 yĕhûdâ, yĕdêhem |
| has **read**. (16) | mel**ek** YĔHÛDâ | 3 ʾăšer, ʾăšer, ʾăšer |
| | taḥat ʾĂŠER | 3 taḥat, wayqaṭ, ḥămāt |
| On account of WHICH | ʿăzāvûnî | 3 hazzeh, hassēpher, hazzeh |
| they have **aban**doned **me** | wayqaṭṭĕrû LĔʾLŌhîm | 3 azzeh, ʿăza, azzeh |
| and have made offerings to **other** | ʾăḥērîm | 3 hîm, rîm, hem |
| GODS, | | |
| so **that** they **vex** **me** | lĕ**ma**ʿan **hak**ʿîsēnî | 3 hîm, hem, ḥămātî |
| **with** ALL the **work of** their HANDS, | **bĕ**KŌL **ma**ʿăśēh YĔDÊH**em** | 3 ha, ḥă, ha 3 î, î, î (final) |
| so is kin**dled** | wĕniṣṣĕtâ | 3 sēnî, śē, ṣĕtâ 3 kol, kol, qôm |
| **wrath** of **mine** | ḥămātî | 3 bĕkōl, bammāqôm, tikbeh |
| **against** THIS | bamMĀQÔM | 3 ma, ma, mā + māqôm |
| PLACE, | | |
| and it will not be QUENCHED.' (17) | HAZZEH wĕlōʾ tiKBEH | 2 māqôm hazzeh (inclusio) |

The first three verses of Huldah's speech show clear triplet soundplays (mostly of syllables, and some words), no less intense and no less consistent than that seen heretofore in other lyrical prophetic texts. This pattern comes through in spite of the Deuteronomistic tradition's narrative style and shaping of the text. Some may say that this tradition simply imitated the women's lyrical pattern and put the words into Huldah's mouth. If this is to be supported, evidence for it must be brought forth that shows Huldah's represented oracle follows a Deuteronomistic tradition, ideology, or terminology *more than* a prophetic tradition, or that the rendering here in some way blocks a lyrical oracle with prophetic message. The above analysis does not support this. Huldah's words are represented to respond to the previous figures' speeches, not only to the king, but to the officials and high priest. Rather than interpret that the woman prophet is simply co-opted, it would seem more accurate to suggest that she may have been a key figure in a Deuteronomistic establishment, as a prophet, and may have helped shaped its rhetoric. Further examination of the specific terms she uses, as compared with the terms used in lyrics of other prophets might shed further light on this question. The remainder of her speech is as follows.

| *(female)* | wĕʾ**el** - | *(triplets)* |
|---|---|---|
| And to | | |
| the king of Judah, | ***MELEK YĔHÛDÂ*** | 3 ʾel, ʾēlāyw, ʾĕlōhê (+2 ʾ**et**) |
| who sent you | haššō**lē**aḥ ʾ**et**kem | 3 yĕhûdâ (yĕdêh, yĕhûdâ above) |
| to inquire of YHWH, | **li**drōš ʾ**e**t - ***YHWH*** | |
| thus shall you say to him; | ***KŌ*** tōʾ***MĔR***û ʾ**ē**l**ā**yw | 4 kō, kō + kō, ko (above) |
| Thus says YHWH, God of Israel: | ***KŌ*** - ***ʾĀMAR YHWH*** ʾ**ĕ**l**ō**hê ***YIŚRĀʾĒL*** | 2 YHWH + 2 YHWH (below) |
| ʻThe words that | had***DĔVĀR***îm ***ʾĂŠER*** | 3 ʾăšer, ʾăšer (+1 below) |
| you have heard, (18) | ***ŠĀM***āʿt***ā*** | 3 šām, šom, šām (below) |
| because your heart | yaʿan r**ak**- | 3 rak, ʿăkā, māq |
| was penitent, | lĕvāvĕ**k*ā*** | 3 kā, kānaʿ, kā |
| and you humbled yourself before YHWH, | wattik**kā**n***a*ʿ** mippĕnê ***YHWH*** | 3 dĕvār, dibbar (+divrê above) |
| when you heard that | **bĕ*ŠOM*ʿăk*ā*** ***ʾĂŠER*** | |
| I spoke | ***DIBBAR***tî | |
| against this place, | ʿ**al**-***HAMMĀQÔM HAZZEH*** | 3 šām, ham, šām |
| and against its inhabitants, | wĕʿ**al**-yōšĕvāyw | 3 ʿal, wĕʿal, wĕl |
| to become | **li**hyôt | 3 lihyôt, lĕšammâ, liqlālâ |
| a desolation | **lĕ*ŠAM*m*â*** | 3 wĕliq, wattiq, wattivkeh |
| and a curse, | **wĕliqlāl*â*** | 2 ĕgā, ĕga (+kā) |
| and you tore your clothes | **wattiqr*a*ʿ** ʾet-bĕ**gā**dêk***ā*** | 3 ānāy, ʾānōkî, nĕ |
| and you wept before me, | **watti**vkeh lĕph**ā**n**ā**y | 3 gam, šām + šālôm (below) |
| so also I | wĕ**gam** ʾ**ā**n**ō**k***î*** | 7 kā, kā, tā, kā, nâ, kā, rāʿâ (v.20) |
| have heard (you),' says YHWH. (19) | ***ŠĀM***aʿt*î* **nĕ**ʾum-***YHWH*** | |
| ʻTherefore, look! I will gather you | lākēn h**inn*î*** ***ʾŌSIPH*k*ā*** | 2 ʾōsiphkā, neʾĕsaphtā |
| to your ancestors, | ʿ**al** - ʾă*VŌTÊKĀ* | 2 vōtêkā, vrōtêkā |
| and you shall be gathered | **wĕne*ʾĔSAPH*t*ā*** | 3 ʿal, ʾel, āl |
| to your grave | ʾ**el** - qi*VRŌTÊKĀ* | 3 neʾĕ, ʾênâ, ʿênêkā 2 bĕ, bĕ |
| in peace; | **bĕ***ŠĀLÔM* | 1 ʾănî (+ hinnî, ʾānōkî above) |
| and your eyes shall not see | wĕlōʾ-tir**ʾên*â*** **ʿênêk*ā*** | 2 rāʿâ mēvîʾ (above, inclusio) |
| all the disaster that I will bring | **bĕ*KŌL*** hā***RĀʿÂ*** ***ʾĂŠER***- ʾ**ănî** | 4 hammāqôm hazzeh (total) (inclusio) |
| on this place.'" (20abc) | ***MĒVî*ʾ** ʿ**al**-***HAMMĀQÔM HAZZEH*** | |

For the purposes of this study, the primary conclusion to draw is that even the Deuteronomistic corpus has evidence of preserving the women's triplet-sound composing tradition in representing this woman prophet.

## Excursus: A Woman Prophet in Habakkuk 3?

A number of scholars have noted linkages between lyrics of songs regarded as some of the older poetry of the Bible to the song in Habakkuk 3:1–19, particularly terms and imagery in the Song of Deborah and older psalms. The poems of Habakkuk are usually dated from the late seventh to early sixth century BCE. Steve Cook has suggested that Habakkuk 3, as a victory song genre (for YHWH), was a woman prophet's lyrical composition based on the singer's use of the term ('does'; *ʾayyālôt*) to describe 'herself' in v. 19[2]: "YHWH, my Lord, is my strength; he makes my feet like the feet of deer, and makes me tread upon the heights."[3] Cook suggests that the deer (or 'doe') symbolized women victims in wartime, as captured prizes, based on the motif in other texts and in other cultures. He concludes, nevertheless, that a woman lyricist's song with its glorifying YHWH as holy warrior here serves to legitimate androcentric militarism, and in his interpretation, served the interests of this woman at the expense of other women.

While I am obviously sympathetic to the search for women's composing voices in biblical texts, and while it is certainly the case that some women would have adopted the culture's militarism and belief that YHWH fought for Israel, in my view, it is not sound procedure to draw a conclusion that this song was composed by a woman, based on one simile that purports to represent women's experience. This same Hebrew feminine word and simile is used to describe *two men* in lyrics elsewhere: for example, in first-person speech, David is represented to describe himself with the very same term (*ʾayyālôt*) in the praise and thanksgiving (or victory) song also attributed to him in 2 Sam 22:1–51 (v. 34); and, the term describes Naphtali in the song attributed to Jacob in Gen 49:21. If it is the animal's admired characteristic that is drawn upon to describe a person, gender does not matter. In all three of these songs, the animal's feature is a positive simile for the person, not an allusion to negative experience,

2. Cook, "Habakkuk 3, Gender, and War."

3. NRSV.

even though having been pursued may have been a precipitating cause for escape.[4]

Further, an examination of the lyrics of Habakkuk 3 does not produce a pervasive triplet syllable sound-repetition pattern as found in numerous other texts where a woman was, or women prophets were, attributed as composing singers. Instead, this song exhibits a predominance of doublet soundplays suggestive in many other texts of a male composer/singer.[5] It is possible that not every woman composer used this identified triplet compositional technique. Nevertheless, for Habakkuk 3, there is no strong implicit evidence for a woman composer. The composer may have been influenced by the Song of Deborah, or by the victory-song genre modified by some women in praise of YHWH, but the simile is certainly not conclusive, and the sound pattern strongly suggests a male lyrical tradition is being followed.

4. On the use of the deer image with this term (found apparently in only six places in the Bible) to describe the weakness of humans in Jeremiah and Lamentations, see Lee, *Singers of Lamentations*, 94.

5. I find only two triplet soundplays: in v. 2 there is *bĕqerev, bĕqerev, bĕrōgez,* but this is in a verse that has four other doublet soundplays; second, in v. 8, there is *hār, hār, hār,* yet this is arguably part of a larger quadruple soundplay; in fact there are three other quadruple soundplays in this verse alone. Both of these triplets, therefore, do not constitute anything more than an exception in a song dominated by doublets and multiples of two.

# CHAPTER 6

# Texts in the Book of Jeremiah

THIS STUDY NOW TURNS to the book of Jeremiah, the original context of which is close chronologically to the timeframe of Huldah, probably with some overlap. The introduction to the book of Jeremiah dates the prophet's oracles from the thirteenth year of Josiah's reign (627) until the collapse of Jerusalem in 587 BCE. Scholars generally agree that the shorter text of the Septuagint edition of Jeremiah is a translation of an older Hebrew version than the MT, the issues of which relate more to the prose sections of the book, though LXX variants on poetic texts will be noted where significant.[1]

A number of scholars have noted the dialogical nature of the poetry of the book of Jeremiah.[2] Several texts will be examined for Hebrew lyrical sound-repetition patterns in the book, which may offer possibility of finding any women's prophetic voices embedded in the book. This analysis presents a beginning assessment of texts in Jeremiah, not a full treatment, which is beyond the scope of this study.

For two poetic texts some commentators have suggested that personified female Jerusalem speaks, mediated by the male prophet: Jer 4:19–21 and Jer 10:19–21.[3] In my previous work, I have analyzed these

1. For a review of scholarship on this, see Allen, *Jeremiah*, 2–4.

2. See especially Biddle, *Polyphony and Symphony*, 1–13; Fretheim, *Jeremiah*, 6.

3. Apart from female voices in Jeremiah and in Lamentations, Jerusalem or Zion portrayed as speaking herself, as rendered by a prophetic voice, is found in Isa 49:14, 21 and Jer 4:31; Isa 61:10–11 is often interpreted as the city persona speaking, but the speech is not introduced as such; the female persona is briefly *called to sing* in Isa 52:9; 54:1; and Zech 9:9. The female city persona's speech is briefly *referred to* in Isa 29:4; 51:3; and Mic 4:10. Creating confusion for interpreters, biblical texts include

passages in relation to very similar passages of a female voice in the book of Lamentations, comparing speakers' uses of genres, imagery (similes and metaphors), terminology, content and themes, and poetic technique. I concluded that more than personifications of Jerusalem/Zion, these female voices were likely the rendering of a woman composer in the context, perhaps a woman lament singer or prophet, as this voice or these voices offered a very different perspective from Jeremiah and from other voices in Lamentations.[4] Indeed, they offer both a theological and sociopolitical challenge in the context. In addition to these two texts, sections of Jeremiah 8–9 and Jeremiah 31 will be examined presently, the former as it refers to women lamenters/mourners, and the latter as the passage offers an empathetic portrayal of Rachel as figurative mother.

## Jeremiah 2

As in the book of Isaiah, comparisons with the represented male prophet's speeches in Jeremiah are important. The first oracle in the book of Jeremiah following his call, with Jeremiah as implied composer/performer, is in Jer 2:1–2. The sound repetition pattern is analyzed below:

| | | |
|---|---|---|
| I remember<br>of you the devotion of your youth,<br>the love you had as a bride,<br>you went after me<br>in the wilderness,<br>in a land<br>not sown. (2c)<br><br>Holy was Israel to YHWH,<br>first fruits of his harvest.<br>All who ate of it were held guilty;<br>disaster came upon them,<br>says YHWH. (3) | zākartî<br>lāk ḥesed nĕʿûrayik<br>ʾahăvat kĕlûlōtāyik<br>lektēk ʾaḥăray bammidbār<br>bĕʾereṣ<br>lōʾ zĕrûʿâ<br><br>qōdeš yiśrāʾēl laYHWH<br>rēʾšît tĕvûʾātōh<br>kol -ʾōkĕlāyw yeʾšāmû<br>rāʿâ tāvōʾ ʾălêhem<br>nĕʾum -YHWH | *(doublets)*<br>2 zāk, lāk 2 kar, ḥăr<br>2 zākartî, zĕrûʿâ<br>4 zāk, lāk, lektēk<br>2 ayik, āyik 2 lō, lōʾ<br>2 ʾahăvat, ʾaḥăray<br>2 bammidbār, bĕʾereṣ<br>2 qō, ko 2 yiś, yeʾš<br>2 YHWH, YHWH<br>2 la, lê 2 eš, rēʾš (yeʾš)<br>2 tĕvû, tāvōʾ<br>2 kol-ʾōkĕl 2 āmû, ĕʾum<br>2 rē, rāʿâ 4 ʾēl, ol, ĕlā, ʾălê |

The doublet sound pattern in Jeremiah's lyricizing is clear and consistent. The very first verse personifies Jerusalem as female, as doting bride, and is reminiscent of such imagery in the lyrics of Hosea (Hos 2:2–20) and

exhortations to speak or sing to female Jerusalem, to women mourners, and as I shall argue, to women prophets.

4. Lee, *Singers of Lamentations*; idem, "Singers of Lamentations: (A)Scribing (De) Claiming Poets and Prophets," 33–46; idem, "Prophet and Singer in the Fray," 190–209.

other prophetic texts,[5] which have been roundly criticized, and rightly so, by feminist interpreters when their lyrics become misogynist, depicting YHWH as abusive husband.[6] This Jer 2:1–2 text shows that Jeremiah, like other male prophets who personified the city or people as female all appear to have composed this theme with a doublet sound pattern, even though the content is about a female persona. In an earlier study,[7] I translated v. 2 as follows, suggesting a threefold content:

> I've remembered your youthful devotion,
> your bridal love,
> your going after me in the wildernesss,
> in a land not sown.
> (2:2b–c)

Yet, the Hebrew soundplays conveying the content through *doublet* syllable repetitions do shift the emphasis (suggested by the English), ironically and subtly, away from full focus on personified Jerusalem *to the relationship* between YHWH and the people personified as female. For example, the doublets emphasize,

> "I remember you /
> your youth, your being a bride /
> love, following me /
> I remember, not sown."

In this case, the doublets suggest, in my view, a more endearing reminiscence by YHWH at least here, rather than a matter-of-fact statement overbearingly weighted on the female object or vehicle of the metaphor. The soundplays throw as much emphasis on YHWH as partner; several

5. For the wilderness motif used by prophets, see Talmon, "'Desert Motif' in the Bible," 31–63.

6. Jeremiah is also criticized for such extreme lyrics, as in Jer 2:20–25; 3:1–4, 6–10; 4:30–31; 13:20–27; while misogynous biblical lyrics are not the primary focus of the present study, differences in lyrics composed by different genders will shed some light on this issue; for a recent overview of work in this area in Jeremiah, see Shields, "Impasse or Opportunity," 290–302, and Brenner, "Response to Mary E. Shields," in ibid., 303–6; also earlier, e.g., Kaiser, "Poet as 'Female Impersonator,'" 164–82; Brenner, "On Prophetic Propaganda," 256–74; Bauer-Levesque, *Gender in the Book of Jeremiah*; Baumann, *Love and Violence*; Maier, *Daughter Zion, Mother Zion*; O'Brien, *Challenging Prophetic Metaphor*; Newsom et al., *Women's Bible Commentary*.

7. Lee, "Exposing a Buried Subtext," 87–122.

soundplays with 'I remember' and another with 'after me' render the deity's words dwelling upon the mutuality of the relationship,[8] not simply on the deity's hierarchical power over the female. This example shows how translation without soundplay in mind can change the lyrics' artistic effect to emphasize meaning(s) differently than what might have been heard and understood by a fluent Hebrew-speaking audience, even though every hearer may hear different nuances, of course. Lyrics produce multiple meanings and interpretations, but *how these are produced* by the artist in the ancient culture, in its indigenous language, is important in order to be true as much as possible to the texts' voices. In the above verse *the only term* that does not bear fully a doublet sound repetition (i.e., two consonants repeated of its root or form) is *ḥesed*; the many doublet soundplays circle around this term, integral to a covenant relationship, as if to highlight its centrality and importance. What is *not repeated* in sound is thereby emphasized, disrupting the expected pattern.

Nevertheless, Jeremiah's lyrics do go on using at times the female personification of Jerusalem in misogynistic type language, as soon as in 2:20–25. The practice of oral tradition in which the older generation teaches the younger, not only the way of composing lyrics with sound patterns, but also the formulas and themes that are vehicles for cultural practice, can mean perpetuating what is criticized and understood today as misogynistic rhetoric and cultural practice. One can only assume that the young Jeremiah learned in part from his forebears, earlier male prophets, how they lyricized, and from his understanding of receiving words from the deity. Yet it is also the practice of oral tradition that has always allowed for innovation, and whether lyricists choose to push back the limits of what is accepted into new ideas and practices. Most of the voices in the book of Lamentations (below) do just this, innovate oral traditional lyrics and content for lamenting in severe crisis, to question God,

8. Shields, "Impasse or Opportunity," 295, makes an excellent and needed point, following Maier (*Daughter Zion, Mother Zion*, 98–99) and Baumann (*Love and Violence*, 57–81) that too often interpreters 'read into' biblical texts (about the relationship of God and Israel, represented as female) modern ideas of mutually loving relationships and forget the ancient political practice of a covenant between a superior and subordinatre party, or on the other hand, simply overlook violence by God against 'his' partner. There is also a danger of reading every text about the relationship of God and people (especially rendered as female) as *only* hiercharchical and abusive of power, and moreover, assuming that the entire Hebrew Bible presents only this. Drawing such a modern, patronizing conclusion without critically examining each text may erase or miss any dissenting views of the indigenous people in their texts, including women. This would not be a postcolonial approach.

and implicitly challenge prophetic theology. The question here will be whether the triplet and doublet sound-artistry traditions will be (were) employed by the tradents for innovation in this ultimate crisis for ancient Israel, including in terms of gender relations.

## Jeremiah 11

Jeremiah himself is portrayed as lamenting and questioning God when he is persecuted by the community for following God's call to announce judgment and impending destruction. An examination of Jeremiah's first lament in Jer 11:18–20[9] (below) also shows the doublet sound pattern is dominant, yet it simply serves as a vehicle for his creativity, as has been true for other lyricists already considered. However, while the doublet pattern prevails, Jeremiah's represented lyrics also suggest him using, more than other male prophets, some triplet soundplays for emphasis, as part of fourfold soundplays (see below).

| *(male)* | | *(doublets, some triplets)* |
|---|---|---|
| But YHWH made it known to me,<br>and I knew;<br>then you showed me<br>their deeds.[1] (18)<br>But I (was)<br>like a lamb<br>gentle,<br>led to slaughter. | *WAYHWH HÔDÎ'ANÎ*<br>wā'*ĒDĀ'Â*<br>'āz *HIR'ÎTANÎ*<br>*MA'ALLÊHEM*<br>**wa**'*ĂNÎ KĔ***ke**veś<br>**'allûph**<br>**yûval liṭvôaḥ** | 2 ôdî'a, ēdā'<br>2 hôdî'anî, hir'îtanî<br>3 hôdî'anî, ēdā', hir'îtanî<br>+ yāda'tî (below) = 4<br>3 ma'all, 'all, val + 'ālay = 4<br>2 hir'ît, liṭ<br>3 anî, anî, wa'ănî + wĕni = 4<br>2 kĕke 4 val, vôaḥ +vû, vôt |
| And I did not know<br>that against me they devised<br>schemes,<br>"Let us destroy<br>the tree with its fruit,[2]<br>let us cut him off<br>from land of the living; his name<br>will not be remembered<br>any more!" (19) | **wĕ***LŌ'-YĀDA'***tî**<br>*KÎ -'ĀLAY ḤĀŠĔVÛ*<br>**ma***ḤĂŠĀVÔT*<br>**našḥîtâ**<br>**'ēṣ** bĕ**laḥmô**<br>wĕ*NIKRĔTE***nnû**<br>**mē'ereṣ ḥayyîm ûšĕmô**<br>*LŌ'*-**yizzākēr 'ôd** | 2 kĕke 'all, kî-'ālay<br>2 lō'-yāda'tî, lō'-yizzākēr<br>3 ḥāšĕvû, ḥăšāvôt, našḥîtâ<br>3 na, ni, nû 2 'ēṣ, 'ereṣ<br>2 wĕnikrĕtennû<br>wa'ănî kĕkeveś (above)<br>2 mē'ereṣ ḥayyîm +<br>ma'allêhem (above) |
| But, YHWH of hosts,<br>who judges righteously,<br>who examines<br>the inmost self[3] and the mind,<br>let me see your retribution<br>upon them,<br>because unto you I have revealed<br>my strife.[4] (20) | *WAYHWH* **ṣĕvā'ôt**<br>**šōphēṭ ṣe**deq<br>bōḥēn<br>*KĔLĀYÔT* wālēv<br>**'er'eh** *NIQMĀTKĀ*<br>*MĒHEM*<br>*KÎ 'ĔLÊKĀ* gillîtî<br>**'et-rîvî** | 5 ôt, mô, mô, 'ôd, 'ôt (final)<br>2 waYHWH, waYHWH (above)<br>4 ṣĕvā'ôt ṣedeq šōphēṭ bōḥēn<br>2 kĕlāyôt, kî 'ēlêkā 2 kî, kî<br>3 niqmātkā + nikrĕtennû,<br>'ănî kĕkeveś (above)<br>2 mēhem, ma'allêhem (inclusio)<br>4 'er'eh, 'et-rîvî (+'ēṣ, 'ereṣ) |

[1] NJPS.
[2] Literally, 'bread'.
[3] Author's translation.
[4] Author's translation.

9. Following NRSV unless otherwise indicated.

Several triplet soundplays above are embedded in his lament and disrupt the dominant doublet pattern, serving for emphasis; they poignantly focus on the most personal angst of the prophet, whose life is being threatened: *hôdîʿanî, wāēdāʿ, hirʾîtanî* (YHWH "made it known to me and I knew, you showed me"); *ʿanî, anî, ʾănî* ("me," "me," "I"); and *ḥāšvû, ḥăšāvôt* + *našḥîtâ* ("they devised schemes," "let us destroy" him). These triple syllable or word sound repetitions in each case are followed by a fourth sound repetition a little distance away from the cluster, thus 3+1=4. What might be an explanation for this feature? In my view, superficial answers are that Jeremiah is imitating or impersonating women's style. More deeply, perhaps, he has made the tradition of women's lyrical expression a part of his consciousness and experience, either as part of his gender identity, or perhaps because the context of suffering has brought the male prophet into close proximity and identifying with women's expressions of lament and mourning. This prophet is in a vulnerable state as a man; his state is analogous perhaps to how women could be vulnerable in the culture, particularly in time of war. It is important to note here that a feature seen already in women's represented lyrics included the use of a *doubled* word she joined to an added syllable sound to make a triplet (2+1=3). When this dynamic appears in a dialogical context, the lyricist may be quoting another and adding a soundplay (and line or phrase). Could it be that Jeremiah was quoting a woman's or women's lament lyrics with whom he was associated and creatively adding his own line for fourfold soundplays, perhaps with them in dialog? Further analysis, beyond the present study, is necessary for a full understanding of how the book of Jeremiah portrays the male prophet's lyricizing in terms of soundplay. A preliminary assessment suggests that in two different genres—a judgment oracle and a lament—this prophet employs the doublet-sound composing tradition associated with men, yet in this lament, he also employs a triplet pattern typical of women's composing.

The analysis turns now to several texts in the book of Jeremiah in which women are identified as speakers, female persona, or sympathetic subjects: Jer 4:19–21; 10:19–25; 8:18–9:3, 17–22; and 31:15–17. Only in Jer 31:15–17 is the female speaker introduced as Rachel; in the other texts, the female speaker is *unintroduced*, which raises the question of whether this voice is more than simply a personification (who is typically introduced by the prophet), as many interpreters assume.

## Jeremiah 4

Some commentators suggest that Jer 4:5–31 reflects a likely context of an alarm about the sixth-century invasion by the Babylonians from the north of Judah and Jerusalem, and unfolding destruction. Within this passage, most commentators usually regard that Jeremiah is the primary voice speaking what YHWH charges him to say (v. 5a–b), and that personified Jerusalem also speaks in vv. 19–21,[10] though some think this is yet Jeremiah's own lament. The chart below lays out the sound patterns of the different voices.[11] It suggests a male prophet (doublet soundplays) speaking on behalf of YHWH in 4:4–9.[12]

| *(male)* | | *(doublets)* |
|---|---|---|
| Proclaim in Judah, | haggîdû vîhûdâ | 10 final û |
| and in Jerusalem, | ûvîrûšālaim | 2 vîhûdâ, ûvîrûšālaim |
| Announce and say: | hašmîʿû WĔʾIMRÛ | 2 wĕʾimrû, wĕʾimrû |
| "Blow[1] the horn[2] in the land!" | tiqʿû ŠÔPHĀR bāʾāreṣ | 4 šôphār bāʾāreṣ, |
| Cry out, | qirʾû | ʿārê hammivṣār |
| project, and say: | malʾû WĔʾIMRÛ | 2 mivṣār, mēvîʾ |
| "Assemble, and let us go | hēʾāsphû wĕnāvôʾâ | 4 haggîdû, hašmîʿû, |
| into the fortified cities!" (5) | ʾel-ʿĀRÊ hamMIVṣār | hēʾāsphû, hāʿîzû |
| Raise a signal:[3] | ŚĔʾÛ-NĒS | 2 śĕʾû-nēs, ṣiyyônâ |
| To Zion. | ṢIYYÔNÂ | 2 ôn, ôn |
| Take refuge, do not delay! | hāʿîzû ʾal - taʿămōdû | 2 taʿă, rāʿâ 2 ʾal, ʿālâ |
| For evil I bring | KÎ rāʿâ ʾānōkî MĒVÎʾ | 2 ʾānōkî, āphôn 2 kî, kî |
| from the north, | miṣṣāphôn | 2 šever (+ šôphār above) |
| a disaster great. (6) | wĕŠEVER gādôl | 2 gādôl (+ haggîdû above) |
| Has come up a lion | ʿālâ ʾARYĒH | 2 gādôl, gôyim 2 nāsaʿ, yāṣāʾ |
| from his thicket: | missubbĕkô | 4 ʿālâ ʾaryēh, |
| And the destroyer of nations | ûmašḥît gôyim | lāśûm ʾarṣēk, |
| has set out, | nāsaʿ | lĕšammâ ʿārayik + |
| has departed | yāṣāʾ | ʾel - ʿārê (above) |
| from his place, | mimmĕqōmô | 4 miṣṣāphôn, missubbĕkô, |
| To make your land | LĀŚÛM ʾARṢĒK | mimmĕqōmô, mimmennû |
| a desolation; your cities | LĔŠAMMÂ ʿĀRAYIK | (v.8 below) |
| shall be ruined, without inhabitant. (7) | tiṣṣênâ mēʾên yôšēv | 2 tiṣṣ , miṣṣ 2 ênâ ʾên |

1 *qere*.
2 Literally, the shofar.
3 Holladay, *Jeremiah 1*, 140, notes the parallel in 6:1: 'fire signal.' LXX has 'flee'.

10. E.g., Volz, *Prophet Jeremia*, 56, identified Jerusalem / Daughter Zion's speech in Jer 4:19–21.

11. Following NJPS unless otherwise indicated.

12. Lundbom, *Jeremiah 1–20*, notes several doublet soundplays with *ʿaryē, ʿ arṣēk, ʿārayik, and ʿārê* in Jeremiah's rhetoric across vv. 5–8.

Verse 5 above appears to be the desperate voice of people in outlying areas trying to run and escape to find protection in the fortified cities. Verses 6 and 7 suggest Jeremiah's voice (doublet soundplays) speaking for YHWH. The prophet then raises a call (in v.8 below) for a group[13] to utter laments of mourning: that is, to utter a dirge-type lament (cf. Jeremiah 9).

Instead, what immediately ensues is an interjecting voice in v. 10, using *triplet* soundplays, speaking a lament *prayer* of complaint to YHWH. Lyrical in form, it had been considered a prose insert,[14] though numerous commentators regard it as poetry. Most regard the complaint to YHWH in defense of the people in v. 10 as Jeremiah's voice.[15] However, while there are non sequiturs in the arrangement of utterances at times, still it is somewhat surprising for Jeremiah's voice to break the flow here, to suddenly stop speaking severe judgments for YHWH while describing the invasion; if anything one would expect Jeremiah to utter a dirge or express mourning, since he just called for that. It is impossible here to know whether this call and response of speakers originated this way from the context, or whether a prophet or scribe later arranged the voices together when writing their utterances. If a prophet or scribe were trying to represent the voices of the context, there may have been an approximation of the flow of the rhetoric, or a scribe may have lent his or her interpretation to it. Some might say that what we have entirely in the text is only the view of a scribe or final redactor.[16] In any event, in the analyses of this study, a triplet sound-repetition pattern is suggestive of a woman's voice in v. 10, so let us consider 4:8–10.

13. Masculine plural imperative, but Hebrew usage of the form can, and likely here, includes women.

14. Still NRSV and NJPS. Althann, *Philological Analysis*, 58–72, argued for vv. 9–12 also being poetry.

15. I myself interpreted it as such previously; Lee, *Singers of Lamentations,* 56, primarily because elsewhere Jeremiah is portrayed as complaining to YHWH in defense of the innocent who suffer at the hand of those who exploit, and he critiques false prophets (Jer 12:1; 14:13); however, in light of the lyrical form and triplet sound pattern here, I have had to rethink this view. Just because Jeremiah expresses these concerns elsewhere does not mean that only he could have uttered this line and not someone else.

16. I am not willing to concede that a scribe or redactor had that much power over the poetic sources.

| | | |
|---|---|---|
| *(male)* | ʿal-zōʾt | *(doublets)* |
| For this, | ḥigrû śaqqîm | 4 ḥigrû, siphdû, hêlîlû + |
| put on sackcloth,[1] | siphdû | mimmennû |
| mourn | wĕhêlîlû | 2 qōmô, qîm 2 lîlû, lōʾ |
| and wail; | kî lōʾ-šāv | 4 ḥărôn, hāyâ, hahûʾ |
| Indeed! it has not turned away— | ḥărôn ʾaph - *YHWH* | 1 kî 2 lōʾ-šāv +yôšēv(above) |
| the blazing anger of YHWH— | mimmennû | 2 siph, ʾaph 2 mennû, nĕʾum |
| from us. (8) | wĕhāyâ vayyôm - | 2 YHWH, YHWH |
| And it shall be | hahûʾ nĕʾum-*YHWH* | 2 vayyôm, yōʾvad |
| in that day —declares YHWH— | yōʾvad *LĒV*- hammelek | 2 lēv-hammelek, |
| Shall fail the mind of the king | wĕ*LĒV* haśśārîm | lēv haśśārîm 2 ham, šam |
| and the mind of the nobles | wĕnāšammû | 2 śārîm, śaqqîm (above) |
| and be appalled | hakkō*HĂNÎM* | 2 hakkōhănîm, hannĕvîʾîm |
| the priests, | wĕ*HANNĔVÎʾÎM* | 2 yitmāhû + hahûʾ (above, |
| and the prophets | | |
| shall stand aghast. (9) | yitmāhû | inclusio) |
| | | *(triplets)* |
| *(female)* | wāʾ*ŌMAR* ʾăhāh | 3 ăhāh, ʾădōnāy, ʾākēn |
| But I said:[2] Aha! | ʾădōnāy *YHWH* | 1 YHWH +2 above=3 |
| Lord YHWH! | ʾākēn *HAŠŠĒʾ* | 3 haššēʾ, hiššēʾtā, hazzeh |
| But[3] surely | *HIŠŠĒʾ*tā *LĀʿĀM* | 3 lāʿām, lîrûšālaim, šālôm |
| you deceived | *HAZZEH* wĕlîrû*ŠĀLAIM* | 3 ʾākēn , lākem, nāgʿâ |
| this people | lēʾ*MŌR* *ŠĀLÔM* | 2 ʾōmar, ʾmōr 3 lî, lē, lā |
| and Jerusalem, | *YIHYEH* | 5 šēʾ, šēʾtā, šā, šā, eš |
| saying: "Peace | lākem | 3 ʾākēn, lākem, āgĕʿâ |
| there will be | wĕnāgĕʿâ ḥerev | 6 hāh, ha, hi, ha, ḥe, ha |
| for you." | ʿad - hannāpheš | 3 nā, nā + nāy (above) |
| Yet the sword touches | | 2 ʿad-hanā + ʾăhāh ʾăd(above) |
| against the throat![4] (10) | | |

[1] A group of people are called upon to lament and wail.
[2] LXX[a] has "and they said." Allen suggests their message of peace "was permitted by—though not derived from—Yahweh" (following McKane, *Jeremiah*, 94-95).
[3] Translating the contrary statement of what precedes following the verb *ʾmr* (BDB: 38); NRSV has "how utterly you have deceived this people…."; Lundbom, *Jeremiah 1-20*, 339, has "you have really been deceptive to this people," and following Muffs (1992:29) suggests "This is more than an expression of shock and surprise; Jeremiah is conveying strong opposition to Yahweh and comes dangerously close to blasphemy. He is implying that Yahweh is responsible for the prophets preaching peace." The verb is the same as used by Eve in Gen 3:13 to say the snake "deceived" her.
[4] Lundbom, *Jeremiah 1-20*, 339, notes the Ugaritic cognate of Hebrew *nepheš* can also mean 'throat'.

Verses 8–9 above bear the doublet pattern of a male voice, but then an unidentified voice interjects using a *triplet* syllable sound pattern in v. 10. The voice sounds like a prophet's complaint[17] to God on behalf of the people, which is why virtually all commentators suggest this is Jeremiah speaking. I propose here that it is *a woman prophet* interjecting, whose voice has followed soon after Jeremiah called for a group to put on sackcloth, to lament, and to wail (v. 8)—women were supposed to raise the dirge laments and express mourning. Yet this woman's voice has uttered not a dirge, as directed, but *a lament prayer* to YHWH.[18] The overall

17. Without clear reasoning at times, commentators attribute some laments to Jeremiah and some to Jerusalem.

18. For God's *prohibition* of prayer at a certain point in Jeremiah, see Lee, *Singers of Lamentations*, 69, 80.

passage suggests a context of urgency and crisis in which prophet and mourners are together. While it is conceivable that a female mourner or lamenter (with triplet soundplay) uttered the direct complaint to YHWH in v. 10, it would be more likely that this is a woman prophet's voice issuing such a charge of divine deception, especially as this plaintiff speaks about false prophets.[19] In fact, it is reminiscent of Abraham's interjection with God about the intended destruction of Sodom and Gomorrah, and of Moses' intervention pleading with YHWH in the golden-calf incident (on the matter of the woman prophet's addressing the problem of YHWH's anger, see below in Jeremiah 10).

An apparent response to the female voice next comes (below; v. 11) in doublet soundplays; it is unclear whether it is YHWH or Jeremiah speaking to her, or Jeremiah speaking for YHWH. The one responding, more likely YHWH, repeats her phrase—"this people and Jerusalem." Rather than address her charge, however, the voice reiterates the coming destruction using a metaphor of a searing 'wind' (or *rûaḥ*), especially important as it is YHWH's wind or destructive energy that arrives, yet in the form of the invading enemy (as below). (This lyric with *bammidbār derek* is similar to that in Isa 40:3, though here for judgment, there for YHWH's way of rescue through the desert.) An important element of the interpretation of the reply here is the term, *bat-ʿammî* in v. 11, which it is not necessary to translate as a personification of the city or nation.[20] Moreover, there is no reason why a personification has to be the object here: there is no preposition preceding *bat-ʿammî* (contra NRSV's "toward"); nor is it necessary that *derek* be in construct relationship with *bat-ʿammî*. Rather, 'daughter of my people' may be a referent to a real person, a woman, alluded to in the context,[21] thus a vocative as translated

19. Likewise, in Jer 8:11, I suggest YHWH's voice addresses *bat-ʿammî* again regarding false prophets: "They have treated the destruction, *bat-ʿammî*, carelessly, saying 'peace, peace' when there is no peace."

20. Nearly all commentators simply assume that *bat-ʿ ammî* is intended to be congruous with *bat-ṣiyyôn*, or Daughter Jerusalem; however, *bat-ʿammî* does not follow the same grammatical pattern as 'Daughter Jerusalem' or 'Daughter Zion,' which are appositional constructions. 'My people' is not a proper noun. In fact, the prophet Ezekiel refers to women prophets in his context as '*daughters of your people*' (*bĕnôt ʿammĕkā*) whom he is called to criticize as false prophets, and he is regularly called 'son of man' (certainly a real person); a more positive reference to women prophets as "your daughters" (*bĕnôtêkem*) is in the well-known text of Joel 2:28 (3:1); cf. Bowen, "Daughters of Your People," 417–33.

21. For a discussion of the prophet Jeremiah's peculiar use of the term *bat-ʿammî*, see Henderson, "Who Weeps in Jeremiah viii 23 (ix 1)?," 191–206; on Jeremiah's use of

below, as YHWH addresses her as the one who just lamented in v. 10. The sound pattern that follows, then, in v. 12–13, dominated by triplets, suggests the woman prophet responds in turn with an implication that she has felt the wind or *rûaḥ* of the coming enemy,[22] but will 'now' even utter judgments against 'them.' Her lyrics describe the chariots and horses of the enemy, a motif seen in women's lyrics earlier. Some interpreters view God as speaking in v. 12, but the translation of 'to me' or 'for me' (*lî*) is problematic; God's wind would not come to the deity (NJPS translates "against me"; NRSV "from me").[23] But after the (proposed) woman's voice describing the enemy in v. 13, she says "woe is us, we are doomed"). This is a prophetic voice. If all these lines were simply Jeremiah speaking in vv. 12–13, it seems unlikely that his perspective would shift so radically and so quickly from agreeing with and uttering God's condemnations and destroying punishment of the people by the enemy (vv. 5–9) to accusing God of deception (v. 10) to critiquing the enemy (v. 12) and finally would return to strident condemnations of personified Jerusalem (v. 14). Instead, more simply, *another* prophetic voice (identified by a clear, different lyrical pattern [vv. 12–13] and suggested to be a woman prophet), who has uttered a complaint about God's bringing the punishing enemy, now will critique this enemy's injustice against her people. Thus the text suggests two different 'true' prophets in some disagreement about YHWH's actions to punish in this way.

---

the phrase as a term of endearment for an individual, rather than a personification, see Lee, *Singers of Lamentations*, 63–65. In Jer 6:26, Jeremiah addresses *bat-ʿammî* with a vocative, calling her to mourn and lament. This term in the Bible first appears in the text, Isa 22:4, and only once in the book of Isaiah.

22. Lundbom, *Jeremiah 1–20*, 344, notes the doublet soundplay with *mālē* and *mēēlle* in v. 12, but in fact these two are part of a *triplet* soundplay also with *ya ʿăle* in v. 13.

23. Allen's translation, *Jeremiah*, 63, "at my behest" gets at an implied meaning 'for me.'

| | | |
|---|---|---|
| *(male-YHWH)*<br><br>At that time,<br>it will be said about 'this people and Jerusalem':<br><br>A wind searing from the heights[1]<br>onto the desert, a path,[2]<br><br>Daughter of my people,<br><br>not to winnow<br>and not to fan. (11) | BĀ'ĒT hahî'<br>yē'āmēr LĀ'ĀM-<br>hazzeh<br>wělîrûŠĀLAIM<br>RÛAḤ ṣaḥ ŠĔPHĀYÎM<br>bammiDBĀR DERek<br>BAT - 'AMMÎ<br>LÔ' lizrôt<br>wěLÔ' lěhāBAR | *(doublets)*<br>2 bā'ēt hahî', bat 'ammî<br>2 'ām, 'ām<br>2 lā'ām-hazzeh wělîrûšālaim<br>+ lā'ām hazzeh wělîrûšālaim (above)<br>2 ze wělîrûšālaim,<br>ṣaḥ šěphāyîm<br>2 bammidbār 2 dbār, derek<br>2 bār, bar<br>4 lô' li, lô' lě |
| *(female)*<br>A wind blast<br>from these[3] comes to me:<br>Now<br>also I<br>I will speak justice<br>against them. (12)<br><br>Look!<br>like clouds<br>he ascends,[4]<br>and like a whirlwind his chariots,<br>swifter than eagles<br>his horses.<br>Woe to us!<br>Indeed, we are ruined! (13) | RÛAḤ MĀLĒ'<br>MĒ'ĒLLEH yāvô' lî<br>'attâ<br>gam-'ănî<br>'ădabbēr mišpĀṬÎM<br>'ÔTĀM<br>hinnēh<br>ka'ănānîm<br>YA'ĂLEH<br>wěkassûphâ markěvÔTĀYW<br>qallû minněšārîm<br>sûsāyw<br>'ÔY LĀnû<br>kî šuddāděnû | *(triplets)*<br>2 rûaḥ (+rûaḥ above)<br>3 mālē', mē'ēlleh + ya'ăleh<br>3 'attâ, 'ănî, 'ădabbēr<br>3 'attâ + bā'ēt hahî',<br>bat 'ammî (above)<br>3 āṭîm, 'ôtām, ôtāyw<br>3 îm, îm, îm<br>3 'ănî, hinnēh, 'ănānîm<br>3 ka, ka, qa<br>3 mar, minněšār<br>3 ya'ăleh, qallû, 'ôy lānû<br>3 û, û, û (final)<br>3 ānû + 'ănānîm, 'ănî (above)<br>3 sûphâ, sûsāyw, šuddād |

1 *šěphāyîm* suggests bare places or wind-swept heights (BDB:1046). LXX is of no help, translating a moral interpretation ('a spirit of error'; Carroll, *Jeremiah*, 162).
2 MT has the noun form, *derek*, which need not be in construct with *bat-'ammî,* as the lyrics of v. 11 are elliptical. Even with repointing a verb, one expects a feminine verb with *rûaḥ* (though the apparent Qal participle of *ṣḥḥ* with *rûaḥ* is masculine, and *rûaḥ* can be masculine; BDB:924). Yet the plural 'them' in v. 12, if referring to the enemy associated with *drk* in v. 11, should be 'they tred.' Yet, in v. 13 the enemy is referred to with masculine singular suffixes.
3 *Mē'ēlleh* ('from these') must refer to a wind blast coming from the enemy invaders that the voice discerns as coming 'to me,' but then emphasizes "Now, *even I* (or 'also') I will bring charges against them."
4 NJPS suggests the 'he' refers to the invader.

The doublet pattern continues in vv. 14–18, suggestive of Jeremiah's voice. These verses include his personifying Jerusalem as female in vv. 14, 17, and 18. Interpreters differ on whether vv. 19–21 is Jeremiah's anguished utterance[24] or the voice of personified Jerusalem.[25] I have suggested previously

24. E.g., Fretheim, *Jeremiah*, 99; Allen, *Jeremiah*, 69. For a review of views, see Bauer, *Gender in the Book of Jeremiah*, 63–66. Following Kaiser, "Poet as 'Female Impersonator,'" 164–82, Bauer, *Gender in the Book of Jeremiah*, 63–64, suggests that "Jeremiah in labor pain takes on a female persona." While this theory is interesting (a version of 'imitation'), it maintains the status quo that women's voices are all constructs of male prophets and tends to discourage closer examination of texts for real women's contributions as lyrical composers.

25. Carroll, *Jeremiah*, 167, or Judah.

that it may be the composition of a woman lamenter or prophet.[26] In applying the syllable sound-repetition 'test' to this text, I find that it bears doublets of words, yet these are part of triplet soundplays. This suggests a woman's voice (prophet or lamenter) who laments on behalf of the city and people.[27] In every other case considered, where a male prophet personifies the city as female, he renders with doublet soundplay only.

| *(female)* | | *(triplets)* |
|---|---|---|
| | MĒʿAY | 3 mēʿay, mēʿay, hōmeh |
| My insides,<br>My insides! I labor in anguish![1] | MĒʿAY ʾĀḤîlâ | 3 ʾāḥîlâ, ʾaḥărîš, hāʾāreṣ |
| The walls of my heart! | qîrôt LIBBÎ | 3 libbî, li, lîbbî |
| | | 5 ôt, hō, lōʾ, qôl šô |
| Beating wildly—my heart![2] | hōmeh-LÎ LIBBÎ | 3 qîrôt + kî qôl, kî |
| I will not keep silent; | lōʾ ʾAḤĂRÎŠ | 3 ʾaḥărîš, šāmaʿtî, naphšî |
| Indeed! the blare of the horn, | KÎ QÔL ŠÔPHĀR ŠĀMAʿtî | 3 hōme, šāma, milḥāmâ |
| my soul<br>hears,[3] | naphšî | 6 šôphār (2), šever (2),<br>šuddĕd (2) |
| the alarm<br>of war. (19) | tĕrûʿat<br>milḥāmâ | 3 tĕrûʿat, yĕrîʿōtāy, mātay |
| Disaster<br>upon disaster has befallen, | ŠEVER<br>ʿal-ŠEVER niqrāʾ | 3 šuddĕdâ, šuddĕdû +<br>šuddādnû (v. 13 above) |
| Indeed! ravaged is all the land. | KÎ ŠUDDĔDÂ KOL-HĀʾĀREṢ | 3 qôl šôphār, šuddĕdâ kol |
| Suddenly ravaged[4] are my tents, | pitʾōm ŠUDDĔDÛ ʾōhālay | qôl šôphār |
| in a moment, my curtains.[5] (20) | regaʿ yĕrîʿōtāy | 3 ōhālay, ʿōtāy, ʿad-mātay |
| | ʿad - MĀTAY | 3 hāʾāreṣ, ʾerʾeh-nnēs, ʾešmĕʿâ |
| How long<br>must I see standards, | ʾERʾEH-NNĒS | 3 mātay + mēʿay, mēʿay<br>(above, inclusio) |
| and hear | ʾEŠMĔʿÂ | |
| the blare of the horn? (21) | QÔL ŠÔPHĀR | 2 qôl šôphār, qôl šôphār<br>(above, inclusio) |

[1] *Kethiv*, from *ḥûl*, but following some Q manuscripts that have the form of this verb, *ʾāḥîlâ* (for better soundplay), rather than *ʾāḥûlâ*, both Qal cohortative, or perhaps hifil. "Writhe in pain" (NRSV, similarly NJPS) miss the allusion of the term used for a woman in labor, as emphasized in Bauer, *Gender in the Book of Jeremiah*, 63, and by feminist interpreters.
[2] NRSV.
[3] *Kethiv*.
[4] Lundbom, *Jeremiah 1-20*, 345, 353, notes that the term *šdd* occurs 29x in the book of Jeremiah, and that 'tents' likely refers to personal dwellings throughout the land.
[5] NRSV.

In 4:22–31 below, the lyrics are dominated by doublet soundplays, thus suggestive of the male prophet's oracles.[28] This includes the notable

26. I will not include the full argument here; see Lee, *Singers of Lamentations*, and later publications.

27. In a previous study—Lee, *Singers of Lamentations*, 50–51—I called this woman "Jerusalem's poet" to distinguish her as a possible woman lyricist from the female personification, suggestive of a tradition of women singers in performance dialogue with prophets, possibly related to women as lament singers.

28. One exception is in v. 22, a triplet repetition of 'they' (*hēmmâ*) in the critique of 'my people'; six other doublet soundplays in the verse override the triplet, which is for emphasis. In my previous study, I suggested that perhaps Jerusalem's poet spoke this line, but doublets suggest a male prophet.

undoing of creation, echoing and reversing Genesis 1. The entire passage closes in vv. 30–31 with the male prophet, using *doublet soundplays*, rendering more female personifications—of the people as a woman vainly beautifying herself, and of Daughter Zion fainting before killers or rapists.

In the above analysis or reading of the texts, based on Hebrew sound patterns suggested to represent composing/performing speakers, I find that the male prophet's speech is in line with YHWH's rendered perspective and voice, and the female prophet expresses dissidence or dissonance with them. An analysis next of the voices in Jeremiah 10 will see where this might lead, since this chapter shows parallel with Jeremiah 4.

## Jeremiah 10

Most commentators see the opening of Jeremiah, 10:1–16, as a separate section focused on the idols or gods of other nations. Thus the treatment here begins with Jer 10:17–25.[29] The opening voice is YHWH's, in doublet sound pattern, suggested to be uttered by Jeremiah. The imperative ('gather up your bundle') is in second-person feminine singular; most interpret this to be directed at the persona of Jerusalem; however, the female voice who utters a response below uses a triplet repetition pattern. If she were Jerusalem speaking, rendered by a male prophet, this analysis would assess that her voice should be in doublet soundplays. Thus I propose instead a woman prophet is giving utterance, not with metaphorical language, but in serious distress during the invasion of war, suggesting the land has been gravely under siege.

29. Author's translation.

| *(male)* | | *(doublets)* |
|---|---|---|
| Gather up from the ground,<br>your bundle<br>Woman living[1] under siege! (17)<br>For thus says YHWH:<br><br>Look! (I am) slinging out<br>the inhabitants of the land<br>at this time,<br>and I am pressing<br>them out,<br>that they may be detected."[2] (18) | ʾispî mē*ʾEREṢ*<br>kinʿātēk<br>*YŌŠEVET* bammāṣôr<br>kî-kō ʾāmar YHWH<br>hinnî qôlēaʿ<br>ʾet-*YÔŠVÊ* hā*ʾĀREṢ*<br>bappaʿam hazzōʾt<br>wahăṣērôtî<br>lāhem<br>lĕmaʿan yimṣāʾû | 2 pî, pa<br>2 ʾereṣ, ʾāreṣ 2 ar, ʾār<br>4 ammā, ʾāma, aʿam, maʿan<br>2 yōševet, yôšvê 2 ʾām, ʿam<br>2 ki, kî 2 ba, ba<br>2 kō, qô 2 kin, hin<br>6 mēʾereṣ, māṣôr, hāʾāreṣ,<br>hazzōʾt, hăṣērôtî, yimṣāʾû<br>2 lāhem, lĕmaʿan |
| *(female)*<br>Woe is me<br>because of my hurt! Gushes[3]<br>my wound. But I,<br>I said,<br>"Ah!<br>this is my piercing,[4] and I bear it."[5]<br>My tent is ravaged,<br><br>and all my cords<br>are broken;<br>my children[6] went out from me,<br><br>and they are no more;<br><br>there is no one stretching out<br>any more<br>my tent, or setting up<br>my curtains. (19-20) | ʾôy lî<br>ʿal-šivrî naḥlâ<br>makkātî *WAʾĂNÎ*<br>*ʾĀMARTÎ*<br>ʾak<br>zeh *ḤŎLÎ* *WĔʾEŚŚĀʾENNÛ*<br>*ʾĀHŎLÎ* šuddād<br>wĕkol - *MÊTĀRAY*<br>nittāqû<br>bānay *YĔṢĀʾUNÎ*<br>wĕʾênām<br>ʾên-nōṭeh<br>ʿôd<br>*ʾĀHŎLÎ* ûmēqîm<br>*YĔRÎʿÔTĀY* | *(triplets)*<br>1 ʾôy lî +<br>3 ḥŏlî, ʾāhŏlî, ʾāhŏlî (below)<br>9 î (final) (in vv. 19-20)<br>3 makkātî, ʾak, nittāqû<br>3 ḥŏlî, āhŏlî, kol<br>1 šuddād (+ 2x in 4:20 = 3)<br>6 makkātî, ʾāmartî,<br>ʾak, mêtāray,<br>nittāqû, mēqîm<br>3 waʾănî, wĕʾeśśāʾennû,<br>yĕṣāʾunî<br>3 bānay, wĕʾênām, ʾên-nō<br>3 mêtāray, bānay, yĕrîʿôtāy<br>3 ōṭeh, ʿôd, ʿôtāy |

1 *Qere*. NRSV has "you who live" but the Hebrew has, grammatically, "woman living"!
2 Contra NRSV, translating *hăṣērôtî* in v. 18b as hiphʿil of a sense of *ṣrr* (to restrict, make narrow, BDB:864), suggesting besieged inhabitants holed up within a town, to cause enough distress to 'press' or force them out; that YHWH intends to create vulnerable refugees is a stunning statement. The LXX phrase used here, εν θλίψσει, is also suggestive of both 'compression' and 'distress' (BAG, 362); 'that they may be detected' translates *yimṣāʾû* as a nifal imperfect, foll. LXX.
3 An unusual verbal form of the noun *nḥl* ("torrent" or "wady" that flows), rather than from *ḥlh* (as Holladay, *Jeremiah I*, 342; to be "weak, sick"); cf. Jer 14:17 and Lam 2:18.
4 Author's translation, from *ḥll*, to 'pierce', not "this is my punishment" (NRSV).
5 The usual translation here of "I must bear it" reads into the text that this is the guilty female persona.
6 LXX has "my flock" instead of the verb "gone out": "my children and my flock are no more."

In the above passage, the woman's voice renders herself distraught to the utmost; the usual rhythm and triplet pattern in v. 19 is so fragmented, compared to the usual flow, as to be nearly indiscernible, suggestive of broken speech. From her interjection *ʾôy lî* ('woe is me') to triple *ḥŏlî, ʾāhŏlî, ʾāhŏlî* (my wound/my tent/my tent) to the *nine* final *î* sounds ('me'), plus *three* final *ay* sounds ('my')—the effect is far more than a repetitive 'oh me, oh me, oh me.' Yet a few syllables (in v. 19) she picks up, and forms the usual triple soundform (v. 20), whether in the midst of destruction or later, but sounding like one truly wounded, sitting alone among the ruins of her tent-house, looking around at the devastation and loss of normalcy.[30] She ironically mumbles in minimal words how there is no one available to help her restore her home, much as people do in a state of shock—after warfare or a natural disaster has torn through their homes—sadly wandering in the ruins talking to themselves. It is the case that the 'wound' is used metaphorically by Jeremiah, but it should not simply be discounted here that a real person in the context has suffered real destruction and wounding.

The ensuing three verses (10:21–23) after the above convey a doublet soundplay pattern, with the male voice further commenting on the stupidity of the leaders for not 'seeking' YHWH (implying through not consulting them, the prophets; v. 21), a further alarm of the approaching enemy (v. 22), and a comment on the inability of humans to control their behavior (v. 23).

However, 10:24–25 resumes the triplet pattern; (the) female voice *again* expresses a lament prayer directly to YHWH, with more measured tone, yet still with imperatives, asking to be fairly 'corrected' with divine *justice, not anger*, implying the same request for the people. That she laments is highly ironic because in the book of Jeremiah, YHWH has reached a point of refusing to hear prayer (Jer 7:16; 11:14; 14:11), which is further ironic since prayer is the vehicle for confession. Yet, the woman prophet implicitly still critiques divine involvement in excessive punishment and their abandonment to destruction. As I have argued elsewhere, this critique of God's anger in the midst of this crisis is unprecedented, not found in the complaints of Jeremiah,[31] which do not appear until later in the book, but her laments are continuous with the woman's voice in the book of Lamentations. Indeed, her appeal is one of the most stunning theological challenges in the entire Hebrew Bible. This becomes much more apparent when the voice in Lamentations decries God's allowing the deaths of innocent children, thus calling into question 'corporate' punishment. For this reason, I have moved from the position that this voice might have been a singer of lament only to the position that the voice is of a woman prophet to utter such a bold challenge before God. The only psalmic confessions that come close to this plea in Jer 10:24 are in Ps 38 ("O YHWH, do not reprove me with your wrath or *correct* me

30. On the book of Jeremiah addressing trauma, see Kathleen O'Connor, *Jeremiah: Pain and Promise.*

31. Lee, *Singers of Lamentations,* 7. Verse 24 has a close parallel to Psalm 79:6–7. Most scholars attribute these lines to Jeremiah; e.g., Lundbom, *Jeremiah 1–20,* 608.

with your *anger*") and similarly Ps 6, but they do not ask YHWH to correct instead according to *justice*, as the voice does here in Jer 10:24.[32]

| *(female)* | | *(triplets)* |
|---|---|---|
| Correct me, YHWH, | yassĕrēnî YHWH | 3 ya, YH, ya‘ăqōv |
| but with justice; | ʾak- BĔMIŠPĀṬ | 3 ēnî , pen...ēnî |
| not with your anger, | ʾAL- bĕʾappĕkā | 12 k or q sounds |
| lest you bring me to nothing. (24) | pen-tam‘iṭēnî | 3 pā, pĕ, pe |
| Pour out your wrath | šĕphōk ḥămātĕkā | 3 bĕ, bĕ, bĕ |
| on the nations | ʾAL-haggôyim | 3 mišpāṭ, ʾappĕkā, mišpāḥôt |
| that do not know you, | ʾĂŠER LŌʾ-yĕdā‘ûkā | 3 ʾal, ʾal, ʾal |
| and on the peoples | wĕʾAL MIŠPĀḤÔT | 2 lōʾ-yĕdā‘ûkā, lōʾ |
| that on your name | ʾĂŠER BĔŠIMkā | 3 šĕ, ʾăšer, ʾăšer |
| do not call; | LŌʾ qārāʾû | 4 kā , kā , kā , kā (final) |
| for they have devoured Jacob; | kî-ʾĀKĔLŪ ʾET-ya‘ăqōv | 3 kî -ʾākĕlû, waʾăkāluhû, waykalluhû |
| they have devoured him | waʾĂKĀLUHÛ | 6 û (final; 3 hû) |
| and consumed him, | wayKALLUHÛ | 3 qā, kā, ka 2 ʾet, ʾet |
| and his habitation | wĕʾET-nāwēhû | 3 tam, ḥăm, šam |
| have laid waste. (25) | hēšammû | |

## Jeremiah 8 and 9

An assessment of the sound patterns in Jeremiah 8 and 9 reveals that these texts are dominated by doublet soundplays. This is ironic since in these chapters women are called upon to raise laments (dirges) for the ongoing destruction. While the texts are very important for the information that women customarily composed and sang such laments, the texts themselves do not give us their actual songs. Rather, the texts simply have the male prophet rendering YHWH's calling for the women to come lament. The lyrics in the text (in doublet soundplay) are what YHWH through the male prophet is telling them to sing.

On the other hand, Jer 8:19a, 21, 22, and 23 all contain Jeremiah's references to *bat-ʿammî*. Again, most commentators interpret his reference as to the female persona of Jerusalem 'destroyed.' This is understandable since there are regular uses of personified Jerusalem by Jeremiah. However, in Jer 10:19 the sound pattern suggests the voice of a woman, not a personification (whose voice invariably is rendered by male prophets' doublet soundplays). There *bat-ʿammî* cried out in anguish using three different verbs for injuries. I would argue that there is no clear evidence as to why, therefore, in Jer 8:19a Jeremiah must be referring to a

32. Lee, *Singers of Lamentations*, 70.

personification rather than a real person in the portrayed intensity of war and violence against the people.

It is true that Jeremiah uses the term *šeber* as a leitwort in his utterances and does use it at times metaphorically, suggestive of the people's wound (i.e., sin or wrong) that needs healing; yet it is also likely, as with most prophetic speech, that he exploits variations on its meaning. Are we to assume that prophets who composed utterances represented in the Bible were never touched or harmed physically by what happened? This rather flies in the face of likely reality.

If Jeremiah is not using *bat-ʿammî* as a personification, then this leaves the possibility that the wound the woman referrred to was real, perhaps from an attack where she resided. (A person in a war context lamenting as though truly injured, when they are only speaking metaphorically of their emotion or sympathy, might be regarded with disdain when thousands are falling injured or dead all around them.) By v. 23, Jeremiah laments not only for her but also for 'those slain of the daughter of my people,' suggesting those with her who were killed, i.e., perhaps her family or village. Thus the excerpt below (8:18–23) may be interpreted not as metaphorical but as alluding to real suffering in the context, beginning with what appears to be the woman's voice in v. 18, with triplet soundplays.[33] The remaining lines are by the male prophet.

33. Verses. 19bc–20 are quoted speeches of others. The phrase in Jer 9:6 [7] appears to be a corruption in the text; Holladay's solution works best: *bat* should be *bĕtat* (construct of the root *bth*, 'ruin' as in Isa 5:6), or 'ruin of my people' not 'Daughter of my people' (Holladay, *Jeremiah 1*, 297–98). In Jer 14:17, the phrase 'virgin Daughter of my people' appears in the MT (in a passage similar to Jer 8:21–23 and 10:19), but 'virgin' is not in the LXX, which has "because the daughter of my people was shattered with a fracture and with a very grievous blow . . . " in a passage that also describes the casualties of war for those slain in the field (*New English Translation of the Septuagint: Ieremias*, 894).

| | |
|---|---|
| *(female)* | |
| My joy has gone, | mavlîgîtî ʿălê |
| grief is upon me, | yāgôn ʿālay |
| my heart is faint.[1] (18) | libbî dawwāy |
| *(male)* | |
| Listen! the voice of | hinnē-qôl |
| a cry for help by[2] | šawĕʿat |
| the daughter of my people[3] | BAT-ʿAMMÎ |
| from the land, | mēʾereṣ |
| from afar … (19a) | marḥaqqîm |
| For the hurting of the daughter of my people, | ʿal-ŠEBER BAT-ʿAMMÎ |
| I am hurt, | hošBĀRĕttî |
| I mourn, dismay | qādartî ŠAMMâ |
| seizes me. (21) | heḥĕziqātĕnî |
| Is there balm —none in Gilead?! | haṣŏrî ʾÊN bĕgilʿād |
| Or a healer[4] —none there?! | ʾim-rōphēʾ ʾÊN ŠĀM |
| Oh why has it | kî maddûaʿ |
| not gone forward, | lōʾ ʿālĕtâ |
| the healing of | ʾărukat |
| the daughter of my people? (22) | BAT-ʿAMMÎ |
| Would my head were a spring, | mî-yittēn rōʾšî mayim |
| and my eyes a fountain of tears, | wĕʿênî mĕqôr dimʿâ |
| so that I might weep day | wĕʾekveh yômām |
| and night | wālaylâ |
| for those slain of[5] the daughter of my people! (23) | ʾēt ḥalĕlê BAT-ʿAMMÎ |

[1] Also the female speaker in Lam 1:22 says "my heart is faint (*dwy*)." The root *dwh* can refer to sickness or injury, but also to the weakness caused by menstruation (BDB:188), thus a word familier to women.

[2] It would be the same construction if the text said, 'Listen, the voice of a cry for help (or deliverance) of (by) Jeremiah from the land.' Why would the prophet who is presumed to be in Jerusalem say that personified Jerusalem is crying from a distance from the land?

[3] Both NRSV and NJPS translate this phrase as "my poor people," thus removing the female referent.

[4] Translating a less modern, more traditional term.

[5] Both NRSV and NJPS have "for the slain of my poor people."

## Jeremiah 31

The last passage to consider for this analysis in Jeremiah is chapter 31, which renders the weeping of Rachel for her exiled children (31:15–17), beloved mother in Israel. This text shows pervasive triplet syllable sound repetitions, suggestive of a woman prophet's oracle of comfort or salvation, or perhaps several joined together. The portrayal of a figure symbolic of Israel as a suffering mother, without the rhetoric of blame or sin, is in stark contrast to the male prophets' personifying the people as unfaithful wife. Perhaps the woman prophet suggested in these earlier texts in the book of Jeremiah later was called to give voice to the sufferers with this comfort oracle. The focus on the children is also a central theme by the voice of the woman in Lamentations (below), as it was in Jer 10:20.[34]

| | | |
|---|---|---|
| Thus says YHWH: | *KŌ 'ĀMAR YHWH* | *(triplets)* |
| A voice in Ramah is heard, | qôl bĕ*RĀMÂ* nišmāʿ | 3 bĕrāmâ, tamrûrîm, rāḥēl |
| lamentation | nĕhî | 3 ni, nĕhî, bĕkî |
| weeping | *BĔKÎ* | 3 bĕkî, akkâ, bānêhā |
| bitterly. | ta*MRÛRÎM* | 3 bĕkî, mĕvakkâ, mibbekî (below) |
| Rachel is weeping | rāḥēl *MĔVAKKÂ* | 3 ēl, ʿal, ʿal |
| for her children; | *'AL - BĀNÊHĀ* | 6 nĕhî, bānêhā, mē'ănâ, hinnāḥēm, bānêhā, 'ênennû |
| she refuses | mē'ănâ | 3 ʿal-bānêhā, ʿal-bānêhā + vānîm (below) |
| to be comforted | lĕhinnāḥēm | 2 kō 'āmar, kō 'āmar |
| for her children, | *'AL - BĀNÊHĀ* | 4 YHWH |
| because | kî | 2 qôl, qôl (above) |
| they are no more. (15) | 'ênennû | 3 minʿî, mibbe, middi |
| Thus says YHWH: | *KŌ 'ĀMAR YHWH* | 3 qôlēk, ekî, ʿênayik |
| Keep your voice | minʿî qôlēk | 2 kî, kî (above) |
| from weeping, | *MIBBEKÎ* | 4 yēš, wĕš, yēš, wĕš |
| and your eyes | wĕʿênayik | 3 śākār, šāvû, šāvû |
| from tears; | middimʿâ | 3 śākār, 'ereṣ, 'aḥăr |
| for | kî | 3 wĕšāvû, wĕyēš, wĕšāvû |
| there is a reward for your work, | *YĒŠ ŚĀKĀR LIPH'ULLĀTĒK* | 3 tēk, tiq, tēk |
| says YHWH: | *NĔ'UM-YHWH* | 3 liphʿullātēk, lĕ'aḥărîtēk, ligvûlām |
| they shall return from enemy-land; | *WĔŠĀVÛ* mē'ereṣ 'ôyēv | 2 nĕ'um, nĕ'um |
| there is hope for your future, | WĔYEŠ-*TIQ*wâ *LĔ'AḤĂRÎTĒK* | |
| says YHWH: | *NĔ'UM-YHWH* | |
| they shall return—your children— to their own country. (16-17) | *WĔŠĀVÛ* vānîm *LIGVÛLĀM* | |

34. On this theme, see Linafelt, *Surviving Lamentations*.

# CHAPTER 7

# Texts in the Book of Lamentations

## Lamentations 1[1]

THERE ARE TWO MOST surprising findings with the book of Lamentations using this sound-pattern analysis. First, whereas the well-known acrostic in Lamentations implies a 'dictating' of the form of the poetry, as will be seen it has *little effect* on the lyricists' use of pervasive sound patterns overall in Lamentations 1–2. Second, the first verses of Lamentations 1 bear a triplet syllable-sound repetition pattern, suggestive that *a female lyricist opens the book*. A doublet sound pattern, suggestive of a male voice, picks up in v. 3 and continues through v. 9b. I had noted in my previous work that the male voice expressed a prophetic theology of punishment, and used a communal dirge-type genre in Lamentations 1, in contrast to the woman speaking in v. 9c and following. I had also noted that the perspective of the first chapter was more sympathetic than that found in most male prophets, that the usual personification of the city as unfaithful wife is not present here.[2] It has become clearer, now applying

1. There has been a flurry of new commentaries and studies on Lamentations in the last fifteen years; for those that especially focus on women and female imagery in the book, see Brenner and Van Dijk-Hemmes, *On Gendering Texts*; O'Connor, *Lamentations and the Tears of the World*; O'Connor, "Lamentations," *Women's Bible Commentary* (1998; 2012); Linafelt, *Surviving Lamentations*; Lee, *Singers of Lamentations*; Mandolfo, *Daughter Zion Talks Back to the Prophets*; Maier, *Daughter Zion, Mother Zion*; and Pham, *Mourning in the Ancient Near East.*

2. Lee, *Singers of Lamentations*, 85. Since the unfaithful-wife motif is missing, Jerusalem's rape, noted by several commentators as rendered in vv. 8–10, is what the enemy does to her (on two levels: what happened to individual women, and what happened to the symbolic city with sanctuary invaded). But that the other voice says

this sound-repetition analysis, that this tone in Lamentations 1 is due to the empathy of both a female and a male voice in Lam 1:1–4. The triplet sound pattern suggests a female voice in vv. 1–2, who also personifies the city as female, but *as a widow*. Not only in ancient Israelite culture, but in traditional cultures worldwide today, the plight of and compassion for the widow is primarily a woman's concern. And it is this voice that first makes the well-known utterance—"there is no one comforting her." By v. 5, however, the male voice with doublet soundplays begins to emphasize the *female city-persona's sin* and consequences of 'her' punishment.

As I have argued previously, the woman speaking through much of the second half of Lamentations 1 and again in Lamentations 2, rather than being the voice of the personified city that is a construct by another poet (usually deemed male), instead is more likely rendered by a woman composer/performer,[3] arguably a prophet, who also deeply identified with and served Jerusalem, and so speaks on the city's behalf.[4] Gerlinde Baumann, following the lead of S.D. Goitein[5] and Fokkelien van Dijk-Hemmes,[6] noted that in contrast to the female persona of the marriage metaphor in texts rendered by male prophets, here in Lamentations the 'woman' is given more of a voice,"[7] and that "the created person is more than a fiction."[8] Goitein's emphasis on women typically singing 'lament' (as in the dirge genre and mourning for the dead) led him to suggest words like theirs likely influenced the composition of Lamentations.

---

YHWH allowed the enemy to wreak violence as punishment for Jerusalem's sin makes this linkage misogynistic by suggesting the female persona deserved this treatment.

3. Lee, *Singers of Lamentations*, 75–194.

4. Lee, "Singers of Lamentations," 33–46.

5. Goitein, "Women as Creators," 27.

6. Van Dijk-Hemmes, *On Gendering Texts*, 86.

7. Baumann, *Love and Violence*, 167–74, suggests the metaphor of marriage is more subdued in the book of Lamentations than in prophetic books, but it still sets the context; she notes that while language like 'whore' and 'prostitute' and explicit violent punishment of the wife by YHWH are missing here, it is clear in the text that YHWH is still considered the punisher of Jerusalem (by the violence of enemy destruction).

8. On this point, Baumann, *Love and Violence*, 171, cites Lanahan, "Speaking Voice," 41, even though he still posited a single poet ('he') creating the voices. However, the question to the fore is, where is this woman's voice coming from, and *how* is she given voice? I would suggest that no one 'constructed' her voice; rather, this was a real woman lyricist in the context who *had voice, was a voice,* and spoke by composing lyrics; someone received her words as important and included them in the canon—that point is extraordinary and suggests a different picture than simply a 'patriarchal' scribal and canonizing process.

This is helpful; however, as I have argued previously, the woman's voice in the book of Lamentations eschews *that* genre (dirge), which tradition expected her to sing (thus also as YHWH summoned women to do in Jeremiah 9), *in favor of* direct lament prayer to YHWH; in fact she defies YHWH's earlier prohibition of lament prayer. Further, there are two key reasons why it is legitimate to look for a real woman's voice represented in Lamentations, beyond simply a persona constructed by prophetic rhetoric. First, though written, the text still reflects an oral-traditional culture in which voices typically represent different individuals in a performative context. Second, the proposed female voice's perspective, compared to the male's, initially in Lamentations goes much further than his standard prophetic theology, to depict and grapple with the nature of the punishment and experience of suffering, especially of the innocent population.[9] These two rationales link to an oral-poetic method that also finds here the two different sound patterns, proposed to be employed by male and female composing voices. As below, the Hebrew text suggests at least two different composer lyricists in Lamentations: female and male.

It is also the case, however, that by the end of Lamentations 1, the woman's lyrics so blend her own suffering with that of the city's population that she virtually melds with the city persona, for example, when she says, "there is no one comforting *me*." It may be noted that in a similar manner Jeremiah's laments in the book of Jeremiah reflect not only his own suffering but that of the city inhabitants and the exiles. Should someone in the context of crisis address Jeremiah as 'Israel', for example, he and his composed utterances would carry double meaning through both his prophetic experience of suffering and his standing symbolically as a figure representing the people. The difference between the female singer in Lamentations and a typical lament singer of an individual lament is that an individual singer might sing of his or her suffering and the city's, but would not sing of "my warriors, my young women, my young men" as though responsible for them. However, a prophet serving the role of a mother (or father) to the community could indeed speak this way.

9. O'Connor, "Lamentations," *Women's Bible Commentary* (2012), 282, notes the important message of the female voice in Lamentations (albeit as a personification): "Daughter Zion's voice evokes the pain of women who have lost their children, who know sexual abuse, who are victims of war and famine. To pray with daughter Zion is to join with the struggles of women around the globe. It is to reject victimhood by embracing the anger that can provide energy to transform relationships."

The prophetic theology of destruction as punishment might elicit such a female prophetic voice also to speak of 'my transgressions' that YHWH has made the city pay for. (It is interesting to remember that God had told Jeremiah in his call that he would make him *like a fortified city.*) Perhaps this woman prophet's call was similar, likened to the city whose prophet she also was. Huldah was a prophet assigned to Jerusalem, though her only utterance seems very different than the female voice in Jeremiah and Lamentations below. In previous studies I called the woman composer of the woman's voice in Lamentations 'Jerusalem's poet,' yet every indication of the text and the context point to the likelihood that she was *an unnamed prophet*. That later tradition attached the name Jeremiah to the book (as singing '*qinot*') may have been for three possible reasons, not mutually exclusive: first, perhaps a sympathetic scribe or prophetic circle wanted to include the woman prophet's utterances and so hid them behind Jeremiah's authoritative name from the context, for Jeremiah himself did his share of strident lamenting; second, women were associated with singing qinot, and though the book is not primarily these but is lament prayer, this title preserves the woman's voice; and, third, possibly, the woman prophet and Jeremiah finally joined together in protest in the context.

The sound patterns of male and female speakers across the entirety of Lamentations 1 are as follows. As before in other texts that convey triplet sound repetitions, also here, the female lyricist's occasional use of doubled words for emphasis, obvious on the surface, yet *hides* the underlying *triplet* sound pattern: e.g., *rabbātî, rabbātî, śārātî;* and *hāyĕtâ, hāyĕtâ, hāʿîr* (in v. 1).

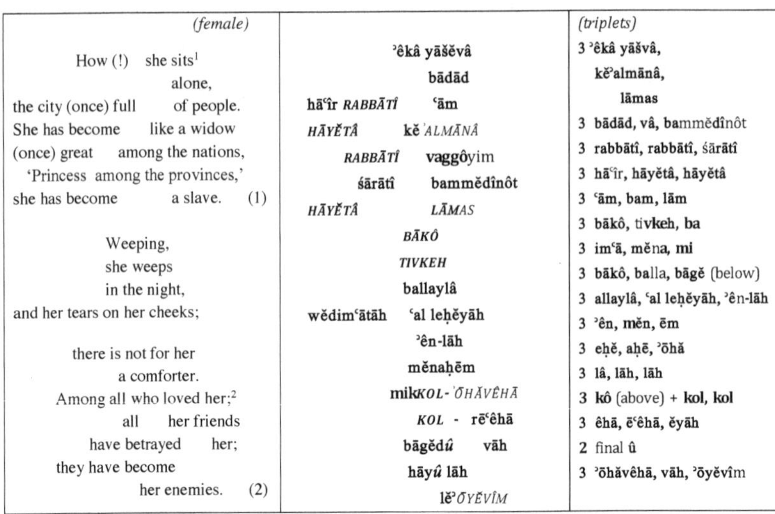

| *(female)* | | *(triplets)* |
|---|---|---|
| How (!) she sits[1]<br>alone,<br>the city (once) full of people.<br>She has become like a widow<br>(once) great among the nations,<br>'Princess among the provinces,'<br>she has become a slave. (1)<br><br>Weeping,<br>she weeps<br>in the night,<br>and her tears on her cheeks;<br><br>there is not for her<br>a comforter.<br>Among all who loved her;[2]<br>all her friends<br>have betrayed her;<br>they have become<br>her enemies. (2) | **ʾêkâ yāšĕvâ**<br>**bādād**<br>**hāʿîr *RABBĀTÎ* ʿām**<br>***HĀYĔTÂ*** **kĕ** *ʾALMĀNÂ*<br>***RABBĀTÎ*** **vaggô**yim<br>**śārātî bammĕdînôt**<br>***HĀYĔTÂ*** *LĀMAS*<br>***BĀKÔ***<br>***TIVKEH***<br>**ballaylâ**<br>**wĕdimʿātāh ʿal leḥĕyāh**<br>**ʾên-lāh**<br>**mĕnaḥēm**<br>**mik***KOL*- *ʾŌHĂVÊHĀ*<br>***KOL*** **- rēʿêhā**<br>**bāgĕd*û* vāh**<br>**hāy*û* lāh**<br>**lĕʾ***ŌYĔVÎM* | 3 **ʾêkâ yāšvâ,**<br>**kĕʾalmānâ,**<br>**lāmas**<br>3 **bādād, vâ, bam**mĕdînôt<br>3 **rabbātî, rabbātî,** śārātî<br>3 **hāʿîr, hāyĕtâ, hāyĕtâ**<br>3 **ʿām, bam, lām**<br>3 **bākô,** ti**vkeh, ba**<br>3 **imʿā, mĕ**na**, mi**<br>3 **bākô, ba**lla**, bāgĕ** (below)<br>3 **allaylâ, ʿal leḥĕyāh, ʾê**n-**lāh**<br>3 **ʾên, mĕn, ēm**<br>3 **eḥĕ, aḥē, ʾōhă**<br>3 **lâ, lāh, lāh**<br>3 **kô** (above) + **kol, kol**<br>3 **êhā, ēʿêhā, ĕyāh**<br>2 final **û**<br>3 **ʾōhăvêhā, vāh, ʾōyĕv**îm |

[1] Author's translation, unless otherwise indicated.
[2] I translate this way rather than use the term "her lovers" (or "allies" would capture the political dimension), which is pejorative prophetic judgment rhetoric assumed by translators, when the lyrics do not require it, especially as the woman's voice here is sympathetic to Jerusalem, whose leaders have failed her.

The empathetic portrait of Jerusalem by the woman's voice above is followed by an empathetic male voice using pervasive doublet soundplays (or multiples of two), personifying first Judah as female in v. 3, then Zion as female in v. 4. In v. 3 he uses *eight* repetitions of both *o* sounds and final-*a* sounds to emphasize exiled Judah's suffering.

| | | |
|---|---|---|
| *(male)* | | *(doublets)* |
| Exiled Judah (is), | gālĕtâ yĕhûdâ | 2 gālĕtâ, gûhā (below) |
| with suffering | mē‘ōnî | 2 yĕhûdâ, ‘ăvōdâ |
| and hard servitude. | ûmērōv ‘ăvōdâ | 2 mē‘ōnî, mērōv 2 ōv ‘ăvō |
| She lives | hîʾ yāšĕvâ | 2 vaggôyim (vaggôyim v. 1) |
| among the nations; | vaggôyim | 8 long ‘o’ sounds 8 final ‘a’ |
| not finding | lōʾ māṣĕʾâ | 2 hîʾ, hi 2 vâ, va |
| a resting place. | mānôaḥ | 2 māṣʾēâ, mānôaḥ |
| All her pursuers | kol-rōdĕphêhā | 1 kol (+3 kol/kô above=4) |
| have overtaken her | hiśśîgûhā | 2 ōdâ, ōdĕ 2 im, îm |
| amidst her distress.[1] (3) | bên hamṣārîm | 10 final hā sounds (vv. 3-6) |
| *(male)* | | |
| Roads to Zion | darkê ṣiyyôn | *(doublets)* |
| mourn, | ʾăvēlôt | 2 darkê + rōdĕphê (above) |
| (empty) of anyone | mibbĕlî | 2 ʾăvēlôt + ‘ăvōdâ (above) |
| coming to | bāʾê | 2 vēl, bĕl |
| festival; | mô‘ēd | 2 mi, mô |
| all her gates | kol-šĕ‘ārêhā | 2 bĕlî, bāʾê |
| are ravaged, | šômēmîn | 2 kol…êhā, kō…êhā |
| her priests | kōhănêhā | 2 šĕ, šô |
| are groaning, | neʾĕnāḥîm | 2 mîn, îm |
| her young women | bĕtûlōtêhā | 2 ănêhā, ĕnāḥîm |
| grieving, | nûgôt | 3 êhā, êhā, êhā (‘her’) |
| and she is bitter. (4) | wĕhîʾ mar-lāh | 2 tûlōt, nûgôt |

[1] Esentially NRSV.

The male voice's empathy gives way to judgment rhetoric, however, in v. 5, with his description of YHWH's punishment of Zion for her transgressions, causing her suffering.

| | | |
|---|---|---|
| *(male)* | | *(doublets)* |
| Her foes are the head, | *HĀYÛ ṢĀR*êhā lĕrōʾš | 2 hāyû, hālĕkû |
| her enemies prosper, | ʾōyĕvêhā šālû | 2 rōʾš, rōv |
| for YHWH has grieved her for her | kî- YHWH hôgāh ‘al rōv- | 4 êhā, êhā, êhā, êhā |
| many transgressions. | pĕšā‘êhā | 2 šālû, hālĕkû |
| Her children have gone, | ‘ôlālêhā hālĕkû | 4 šāl, ‘al, ‘ôlāl, hāl |
| captive | šĕvî | 2 ālê, ālê |
| before the face of the foe. (5) | *LIPHNÊ-ṢĀR* | 2 pĕ, phnê |
| | | 2 hāyû ṣārêhā, hāyû śārêhā |
| *(male)* | | 2 wayyēṣēʾ, wayyēlĕkû |
| Has gone out from Daughter Zion[1] | wayyēṣēʾ mibbat-ṣiyyôn | 2 yēṣēʾ mi, māṣĕʾû mir‘eh |
| all her nobility; | kol-hădārāh | 2 kol, kĕ (+kōl below) |
| her princes have become | *HĀYÛ ŚĀR*êhā | 2 hădārāh, hāyû śārêhā |
| like deer; | kĕʾayyālîm | 2 śār + ṣār (above) |
| they do not find pasture | *LŌʾ*-māṣĕʾû mir‘eh | 2 yēlĕkû, vĕlōʾ-kōaḥ |
| they walk | wayyēlĕkû | 2 lōʾ, lōʾ 2 û, û |
| without strength | vĕ*LŌʾ*-kōaḥ | 2 liphnê + liphnê (above) |
| before the face of the pursuer. (6) | *LIPHNÊ* rôdēph | 2 rôd + dār (above, inclusio) |

[1] Qere, as the lines are very short.

The male voice goes on with doublet soundplays next to personify female Jerusalem in vv. 7–9b, first speaking of her suffering and rape, and the actions of the enemy, but then following in v. 8 with lyrics about her sin. With lyrics that can only be troubling to modern readers with regard to a victim of abuse, he emphasizes that she is the cause of her misfortune.[10] He then says, "there is no one comforting her,"[11] echoing the female voice in v. 2a. Just here the woman's voice breaks in with a quick response in v. 9c, in what sounds like the city speaking, yet it is *to* YHWH:

> Look! YHWH, at my suffering![12] How the enemy gloats!"
> *rĕʾē* YHWH *ʾet-ʿonyî kî higdîl ʾoyēv*

It will be suggested that this is in fact the woman lyricist's voice and not the male speaker's construct, because a triplet soundplay will unfold from this verse, to her voice again in v. 11c, and into her longer speech across vv. 12–22. In these lyrics, she speaks on behalf of the city in more personal terms with first-person speech, beginning a long passage in which she describes YHWH's punishing violence by his anger. Four striking triplet soundplays (in vv. 11c–12) convey her misery—including "look! /I am/ look!" (*habbîṭâ, hāyîtî, habbîṭû*) and "you who pass by / pain/ like my pain *(kem kol-ʿōvĕ, makʾôv, kĕmakʾōvî)*—brought on by YHWH, who "grieved / (with his) burning/anger" *(hôgâ, ḥărôn, ʾappô).*

10. On this section of the text and these issues, see Lee, *Singers of Lamentations*, 102–8, in which I suggest that the voice of these lines is generally more sympathetic to the female persona than previous male prophetic rhetoric. Nevertheless, the linkage mentioned above of rape and sin is a misogynistic use of rhetoric and theologically more than problematic.

11. To say that 'there is no one comforting her' after he has spoken of her sin may imply that no one *should* comfort her because she is getting what she deserves. His use of the refrain, therefore, is different from the use of the 'no comfort' motif by the first voice.

12. The term can be translated 'rape.'

| *(female)* | | *(triplets)* |
|---|---|---|
| See YHWH!<br>and look<br>how I am despised! (11c)<br><br>Ah! unto you,<br>all who pass by the way–<br>Look! and see<br>if there is any pain<br>like my pain<br>with which he afflicted me,<br>with which YHWH grieved<br>on the day of his burning<br>anger! (12) | **rĕ᾿ē** ***YHWH***<br>wĕ**habbîṭ*â***<br>kî **hāyîtî** **zôlēl*â***<br>**lô᾿ ᾿ălêkem kol-ʿōvĕrê derek**<br>**habbîṭ*û* ûrĕ᾿*û***<br>ʾim-**yēš** **mak᾿ōv**<br>**kĕmak᾿ōv*î***<br>**᾿ăšer ʿôlal l*î***<br>**᾿ăšer** **hôg*â*** ***YHWH***<br>**bĕyôm** **ḥărôn**<br>ʾapp***ô*** | **3 rĕ᾿ē YHWH, rĕ᾿û**<br>(+**rĕ᾿ē YHWH** v. 9 above)<br>**3 YHWH, YHWH** (+ 1 above)<br>**3 habbîṭâ, hāyîtî, habbîṭû**<br>**3 zôlēlâ, lô᾿ ᾿ălê, ʿôlal lî**<br>**3 kem kol-ʿōvĕ,**<br>**mak᾿ôv,**<br>**kĕmak᾿ōvî**<br>**3 û ûrĕ᾿û**<br>**3 yēš, ᾿ăšer, ᾿ăš**er<br>**3 bî, bî, bĕ**<br>**3 hô, ḥărôn,** ʾapp**ô** (+**2 ô**) **=5** |

In the above lyrics, the female voice occasionally repeats a word for emphasis, as in v. 1, and joins it to a like-sounding term for triplet soundplay, but for the most part her sound repetitions are in three *syllables*, very often with two consonants repeated in adjoining syllables across three different words. The same type of syllable-consonantal repetition is utilized by the male voice, only in doublets, not triplets.

| *(female)* | | *(triplets)* |
|---|---|---|
| From on high<br>he sent fire, into my bones<br>he made it sink.[1] He stretched<br>a net for my feet<br>and turned me back.<br>He made me desolate,<br>all the day long,<br>faint.[2] (13)<br><br>Fastened is the yoke of my<br>transgression,<br>by his hand,<br>lashed tight,[3] his yoke<br>upon my neck.<br>It depletes<br>my strength.<br>Adonai<br>gives me<br>into the hands of those<br>I cannot<br>withstand.[4] (14)<br><br>He cut down all my mighty ones –<br>Adonai<br>in my midst!<br>He proclaimed against me a time<br>to crush<br>my young men. | **mimmārôm**<br>**šālaḥ-᾿ēš bĕʿaṣmōtay**<br>**wayyirdennâ pāraś**<br>**rešet lĕraglay**<br>**hĕšîvanî ᾿āḥôr**<br>**nĕtānanî šōmēmâ**<br>**kol - hayyôm**<br>**dāwâ**<br>**niśqad ʿōl pĕšāʿay**<br>**bĕyādô**<br>**yiśtārĕgû ʿālû**<br>**ʿal-ṣawwā᾿rî**<br>**hikšîl**<br>**kōḥî**<br>**nĕtānanî**<br>**᾿ădōnāy**<br>**bîdê**<br>**lō᾿-᾿ûkal**<br>**qûm**<br>**sillâ kol-᾿abbîray**<br>**᾿ădōnāy**<br>**bĕqirbî**<br>**qārā᾿ ʿālay môʿēd**<br>**lišbōr**<br>**baḥûrāy** | **3 mimmārôm,** šōmēmâ,<br>yôm<br>**3 mā, mō, mâ**<br>**3 ennâ, anî, anî 3 ra, re, ra**<br>**3 ᾿ēš, reš, hĕš** (+**šā, šō**) =**5**<br>**2 yôm, yôm** (above,<br>inclusio)<br>**2 dāwâ + dennâ** (inclusio)<br>**3 niśq, yiś, hikš**<br>**3 ʿōl, ʿāl, ʿal**<br>**3 ʿay + ay, ay** (above)<br>**3 šāʿay, ṣawwā᾿ + ṣ**mōt**ay**<br>**6 î** (final) (above)<br>**3 ad, ādô, ᾿ădō**<br>**3 gû ʿālû, ᾿ûkal, qû**<br>**3** niś**q**ad, bĕyād, bîdê<br>**3 nĕtānanî, nāy**<br>**3 ʿāl, ʿal, al 3 kō, kal, qû**<br>**3 sillâ** +hikšîl, **šālaḥ** (above)<br>**3 kol**, qir, qār<br>**3 ᾿abbîray, ᾿ădōnāy, ʿālay**<br>**3 bîr, bōr, baḥûr**<br>**3 ᾿abbîray, ᾿ădōnāy, baḥûrāy**<br>**3 ray, rā᾿, rāy 4 ay, ay, ay, ay**<br>**5 bî, bĕ, bî, bō, ba** |

[1] Hillers, *Lamentations*, 72.
[2] Though 'weak' might be a better translation, I use the term 'faint' here because it is the same term used by the proposed woman's voice in Jer 8:18, 'my heart is faint.'
[3] NJPS.
[4] NJPS.

In v. 14 above, the woman lyricist composes a triplet soundplay for a graphic image of YHWH putting the yoke on her neck as though she were an animal, "fastened / by his hand /Adonai" (*niśqad, bĕyād, ʾădōnāy*), and an overlapping soundplay of "fastened / lashed tight / it depletes" my strength (*niśqad, yiśtārgû, hikšîl*). In this and the following v. 15a–b, one can see her use of the term 'Adonai' within soundplays, perhaps a reason for its use instead of YHWH, though there have been texts heretofore where the name of YHWH or the term Elohim are also used for soundplay effect.

There are occasional interjections in this passage by the male voice, using doublet soundplays (vv. 10, 11ab, 15, 17). In what unfolds below, there is a surprising, apparent growing dialog between the female voice and male voice, with growing sympathy from him of her perspective, a dialog which will grow even closer in Lamentations 2. The male voice below appears to have a triplet soundplay speaking of Judah being destroyed as in a winepress, until one recalls where he left off his utterance above in v. 11, when he used the verb *nātĕnû,* thus completing here a fourfold apparent onomotopoeia. This brings forth an expression of weeping from the woman's voice; what appears to be only a doubled word in translation is a compelling triplet soundplay: 'I am weeping, my eyes, my eyes' (*ʾănî, ʿênî, ʿênî*). This repetition is very similar to the woman's voice in Jer 4:19: 'my insides, my insides, beating wildly (*mēʿay, mēʿay, hōme*). Here, the woman returns to her refrain ("a comforter is far from me") (*rāḥaq mimmennî mĕnaḥēm*) and laments for her children. The male voice responds quickly: "No one is comforting her (*ʾên mĕnaḥēm lāh*).

| | | |
|---|---|---|
| *(male)*<br>A winepress—<br>Adonai trampled,<br>Virgin<br>Daughter Judah! (15) | **gat**<br>**dārak ʾădōnāy**<br>**livtûlat**<br>**bat-yĕhûdâ** | *(doublets)*<br>**4 gat, lat, bat** (+**nātĕnû**, his voice v. 11: "they give")<br>**2 dārak** + **qārāʾ** (above)<br>**2 liv, lat 2 dā, dâ** (chiasm) |
| *(female)*<br>For these things<br>I am weeping.<br>My eyes,<br>my eyes, run with tears!<br>Because far away from me<br>is a comforter,<br>restoring<br>my life.<br>My children are devastated,<br>because the enemy overpowers. (16) | **ʿal-ʾēlle** *ʾĂNÎ* **vôkiyyâ**<br>*ʿÊNÎ*<br>*ʿÊNÎ* **yōrĕdâ** *MAYIM*<br>***KÎ*-rāḥaq** *MIMM***ennî**<br>***MĔNAḤĒM***<br>**mēšîv**<br>**naphšî**<br>**hāyû vānay šômēmîm**<br>***KÎ* gāvar ʾôyēv** | *(triplets)*<br>**3 ʾănî, ʿênî, ʿênî 3 vô, vā, var**<br>**3 ki, kî, kî** (+ **6** below=**9**)<br>**3 rāḥaq+dārak, qārāʾ**(above)<br>**3 mayim, mimm, mĕnaḥēm**<br>**3 šîv, šî, šô**<br>**7 ma, mi, me, mĕ, mē, mî**<br>**3 na, na, nay**<br>**2 gāvar, gat** (inclusio) |
| *(male)*<br>Zion stretches out her hands.<br>No one is<br>comforting her.<br>YHWH has commanded<br>against Jacob<br>those around him<br>(to be) his foes. Jerusalem<br>has become one cast out/banished<br>among them. (17) | **pērĕśâ ṣiyyôn bĕyādêhā**<br>**ʾên**<br>***MĔNAḤĒM* lāh**<br>**ṣiwwâ YHWH**<br>**lĕyaʿăqōv**<br>**sĕvîvāyw**<br>**ṣārāyw hāyĕtâ yĕrûšālaim**<br>**lĕniddâ** *BÊNÊHEM* | *(doublets)*<br>**2 mĕnaḥēm + mĕnaḥēm** (above)<br>**2 ʾên, mĕnaḥēm**<br>**2 dêhā, dâ**<br>**4 ṣi, ṣi, sĕ, ṣā 2 lĕ, lĕ**<br>**2 mĕnaḥēm, bênêhem**<br>**2 bĕyādêhā, hāyĕtâ**<br>**2 lāh, laim** |

The woman's voice resumes in v. 18 in what I have previously called a defiant statement, reminiscent of Jeremiah's lament in Jer 12:1,[13] where here she takes issue (contends; *marah*) with YHWH's previous messages of judgment for destruction, upon witnessing all the devastation and suffering.[14] Her voice in v. 20 continues to sound much like the woman's voice in Jer 4:19. A case could be made that it is the same woman prophet in this context. For the third time in this passage she calls upon YHWH to "Look" (*rĕʾē*) upon what is happening. Her appeal "Hear now! (*šimʿû-nāʾ)* all peoples" is a term used by prophets (as also uttered by the proposed woman's voice in Mic 6:1).

13. I am indebted to Holladay, "Style, Irony," 50, for the link to Jeremiah 12 and an alternative reading (suggested bitter sarcasm) to the simple traditional confessional view taken by most commentators.

14. For use of the term 'rebel' (*mrh*) to criticize the people's behavior for not obeying or trusting God, see Jer 4:17; 5:23; Num 20:24; Deut 9:23–23; Ps 78:8; 105:28; the verb also has the connotation 'to disagree' or 'to be contentious' (BDB, 598).

| *(female)* | | *(triplets)* (above) |
|---|---|---|
| Innocent (righteous) is YHWH, | **ṣaddîq hû᾽** *YHWH* | 1 **ṣaddîq** + **niśqad, bĕyād** (in |
| but his edict I contend against. | *KÎ* phîhû *MĀRîtî* | v. 14 above) = 3 |
| | **šimʿû-nā᾽** | (echoes 4 ṣ above) |
| Hear, now! | **kol-hāʿammîm** | 3 **hû᾽, hû, ḥû** 3 **kol, k᾽ō, kō** |
| all the peoples,[1] | **û***RĔ᾽û* **mak᾽ōvî** | 3 **ʿû, û, û** (final) |
| and see my pain. | | |
| My young women | **bĕtûlōt***ay* | 3 **mārîtî, mak᾽ōvî, vašševî** |
| and my young men | **ûvaḥûr***ay* | 3 **ûrĕ᾽û, bĕtûlōtay, ûvaḥûray** |
| go into captivity. (18) | **hālĕkû vašševî** | 15 **û** sounds (total) |
| I called out to those who loved me | **qārā᾽tî** *LAM᾽***ahăv***ay* | 3 **rĕ᾽û, rimmûnî, rĕ᾽ē** |
| —they deceived me; | **hēmmâ rimmûnî** | 3 **rĕ᾽ēh** YHWH (+ vv. 9, 11) |
| my priests | **kōhăn***ay* | 3 **lam᾽a, hēmmâ, rimmû** |
| and my elders in the city | **ûzĕqēn***ay* **bāʿîr** | 3 **nî, nay, nay** |
| perished; | gāwāʿ*û* | 6 **ay** (endings) |
| | | 3 **lam, lām, šām** (below) |
| indeed they seek | *KÎ* - *VIQŠÛ* | 3 **viqšû, yāšîvû, naphšām** |
| food for themselves | ᾽ōkel *LĀMÔ* | 4 **kî** (9 total by this voice) |
| to restore | **wĕ***YĀŠÎVÛ* | 3 **ṣar, marmār** |
| their very lives. (19) | ᾽et-*NAPHŠĀM* | 3 **marmār, mār, mār** (4) |
| Look! YHWH, | *RĔ᾽ĒH YHWH* | 3 **mēʿay, marmār** |
| indeed I am distressed! | *KÎ* - **ṣar-lî** | 3 **libbî, bĕqirbî, kî** |
| My insides | **mē***ʿay* | 13 **î** (final) |
| churn. In tumult | *ḤŎMARMĀRÛ* **nehpak** | 3 **kî, qi, kî** |
| is my heart | **libbî** | 3 **ḥŏmar, miḥûṣ, ḥerev** |
| within me. | **bĕqirbî** | 3 **bî, bî, babbayit** |
| Indeed, contending I | *KÎ* *MĀRÔ* | 3 **mārô mārîtî** + **mārîtî** |
| am contentious! | *MĀRÎTÎ* | (above, inclusio) |
| (because) in the street | **miḥûṣ** | 3 **babbayit, bĕqirbî, bāʿîr** |
| the sword bereaves, | šikkĕlâ-*ḤEREV* | 7 **m** sounds (above) |
| in the house–ah! death![2] (20) | **babbayit kammā**wet | |

[1] *Qere*.
[2] Reading the *kaph* as asseverative.

In v. 21, the woman's voice composes a triplet soundplay, again with her refrain, they hear how "I groan: 'there is no comforter for me'": *ne᾽ĕnāḥâ, ᾽ānî ᾽ên, mĕnaḥēm*. She laments of her enemies who rejoice over her trouble, much as a lamenter in the Psalms might convey, but also much like Jeremiah lamented about his enemies as a prophet persecuted, and called for God's judgment upon them. As is often the case, she ends her lyrics in a passage with a doublet soundplay as an inclusio, here with *libbî* ('my heart'), which she uttered once in v. 20 above.

| | | |
|---|---|---|
| *(female)* | | *(triplets)* |
| They hear how I groan: | ŠĀMĔʿÛ KÎ NEʾĔNĀḤÂ | 3 šāmĕʿû kî, šāmĕʿû, śāśû kî |
| 'none comforting me.' | ʾĀNÎ ʾÊN<br>MĔNAḤĒM LÎ | 3 kî neʾĕnāḥâ, ʾānî ʾên, mĕnaḥēm |
| All my enemies | KOL-ʾōyĕvay | 3 kî neʾĕnāḥâ, ʾānî ʾên, kāmônî (below, inclusio) |
| hear of my trouble; | ŠĀMĔʿÛ RĀʿĀTÎ | |
| they rejoice that you | ŚĀŚÛ KÎ ʾattâ | 2 kî , kî (9 total) |
| have done it. | ʿāśîtā | 3 āʿātî, ʾattâ, āʾtā |
| Bring on | hēVĒʾtā | 6 î (final) |
| the day You proclaimed, | yôm - qārāʾtā | 6 final tî , tâ, tā, tā, tā + initial tā (below) |
| that they be | wĕyihyû | 2 ônî + ʾānî (inclusio) |
| like I am! (21) | kāmônî | 3 kām, tām, lām |
| Let it come, all their evil | tāVŌʾ KOL-RĀʿĀTĀM | 3 rāʿātām, rabbôt + rāʿātî (above) |
| before your face and deal with them | lĕphānêkā wĕʿÔLĒL LĀmô | |
| just as you dealt with me, | kaʾăšer ʿÔLALTĀ LÎ | 3 ʿôlēl lāmô, ʿôlaltā, lî ʿal |
| for | ʿal | 6 lĕ, lēl, lā, lal, lî, li |
| all my transgressions. | KOL - pĕšāʿāy | 3 ʿāy, ay, āy |
| For many are my groans, | kî -RABBÔT ʾanḥōtay | 3 kol, kol + kol (above) |
| and my heart is faint. (22) | wĕLIBBÎ dawwāy | 2 libbî + libbî (v. 20 above, inclusio) |

## Lamentations 2

Lam 2 opens with the male voice continuing to describe *personified* Daughter Zion, yet now he also greatly emphasizes YHWH's destroying actions against her. As in Lamentations 1, he very often repeats terms referring to the female personified city ('Daughter Zion' in 2:1, 4, 8, 10; 'Daughter Judah' in 2:2, 5; Zion in 2:6; 'Daughter Jerusalem' in 2:13a, 15; and 'Virgin Daughter Zion' in 2:13b).[15] In light of all these terms, it is no wonder that a 'real woman's' voice in the text gets lost in the flood of allusions to the city persona.[16]

However, there is a clear shift by the male voice from city personification *to real people in the city* after v. 9. In v. 10 he alludes to "the young girls (plural, *bĕtûlōt,* or virgins) *of* or *in* Jerusalem" who are mourning on the ground. The male voice appears to become personally involved in the grieving as a witness, as in v. 11 he says, "My eyes are strained

15. In the latter instances, the male voice addresses these directly, taken to be personifications of the city, yet the male voice speaks to them as though they were a real person. It may be that the originating context had the male voice addressing a woman lamenter or a woman prophet.

16. I have a suspicion that these many appellatives for the female city personified may have been added later by a scribal tradition intent on hiding the woman prophet's voice in the guise of a sinful Jerusalem. Yet, the triplet soundplays ring through from the women's lyrical tradition.

with weeping, my insides churn, my bile is poured out upon the ground because of the destruction, Daughter of my people (*bat- ʿammî*), because children and infants faint in the streets of the city." Here he uses the term, *bat- ʿammî,* seen in Jer 4:11 and elsewhere, argued in that book to be a referent for a female prophet. It is often used by Jeremiah. Thus I translate here the phrase as the male voice's addressing her *about* the destruction, not 'the destruction *of* Daughter of My People.' He is overcome with the sight of children's suffering and deaths, and thus is expressing a tone now very similar to hers. This verse sounds much like his 'aside' to a companion in the context. If so, if he addresses a woman prophet, it must be the same woman's voice of Lamentations 1. A few verses later, he will appeal *to her*, I shall argue, to raise her own voice (again).

Further along, in Lam 2:18–19, the male voice directly addresses "'Wall' (*ḥômat*) of Daughter Zion," asking her to cry out. It is possible (and most regard it as such) that the poet is still personifying city structures that might be given a vocal expression, as previously he said, "He (YHWH) caused to mourn rampart and wall (*hōmâ*) . . ." (2:8c). An examination of Lamentations 2 shows that the male voice uses this term 'wall' several times. He begins by describing how YHWH, in becoming like their enemy, allowed the invader to destroy 'the walls (*hōmōt*) of her palaces' (2:7b). Then he says, YHWH "devised to lay in ruins the wall (*ḥômat*) of Daughter Zion" (2:8a); then, as above, "rampart and wall (*hōmâ*)" mourn (2:8c).

As noted, in 2:10 the male voice shifts focus to actual persons *in* the city suffering (elders, young girls, infants, babies, mothers, prophets), and describes the gloating enemy. It is precisely at the end of this long section (vv. 10–17) that he says,

> "Cry out 'their heart' to Adonai, *Wall* of Daughter Zion!
> Let tears run down
> like a torrent, day and night.
> Do not give yourself to numbness;
> do not let cease the 'daughter' of your eye.[17] (18)
>
> Stand up, cry out in the night!
> —at the head of every watch.
> Pour out your heart like water,

17. Normally the Hebrew phrase refers to the pupil of the eye but here appears to be used for a doublet soundplay with *bat-ṣiyyôn*. A cognate in Ethiopic also means the pupil of the eye (BDB, 123).

before the face of Adonai!
Lift up your hands to him
for the lives of your children,
fainting for hunger
at the head of every street!" (19)

I propose here that the male voice uses the term 'Wall' as an appellative to appeal to a real woman in the context, asking her to rise up and speak. This ingenious use of lyric will apparently evoke 'her' voice, rendered in the verses to follow (indicated by her triplet soundplays). If the male voice simply wanted to refer to the persona of Zion to speak, he need not refer to her as 'Wall' (previously in 1:8 he says, "she [Jerusalem] groans").

So why might the male voice now use this term as a metaphor for a real woman in the context?[18] I would suggest that he naturally alludes to her typical post or locale on a wall elevated in, or around, the city; here he encourages her to lament and cry out using the symbolism of the 'night watch' (v. 19) at which a sentinel might voice an alarm or give account of what is happening; it is *a metaphor and simile used regularly for prophets* in the Bible. The emphasis is very strong that he calls for her to raise her voice; he uses *five* feminine imperative verbs and *two* jussive feminine verbs. As will be seen in the discussion of Isa 40:9, there is a need to distinguish between a woman prophet crying out *on behalf of* the city, and the notion that the city itself is to cry out.

It is notable that in Jer 4:19, the woman's voice (proposed to be a prophet's voice), cried out in anguish using the same term, 'wall', with an unprecedented phrase in the Bible, referring to "the walls of my heart *(hōme-lî libbî)*." While this too may be interpreted as the city persona referring to its walls, it may also refer to a prophet for whom the city walls were dear and endangered, as well as a place from which they uttered oracles (again, the sentinel motif). Regardless of the sorting out of 'persona' from person, the woman's voice does respond and cry out in vv. 20–22 (as below, where her triplet soundplays appear again) following the male (prophet's?) appeal to her using *doublet* soundplays.

18. It is likely that there was a mixing of the metaphorical and the 'real-life' referent in the lyrics of Lamentations and of prophetic books. Whether this was due to a heavy use of the metaphorical by speakers in an oral culture immersed in lyric, or due to later scribal joining of these together so that the difference is not always clear, is impossible to sort out with certitude. Yet, neither is it a fully critical approach to regard all female voices simply as personifications, while male voices are automatically deemed prophets.

| | | |
|---|---|---|
| *(male)* | | *(doublets)* |
| Cry out[1] | ṣāʿaq | 2 ṣāʿaq, ṣiyyôn |
| their heart to Adonay, | *LIBBĀM* ʾel-ʾădōnāy | 2 ʾădōn, ṣiyyôn |
| O Wall of | ḥômat | 2 ḥômat, hôrîdî |
| Daughter Zion! | *BAT-* ṣiyyôn | 2 ḥôm, yôm 2 bat, bat |
| Let run down like a torrent | hôrîdî kannaḥal | 4 mat, bat, gat, bat |
| tears, day and night; | dimʿâ yômām wā*LAYLÂ* | 2 bām, mām |
| Do not give yourself to numbness; | *ʾAL-TITTĔNÎ* phûgat lāk | 2 ʾal-tittĕnî, ʾal-tiddōm |
| do not let cease the 'daughter' of | *ʾAL-TIDDŌM* *BAT* - ʿênēk | 2 laylâ, lāk |
| your eye. (18) | | 2 ṣāʿaq, lāk |
| Stand up, | qûmî | 2 rōnnî + hôrîdî (above) |
| ring out in the night![2] | rōnnî va*LLAYLÂ* | 2 vallaylâ + laylâ (above) |
| –at the head of | lĕ*RŌʾŠ* | 2 rōʾš, rôt 2 šiphkî, pĕnê |
| the watches. | ʾašmurôt | 2 kammayim + kannaḥal (above) |
| Pour out | šiphkî | 2 libbēk + libbām (above) |
| like water | kammayim | 2 ʾădōnāy + ʾădōnāy (above) |
| your heart, | *LIBBĒK* | 2 kammayim, kappayik |
| in front of the face of Adonai! | nōkaḥ pĕnê ʾădōnāy | 2 ayik, ayik |
| Lift up to him | śĕʾî ʾēlāyw | 2 nō, ne |
| your hands | kapp*AYIK* | 2 bĕrāʿāv, bĕrōʾš |
| for the lives of your children, | al-nepheš ʿôlāl*AYIK* | 2 ʿôl, kol 2 im, îm |
| the ones fainting | hāʿăṭûphîm | 2 bĕrōʾš, lĕrōʾš (above, inclusio) |
| for hunger | *BĔRĀ*ʿāv | |
| at the head of every street! (19) | *BĔRŌʾŠ* kol - ḥûṣôt | |

[1] One expects an imperative feminine form, yet this appears abbreviated, perhaps for the doublet soundplay with *lāk* ('to or for yourself," with second feminine singular suffix). Or perhaps 'their heart' should be regarded as the subject ('their heart cries out'), with the implication that she should raise their cry for them, as apparent in the following lines with feminine imperatives.

[2] Qere.

It should be noted that while the woman's voice will next make direct reply to the male voice and cry out, his imperative was simply an encouragement, as she has obviously already been lifting her voice, and *to* YHWH. In fact, she starts by simply repeating what she already said twice before, 'Look YHWH and see!' completing a triple repetition (also in 1:9, and 11). What is most notable is that the male voice above can be interpreted as coming over to her side in more fully understanding her complaints about and to YHWH, and their need for a comforter. Her voice, below, becomes more vociferous, with a tone of anger coming through, especially with regard to the lost lives of her little children, blaming YHWH for allowing their killing because of his anger. She says bitterly, with anguish: "there was not one who *escaped / of the little ones I guided / and made a brood*'": *pālîṭ, ṭipaḥtî, ribbîtî.* "The enemy finished them off . . . and you showed no pity": *killām . . . lōʾ ḥāmāltā* (inclusio).

| *(female)* | **rĕʾē YHWH** | *(triplets)* |
|---|---|---|
| Look YHWH! | **wĕhabbîṭâ** | 3 **ṭâ, tā, nâ** (final) |
| and see! | **lĕmî** *ʿÔLALTĀ KŌ* | 3 **ʿôlaltā kō, tōʾkalnâ, ʿōlālê** |
| To whom have you dealt so? | **ʾim -** *TŌʾKALNĀ* | 6 **mî, ʾim, îm, îm, ʾim, mi** |
| Should they eat | **nāšîm** | 2 **nāšîm, bĕmiqdaš** |
| —women— | **piryām** *ʿŌLĀLÊ* | |
| their offspring?! Children | **ṭippuḥîm** | |
| they brought up? | | |
| Or should be killed | **ʾim -yēhārēg** | |
| in the sanctuary of Adonai | **bĕmiqdaš ʾădōnāy** | 3 **hārēg, ʾāreṣ, naʿar** |
| priest | **kōhēn** | |
| and prophet ?! (20) | **wĕnāvîʾ** | 3 **nāvîʾ, na, nāph** |
| They lie on the ground in the streets, | **šākvû lāʾāreṣ** *ḤÛṢÔT* | |
| young | **naʿar** | 2 **šākvû, zāqēn** |
| and old. My young women | **wĕzāqēn bĕtûlōtay** | 3 **ōnāy, ōtay, ûray** |
| and men | **ûva***ḤÛR***ay** | |
| fall by the sword. | **nāphlû ve***ḤĀR***ev** | 3 **ḥûr, ḥārev, hāragtā** |
| You have killed | *ḤĀRAGTĀ* | 3 **hāragtā, ṭāvaḥtā, ḥāmāltā** |
| on the day of your anger; | *BĔYÔM ʾAPPEKĀ* **ṭāvaḥtā** | 3 **bĕyôm ʾappekā + kĕyôm,** |
| you slaughtered | | **bĕyôm ʾaph** (below) |
| and you did not pity. (21) | *LŌʾ ḤĀMĀLTĀ* **tiqrāʾ** | 2 **lōʾ ḥā + lāʾ...ḥû** (above) |
| You called | *KĔYÔM* **môʿēd** | |
| like on a feast day | **mĕgûray** | 3 **hāragtā, lōʾ ḥāmāltā,** |
| for my neighbors[1] | **missāvîv** *WĔLŌʾ HĀYĀ* | **wĕlōʾ hāyâ** |
| all around. And no one | | |
| on the day of the anger of YHWH | *BĔYÔM ʾAPH* - *YHWH* | 3 **môʿēd, mĕgûray, missāvîv** |
| escaped or survived, | *PĀLÎṬ* **wĕśārîd** | 3 **ʾaph, pālîṭ, paḥtî** |
| the little ones I guided | **ʾăšer-***ṬIPPAḤTÎ* | 3 **pālîṭ, ṭipaḥtî, bîtî** |
| and made a brood, | | |
| the enemy has finished off. (22) | **wĕri***BBÎTÎ* **ʾōyĕvî killām** | 2 **killām + ḥāmāltā** (above, inclusio) |

[1] Gordis, *Lamentations*, 169, suggests this is a *talḥin* (wordplay with two intended meanings) in which the root *gwr* at once refers to "neighbors" sojourning around Jerusalem as well as the "terrors" surrounding her.

Numerous scholars have made the connections between the lyrics of Deutero-Isaiah responding to laments in Lamentations. To Deutero-Isaiah this study now turns, not in order primarily to discern fully those links, but to push on toward consideration of how some texts there link with the women's proposed prophetic voices here, and whether the signature feature of triplet soundplays by the women's tradition is evident in Deutero-Isaiah.

## CHAPTER 8

# Texts in Isaiah 40–55

THIS CHAPTER MOVES TO the context of the sixth century BCE suggested by Isaiah 40–55, after Jerusalem was destroyed, Judah devastated, and the exiles sent to Babylon. It is beyond the scope of this study to analyze completely the sound patterns across Isaiah 40–55, so here is first examined Isaiah 40, since several scholars have suggested that a woman prophet may be included in this text, based on several feminine grammatical forms. Some have used Isaiah 40 as a springboard for the larger question of whether 'Second Isaiah' *was* a woman prophet,[1] or whether this section as a whole includes the utterances of a woman prophet or prophets.[2] While the former treatments are important for raising the question, here I cannot agree there is evidence that *the whole* of Isaiah 40–55 portrays either only a single male voice (poet, prophet, or author) or only a single female voice (poet, prophet, or author).[3] Multiple lyri-

1. Stone, "Second Isaiah," 85–99; McEvenue, "Who Was Second Isaiah?," 213–22.

2. Particularly the term *mĕbaśśeret* (in 40:9) has been viewed by some scholars as likely or possibly referring to a female prophet, including Stone (1992), McEvenue (1997), and recently, Goldingay and Payne, *Isaiah 40–55*, 44–49, who note, in order "to leave open the question about the prophet's gender, we will seek to avoid referring to this prophet as 'he'" (48); thus also Tiemeyer, *For the Comfort of Zion*, 17–18, 29–30, 279–85, and for a convincing argument for translating "herald to Zion" in light of grammatical usages in the whole chapter, agreement in most of the ancient versions, and by a number of earlier scholars.

3. I avoid use of the term 'author' as it invokes presumptions of modern writing and neglect of processes of composing/performing in oral-traditional cultures. Gendered grammar or descriptions allude to a male prophet or male prophets as speakers in Second Isaiah in 51:16; 52:7; and perhaps 49:1–6 and 50:4–9, unless the latter allude to a male 'servant' or Israel, and not a prophet. Stone, "Second Isaiah," 88, with a

cal prophets or prophetic voices with differing perspectives and styles are suggested within Isaiah 40–55, as some scholars have suggested.[4] I am in agreement that a woman prophet is included in Isaiah 40, based on feminine grammatical markers (as below), and this analysis will search for further possible evidence based on the sound patterns of the lyrics.[5] As has already been noted, especially in this historical time of profoundest crisis, with the breakdown and failure of most authority structures, not only would more voices likely be at play, but also women would likely have had more freedom to contribute.[6] Yet it should not be forgotten that in the biblical tradition it is still a claim that God decides who is called to speak and when, though cultural structures and obstructions may have denied prophetic women their voices, or failed to give them credit or attribution.[7] In light of the previous history and portrayal of prophets in Israel, informed reason would suggest that for the anonymous composers of these chapters (and on through Isaiah 66) we may have both male and female prophets represented, but the evidence must be more fully weighed.

While some scholars have hypothesized whether and how Isaiah 40 is a 'prologue' to the larger corpus, have generally dated layers of redaction of verses suggestive of different 'editions' of the work, and asked whether Isaiah 40 exhibits 'authorial unity,'[8] this analysis sets aside these historical and literary questions as more apropos for modern cultures' concerns. An oral-poetic, postcolonial approach utilized here regards Isaiah 40 as a representation of an indigenous, oral-traditional culture's tendency to

---

feminist and reader-response approach makes an important point: "We begin to locate a woman's voice by listening for it."

4. E.g., on the unlikelihood of a single prophet represented in Isaiah 40–55 since other prophets are understood to be responsible for other parts of the book, see Clements, "Beyond Tradition-History," 111; others open to multiple prophets in Isaiah 40–55 include Goldingay and Payne, *Isaiah 40–55*, 44–49; and Tiemeyer, *For the Comfort of Zion*, 14–25; many scholars, however, work from the premise that Deutero-Isaiah was one prophet or author; e.g., Williamson, *Book Called Isaiah*. I was not able to review the recent publications: Bautch and Hibbard, *Book of Isaiah* (2014); and Tiemeyer and Barstad, *Continuity and Discontinuity* (2014).

5. Fokkelman, "Stylistic Analysis of Isaiah 40:1–11" 68–90, addressed some of the alliteration and assonance in Isaiah 40, noting Alonso Schökel's recognition of 'binary' and 'tertiary' tension in the lyrics, especially in vv. 6–8 (Alonso Schökel, *Manual of Hebrew Poetics*, 56).

6. Following the insight of Hackett, "In the Days of Jael," 19.

7. Goldingay and Payne, *Isaiah 40–55*, 48, suggest that a woman prophet contributing to Isaiah 40–55 may be a reason why the corpus was left anonymous.

8. See the review of options in Tiemeyer, *For the Comfort of Zion*, 337–39.

have multiple voices, sometimes in dialogue, who performed prophetic utterances, as well as songs of lament and praise, which may or may not have been uttered at the same occasion.[9] This does not preclude writing, of course, but oral composition and performance would not have simply disappeared during or after the crisis, whether in Judah or Babylon, but in fact would have been of tantamount importance when social structures collapsed. Thus, it is logical to expect that Isaiah 40 preserves and sets forth as the opening for this context a plural representation of voices that were operative (the dating of which is impossible to determine), and who may be included through some or all of the corpus. Tracing these voices, where possible, by their perspectives, use of sound patterns, other poetic techniques, particular terms, genres, themes, and theology may contribute to understanding the contributions of several extraordinary (yet anonymous) individuals who created the rich tapestry that is Isaiah 40–55 (and perhaps beyond). Of course, even this is an interpretive process, yet must be grounded in textual evidence and probabilities. My main aim in this study is to begin to discern whether the proposed sound patterns associated with female and male composing is evident or clear in this corpus.

As has been oft noted and examined, Second Isaiah contains extensive imagery of cities as female, particularly Zion/Jerusalem, receiving prophetic comfort/salvation oracles, and striking imagery of God as mother[10] and as midwife.[11] Thus, also briefly considered here will be the poignant Isa 49:13–21 passage that renders Zion's lament of being forgotten along with God's portrayed self-references like a mother, also found in Isa 42:14–15. Sympathetic female personification and female imagery for God are not sufficient, of course, to conclude a woman prophet's voice is responsible for such compositions, but the particular imagery of God as mother, and the feminine grammatical indicators in Isaiah 40, do call

9. Alternatively, to regard voices as simply constructions of personae by a single, monolithic, master 'author' ignores that in ancient cultures there were often numerous oral composers in a community, and oral composition regularly involved antiphonal performance, in the same or different settings. The present analysis is in line with Trible's groundbreaking work aiming to uncover "neglected traditions to reveal countervoices," *God and the Rhetoric of Sexuality*, 202 (cited in Stone, "Second Isaiah").

10. Trible, *God and the Rhetoric of Sexuality*, 51–52; Gruber, "Motherhood of God," 351–59; Gruber, "Feminine Similes Applied to the LORD," 75–84; Schmitt, "Motherhood of God and Zion as Mother," 557–69; Stone, "Second Isaiah," 96; Dille, *Mixing Metaphors*; Løland, *Silent or Salient Gender?*

11. Claassens, *Mourner, Mother, Midwife*, 41–63; this motif is also in Isa 66:7–12; see the study by Franke on this in "'Like a Mother I Have Comforted You,'" 35–55.

for serious exploration of the question of women prophets' voices *of composition* in the corpus.

## Isaiah 40: Multiple Voices and the Reluctant "Herald" to the City

Isaiah 40:1[12] opens with a profound and unadorned comfort oracle.[13] This long-awaited communication from YHWH to the people must have come as a clarion to a stunned audience that had experienced devastation, traumatic loss, and a sense of abandonment by their God, marked by a long divine silence.[14]

12. For the following texts, the NJPS will provide the basis for translation, unless indicated otherwise, with occasional reordering of terms from the English to capture the Hebrew emphases of sound patterns. Of note is the NJPS translation of the Hebrew in v. 9: "O herald of joy to Zion . . . O herald of joy to Jerusalem," which indicates a female voice in the context portrayed.

13. Along with Blenkinsopp, *Isaiah 40–55*, 179, I regard the voice of 40:1 as a prophet, lacking clear evidence of a voice from the heavenly council. Many commentators interpret that Isaiah 40 contains a dialogical scene with the heavenly council involved in commissioning a prophet or prophets, following Rowley, "Council of Yahweh," and others. While there are arguments for and against this conjecture (there are precedents for the divine council in other biblical texts), it becomes speculative as to which lines render a divine messenger speaking and not a prophet, since they will likely have the same message. In either case a plurality of addressees are to speak comfort. Brueggemann, *Isaiah 40–66*, 17, emphasizes the important point that the comfort is coming *from* YHWH.

14. In the book of Lamentations, God is never rendered speaking to the people left in Jerusalem, or in the land, after the Babylonian devastation. Also, on God's refusal to hear lament or prayer in the book of Jeremiah after a certain point, see Lee, *Singers of Lamentations*, 69, 80, 117.

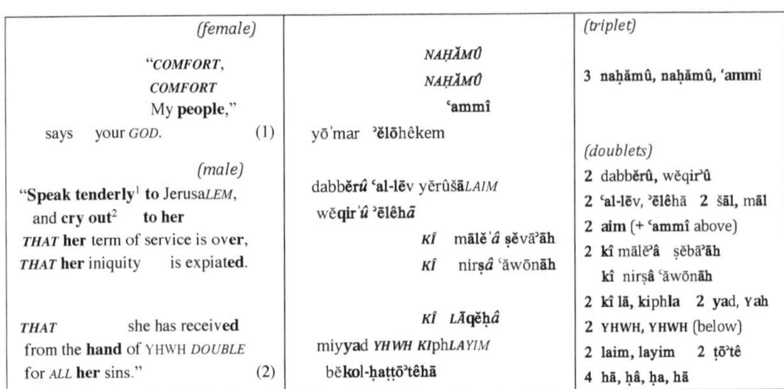

| *(female)* | | *(triplet)* |
|---|---|---|
| ***"COMFORT,***<br>***COMFORT***<br>My **people,"**<br>says your *GOD.* (1) | ***NAḤĂMÛ***<br>***NAḤĂMÛ***<br>**ʿammî**<br>yōʾmar **ʾĕlō**hêkem | **3 naḥămû, naḥămû, ʿammî** |
| *(male)*<br>**"Speak tenderly**[1] **to** Jerusa*LEM*,<br>and **cry out**[2] **to her**<br>***THAT* her** term of service is ov**er**,<br>***THAT* her** iniquity is expiat**ed**.<br><br>***THAT*** she has receiv**ed**<br>from the **hand** of YHWH *DOUBLE*<br>for *ALL* **her** sins." (2) | dabb**ĕrû** **ʿal-lē**v yĕrûš**ā***LAIM*<br>wĕ**qir**ʾ**û** **ʾēlêhā**<br>***KÎ*** mālĕʾ**â** **ṣ**ĕvāʾ**āh**<br>***KÎ*** nirṣ**â** ʿăwōn**āh**<br><br>***KÎ*** ***LĀ*qĕḥâ**<br>miy**ya**d ***YHWH KI*ph*LAYIM***<br>bĕ**kol-ḥaṭṭōʾtêhā** | *(doublets)*<br>**2 dabbĕrû,** wĕqirʾ**û**<br>**2 ʿal-lē**v, **ʾēlê**hā **2** š**āl, mā**l<br>**2 aim** (+ **ʿammî** above)<br>**2 kî** mālĕʾ**â** ṣĕbāʾ**āh**<br>**kî** nirṣ**â** ʿăwōn**āh**<br>**2 kî lā, kiph**la **2 ya**d, Yah<br>**2 YHWH, YHWH** (below)<br>**2 laim, layim 2** ṭōʾtê<br>**4 hā, ḥâ, ḥa, hā** |

[1] Literally, 'speak to the heart of' Jerusalem. This is a phrase seen elsewhere where a male figure especially speaks to a woman for endearment, consoling, or power in persuasion (Ruth 2:13; Gen 34:31; Hos 2:14); however, compare its use in Joseph's speech to his reconciled brothers (Gen 50:21).
[2] Translating *qr'* here exactly the same as in verses below, to show the repetitions. Muilenburg, *Isaiah 40-66*, 425, noted that the term is used more than 30 times in Isa 40-55.

The double use of the word 'comfort' by the first voice, obvious in translation, yet obscures a surprising and poignant *triplet* soundplay in Hebrew with '*my people*' (*naḥămû, naḥămû, ʿammî*). The voice of v. 2 on the other hand proceeds with doublet soundplays. Thus I suggest these are two different prophetic voices, and the significance of this will be tracked below. The first voice of Isaiah 40 is suggested to be female by the triplet pattern.[15] This proposed woman prophet utters God's address *not simply* with that one word "comfort" repeated in reply to "no one is *comforting*" Jerusalem (Lam 1:2)—uttered by the woman's voice in the book of Lamentations.[16] For she, too, had lamented with triplet soundplays, referring to the 'people' (*ʿām*) absent from the city, like a widow (*ʾalmānâ*), like a 'slave' (*lāmas*), for whom with tears 'on her cheeks, there was not for her a comforter": *ʿal leḥĕyāh / ʾên-lāh / mĕnaḥēm*. The woman's voice of Isa 40:1 now consoles the lamenting voice also with triplet soundplay: *naḥămû, naḥămû, ʿammî* ("comfort, comfort, my people").

Without engaging the debate of the social location of the Isaiah prophets here and their audience (Judah or Babylon), the question must

15. Alternatively, for those holding to a divine-council scenario, perhaps this is a female voice in the council.

16. A number of commentators, following Gottwald, *Studies in the Book of Lamentations*, 45, note that the 'comfort' message in Isaiah 40–55 is an answer to Lamentations that there is no one to comfort Jerusalem; e.g., Westermann, *Isaiah 40–66*, 34, who also suggested the "duplication" of words was a stylistic feature of his [the one prophet's, deutero-Isaiah's,] preaching.

be raised as to whether the earlier (proposed) woman prophet in Lamentations, active during and after the devastation in Jerusalem, and this proposed woman prophet now comforting Jerusalem in Isa 40:1 might be represented by the texts to be *the same person*. As will be seen below, I will argue that this woman prophet of Isa 40:1 is not implied to be the same voice as in Lamentations, but that she (now) is likely *answering her* in an extraordinary 'call-and-response' scenario that has transcended decades, to say that YHWH has not forgotten.[17]

A second prophetic voice continues the comfort speech (above, v. 2), clearly favoring doublet soundplays (so implied to be male); for example, "Speak tenderly to Jerusalem and cry out to her" (*dabbĕrû, wĕqirʾû; ʿal-lēv, ʾēlêhā*). However, he directs his message not to 'the people' as the first voice does, but *to the female personified* Jerusalem, and further interprets that the matter of 'her' punishment has been fulfilled, with standard prophetic theology. The first mention of YHWH, then (and in all of Isaiah 40), is this voice's *negative* reminder of the punishment by YHWH's hand. (The first voice used *ʾĕlōhîm*, not YHWH.) While at first glance v. 2 appears to contain a female voice's triple use of *kî*, when the explanation of punishment (in v. 2b) is separated from the actual announcement of comfort (2a), there is discerned a double use of *kî* in the announcement, and a double *k* alliteration in the explanation (*ki lā + kiphlayim*). This second (male) voice uses an extraordinary number of *twelve* doubled sound pairs *in one verse*! Thus, the contrast between him and the first voice is significant already in Isaiah 40—the restraint of the first voice, and the lengthier speech of the second (male) voice—yet both offer poignant lyrics for the context.[18] Both address a plural group, likely prophets, also calling them to express comfort.[19]

17. It is or will be impossible to determine whether these two proposed women prophets' lives overlapped in real time, or whether the latter speaks to the former in some kind of a mystical conversation (?) Here I avoid the simple explanation that the latter might simply 'imagine' the former as a literary construct, since traditional indigenous cultures practiced more than this in communicating with their ancestors.

18. Seitz, "Divine Council," 229–47, suggests that vv. 3–5 are not a prophet's words but the words of a divine messenger, though the text itself is not explicit about this; further, Seitz offers a sweeping statement (245) that in Isaiah 40–55 no longer do we have a prophet or prophets "giving rise to that literature as original oral speaker" but "we have written oracles." The evidence for this claim is insufficient.

19. Blenkinsopp, *Isaiah 40–55*, 179–80, following the Targumist and most of the medieval commentators, understands that a plural group of prophets are addressed, and a divine council is not evident.

This male prophetic voice, or another male, goes on to speak three more verses with many more doublet soundplays (vv. 3–5, conveying the well-known lyrics about preparation of YHWH's passage through the desert, as though for a king[20]).

| (male) | | (doublets) |
|---|---|---|
| A *VOICE*<br>is ***CRYING OUT***:<br>"**In the desert** clear<br>a **road** for ***YHWH***!<br>Level **out**<br>**in the wilderness** a *HIGHWAY*<br>for **our** God! (3)<br><br>Let ***EVERY*** valley be raised,<br>***EVERY*** *HILL*<br>and **mount** be **low**.[1]<br>Let **be**<br>the *RUGGED GROUND* *LEVEL*<br>and the *RIDGES*<br>*A PLAIN*.[2] (4)<br>And shall *APPEAR*<br>the **Pre**sence[3] of ***YHWH***,<br>And they shall behold (it)—<br>***ALL*** life, as **one**,<br>**For mouth** of ***YHWH*** has **spoken**." (5) | ***QÔL***<br>***QÔRĒ***'<br>**ba**mmid**bār** **pannû**<br>**derek** ***YHWH***<br>***YAŠŠ***ěr**û**<br>**bāʿărāvâ** *MĚSILLÂ*<br>***LĒ'LŌHÊ*nû**<br>***KOL*-gê**ʾ **yinnāśē**ʾ<br>**wě*KOL-HAR***<br>**wěgivʿâ** ***YIŠ*pāl*û***<br>**wěhāyâ**<br>h*E'ĀQŌV* *LĚMÎŠ*ôr<br>**wě*HOR*kā**sîm<br>*LĚVIQ'Â*<br>**wě**nig**lâ**<br>**kěvôd** ***YHWH***<br>**wě**rāʾû ***KOL***-b**āś**ār **yaḥ**d**ā**w<br>**kî pî** ***YHWH*** **dibbēr** | **2** **q**ô**l** **q**ô**r**<br>**4** **û, û, û, û** (final)<br>**2** **ba**mmi**dbār, bāʿărāvâ**<br>**2** **nû, nû**<br>**2** **dbār, der**<br>**3** **yaššěrû, yinnāśē**ʾ, **yiš**pāl**û**<br>**2** **měsillâ, lěmîš**ôr **2 gê**ʾ, **gi**<br>**2** **kol, kol** **2** **yi, yi**<br>**2** **wěkol-har, wěhorkā**<br>**2** **pannû, pālû**<br>**2** **wěgivʿâ, wěhāyâ**<br>**2** **heʿāqōv lě, lěviqʿâ**<br>**2** lě**viqʿâ, wěniglâ**<br>**2** **lěv, kěv**<br>**2** **kěvôd** YHWH…yaḥ**dā**w<br>**kî** pî YHWH **di**bbēr<br>**2** **kî** pî **7** **'l'** sounds<br>**2 kol** (inclusio w/**qôl** in v. 3) |

[1] This verb is qal in MT not hip'il.
[2] Watson noted the prophet's soundplay with *'āqōb* and *biq'â*, cited in Goldingay and Payne, *Isaiah 40-55*, 77. Definite article *ha* and preposition *lě* are also part of this doublet soundplay: *he'āqōv lě… lěviq'â.*
[3] Or 'glory'.

Next, in v. 6 below, there is both a parallel with v. 3 ("a voice is crying out"), yet also a shift as numerous commentators note. Verse 6 opens with, "a voice is saying, 'cry out'" (or 'proclaim' as a prophet). It is unclear whether the exhorter is a male prophet who just spoke in v. 2 or vv. 3–5, or another person's voice. In any case, a kind of response follows in v. 6 of a prophet discouraged, beyond the typical reluctance of biblical prophets.[21] The NRSV and NJPS render this voice as "but *I said* (*wě'āmar*)" what shall I cry? (following the MT).[22] However, the

20. The concept of a highway for a deity was known and lyrically expressed also in Babylon; Westermann, *Isaiah 40–66*, 38; Muilenburg, *Isaiah 40–66*, 427, notes the same, but does not preclude an allusion to the motif of the Hebrews' Exodus out of Egypt. Fokkelman, "Stylistic Analysis," 71, observes the quadruple alliteration with the *ki* sound, beyond the triple repetition of *kî*.

21. Thus also Westermann, *Isaiah 40–66*, 43. Goldingay and Payne, *Isaiah 40–55*, 79, note that with this voice's response "a conversation develops" in the passage.

22. A number of versions and interpreters also point and translate 1QIsa[a] the same

Qumran scroll (1QIsa[a]) has *wmrh*, which can be pointed as a feminine participle, "but *she was saying*, 'what shall I cry'?"[23] This nicely parallels the just-mentioned masculine participle used for the voice in v. 6 calling her to speak, thus a gender-matched parallelism. One can imagine a scribe preserving a description of two prophetic speakers. Not only does it appear the older Qumran scroll here kept a term referencing a woman, but even in the MT, a triplet pattern unfolds in v. 6 (*ʾōmēr, ʾōmrâ, mâ*) in order to introduce what I propose is a second female prophet's voice, just as a *doublet* pattern introduced a male prophetic voice in v. 3, above (*qôl qôrēʾ*).

If the only evidence in the texts were the triplet pattern in v. 1 and this variant feminine grammatical form in the older textual manuscript of v. 6, it still may not be enough to posit female prophets. However, what ensues in vv. 6–7 below (and later in the chapter with numerous feminine grammatical forms) is *another, lengthier use of triplet soundplays*, reflective of a women's lyrical tradition.

as the first-person verb of MT; however, the final *hê* on the end of the term is not adequately explained in this case as a cohortative expressing strong determination or desire, which is the *opposite* of the tone of the voice—reluctance to speak. Seitz, "Divine Council," 235fn21 and other scholars note there are numerous examples in 1QIsa[a] of this form of a lengthened first-person singular imperfect verb, and thus 'false cohortatives,' so that the occurrence here in Isaiah 40 of 1QIsa[a] was not a cohortative. However, the form is also a feminine participle.

23. The final *heh* in 1QIsa[a] suggests a feminine participle, also suggested in Petersen, *Late Israelite Prophecy*, 20, 46–47, following a reading from S. Dean McBride; I translate the same but do not believe it alludes to the purported 'herald, Zion,' but rather to a female prophet, in light of the gendered Hebrew sound patterns analyzed here; thus McEvenue, "Who Was Second Isaiah?," 218–21; the quick dismissal of this possibility is curious by Goldingay and Payne, *Isaiah 40–55*, 81, following Seitz, "Divine Council," 234–37, given their openness to the possibility of a woman prophet in the texts and their preference for 'herald to Zion' rather than 'Zion Herald' in v. 9 (86). Likewise, Tiemeyer, *For the Comfort of Zion*, 15–16, does not adopt "she said" for the form in 1QIsa[a], since the 1QIsa[a] term *could be* first person, agreeing with LXX and Vulgate, and yet Tiemeyer shows how the versions (LXX, Targum, and Vulgate) *removed the feminine participle* of v. 9. Perhaps the MT similarly overwrote the feminine form *here* from discomfort about a female prophet. In any case, 1QIsa[a] is the older text and allows for "she was saying." This piece of the puzzle is important for distinguishing voices in Isaiah 40, which I do not regard as a single 'authorial' unity.

| | | |
|---|---|---|
| *(female referred to)*<br>*A VOICE* ***IS SAYING***: "***CRY OUT***!"<br>But she ***IS SAYING***,[1]<br>"**What** shall ***I CRY***?"[2] | *QÔL* ***'ŌMĒR QĔRĀ'***<br>wĕ ***'ÔMĔRÂ***<br>**mâ** ***'EQRĀ'*** | *(triplets)*<br>3 **qôl, qĕrā', 'eqrā'**<br>3 **'ōmēr, 'ômĕrâ, mâ** |
| *(female)*<br>***ALL*** *THAT LIVES*<br>is ***GRASS***, and<br>***ALL*** its *LASTING* goodness[3]<br>**like** a ***FLOWER***<br>of *THE FIELD*: (6)<br>**Withered** (the) ***GRASS***,<br>**collapsed** (the) ***FLOWER***,<br>**Because** breath of ***YHWH***<br>**has blown** against it.<br>So,<br>(just) ***GRASS*** (are)<br>the ***PEOPLE***."[4] (7) | ***KOL*** - *HA*bb*ĀŚĀR*<br>***ḤĀṢÎR***<br>wĕ***KOL*** - *ḤAS***dô**<br>**kĕ*ṢÎṢ***<br>*HAŚŚ***ādeh**<br>**yāvēš** ***ḤĀṢÎR***<br>**nāvēl** ***ṢÎṢ***<br>**kî** rûaḥ **YHWH**<br>**nāšĕvâ** bô<br>**'ākēn**<br>***ḤĀṢÎR*** **hā** ***'ĀM*** | *(triplets)*<br>3 **qôl, kol, kol**<br>3 **habbāśār, ḥasdô, haśśādeh**<br>3 **ḥāṣîr, ḥāṣîr, ḥāṣîr**<br>2 kĕ**ṣîṣ, ṣîṣ** (+3 ḥāṣîr) = **5**<br>3 **yāvēš, nāvēl, nāšĕvâ**<br>3 **kĕ, kî,** 'ākēn<br>1 **rûaḥ YHWH**<br>1 **hā'ām** (inclusio w/1st voice's mention of **'ām**, v. 1)<br>7 **ha** sounds (initial) |
| *(male)*<br>" '**Withered** (the) ***GRASS***,<br>**collapsed** (the) ***FLOWER***,'—<br>But the ***WORD*** of<br>***OUR GOD***<br>**stands up firm** *FOREVER*."[5] (8) | **yāvēš** ***ḤĀṢÎR***<br>**nāvēl** ***ṢÎṢ***<br>**ûdĕvar-**<br>***'ĔLŌHÊNÛ***<br>**yāqûm** ***LĔ'ÔL*****ām** | *(doublets)*<br>2 **yāvēš ḥāṣîr**<br>**nāvēl ṣîṣ** (repeats v. 7a)<br>2 **dĕvar**, di**bbēr** (v. 5 above)<br>2 **'ĕlōhênû** (above)**, lĕ'ôl**ām<br>2 **yāqûm** ('**ākē**n above)<br>2 **yā, yā 2 ām** (hā'**ām** above) |

1 Following 1QIsa[a] (and pointing *wĕ'ômĕrâ*), not MT (*wĕ'āmar*).
2 Goldingay and Payne, *Isaiah 40-55*, 82, remind that *mâ* ('what') may also be translated '*how can*' I cry.
3 An unusual but poignant use of *ḥesed*, applied to humans like plants, creating an image of those who are steadfast, good, and beautiful, but collapse or fade; see Muilenburg's discussion, *Isaiah* 40-66, 429-30.
4 Translating not "man" (NJPS) but 'the people,' important for God's covenant people sent into exile; also noted by Fokkelman, "Stylistic Analysis," 68-90; 73. BHS and some commentators, including Fokkelman, propose deleting the last three words of v. 7, in the interests of "absolute parallelism" (69); this tendency to excise text that does not fit with one's idea of what Hebrew poetry or prophecy should be may erase a female prophet's voice by removing the triple repetition of 'grass' in vv. 6-7, but also removes 'the people,' a key for Isa 40 and this prophecy.
5 Blenkinsopp, *Isaiah 40-55*, 178.

This proposed discouraged prophet's dissonance with the call to speak she renders with nature imagery and laments the people's fleeting and frail existence as being like 'grass,' repeated three times, *ḥāṣîr, ḥāṣîr, ḥāṣîr,* and like the collapsing or fading flower. Three verbs bear a triplet soundplay—'withers,' 'collapses,' and 'blows': *yāvēš, nāvēl, nāšĕvâ*. She says the people suffered this fate because "(the) breath of YHWH has blown against it" (v. 7b; *kî rûaḥ* YHWH *nāšĕvâ bô*). Her resigned discouragement echoes the same imagery in judgment oracles earlier in Isaiah[24]—likely from having seen and experienced firsthand the traumas of devastation of the people of Jerusalem and Judah over many years. Such discouragement might be burdened further by the fresh reminder from the male prophet above that the devastation was YHWH's punish-

24. For a link of this text to a 'fading flower' alluded to in Isa 28:1, 4, as well as the 'grass' in Isa 37:26, see Seitz, "Divine Council," 242; *Zion's Final Destiny*, 197–98.

ment—yet, this prophet's struggle was important to have been included in this passage.[25]

Just as importantly as the imagery from First Isaiah, this discouraged prophet's words and demeanor clearly echo the harsh complaint to YHWH expressed by the (proposed woman prophet's) voice in Jer 4:10 and 12. In that text, the nature of divine punishment of the people was notably in the specific form of a *searing 'wind'* (*rûaḥ*) that YHWH was sending in the form of the Babylonian destroyers (Jer 4:11). This congruence raises the question of whether these two voices might be implied to be the same person, especially if this voice in Isaiah 40 has a social location in Jerusalem. Such envisioning of nature as bearing God's manifestation was heard in the women's prophetic voices in the Song of the Sea, the Song of Deborah, as well as in First Isaiah texts. However, this Isaiah 40 prophet conveys *an ironic reversal*—nature and her people receive the negative impact of YHWH as destroyer, not creator. Psychologically, emotionally, spiritually, she is not portrayed as accepting that this YHWH, who was said to destroy, now will, or can, have a positive overture toward the people.[26] Given this voice's poignant lyrical artistry, I would not agree with Fokkelman's severe judgment and dismissal of this speaker, according to which the speaker "remains impersonal"; Fokkelman further asserts that "any spark of individual vitality is gone."[27] To the contrary, it is not surprising

25. A number of commentators note the difficult task of the prophet or prophets in Isaiah 40–55 to convince the people about the new message and YHWH now comforting them; Goldingay and Payne note the rabbinic discussion in *Pesiqta' de Rab Kahana* that Jerusalem refused the comfort of ten prophets because "each had also been a discomforter" (*Isaiah 40–55*, 66). Heffelfinger, *I Am Large, I Contain Multitudes*, 101–105, fn 84, points to numerous texts in Deutero-Isaiah with "the tensions, emotions, and conflicts that are bound up in the notion of reconciliation between YHWH and Israel," (33) the "mind change [*nḥm*] in YHWH from wrath to comfort" (105), and the "disjunction" between claims of YHWH's comfort and divine angry speeches (111). On the critique of YHWH's excessive wrath by female voices in Jeremiah 10 and in Lamentations 2 and 3, see Lee, *The Singers of Lamentations*, 55–73; 114–17; 124–44; 159; 167–77; 186–94.

26. Goldingay and Payne, *Isaiah 40–55*, 49, note that overall Second Isaiah "seeks to rehabilitate YHWH in the eyes of the people."

27. Fokkelman, "Stylistic Analysis of Isaiah 40:1–11," 79–81. In Fokkelman's treatment, the two voices in vv. 6–8 are both male; he notes that the "complainer" is responded to by a voice (v. 8) who "knows that he [himself] belongs to the religious community and is connected with God," implying strongly that the previous voice is not (connected or belonging). Yet Fokkelman goes on about the voice of v. 8: "The poet is so magnanimous and honest as to allow the voice of defeatism ample opportunity for speaking, but it must not remain uncontradicted" (81).

for the prophetic role that the close of her lyric (above) was explicitly with *the people* ("the people is grass"), echoing the lyric in v. 1: "comfort, comfort, *my people*."[28] Further, the analysis here, rather than conclude that these two expressions for the people (v. 1 and vv. 6–7) are from the same woman prophet, interprets that this voice in v. 6 is responding to the one above, whose message was a call to comfort and to be comforted. The voice in vv. 6–7 is 'not comforted' (yet). Thus in Isaiah 40 there is the possibility of not just one woman prophet, *but two,* based on grammatical forms, soundplay artistry, and perspectives. This will continue to unfold in the chapter.

The discouraged woman prophet's lines in vv. 6–7, however, evoked a quick reply from a male prophetic voice (doublet pattern above in v. 8) who quotes her lyric but ignores her precise lament[29] and concern for the people's frailty or suffering (and implicit critique of YHWH), in favor of his affirming the everlasting "word of our God." His choice of the verb for God's word—it 'stands up firm'—purposefully contrasts the image of plants that fall over. This plurality of voices, even with differing perspectives, was regarded as important by those who preserved and included them in Isaiah 40; no doubt it was part of the immense grappling with their profoundly difficult experiences of survival, faith, and whether a different future could be heard and embraced.

Fortunately, another voice intervenes energetically[30] (below) to encourage the discouraged woman prophet to cry out further, addressing her with *five* feminine imperative verbs. This encouraging voice *also uses a triplet syllable sound pattern* in composing, as below (e.g., *ʿal, ʿălî, ʾal / har, hār, hār / gāvōah, vakkōaḥ, qôlēk / îmî, îmî, ʾimrî),* thus coming from a female prophet. I would argue it is reasonable to assume this is the

28. Westermann, *Isaiah 40–66,* 40–41, and numerous commentators regard the despondent voice as Deutero-Isaiah; while the overall texts do not support just one prophet, Westermann's comment nevertheless well expresses the pathos of the speaker, who "so charged with emotion, perfectly gathers up all the vanquished nation's lamentation and sheer despair . . . that no longer believes in the possibility of any new beginning." In my analysis, this voice is not simply hopeless but exhibits a traumatized yet faithful individual naturally struggling from the destructive experiences, and who also has a theological complaint about how YHWH has treated the people.

29. Baltzer, *Deutero-Isaiah*, 57–58, also calls v. 7 a "lament."

30. Muilenburg, *Isaiah 40–66*, 431, suggests that vv. 9–10, both in form and content, are "more impressive than the foregoing lines. The same imperatives are present, but they are more eager, more intense and impassioned, more imaginative and wide-ranging."

implied woman prophet who opened Isaiah 40 with, "Comfort, comfort, my people, says your God." She replies directly to the two previous speakers' use of the term *bāśār* (the living)—to the male prophet's utterance that all 'flesh' (*bāśār,* or all that lives) will see YHWH's return (v. 5), and to the discouraged woman prophet's depiction of the living (*bāśār*) as like dying vegetation. The encouraging woman prophet (from 40:1) deftly transforms the term into one that *rekindles the prophetic calling* of the discouraged woman (*měvaśśeret;* 'woman herald of joy' or 'good news').

| (exhorting female) | | (triplets) |
|---|---|---|
| UPON a MOUNTAIN **lofty**, | 'AL HAR - GĀVŌAH | 3 **'al, 'ălî, ʾal** |
| GO UP O WOMAN HERALD[1] | 'ĂLÎ-LĀK MĚVAŚŚERET ṣiyyôn | 3 **'ălî-lāk, qôlēk, ʾĕlōhêk**em |
| OF JOY to Zion; | HĀRÎMÎ VAKKŌAḤ | 3 **har, hār, hār** |
| RAISE, **with power**, | QÔLĒK | 3 **gāvōah, vakkōaḥ, qô**lēk |
| **your voice**, | | |
| O WOMAN HERALD | MĚVAŚŚERET **yě**rûšālāim | 2 **měvaśśeret, měvaśśeret** |
| OF JOY to **Je**rusalem— | HĀRÎMÎ | (+ ṣiyyôn) (cf **bāśār** , v. 5) |
| RAISE it, | | |
| HAVE NO **fear**; ANNOUNCE | 'AL-**tîrāʾî** 'IMRÎ | 3 **îmî, îmî, ʾimrî** |
| to (the) **cities** of **Ju**dah: | **lě'ārê** **yě**hûdâ | 3 ṣi**yyôn, yě**rûšālāim, **yě**hûdâ |
| SEE YOUR GOD![2] (9) | HINNĒH 'ĔLŌHÊKEM | |
| SEE the **Lord** YHWH | HINNĒH **ʾădōnāy** YHWH | 3 ṣiyy**ôn**, ʾăd**ōnāy**, ph**ānāyw** |
| with might is **coming**,[3] | bĕḥā**zāq** yāv**ô**ʾ | 3 **ôʾ, 'ô, ô** |
| and **his** arm | û**zěrō** '**ô** | 3 **hinnēh, hinnēh, hinnēh** |
| ruling **for him**. | mōšě**lâ lô** | 3 **ô, ô, ô** |
| | | 3 **ḥāzāq...ôʾ, ûzěrō', śěkārô** |
| SEE! | HINNĒH | 3 ʾăd**ōnāy, ûphě'ullā,** lě**phānāyw** |
| **His** reward | **śěkārô** | |
| (is) with **him**, | 'it**tô** | 3 **lâ lô, lātô** |
| and **his recompense before him**. (10) | **ûphě**'ull**ātô** **lěphānāyw** | |

[1] The term is also found in Ps 68:12.
[2] The word 'behold' does not quite capture the exclamatory aspect of the Hebrew term.
[3] The imperfect verb appears to suggest the unfolding, imminent coming of YHWH, as also the participle for his arm (ironically a feminine noun) 'exercising dominion.'

Th encouraging woman prophet's lyrics parallel the male voice's intent in v. 2 calling for a prophet to speak comfort *to* Jerusalem, only here she makes explicit that it is a woman prophet (the aforesaid) she exhorts to announce the comfort oracle: "Upon a mountain lofty, go up, O woman herald of Zion; raise, with power, your voice."[31] The tendency in recent

31. Following NJPS, but adding 'woman' before 'herald' to make explicit the Hebrew grammar of the feminine term *měvaśśeret.* The only difference in grammar in the admonition between this voice and the male voice calling for prophets to "speak to Jerusalem" in v. 2 is his use of a preposition, whereas here in v. 9 this intent is conveyed instead by the feminine singular participle of the verb, *bsr,* being in a construct relationship with Zion: 'herald of Zion,' that is, Zion's herald, not that Zion *is* the herald. It would be incorrect grammar to insert a preposition 'to' in the first part of v. 9 (before

years to regard *Zion* as the herald, or Jerusalem as the herald, is not supported by Isaiah 40 as a whole or required by the grammar. The exhorting woman prophet's use of the term *mĕbaśśeret* purposefully emphasizes that the time has finally come for joy and good news, not sorrowful resignation. Also in her utterance, she portrays YHWH as coming back to Zion, Jerusalem, and to the cities of Judah, whereas in the male prophet's lyrics in vv. 3–5, the focus was on YHWH coming through the desert. Importantly, the lyric in v.2 was also exhorting prophets to speak explicitly *to* Jerusalem. So also here, the parallel is obvious—the encouraging prophet exhorts a prophet (another female) to utter words *to* Zion, Jerusalem, and the cities, as a 'herald' to them. Whereas the male prophet above announced to Jerusalem the end of her punishment, the encouraging woman prophet here is *the first to announce*, and call for others to announce, that *YHWH is now returning to* Jerusalem and to Judah.[32]

In her own oracle above, the encouraging, exhorting female prophet makes triple use of 'see!' (*hinnē*),[33] and two tight sets of triple final *ô* sounds to emphasize God's coming. She still uses the language of an androcentric culture that renders God with male language to show divine power to rescue the people, even as a royal deity exercising dominion.[34] Her lyrics also participate in the tradition of the old theophanies of YHWH,[35] as in Miriam's and Deborah's lyrics. Other texts in Isaiah 40–55 will render God as female, as will be addressed below.

In what is implied to be a dramatic unfolding, the discouraged female prophet (below) responds to the encouraging woman prophet.

---

Zion) because the herald is being told to go up on a mountain, not yet to speak *to* Zion. Furthermore, this same exhorting speaker does supply the preposition 'to' just following where it is appropriate grammatically: "Announce *to* (*lĕ*) the cities of Judah . . . ." There is no reason why this last sentence is anything less than all-inclusive: the woman herald is called to speak to the cities of Judah, including Zion and Jerusalem. To interpret and translate *mĕvaśśeret ṣiyyôn* as "Zion, Herald" (NRSV, thus an appositional genitive) is an example of the persisting scholarly tendency simply to translate all female voices as personifications of cities or lands. In this case, it would (and has) *erased the woman prophet*. Why the continuing resistance by scholars to a female prophet *to* Zion/Jerusalem?

32. A prophetic depiction of YHWH's earlier departure from Jerusalem and the land is found in Ezekiel 10–11.

33. This 'triad' is noted in Muilenburg, *Isaiah 40–66*, 423, as is the importance of sound across vv. 9–11 for "striking effect."

34. On this imagery for God and similarity to neo-Babylonian ideology, see Blenkinsopp, *Isaiah 40–55*, 186.

35. Westermann, *Isaiah 40–66*, 45.

However, she does not refer to the deity by name, nor as the other woman prophet does she describe God's power in the strength (*beḥāzāq*) of his royal arm (*zĕrōʿ*), but shifts the lyrics (completing a different triplet soundplay) to the image of God like a gentle shepherd who *holds vulnerable lambs in 'his arm'* (*bizrōʿô*). In this, the discouraged woman prophet returns to images of the natural world, rather than the image of YHWH like a political king wielding power and violence. This may prompt the formerly encouraging prophet to shift focus as well just following in v. 12, to the cosmic realm and to God as Creator.

| | | |
|---|---|---|
| *(previous female replies)*<br>*LIKE* a *SHEPHERD*,<br>**his flock** **he** *PASTURES*:<br>**In his arm** **he** gathers **lambs**<br>**in his bosom** **he** carries (them);<br>mother **sheep**<br>he **guides**.[1]<br>(11) | **kĕ***RŌ ʿEH*<br>ʿedr**ô** **yi***R ʿEH*<br>*BIZRŌ ʿÔ* **yĕqa**bbēṣ **ṭĕlā**ʾîm<br>**ûvĕḥêqô** **yi**śśāʾ **ʿālô**t<br>**yĕ**na**hēl** | *(triplets)*<br>3 **rō, rô, rōʿô**<br>3 **bizrōʿô** (+ **bĕḥāz**āq...**ô**',<br>**ûzĕrōʿô** above)<br>3 **rô, rōʿô, qô** 3 **bi, bē, ûvĕ**<br>3 **yirʿe, yĕqabbēṣ, yiśśāʾ**<br>3 **ṭĕlāʾ, ʿālôt , ahēl** |
| *(encouraging female)*<br>*WHO* **measured with** a *HANDFUL*<br>(the) **waters**,[2]<br>**And skies** **with** a handbreadth[3]<br>*GAUGED*,<br>**And** *METED* **with** a *THIRD* **dust**[4]<br>of **the earth**,<br>**And** *WEIGHED* **with** a *SCALE* (the)<br>**mountains**<br>And (the) **hills** **with** a bal**ance**?! (12) | *MÎ-MĀ*dad *BĔŠĀ ʿŎLÔ*<br>*MAYIM*<br>**wĕšā***MAYIM* *BAZZER*et<br>tik**kē**n<br>**wĕ***KOL* *BAŠŠĀLIŠ* **ʿăphar**<br>**hāʾāreṣ**<br>**wĕšā***QAL* *BA*ppe*LES* **hārîm**<br>ûgĕvāʿôt *BĔ*m*Ō ʾZĔ*n*ĀYIM* | *(triplets)*<br>3 **mî-mā, mayim, šā**mayim<br>6 **bĕšāʿōlô, bazzeret,**<br>**baššāliš, bapp**e**les,**<br>**bĕ**mōʾ**zĕ** (+**bizrōʿô** above)<br>3 tik**kēn, kāl, qal**<br>3 **wĕšā, wĕkāl, wĕšāqal**<br>3 ʿ**ăphar, hāʾāreṣ, hārîm**<br>3 **mayim, mayim,** nāyim |

[1] Translating 'drives' seems a bit strong for the imagery here.
[2] 'Handful' to simplify the usual unwieldy translation ('hollow' or 'cup' of hand implied). Q[a] has *my ym* ('waters of the sea'), same consonants but different vowels from *mayim* ('waters'); that larger expanse seems more appropriate for the description here alongside the skies and the earth.
[3] Foll. Blenkinsopp, *Isaiah 40-55*, 187, 189, though he has plural.
[4] LXX deletes 'dust,'' but this deletes the first term of a triplet sound pattern: *ʿăphar, hāʾāreṣ, hārîm.*

Thus, the previously discouraged woman prophet, who said "what shall I cry" finds words of comfort to express, but *stays with her compassionate focus* on the needs of the vulnerable *people* and their plight, and thereby finds an oracle of God like a gentle shepherd.[36] It is interesting that neither female voice refers literally to the "hand" of YHWH in describing the divine power or protection. Perhaps this is because of the negative use of this word by the male voice earlier: Jerusalem "has received *from the hand* of YHWH double for all her sins." This is further ironic in that the 'hand' and 'arm' of YHWH are rendered in numerous biblical texts to describe

36. Muilenburg, *Isaiah 40–66*, 434, suggests, "thus the closing lines [of the first section, including v. 11] strike the note of comfort at the beginning." Blenkinsopp, *Isaiah 40–55*, 187, reminds that the king as shepherd implied justice and care.

God's positive power in rescuing the people earlier from Egyptian slavery. However, the formerly discouraged woman prophet does use a term from the exodus, in lyrics suggested to be Miriam's in Exod 15:13: the image of 'guiding' sheep—*yĕnahēl*; Miriam sang of YHWH with a triplet soundplay: "you led" (*nāḥîta*) the people whom you redeemed (*gāʾāltā);* you guided (*nēhaltā*) them."

The encouraging woman prophet answers her prophetic sister's shepherd-imagery lyrics above (note the overlapping syllable sound repetitions between them), however, by shifting the focus away from God as protector and comforter back to her own previous emphasis on God's power, but now elevated *to the cosmic* level—to God as Creator.[37] This is the *first occasion* in Isaiah 40–55 where the comfort or salvation message *turns* to the cosmic, *in the voice of the woman prophet who initially expressed comfort (40:1), then encouragement*. It is a striking contrast to the other woman prophet's image of the fading grass and flower—as if to console her and all listeners that YHWH is not merely the rescuer of a particular people in a particular place, but is to be recognized as the power behind and through all creation. Once again, these women prophets' voices in Isaiah 40 both emphasize nature in relation to YHWH.

The encouraging woman prophet now emphasizing God's creation next initiates the use of rhetorical questions[38] in order to suggest divine incomparability (also seen in Hannah's song and in Miriam's lyrics: 'who is like YHWH?'; *mî kāmōkâ*). Yet staying in dialog with the other woman prophet, she uses the soundplay above and imagery of the 'arm' to complete a triplet, asking, "who measured the skies with *a handbreadth*?" (*bazzeret*).[39] This perspective is reminiscent of the flow of 'discussion' in the book of Job, from preoccupation with human suffering to God as Creator of the vast cosmos, in order to assure and comfort the people. The importance of this theology cannot be overemphasized, nor should the woman prophet here be underappreciated, and surely these lyrics also bear a link to Genesis 1, regarded as also emerging from the trauma of

37. This interpretation would disagree with those commentators who see the same voice represented in vv. 11 and 12, e.g., Heffelfinger, *I Am Large, I Contain Multitudes*, 102fn74.

38. Westermann, *Isaiah 40–66*, 48–49, suggests that vv. 12–31 fall into the literary category of a "disputation" in order to address and answer the unspoken question and lament: Can our God still really help us? The prophetic answers take the form of "descriptive praise" of God, and Deutero-Isaiah "sets out to revive praise."

39. Or a subdivision of a cubit, the length of the forearm, clarified by Blenkinsopp, *Isaiah 40–55*, 189.

the exilic context. Muilenburg notes that Israel was not preoccupied with cosmogony before Isaiah 40–55, thus the importance of the prophet who was likely also influenced by Babylonian traditions.[40] If a women's lyrical tradition with a signature of triplet soundplays used by women prophets is correct, then women prophets contributed, with creative lyrical sophistication, to this creation theology in dealing with the crisis of exile.

The encouraging woman prophet above, lyricizing about God's role in creating, is next 'answered' by a male prophet below (using *doublet* soundplays), who offers two questions; he carries forward the line of reasoning, but instead reverses the question 'who' to refer *to the human*, and employs a different kind of language, as from a "didactic-sapiential" tradition.[41] His lines are followed by the same female prophet (triplet sound pattern), who resumes her use of terms for measuring, but next focuses on how small the nations are in the eyes of the Creator; they are like dust. Her triple emphasis with the terms "no/no/nothing" *(ʾên, ʾên, ʾayin)* is reminiscent of the triple use of the term *ʾên* in the Song of Hannah ('no one like YHWH').

40. Muilenburg, *Isaiah 40–66*, 443.

41. Blenkinsopp, *Isaiah 40–55*, 191, who also notes that the Babylonian deity, Marduk, when creating the world needed the advice of the wise god Ea.

| *(male)* | | *(doublets)* |
|---|---|---|
| *WHO GAUGED* the **Spirit** of *YHWH*, | *MÎ-TIKKĒN* ʾet-rûaḥ *YHWH* | 2 mî, mî 10 o |
| or (what) man *INFORMED (YHWH)* | wĕʾîš ʿăṣātô yôdîʿennû | 2 tikkēn (+ tikkēn above) |
| of his **plan**?[1] (13) | ʾet-*MÎ* nôʿāṣ | 1 YHWH + 6 ms suffixes) |
| *WHOM* did (YHWH) con**sult**,[2] | wayvînēhû | 2 ʾet, ʾet 2 mišpāṭ, daʿat |
| (who) gave (YHWH) discernment, | | 2 ʿăṣātô, nôʿāṣ 2 rûaḥ, raḥ |
| *TAUGHT HIM* the **way** of just**ice**, | *WAYLAMMĔDĒHÛ* bĕʾōraḥ mišpāṭ | 2 yôdîʿennû, yôdîʿennû |
| *TAUGHT HIM* **knowledge**, | *WAYLAMMĔDĒHÛ* daʿat | 3 wayvînēhû +waylammĕdēhû waylammĕdēhû |
| and (the) **path** of wis**dom**— | | |
| *INFORMED HIM*? (14) | wĕderek tĕvûnôt yôdîʿennû | 6 dî, dē, dē, da, de, dî |
| *(female)* | | *(triplets)* |
| *SEE*, (the) *NATIONS*, | *HĒN GÔYIM* | 3 hēn, zĕn, hēn |
| *LIKE* a drop from a bu**cket,** | kĕmar middĕlî | 3 hēn gôyim, hēn ʾiyyîm, haggôyim |
| and *LIKE* **dust** | ûkĕšaḥaq | |
| on a *BALANCE* | *MŌʾZĔNAYIM* | 3 kĕšaḥaq, kaddaq, kol-hag |
| are *RECKONED*. | neḥšāvû | 3 neḥšāv, mēʾephes, neḥšĕv |
| *SEE*, (the) coastlands | *HĒN ʾIYYÎM* | |
| *LIKE* **fine dust**[3] he **lifts.** (15) | kaddaq yiṭṭôl | 6 kĕ, kĕ, ka, kol, kĕ, kĕ |
| And Lebanon –*NOT ENOUGH* fuel, | ûlĕvānôn *ʾÊN DÊ* bāʿēr | 4 yim, yim, yîm, yim |
| And its beasts–*NOT ENOUGH* sacrifice. | wĕḥayyātô *ʾÊN DÊ* ʿôlâ | 3 da, dê, dê |
| **All the** *NATIONS* | kol-hag*GÔYIM* | 3 ʾên dê, ʾên dê + ʾayin |
| (are) *LIKE* **nothing** | kĕ*ʾAYIN* | 3 ôl, ûlĕ, ʿôlâ |
| (in the) **sight** of **him**, | negdô | 3 neḥšāvû, negdô, neḥšĕvû |
| *LIKE* **non-existence**[4] | kĕʾephes wātōhû | 3 dô, tōhû, lô |
| and emp**tiness.**[5] | | |
| They are *RECKONED* to **him**. (16-17) | neḥšĕvû - lô | |

[1] Translating 'inform' to render the portrayal of human superior attitude or action toward God. LXX adds 'who' is the man, creating a triple repetition of the term where it is unlikely within this doublets passage.
[2] I have substituted YHWH occasionally here for the implied subject or object 'him' (3ms pronominal suffix) referring to YHWH to make clear the contrast with the man's ironic instruction of the deity.
[3] NRSV.
[4] Following 1QIsa[a] that has a kāf instead of a mêm prefix to *ʾps*.
[5] The term *tōhû* is the same as in the phrase in Gen 1:2, "emptiness and void."

The male prophet follows (doublets) with questions about comparing God to a humanly created idol.

| *(male)* | | *(doublets)* |
|---|---|---|
| So *TO* **whom**<br>can you *LIKEN*<br>*GOD*? And **what** *FORM*<br>**compare** *TO HIM*? (18)<br><br>The *IDOL*?<br>A *CRAFTSMAN*[1] shaped it,<br>And a *SMITH* with gold<br>**overlaid** it,<br>**links** of **silver**<br>*SMITHING*. (19)<br><br>*THE MULBERRY* as a gift—<br>a wood that does *NOT* **rot**—<br>he **chooses**.<br>A *CRAFTSMAN*<br>*SKILLED* he **seeks** *FOR IT*<br>*TO MAKE*<br>*A FIRM IDOL* that will *NOT* **topple**.(20) | wě *'EL*-**mî**<br>**tědamměyû**n<br>*'ĒL* **ûma - děmû**t<br>**ta'ar**kû **lô**<br>**ha***PPESEL*<br>nā**sak** *ḤĀRĀŠ*<br>wě*ṢŌRĒPH* **ba**zzāhāv<br>**yěraqqě**'ennû<br>**ûrětuqôt** ke*SEPH*<br>*ṢÔRĒPH*<br>**hamsukkān tě**rûmâ<br>**'ēṣ** lō'-**yirqav**<br>**yivḥār**<br>*ḤĀRĀŠ*<br>**ḥākām yěbaqqeš-lô**<br>**lěhākîn** *PESEL* lō' **yimmôṭ** | 2 'el , 'ēl<br>2 mî, ma<br>2 tědamměyû,<br>ûma-děmût<br>2 tě, ta 2 ha, ḥā<br>2 pesel, pesel<br>2 ḥārāš, ḥārāš<br>2 ṣōrēph, ṣōrēph<br>4 nāsak, hamsukkān,<br>ḥākām, hākîn<br>2 yěraqqě, ûrětuqôt<br>2 yirqav, yivḥār<br><br>2 'ēṣ lō', eš-lô<br>4 lō', lô, lě, lō'<br>2 lō' yimmôṭ (inclusio w/<br>děmût..lô in 18b above) |

[1] Blenkinsopp, *Isaiah 40-55*, 187-88.

The male prophet's lines above are followed by four questions he asks next to a group audience ("you"), challenging them to perceive the 'foundations of the earth.' The earlier, discouraged woman prophet's voice, who spoke of God as shepherd, responds to him. She picks up and carries forward virtually the only two syllables or terms he did *not* double (*hug* and *hā'āreṣ*) and makes *triplet soundplays* out of them. Muilenburg observed the poet's "lyrical triad" "of participial double lines, he that sitteth, . . . spreadeth, . . . bringeth (vv. 22–23), followed by three verbs—each of which is introduced by scarcely (v. 24c)."[42] The formerly discouraged woman prophet also renders God over creation, and (interestingly) portrays God like a woman who stretches out fabric or sets up a tent. She still returns to the frailty of humans, using metaphors of creatures and plant imagery as before, but this time moves her attention to political rulers ('rooted') who can be brought down by the mere breath of God.[43] Movement in this voice is apparent, away from the plight of the people who were victims of rulers and toward their rescue by God's power from that devastating rule.[44] Therefore, she appears to have been released from pre-

42. Muilenburg, *Isaiah 40–66*, 440.

43. Westermann's general comment is appropos: "the exalting of the humble in vv. 29–31 contrasts with the humbling of the exalted in vv 15ff. and 23f" (*Isaiah 40–66*, 61).

44. Brueggemann, *Isaiah 40–66*, 25, notes that such a reversal, in which "princes

occupation about YHWH's past negative actions toward the people, though it is interesting to note that in her speech below she still does not use the name, YHWH, in doing good; instead her participles describe—but refrain from naming—for example, "the One who dwells above the earth."

| | | |
|---|---|---|
| *(male)*<br>*HAVE YOU NOT* known?<br>*HAVE YOU NOT* heard?<br>*HAS* (it) *NOT* been told<br>**from** the **first** to **you**?<br>*HAVE* **you** *NOT* **dis**cerned<br>(the) **foundations**[1] of<br>*THE EARTH*? (21) | *HĂLÔ'* **tēdĕ'û**<br>*HĂLÔ'* **tiš**mā'**û**<br>*HĂLÔ' HUGG***ad**<br>mērō'**š** lākem<br>*HĂLÔ'* **hăvînōtem**<br>**môsdôt** *HĀ'ĀREṢ* | *(doublets)*<br>4 **hălô', hălô', hălô', hălô'**<br>2 **tēdĕ'û, tišmā'û**<br>2 **mērō'š, môsdôt**<br>2 **hă, hā** 2 **ēd, ad** 2 **ōt, ôt**<br>2 **em, em** |
| *(formerly discouraged female)*<br>**The One who** *DWELLS*[2]<br>above the vault of *THE EARTH*—<br>while its *DWELLERS* seem<br>*LIKE* grasshop**pers**—<br>**Who** spread out<br>*LIKE* a curtain[3] the sk**ies**,<br>**stretched them** out<br>*LIKE* a tent<br>for *DWELLING*, (22)<br>**The One who** *BRINGS* potentates<br>to nau**ght**,<br>**rulers** of *EARTH*<br>*LIKE* **nothing** he **makes**– (23) | hay*YŌŠĒV*<br>'**al**-*ḤÛG HĀ'ĀREṢ*<br>wĕ*YŌŠĔVÊ***hā** **ka***ḤĂG***āvîm**<br><br>*HANNÔṬEH* **ka**dd**ōq šā***MAYIM*<br>**wayy***IMTĀḤĒM*<br>**kā'ō**hel<br>lā*ŠĀVET*<br>*HANNÔTĒN* rôzĕ*NÎM* lĕ*'ĀYIN*<br>šōph**ĕṭê** *'EREṢ*<br>**kattō**h*û* **'āśâ** | *(triplets)*<br>3 **yōšēv, yōšĕvê**hā, **šāvet**<br>3 **ḥûg, ḥăg + hug** (above)<br>2 **hā**'āreṣ (completes doublet in v. 21d above)<br>3 **hannôṭeh** (+ **hăvînōte**m above, **hannôtē**n below)<br>3 **'al-ḥûg, kaḥăg, ka**dd**ōq**<br>6 **ka** (5) + **qaš** (below)<br>6 **îm,** ma**yim, yimtāḥēm,** rôzĕ**nîm**, 'āyin<br>3 hā'**āreṣ, 'ereṣ,** bā'**āreṣ**<br>3 **ôṭe, ĕṭê, attō**<br>3 **'āśâ, ûsĕ'ārâ,** ti**śśā**'ēm<br>3 **'aph bal, 'aph bal, 'aph bal**<br>3 **hannôtē**n, kattō**hû, niṭṭā'û**<br>3 **zōrā'**û, **šōrēš, 'āreṣ**<br>3 **bā, bā, vā**<br>3 **'û, 'û, û**<br>2 **giz'ām,** wĕ**gam** 2 **em, 'ēm**<br>3 **nāš, vāš,** qaš |
| *SCARCELY PLANTED*,<br>*SCARCELY* **sown**,<br>*SCARCELY* taken **root in** *EARTH*<br>(is) *THEIR STEM*,<br>When *ALSO* he blows<br>**against them**<br>and they **dry** up, and a **tempest**,[4]<br>*LIKE* **straw, bears them** off.(24) | *'APH BAL* - *NIṬṬ***ā'û**<br>*'APH BAL* - **zōrā'***û*<br>*'APH BAL* - **šōrēš** **bā***'ĀREṢ*<br>*GIZ'ĀM*<br>wĕ*GAM*-n**āš**aph **bāhem**<br>wayyi**vāš***û* **ûsĕ'ārâ**<br>**kaqqaš** ti**śśā'ēm** | |

[1] Simply translating the idea that anyone who observes the earth's structure and forces will understand that a deity has created them.
[2] Translating the triple use of the root *yšb* with the same term. The masculine participle for God who dwells above the earth need not be translated with royal imagery, though the double entendre of a seated royal figure may have been heard in the lyric.
[3] NRSV. Also in Ps 104:2. Walter Brueggemann, *Isaiah 40-66*, 23, notes the potential feminine imagery of God measuring the heavens "as a seamstress might measure cloth." Women also stretched/set out tents.
[4] Translating to capture the wind of a storm.

The male prophet next returns with another question about God's incomparability. Yet he too begins to move his lyrics toward the compassion of the previous woman prophet by drawing attention to how God as Creator[45] is aware of all the host in heaven and on earth, calling them

and rulers are negated" is reminiscent of the lyrics attributed to Hannah (1 Sam 2:7–8).

45. Muilenburg, *Isaiah 40–66*, 443, notes that Second Isaiah uses the root *br'*

each by name. The male prophet sets the stage for his compassionate lyrics to follow, which render Jacob lamenting that he is ignored by God.

| *(male)* | | *(doublets)* |
|---|---|---|
| **So, to** whom can you liken me, | **wĕʾel-mî tĕdammĕyûnî** | 2 **wĕʾel-mî tĕdammĕyûnî** + |
| **that I** can be compared? | **wĕʾešweh** | **wĕ ʾel-mî tĕdammĕyûn** (v. 19) |
| –says the **Holy One**. (25) | yōʾmar **qādôš** | 2 **wĕʾel, wĕʾeš** |
| **Lift** HIGH **your eyes** | **śĕʾû** - MĀRôm **ʿênêkem** | 2 **qādôš** (+**kaqqaš** above) |
| and **see**: WHO CREATED **these**? | **ûrĕʾû** MÎ-VĀRāʾ **ʾēlleh** | 2 **śĕʾû, rĕʾû** |
| The One who SENDS OUT | **ham**MÔṢÎʾ VĔMISPĀR | 2 **ʿênêkem,** ʾ**ônîm** 2 **le, lĕ** |
| **their** host | **ṣĕvāʾām** | 2 **mārôm, mî-vārāʾ,** |
| **to** number **them** | **lĕ**kull**ām** | **vĕmispār, mērōv** |
| Who **calls** them **by name** | **bĕšēm** yiq**rāʾ** | 2 **môṣ, mis** 2 **ʾām, ām** |
| BY GREAT might | MĒRŌV ʾônîm | 2 **vĕmis, bĕšēm** |
| and VAST **power**, | wĕ ʾ**am**MÎṢ **kōaḥ** | 2 **qrāʾ, kōaḥ** 6 **'o' sounds** |
| Not **one** | **ʾîš lōʾ** | 4 **mî, mis, mîṣ, ʾîš** |
| fails to APPEAR. (26) | neʿ**dār** | 4 **mār, vār, pār, dār** |

The male prophet's lament from 'Jacob' below, that he is neglected by God, foreshadows the lament of Zion to come in 49:8–23.[46] The prophet encourages the listener to know that God does "not faint or grow weary" *(lōʾ yîʿaph wĕlōʾ yîgāʿ)*, using a striking doublet soundplay.

| *(male)* | | *(doublets)* |
|---|---|---|
| **Why** do you **say**, O **Jacob**, | **lāmmâ** tōʾ**mar** **ya**ʿăqōv | 2 **lāmm** + **hamm** above |
| and **declare**, O **Israel**, | **ûtĕdabbēr** **yi**śrā ʾĒL | 2 **mâ, ma** 2 **ya, yi** |
| "**Hidden** is **my way from** YHWH, | **nistĕrâ** **darkî** MĒYHWH | 2 **tĕ**dabb**ēr, tĕrâ** |
| and **from** my God, | ûMĒ ʾĔLŌHAY | 2 **dabbēr, dar** 2 **î, î** |
| **My cause** ignored"? (27) | **mišpāṭî** **yaʿăvôr** | 2 **mē**YHWH, **mē**ʾĕlōhay |
| | | 2 YHWH, YHWH |
| Do you NOT **know**? | hă**LÔ**ʾ **yādaʿtā** | 2 **nis, miš** 2 **abbēr, aʿăvôr** |
| Have you NOT **heard**? | ʾim-**LŌ**ʾ **šāmaʿtā** | 2 hă**lô**ʾ, ʾim-lōʾ |
| | | 2 yāda**ʿtā, šāma**ʿ**tā** (+ hă**lô**ʾ |
| | | **tēdĕ**ʿû, hă**lô**ʾ ti**šmā**ʿû above) |
| The GOD of **old** (is) YHWH, | ʾĔLŌHÊ ʿ**ôlām** YHWH | 2 ʾ**ĕlō**hê ʿ**ôlā**m 2 **šām, lām** |
| **Creator** of the **ends** of the EARTH. | bôrēʾ **qĕ**ṣôt **hā**ʾāreṣ | 2 ʾĕlō**hê, bôrē**ʾ |
| He does NOT FAINT | LŌʾ YÎʿAPH | 2 **lō**ʾ **y**îʿaph, **l**ōʾ **y**îg**ā**ʿ |
| and does NOT GROW WEARY; | wĕLŌʾ YÎGĀʿ | 2 **qĕ**ṣôt **hā**ʾāreṣ, **ḥ**ē**q**er |
| there is NO **fathoming** | **ʾên** **ḥē**qer | 2 **l**itvû**nā**tô +miš**pā**ṭî (above, |
| **his under**standing. (28) | litvû**nā**tô | inclusio) |

Here, God's understanding is not for the sake of proving superior wisdom to other deities or humans (as above) but is for the sake of showing divine tender compassion for the people's suffering. The male prophet's

('create') more than any other biblical text.

46. I interpret v. 27 as a prophetic/divine expression of compassion. A question may be, but does not have to be, exasperated.

soundplay *(lōʾ yîʿaph wĕlōʾ yîgāʿ)*, describing how God does not faint or grow weary, evokes a reply, it appears, from the formerly discouraged woman prophet (below), who has been most concerned about the people's suffering. Her lyrics beautifully turn his phrase around, focusing not on God's indefatiguability, but on God's attending to the people's faintness and lack of strength. Her lyrics are most poignant in light of her initial reluctance to speak or to have hope in God's new actions for the people, and, moreover, could be interpreted as implying her own reinvigoration. She draws out and takes further the male prophet's specific term, *yîʿaph* (faint), in his doublet soundplay and composes two key triplet soundplays (*layyāʿēph, yiʿăphû, yaḥălîphû* and *yikkāšēlû, yaḥălîphû, yaʿălû*). Each triplet set is centered on her added term *yaḥălîphû* that conveys the 'restoration' or 'renewal' of human strength to the youths, young men—in essence, to the people, which she renders by a beautiful image from nature, once again. They are like the eagle lifting up to fly. All this has come because, as she says, these have trusted in YHWH, *whom she finally names in a positive way*. The male prophet answers with a gentle extension of her image of people restored.

| *(formerly discouraged female)* | | *(triplets)* (above) |
|---|---|---|
| He *GIVES* **to** the ***FAINT STRENGTH***,[1]<br>and **to** those with *NO* vigor—**might**<br>he **increases**. (29)<br>**Youths**<br>may '***FAINT***<br>and ***GROW WEARY***,'<br>even **young men**<br>***STUMBLE***,<br>***STUMBLE*** down; (30)<br>but the ones *TRUSTING*<br>***YHWH***<br>shall be *RENEWED* (in) ***STRENGTH***<br>and be *LIFTED* (with) new plumes<br>***LIKE EAGLES***.<br><br>*(male)*<br><br>They shall *RUN*<br>***AND NOT GROW WEARY***,<br>They shall *WALK*<br>***AND NOT FAINT***. (31) | **nōtēn** **lay*YĀʿĒPH*** ***KŌAḤ***<br>**ûlĕʾên** **ʾônîm** **ʿoṣmâh**<br>y*ARBEH*<br>**wĕ*YIʿĂPHÛ*** *NĔʿ****ĀRÎM***<br>**wĕ*YIGĀʿÛ***<br>ûvaḥ**ûrîm**<br>***KĀŠÔL***<br>**yik*KĀŠĒLÛ***<br>wĕ**qôyē**<br>***YHWH***<br>*YAḤĂLÎPHÛ* ***KŌAḤ***<br>*YAʿĂLÛ* **ʾē**ver *KANNĔŠ***ārîm**<br><br><br>**yā**rûṣ***û***<br>***WĔLŌʾ YÎGĀʿÛ***<br>***YĒLĔKÛ***<br>***WĔLŌʾ YÎʿĀPHÛ*** | **3 nōtēn, ûlĕʾên** (+**ʾên li...ûnātô**)<br>**3 yāʿēph (+yîʿaph** in v. 28 above, **yiʿăphû** in 30 below)<br>**3 yāʿēph, yiʿăphû, yaḥălîphû**<br>**3 kōaḥ** (**+kōaḥ,** v. 26 + **kōaḥ** below) **3 kōaḥ, qôyē, kōaḥ**<br>**1 ʿoṣmâh** (+ **šāmaʿtā,** yādaʿtā)<br>**1 yarbeh (+ bôrēʾ** above)<br>**1** YHWH (+ **2** above) = **3**<br>**3** YH, **ya, ya 3 rîm, rîm, rîm**<br>**3** yikkāš**ēlû, yaḥălî**phû, **yaʿălû**<br>**3 kāšôl, kāšēlû, kannĕš**ārîm<br>**2** ʾēver, yāʿ**ēph** (inclusio)<br>**2 nĕʿārîm, nĕšārîm** (inclusio)<br>*(doublets)*<br>**2 yārûṣû, yēlĕkû**<br>**2** wĕlōʾ, wĕlōʾ **4** final **û**<br>**1 yēlĕkû** (+ **yaʿălû** above) =**2**<br>**2 yîʿaph û, yîgāʿ û** (above, inclusio) |

[1] NRSV.

Over the course of Isaiah 40's lyrics, it is apparent that there are multiple prophetic speakers/lyricists. Their initial utterances somewhat independent of one another move into a dialogical dynamic in which the voices encourage and influence one another, as is apparent in a close reading and hearing of the Hebrew. The prophets themselves, male and female, offer compelling, inspired lyrics and thus become models of faith, each one different, yet coming to terms with trusting the hope of the messages of comfort and salvation from God to the people in exile, and to the people in Jerusalem and Judah. However, it may be said that the most reluctant prophet in Isaiah 40, here analyzed to be a woman, expresses the profound and realistic struggle and experience of so many exiled Judeans and those left behind in Jerusalem, of not only trusting the message of comfort and rescue, but of trusting the One who is speaking a new message to them.

This analysis has identified two female prophetic voices embedded in Isaiah 40, and one or more male prophetic voices. Distinguishing male and two female voices was based on the syllable sound patterns, gendered grammar, and one woman exhorting another woman. It is less clear whether there is more than one male voice based on content, as there is only one apparent response of a male voice to another, to a female (in v. 8). Perhaps the male voice in vv. 3–5 is a different prophet from the one in v. 2 and in the remainder of the chapter. The two women's voices are initially distinguished from one another as well by their different focus or content. The first is more focused on the people's suffering and weakness, and expresses resignation about their state and YHWH's involvement in contributing to it; the second female voice, which encourages her, focuses more on the imminent arrival of God, who is compassionate Creator, who will intervene for their help. The first female voice eventually joins in this prophetic announcement yet retains her focus on the people's suffering and weakness, yet appears to be renewed and strengthened with them by implicit new trust in God. Her lyrics develop exponentially across Isaiah 40, culminating in her beautiful identification with the eagle restored to flight, to which a male prophet responds affirmingly with added imagery of the newly empowered youth, men, and all of the people who trust in YHWH. A summary of the prophetic voices is in the table below:

| **Females** (*triplet sound pattern*) | **Male** (*doublet pattern*) |
|---|---|
| 40:1 (F1) | |
| | :2, 3–5 |
| :6–7 (F2) | |
| | :8 |
| :9–10 (F1) | |
| :11 (F2) | |
| :12 (F1) | |
| | :13–14 |
| :15–17 (F1) | |
| | :18–21 |
| :22–24 (F2) | |
| | :25–28 |
| :29–31a (F2) | |
| | :31b |
| appr. 15.5 verses | appr. 15.5 verses |

## Isaiah 42:13–16

The analysis of Isaiah 40 in terms of lyrical sound-repetition patterns, as proposed for an indigenous Hebraic women's and men's preferred composing practice in their traditions, points to the need for reconsiderations of all the texts across Isaiah 40–66. While such an exploration awaits further work, for now it is important to mention that an analysis of Isa 42:13–16 bears out the argument.[47]

The verse (42:13) *preceding* the well-known depiction in Isa 42:14–15 of God giving birth like a female is a lyrical third-person description of YHWH as a holy warrior. The prophetic lyricist of this (suggested to be male), below, utilizes a clear *doublet* sound-repetition pattern, and the verbs in a multiple of two, for example: *gibbôr, gabbār; ka, kĕ; yēṣēʾ, yāʿîr, yārîaʿ, yaṣrîaḥ*. While the first part of Isaiah 42 emphasizes the

47. See Darr, "Like Warrior, Like Woman," 560–71, and her brief but important allusion to the 'he or she' who composed it, cited in Stone, "Second Isaiah," 88–89, who posits the likelihood of a woman's voice responsible for these lyrics.

quiet, nonviolent Servant and the joy of rescue and "new things" (v. 9), v. 13 (and the judgments and violence of vv. 18–25) seem to be in some tension with these and with the voice that follows in vv. 14–16, who renders the simile of God as a mother birthing something new.[48]

Katheryn Pfisterer Darr interprets that both similes "share profound intensity and a markedly auditory quality," as both include the shriek or cry of the figure described, and both serve "to underscore Yahweh's power." Darr also links the image of the deity's breath withering plants (in v. 16, below) back to this similar motif in Isa 40:7.[49] That image was rendered, according to this analysis, by a woman prophet *discouraged* by YHWH's allowed destruction of her people. Here, the image that a possible woman prophet renders, of the deity's breath like a mother giving birth (but *not rûaḥ*! and YHWH is not mentioned), transforms the earlier image, redirects it primarily for the creation of a new thing, not destruction. The woman prophet's triplet soundplays—*heḥěš, ʾaḥărîš, ʾeššōm; ěš, ʾeš, ʾeš; ʾaḥărîš, ʾaḥărîv, hārîm; ʾetʾappāq, ʾephʿe, ʾešʾaph*—contain more overlap than usual due to the onomatopoeia in the text. The strong breaths of God cause dessication of the earth ironically while giving birth, even while 'she' (God) as mother 'narrates' this in first person, using key terms from the creation in Genesis (*darkness, light, dry land, herbage*). Here God, like the woman prophet—and like the people in agony in Jeremiah—now also goes through severe pain to bring about a new future. Indeed this language by a woman prophet here *reverses* the birthing pain of a woman prophet suffering as in childbirth (in Jer 4:19) in Jeremiah's context, and reverses that male prophet's depiction of Jerusalem in pain like birthing, or even as raped (Jer 4:31), and makes God the subject who now feels the anguish. Or, from a faith perspective, God *has her make* the divine self the subject in her prophetic lyric.

Though the power of YHWH's breath still has an impact that can be withering (v. 15), and this Creator may with force level the ground for the exiles' return, in this case, the prophet 'shifts down' or reins in YHWH's power, *just as a woman in that culture*, though life-giving, had to rein in her personal power and limit its expression. Instead YHWH is 'moved' to focus on those vulnerable in the community (with impaired vision), whom the deity now gently helps walk, promising at the end not to abandon them or the implied covenant. A definition of a prophet is not only

48. Darr, "Like Warrior, Like Woman, 564, notes that the travailing woman simile for God is unprecedented anywhere else in the Bible.

49. Ibid., 569.

one who spoke for God, but one who *spoke to God convincingly in behalf of what the people needed.*

| *(male)* | YHWH | *(doublets)* |
|---|---|---|
| YHWH[1]<br>like a warrior<br>goes forth; like a fighter[2]<br>He whips up his rage.<br>He yells,<br>He roars aloud,<br>Upon his enemies he charges. (13) | kaggibbôr<br>yēṣēʾ kĕʾîš milḥāmôt<br>yāʿîr qinʾâ<br>yārîaʿ<br>aph-yaṣrîaḥ<br>ʿal-ʾōyĕvāyw yitgabbār | 2 gibbôr, gabbār<br>2 ka, kĕ<br>4 yēṣēʾ, yāʿîr, yārîaʿ, yaṣrîaḥ<br>2 aph, ʿal |
| *(female)*<br>"I have kept silent forever!<br>I have been keeping quiet;<br>I have restrained myself;<br>now like a birthing mother, I groan,<br>I pant,<br>and I gasp<br>all at once. (14) | heḥĕšêtî mēʿôlām<br>ʾaḥărîš<br>ʾetʾappāq<br>kayyôlēdâ ʾephʿe<br>ʾeššōm<br>wĕʾešʾaph<br>yāḥad | *(triplets)*<br>6 heḥĕš, ʾaḥărîš, ʾeššōm, ʾešʾaph + ʿeśbām, wĕśamtî<br>3 ĕš, ʾeš, ʾeš<br>3 ʾaḥărîš, ʾaḥărîv, hārîm<br>3 ʾetʾappāq, ʾephʿe, ʾešʾaph<br>2 yôlēdâ, yāḥad |
| "I am desiccating<br>hills and heights,<br>and all their herbage I dry up.<br><br>And I am replacing<br>rivers with islands,<br>and the marshes I make dry (land).(15) | ʾaḥărîv<br>hārîm ûgĕvāʿôt<br>wĕkol-ʿeśbām ʾôvîš<br>wĕśamtî<br>nĕhārôt lāʾiyyîm<br>waʾăgammîm ʾôvîš | 3 hār, hār, hār<br>3 ûgĕvāʿôt, wĕkol waʾăgammîm<br>3 bām, śam, gam<br>3 ʿeśbām, wĕśamtî + ʾeššōm (above)<br>2 ʾôvîš, ʾôvîš |
| And I help the blind to walk<br>By a road they do not know.<br>By paths they *didn't know*,[3]<br>I lead them.<br><br>I am turning darkness<br>before their faces[4] to light,<br>and rough places<br>to level ground.<br>*These* (are)<br>the promises—<br>I have made them and I have not abandoned them. (16) | wĕhôlaktî ʿiwrîm<br>bĕderek lōʾ yādāʿû<br>bintîvôt lōʾ-yādĕʿû<br>ʾadrîkēm<br>ʾāśîm maḥšāk<br>liphnêhem lāʾôr<br>ûmaʿăqaššîm<br>lĕmîšôr<br>ʾēlleh<br>haddĕvārîm ʿăśîtim wĕlōʾ<br>ʿăzavtîm | 3 îm, îm, îm<br>6 îm, îm, îm, îm, îm, îm<br>3 lōʾ yādāʿû, lōʾ-yādĕʿû + ʿad<br>3 lōʾ, lōʾ, lōʾ<br>3 wĕhôlaktî, maḥšāk, ûmaʿăqašš<br>3 li, lāʾôr, lĕmîšôr<br>3 lĕ, ʾēlleh, wĕlōʾ<br>3 bĕderek, bintîvôt, dĕvārîm<br>3 ʾāśîm, ʿăśîtim, ʿăzavtîm |

1 The verse follows NJPS.
2 The Hebrew imagery is more literal, like a "man of war."
3 MT vocalization suggests not simple repetition of the verb, but a slight variation also for emphasis.
4 The literal translation is more compelling.

Arguably a woman prophet in the text above conveys not only stunning lyrical artistry (with triplet soundplays) but a profound theological development—and a *character* development for YHWH, who is making amends for 'his' earlier destruction and allowing of suffering—now taking responsibility for the impact on his people, and taking care of those likely hurt in the trauma of the exile. While apparently the male prophet and the deity may still revel in warrior imagery (as in v. 13), male bravado gives way to a changed YHWH here and in other texts in Isaiah 40–55 (compared to the deity portrayed in the books of Jeremiah and Lamentations).

## Isaiah 49:13–21

Finally, the poignant Isa 49:13–21[50] passage that renders Zion's lament of being forgotten contains God's portrayed self-references like a mother. In this long passage the *only* verses that convey the doublet sound pattern are vv. 13–14, in which a prophet, apparently male ironically, quotes personified Zion's speech:

| *(male)* | | *(doublets)* |
|---|---|---|
| But said Zion, | **wa**ttōʾmer ṣiyy**ôn** | 2 **wa, wa** |
| "YHWH has forsaken me, | ʿăzāb**anî** **YHWH** | 2 **yô, YH** |
| my Lord | **wa**ʾdō**nāy** | 2 **ôn, ōn** |
| has forgotten me." (14) | šĕkēḥ**ānî** | 2 **anî, ānî** |

This line is followed (vv. 15–21) by a lengthy response primarily in God's voice by a poet using *only triplet soundplays* (the first being three forms of 'forget'—*hătiškaḥ, tiškaḥnâ, ʾeškāḥēk*) to bring a most poignant message: "Can a woman *forget* her nursing child . . . Even these may *forget*, but I will not *forget* you." Thus is proposed also here that the text embeds the women's lyrical tradition, and *a woman prophet answers* Zion's complaint (v. 14) with YHWH's words. Ironically here, and this may be true in other parts of Isaiah 40–66, the doublet pattern suggests that *a male prophet renders the personified female city's* speech in order to convey human suffering, and *a woman prophet renders God's* speech of comfort.

## Conclusion

In summary, what ramifications of this study of texts in Deutero-Isaiah might there be for future understandings of this corpus and the book as a whole? Complete analysis of all the chapters of Isaiah 40–66 might suggest an illuminated rhetorical role of female and male prophets in these contexts. This is extremely important, for the large consensus among both scholars and laypersons is that we simply do not have examples of women prophets' oracles in such contexts. Certainly, a close and complete analysis of the sound patterns found in the male voice of those chapters traditionally referred to as First Isaiah with the later chapters with male voices would be illuminating, to shed light not only on shared artistry, passed

50. Follows the NRSV unless otherwise noted. The previous v. 13 ("Sing for joy, O heavens") is dominated by a doublet sound pattern.

down through the generations, but also on peculiar innovations by the different male prophetic voices in the canonical book of Isaiah. More important, because of the long neglect in examining women's contributions to the biblical texts, the artistry of women's voices from the earlier to the later context must be examined to assess how a women's lyrical tradition, at least suggested by the canonized Hebrew texts, was sustained and developed in particular ways by women 'tradents' over time. From *Hannĕvî'â* (whether one or more women prophets) in the early chapters of the book of Isaiah to the '*Mĕbaśśeret*' in Isaiah 40–55 (whether one woman or more), a clearer picture can certainly be obtained. A closer analysis of the Hebrew may reveal how women prophets passed down their tradition as part of the Isaianic tradition, yet also innovated their lyrics for new situations, particularly arriving in the ultimate crisis for sixth-century Judah/Israel. Finally, also of import will be an assessment of just how the women's lyrics across the book of Isaiah also participated in receiving and innovating lyrics from earlier women prophets and singers in the traditions of Miriam, Deborah, and Hannah.

## Excursus: the Postexilic Context

### Noadiah

The only mentioned woman prophet in the early postexilic context is Noadiah in Neh 6:14. This was in the Persian historical setting, in Jerusalem, after the Judeans returned from exile in the sixth century BCE, during Ezra's priestly leadership and Nehemiah's governorship in Judea in the fifth century. There appear brief references to two figures named Noadiah in the books of Nehemiah and Ezra. The Noadiah receiving somewhat more attention is a woman prophet by this name. Yet, she is only briefly alluded to by Nehemiah in his prayer asking God to remember his enemies—she, the prophetess (*nevi'ah*), and two other men already named, and "the rest of the prophets who wanted to make me afraid." Nehemiah's perspective is portrayed, not Noadiah's, that they had been expressing disagreement or antagonism toward him and his wall-building enterprise. The other Noadiah referred to in this period is in Ezra 8:33; no information of him is given, except that he is male, son of Binnui and a Levite.

## Women Prophets in Postbiblical Judaism

In postbiblical Judaism, a few women not considered prophets in the biblical canon were later called 'prophets' in early rabbinic tradition. These included Hannah, Sarah, Abigail, and Esther. All of these, however, generally fulfilled expected roles of women, though Hannah's individual song of victory included prophetic themes and thanksgiving for God's rescue/salvation. The heroine Judith should rightfully be in consideration as a prophetic figure.

# Conclusion

## Summary

THIS STUDY HAS TRAVERSED and conversed with many texts in the Hebrew Bible across sections of Torah, Prophets and the Writings, and across genres and time periods, in an effort to discern unnamed women's composing voices in some of the prophetic books. As though coming forth from the shadows, and from silence, their voice-sounds began ringing, clear and compelling. This study has explored and analyzed sound patterns in Hebrew lyrics suggestive of women's and men's lyrical composing. Of course it could not treat every text. Yet, a few general conclusions may now be made.

The triplet and doublet soundplay patterns are a pervasive feature in biblical Hebrew poetry or lyrics. Sound repetition in biblical texts has not been thoroughly appreciated for its complexity, and neither in this study was it possible to recognize every single instance of the myriad dynamics of sound artistry in the texts analyzed. Much depends on the hearing of the interpreter. Attention to sound artistry is usually limited to mentioning its presence in a line or a few lines, but not a comprehensive approach. In fact, doublet soundplays have been regarded as the 'typical' in the regular emphasis on parallelism. However, this study suggests that *syllables are the most fundamental units of Hebrew poetry*—the integral elements in lyrical composing, which bear both structure and fluidity for creating, especially where multiple consonants link syllables and produce highly complex sound patterns. The syllable is the building-block for the construction of words and lines that often form complex parallelisms, but sometimes syllable soundplays do not support parallelism.

Further, I have argued that the triplet soundplay pattern is a signature feature of Hebraic women's lyrical composing, which was also utilized by women prophets. This signature soundplay may provide a key to unlocking the presence of unnamed women prophets' utterances in biblical texts, particularly in the prophetic books where multiple voices are discernible. Such voices are often juxtaposed near male prophets' lyrics personifying cities or nations as female, thus clouding the picture at times of the implied speaker. No doubt, there will continue to be disagreement with regard to particular texts, as to whether an implied female *persona* is speaking, or an implied woman *prophet* or other lyricist (such as a lamenter). However, from a basis in Hannah's represented song with pervasive triplet soundplays, corroborated by the women's represented voices in the Song of Songs, and further corroborated by Deborah's implied prophetic voice in Judges 5, and by other texts—a significant burden of argument that *the triplet soundplay was a consistent feature of women's lyricizing* has been made.

While it had been recognized that women prophets sang victory and thanksgiving songs, there had been no way to find evidence either of women prophets' unattributed oracles embedded in prophetic books or for women prophets' *lyrical* judgment oracles, apart from feminine grammatical references. This wide-ranging and detailed study of prophetic lyrics has found, I propose, women's prophetic voices embedded in First Isaiah, Micah, Jeremiah, Lamentations, and Deutero-Isaiah. The signature feature of women's composing, it is proposed, has shed new light on the women's compositional voices in the Song of Deborah and the Song of the Sea, and the triplet signature is reflected in the opening women's story (narrative) of Exodus 1, and even in Genesis 1. Is it possible for scholars and modern-day people to accept that unnamed woman prophets may have uttered lyrical oracles embedded in prophetic books, such as those above, even when not given credit by later redactors? After all, in 2 Kings, the prophetess Huldah is portrayed uttering *a prose indictment* for God. This analysis has shown lingering traces of a triplet sound pattern in her represented speech. Perhaps longstanding assumptions about familiar texts in entire books attributed to one male prophet make those texts appear or 'feel' to be settled with regard to whose voice is speaking, different from new, alternative possibilities. In my view, the differing perspectives of multiple voices in prophetic texts, including some that are in dialog with one another, are much better understood, make more sense, when women were and are given a voice in these contexts.

Some scholars, perhaps using the traditional literary, historical-critical, or theological methods, will not want to 'genderize' texts; they will suggest that it really does not matter if a man or woman composed a text for it to be meaningful to men or women then or today. The latter is true, that texts may be meaningful to all regardless of who composed them. *But it does matter* to discern, where possible, whether a female or male tradition possibly produced a lyrical composition, because women's and men's experiences, perspectives, and ways of speaking *can be different* based on social, cultural and biological experiences. That said, this study one hopes has not promoted a stereotyping of women's speech or views, but has found that women had their own tradition of composing, within which one woman might affirm cultural practices and another woman challenge them. Deborah does not challenge the practice of war against one's enemy, but the proposed woman prophet's voice in Isaiah 11 certainly does, with her vision of a peaceable kingdom that moves past human warfare. The great irony is that in biblical tradition the deity spoke through both men and women, who are both said to be created in God's image, and this implies the God of the Bible did use women's experience and lyrics to give expression to the deity's 'self.'

Newer literary approaches joined to a feminist hermeneutic may prefer to suggest that the Bible is so dominantly patriarchal that there are no women's compositional voices in the texts; the texts were all produced through the male lens in service of male ideologies. While this assumption might seem so, what is the particular argument, based on the whole of the biblical texts, to arrive at this vast conclusion? Or it may be argued that what appears to be a woman's composition was really composed by a man 'imitating' the women's style. Further research into the biblical texts may shed more light on this possibility. However, what many of the texts analyzed here suggest is that men preferred their doublet pattern and women their triplets. Yet, they could regularly employ the opposite in a line or two of their larger composition for emphasis. Therefore, they imitate the other's speech, or rather, better put, they opt for the 'different' to upset expectations for emphasis.

Four methodological approaches, that also affirm the work of the above approaches, would counter the conclusion that the Bible contains only men's compositions. An archaeological approach shows evidences of women performers in ancient Canaan; these are corroborated by numerous allusions to women composer/performers in Israel by biblical texts. An anthropological approach that compares cultures—ancient and contemporary—also affirms the role of women as composer-performers, including in the ancient Near East. Moreover, there we have multiple attestations of utterances recorded representing women prophets. A postcolonial feminist approach challenges the assumption that women were always absent or silent with regard to composing or performing in traditional cultures worldwide, including in the ancient, indigenous culture of Israel. While indigenous cultures may be, and were often, androcentric, this does not preclude women's roles in composing and publicly performing in such oral cultures. Their lyrics provided them, and continue to provide them, an opportunity to challenge and innovate tradition—both current social and religious practices and understandings. From a theological perspective, the question must be raised as to whether the men in control of a purported wholesale patriarchal culture in ancient Israel would have felt free or even been free to completely silence women prophets called by their God. Would they have felt or been free enough to rewrite the utterances of women prophets? The tendency of biblical interpreters through history—scholars and clergy—has often effectively turned a woman prophet's (unattributed) voice into a personification of the female city, even though at times the biblical poetry, grammar, and context do not require or support it. By ignoring the possibility of women's prophecy, we love the message but push aside the messenger and control the vehicle.

As has been observed, those texts that include women's leadership roles and represented voices are often found in contexts of sociopolitical crisis in ancient Israel, of which there were not a few. This explanation is no doubt correct: that in such crises the urgent conditions, and at times the failures of male leadership, meant more opportunity for women. However, it is also important to say that the biblical texts about women leaders in ancient Israel actually suggest that such women also arose and contributed *when there were strong men available* to lead. The women were 'allowed' a place and a voice, even though in some cases their identity was hidden: Miriam with Moses and Aaron; 'Hannevi'ah' with Isaiah; the woman I call 'Šimuna' with Micah; 'Bat-ʿ ammi' with Jeremiah and in Lamentations; the female prophet(s) with male prophet or prophets in Deutero-Isaiah. The presence of these women, it is proposed, simply means that women were always fit to contribute and lead *and were recognized by many for doing so* in spite of the parameters placed on them by the traditional culture and the neglect or erasing of their attributions by those who formed the canon.

In fact, this study has shown from the evidence the Hebrew texts themselves present, extraordinarily, that women and men prophets did at times join together in intricate call and response in making their utterances, in dialogical composing and performing to get their messages across. While certainly scribal activity at times placed their voices side by side in some texts, in other texts the intricacies of lyrics give evidence that it was *in oral composing/performing that true dialogue* between them did take place, still preserved by faithful scribes or redactors or both. And yet there are instances when the woman prophet's voice is singular in its power, beauty, and message, as proposed in the vision of peace in Isa 11:6–9. This study, one hopes, both sheds new light on the singular voices from ancient Israel's indigenous women's lyrical tradition, and gives newfound hope about an ancient *partnership* of women and men together fulfilling their callings from their God, which is an inspiration to see—empowering for women and men today long chagrined at the many instances of the subordination of women in the Bible, in religious traditions, and across cultures still today.

And now to us women: How shall we respond to this proposed uncovering of women's significant contributions in the composing of biblical texts, especially women prophets? With serious skepticism? Or with justifiable anger over millennia of silencing these and so many women? Or with respect for those ancestral, courageous women and men who worked these lyrics into the canon? Or with awe and new appreciation for the extraordinary artistry of Hannĕvî'â and her sisters? In any case, *on these women, our forebears who live on, we cannot turn our backs.* As they were in their time, and still can be today, women biblical prophets are a model of and a warrant for women's leadership, including in ordained ministry—for the calling of a prophet was the highest calling in the Bible.

## Suggestions for Further Work

This study is a beginning. It leaves untouched for analysis many texts in the prophetic books for pursuit of women's voices. For those who are convinced that the triplet sound pattern suggests women's voices, what may be found among the many passages of Second and Third Isaiah? More widely in Jeremiah? In the minor prophets? Moreover, in this study I alluded to some psalms that include triplet soundplays (for example, Ps 113, and also Ps 46). May this key or signature unlock greater knowledge about whether women contributed to composing psalms? Might doublet and triplet sound patterns distinguish speakers with differing perspectives in the Psalms? What about Proverbs 8? What about women's stories? Esther, Ruth. And there are more avenues too numerous to mention.

Given that I have identified possible women's texts, and have compared them to men's texts, what differences are appearing? The first great difference is that prophetic men are often personifying the people, the city, the nation, as female in judgment speeches. We already knew this. What is interesting is that, so far anyway, this is not found so much by women prophets composing, though it remains to be seen how this will play out when more texts are analyzed. The women prophets' voices in this study very often, almost regularly, *invoked nature* in their effort to communicate both divine and human realities (Miriam, Deborah, and the proposed '*Bat-'ammî*', who may have been the reluctant woman prophet in Isaiah 40). Will other texts in Deutero-Isaiah stressing creation or nature's processes be found to be using triplet sound patterns, thus possibly to be women's compositions? It remains to be seen whether this is a greater emphasis of women prophets by more complete analysis of texts. Questions to pursue will be *how* did women's and men's composing traditions render the genders (and everything else) in their stories and lyrics? And how did *individual* women and men (without us having to secure an impossible historical identity) both pass on *and innovate* aspects of these traditions? We will be prepared for women who were complicit in androcentric practices (like Deborah) and those who were more challenging of them (like '*Bat-ʿammî*' in Lamentations). This is nothing new under the sun—that women (and men) do not all think the same. But we must get on with the critical listening, examining, and understanding of the composing of indigenous peoples in ancient Israel.

And now a word about the larger context. Was the triplet-sound composing limited to Israelite women? Might it have been practiced by Canaanite women or in Mesopotamian cultures? Might the Ugaritic cycles, especially those that include stories of Anat, help determine whether this tradition was broader? And in traditional cultures still today, there are evidences of different sound patterns in composing by men and women. Efforts to address these questions and others like them, in my view, are also for the sake of women and men in the world today who cocreate invaluable traditions but also may suffer under old oppressive practices and injustices, sometimes based on gender ideologies, that must be innovated for justice and good. And whether biblical composers were complicit or not in harmful ideologies or practices (who is not?), these tradents were of course addressing much beyond the gender question. A postcolonial, gender-critical, oral-traditional (including writing), indigenous-oriented perspective will affirm which traditions and texts are still constructive and helpful, and which must be criticized as unethical.

In conclusion, the time is long overdue, in history, in academic circles, and in faith communities revering the biblical tradition, to give credit to these faithful women for their extraordinary contributions of lyrical artistry. It is fair to say that for them *syllable sounds were the very breath and blood* that supported the *bone and sinew* of their body of biblical poetry—its beauty, prophetic force, and faith.

Postbiblical Judaism (*Meg.* 14) affirmed Hannah as a prophet, the mother of the prophet Samuel, who overshadowed her in the history of faith. Indeed, were it not for the song associated with her and the 'singular' voice of the tradition that produced it, the women's lyrical *signature* still might have gone unnoticed. For this song is a prime example of an indigenous Hebraic women's lyrical tradition.

So,<br>
sing on with<br>
songs Hannah and<br>
        Hannevi'ah,<br>
          a new<br>
        hearing!

# Bibliography


Ackerman, Susan. *Warrior, Dancer, Seductress, Queen: Women in Judges and Biblical Israel.* ABRL. New York: Doubleday, 1998.

———. "Why Is Miriam Also among the Prophets? (And Is Zippporah among the Priests?)." *JBL* 121 (2002) 47–80.

Albrektson, Bertil et al., eds. *Remembering All the Way: A Collection of Old Testament Studies.* OtSt 21. Leiden: Brill, 1981.

Albright, W. F. *Yahweh and the Gods of Canaan: A Historical Analysis of Two Contrasting Faiths.* The Jordan Lectures 1965. Garden City, NY: Doubleday, 1968.

Allen, Leslie. *Jeremiah.* OTL. Louisville: Westminster John Knox, 2008.

Alonso Schökel, Luis. *A Manual of Hebrew Poetics.* SubBib 11. Rome: Editrice Pontificio Instituto Biblico, 1988.

Alter, Robert. *The Five Books of Moses.* New York: Norton, 2004.

Althann, R. *A Philological Analysis of Jeremiah 4–6 in the Light of Northwest Semitic.* BibOr 38. Rome: Biblical Institute Press, 1983.

Altmann, Alexander, ed. *Biblical Motifs: Origins and Transformations.* Philip W. Lown Institute of Advanced Judaic Studies, Brandeis University. Studies and Texts 3. Cambridge: Harvard University Press, 1966.

Andersen, Francis I., and David Noel Freedman. *Micah: A New Translation with Introduction and Commentary.* AB 24E. New York: Doubleday, 2000.

Anderson, Bernhard. "The Song of Miriam Poetically and Theologically Considered." In *Directions in Biblical Hebrew Poetry*, edited by Elaine R. Follis, 285–96. JSOTSup 40. Sheffield: JSOT Press, 1987.

Atkinson, Clarissa W. et al., eds. *Immaculate and Powerful: The Female in Sacred Image and Social Reality.* The Harvard Women's Studies in Religion Series. Boston: Beacon, 1985.

Bach, Alice. "With a Song in Her Heart: Listening to Scholars Listening for Miriam." In *A Feminist Companion to Exodus to Deuteronomy*, edited by Athalya Brenner, 243–54. FCB 6. Sheffield: Sheffield Academic, 1994.

———, ed. *Women in the Hebrew Bible: A Reader.* New York: Routledge, 1999.

Bal, Mieke, ed. *Anti-covenant: Counter-reading Women's Lives in the Hebrew Bible.* Bible and Literature Series 22. JSOTSup 81. Sheffield: Almond, 1989.

———. *Death & Dissymmetry: The Politics of Coherence in the Book of Judges.* Chicago Studies in the History of Judaism. Chicago: University of Chicago Press, 1988.

———. *Murder and Difference: Gender, Genre, and Scholarship on Sisera's Death.* Translated by Matthew Gumpert. Indiana Studies in Biblical Literature. Bloomington: Indiana University Press, 1988.

Balentine, Samuel E. *Prayer in the Hebrew Bible: The Drama of Divine–Human Dialogue.* OBT. Minneapolis: Fortress, 1993.

Baltzer, Klaus. *Deutero-Isaiah: A Commentary on Isaiah 40–55.* Translated by Margaret Kohl. Hermeneia. Minneapolis: Fortress, 2001.

Bauer-Levesque, Angela. *Gender in the Book of Jeremiah: A Feminist-Literary Reading.* Studies in Biblical Literature 5. New York: Lang, 1999.

Baumann, Gerlinde. *Love and Violence: Marriage as Metaphor for the Relationship between YHWH and Israel in the Prophetic Books.* Translated by Linda M. Maloney. Collegeville, MN: Liturgical, 2003.

Bautch, Richard J., and J. Todd Hibbard, eds. *The Book of Isaiah: Enduring Questions Answered Anew.* Grand Rapids: Eerdmans, 2014.

Beal, Timothy K. "The System and the Speaking Subject in the Hebrew Bible: Reading for Divine Abjection." *BibInt* 2 (1994) 171–89.

Beek, Martinus A., ed. *Studia Biblica et Semitica.* Wageningen: Veenman, 1966.

Ben Zvi, Ehud, and Michael H. Floyd, eds. *Writings and Speech: In Israelite and Ancient Near Eastern Prophecy.* SBLSymS 10. Atlanta: SBL, 2000.

Ben Zvi, Ehud. *Micah.* FOTL 21B. Grand Rapids: Eerdmans, 2000.

Berlin, Adele. *Biblical Poetry through Medieval Jewish Eyes.* Indiana Studies in Biblical Literature. Bloomington: Indiana University Press, 1991.

———. *The Dynamics of Biblical Parallelism.* Bloomington: Indiana University Press, 1985.

Biddle, Mark. *Polyphony and Symphony in Prophetic Literature: Rereading Jeremiah 7–20.* Studies in Old Testament Interpretation 2. Macon, GA: Mercer University Press, 1996.

Bird, Phyllis A. "Images of Women in the Old Testament." In *Religion and Sexism: Images of Women in the Jewish and Christian Traditions,* edited by Rosemary Radford Ruether, 41–88. New York: Simon & Schuster, 1974.

Blenkinsopp, Joseph. "Ballad Style and Psalm Style in the Song of Deborah: A Discussion." *Bib* 42 (1961) 61–76.

———. *Isaiah 1–39.* AB 19A. New York: Doubleday, 2000.

———. *Isaiah 40–55.* AB 19B. New Haven: Yale University Press, 2002.

Boling, Robert G. *Judges.* AB 6A. Garden City, NY: Doubleday, 1975.

Bowen, Nancy R. "The Daughters of Your People: Female Prophets in Ezekiel 13 :17–23." *JBL* 118 (1999) 417–33.

Brenner, Athalya, and Fokkelien van Dijk-Hemmes. *On Gendering Texts: Female and Male Voices in the Hebrew Bible.* BibIntSer 1. Leiden: Brill, 1993.

Brenner, Athalya, ed. *Exodus to Deuteronomy.* FCB 2/5. Sheffield: Sheffield Academic, 2000.

———, ed. *A Feminist Companion to Exodus to Deuteronomy.* FCB 6. Sheffield: Sheffield Academic, 1994.

———, ed. *A Feminist Companion to Judges.* FCB 4. Sheffield: JSOT Press, 1993.

———, ed. *A Feminist Companion to the Latter Prophets.* FCB 8. Sheffield: Sheffield Academic, 1995.

———, ed. *A Feminist Companion to the Song of Songs.* FCB 1. Sheffield: Sheffield Academic, 1993.

———. *The Israelite Woman: Social Role and Literary Type in Biblical Narrative*. Biblical Seminar. Sheffield: Sheffield Academic, 1985.

———. "On Prophetic Propaganda and the Politics of 'Love': The Case of Jeremiah." In *A Feminist Companion to the Latter Prophets*, edited by Athalya Brenner, 256–74. FCB 8. Sheffield: Sheffield Academic, 1995.

———, ed. *Prophets and Daniel*. FCB, 2/8. London: Sheffield Academic, 2001.

———. "Response to Mary E. Shields: About 'Jeremiah' as Reflected in Feminist Eyes." In *Jeremiah (Dis)Placed: New Directions in Writing/Reading Jeremiah*, edited by A. R. Pete Diamond and Louis Stulman, 303–6. Library of Hebrew Bible / Old Testament Studies 529. T. & T. Clark Library of Biblical Studies. London: T. & T. Clark, 2011.

———. "Women Poets and Authors." In *A Feminist Companion to the Song of Songs*, 91–97. FCB 1. Sheffield: Sheffield Academic, 1993.

Brenner, Martin. *The Song of the Sea: Ex 15:1–21*. BZAW 195. Berlin: de Gruyter, 1991.

Brettler, Marc Zvi. *The Book of Judges*. Old Testament Readings. London: Routledge, 2002.

Brooke, George J. "A Long-Lost Song of Miriam." *BAR* 20/3 (1994) 62–65.

Brueggemann, Walter. *Exodus*. In *The New Interpreters Bible*, vol. 1. Nashville: Abingdon, 1994.

———. *Finally Comes the Poet: Daring Speech for Proclamation*. Minneapolis: Fortress, 1989.

———. *First and Second Samuel*. IBC. Louisville: John Knox, 1990.

———. *Isaiah*. Vol. 1, *1–39*. Westminster Bible Companion. Louisville: Westminster/John Knox, 1998.

———. *Isaiah*. Vol. 2, *40–66*. Westminster Bible Companion. Louisville: Westminster/John Knox, 1998.

———. *Israel's Praise: Doxology against Idolatry and Ideology*. Minneapolis: Fortress, 1988.

———. "A Response to 'The Song of Miriam' by Bernhard Anderson." In *Directions in Biblical Hebrew Poetry*, edited by Elaine R. Follis, 285–302. JSOTSup 40. Sheffield: JSOT Press, 1987.

Burns, Rita J. *Has the Lord Indeed Spoken Only through Moses?* SBLDS 84. Atlanta: Scholars, 1987.

Butler, Trent C. *Judges*. WBC 8. Nashville: Nelson, 2009.

Butting, Klara. *Prophetinnen gefragt: Die Bedeutung der Prophetinnen im Kanon aus Torah und Prophetie*. Erev-Rav-Hefte. Biblisch-feministische Texte 3. Knesebeck: Erev-Rav, 2001.

Carroll, Robert P. *Jeremiah*. OTL. Philadelphia: Westminster, 1986.

Caspi, Mishael M., and Julia Ann Blessing. *Weavers of the Songs: The Oral Poetry of Arab Women in Israel and the West Bank*. Washington DC: Three Continents, 1991.

Cassuto, Umberto. *A Commentary on the Book of Exodus*. Publications of the Perry Foundation for Biblical Research in the Hebrew University of Jerusalem. Jerusalem: Magnes, 1967.

Childs, Brevard S. *The Book of Exodus: A Critical, Theological Commentary*. OTL. Louisville: Westminster John Knox, 1974.

———. *Introduction to the Old Testament as Scripture*. Philadelphia: Fortress, 1979.

Claassens, L. Juliana M. *Mourner, Mother, Midwife: Reimagining God's Delivering Presence in the Old Testament*. Westminster John Knox, 2012.

Clements, R. E. "Beyond Tradition-History: Deutero-Isaianic Development of First Isaiah's Themes." *JSOT* 31 (1985) 95–113.

———. *Isaiah 1–39*. NCB. Grand Rapids: Eerdmans, 1980.

Cohen, Norman J. "Miriam's Song: A Modern Midrashic Reading." *Judaism* 33 (1984) 179–90.

Coogan, Michael D. "A Structural and Literary Analysis of the Song of Deborah." *CBQ* 40 (1978) 143–66.

Cook, Steve. "Habakkuk 3, Gender, and War." *Lectio difficilior* 1/2009. http://www.lectio.unibe.ch/09_1/steve_cook_habakkuk_3.html/.

Craigie, Peter C. "Deborah and Anat: A Study of Poetic Imagery (Judges 5)." *ZAW* 90 (1978) 374–81.

———. "Note on Judg 5:2." *VT* 18/3 (1968) 397–99.

Crawford, Sidnie White. "4Q364 & 365: A Preliminary Report." In *The Madrid Qumran Congress: Proceedings, 1991*, edited by Julio T. Barrera and Luis V. Montaner, 1:217–28. 2 vols. STDJ. Leiden: Brill, 1992.

Crenshaw, James L. "Transmitting Prophecy across Generations." In *Writings and Speech: in Israelite and Ancient Near Eastern Prophecy*, edited by Ehud Ben Zvi, and Michael H. Floyd 31–44. SBLSymS 10. Atlanta: SBL, 2000.

Cross, Frank Moore. *Canaanite Myth and Hebrew Epic*. Cambridge: Harvard University Press, 1973.

———. "The Council of YHWH in Second Isaiah." *JNES* 12 (1953) 274–77.

Cross, Frank Moore, and David Noel Freedman. *Studies in Ancient Yahwistic Poetry*. Biblical Resource Series. Grand Rapids: Eerdmans, 1997.

Darr, Katheryn Pfisterer. "Like Warrior, Like Woman: Destruction and Deliverance in Isaiah 42:10–17." *CBQ* 49 (1987) 560–71.

Day, John, ed. *Prophecy and Prophets in Ancient Israel: Proceedings of the Oxford Old Testament Seminar*. Library of Hebrew Bible / Old Testament Studies 531. T. & T. Clark Library of Biblical Studies. New York: T. & T. Clark, 2010.

Day, Peggy L., ed. *Gender and Difference in Ancient Israel*. Minneapolis: Fortress, 1989.

Dempsey, Carol J. "Literary Artistry, Ethical Message, and Some Considerations about the Image of Yahweh and Micah." *JSOT* 85 (1999) 117–28.

Dempster, Stephen G. "Mythology and History in the Song of Deborah." *WTJ* 41 (1978) 33–53.

Diamond, A. R. Pete et al., eds. *Troubling Jeremiah*. JSOTSup 260. Sheffield: Sheffield Academic, 1999.

Diamond, A.R. Pete, and Louis Stulman, eds. *Jeremiah (Dis)Placed: New Directions in Writing/Reading Jeremiah*. Library of Hebrew Bible / Old Testament Studies 529. T. & T. Clark Library of Biblical Studies. London: T. & T. Clark, 2011.

Dijk-Hemmes, Fokkelien van. "Mothers and a Mediator in the Song of Deborah." In *A Feminist Companion to Judges*, edited by Athalya Brenner, 110–14. FCB 4. Sheffield: JSOT Press, 1993.

———. "Some Recent Views on the Presentation of the Song of Miriam." In *A Feminist Companion to Exodus to Deuteronomy*, edited by Athalya Brenner, 200–206. Feminist Companion to the Bible 6. Sheffield: Sheffield Academic, 1994.

Dille, Sarah J. *Mixing Metaphors: God as Mother and Father in Deutero-Isaiah*. JSOTSup 398. Gender, Culture, Theory 13. London: T. & T. Clark, 2004.

Dube, Musa. *Postcolonial Feminist Interpretation of the Bible*. St. Louis: Chalice, 2000.

Durham, John I. *Exodus*. WBC 3. Waco: Word, 1987.

Echols, Charles L. *"Tell Me, O Muse": The Song of Deborah (Judges 5) in the Light of Heroic Poetry*. T. & T. Clark Library of Biblical Studies. Library of Hebrew Bible / Old Testament Studies 487. New York: T. & T. Clark, 2008.

Eskenazi, Tamara Cohn, ed. *The Torah: A Women's Commentary*. New York: Women of Reform Judaism, 2008.

Everson, A. Joseph, and Hyun Chul Paul Kim, eds. *The Desert Will Bloom: Poetic Visions in Isaiah*. SBL: Ancient Israel and Its Literature. Atlanta: SBL, 2009.

Exum, J. Cheryl. "Feminist Criticism: Whose Interests Are Being Served?" In *Judges and Method: New Approaches in Biblical Studies*, edited by Gale A. Yee, 65–90. Minneapolis: Fortress, 1995.

———. "Of Broken Pots, Fluttering Birds, and Visions in the Night: Extended Simile and Poetic Technique in Isaiah." *CBQ* 43 (1981) 331–52.

Fewell, Danna Nolan, and David M. Gunn. "Controlling Perspectives: Women, Men, and the Authority of Violence in Judges 4 and 5." *JAAR* 58 (1990) 389–411.

Finnegan, Ruth. *Oral Poetry: Its Nature, Significance, and Social Context*. Bloomington: Indiana University Press, 1992.

Fischer, Irmtraud. *Gotteskünderinnen: zu einer Geschlechterfairen Deutung des Phänomens der Prophetie und der Prophetinnen in der Hebräischen Bibel*. Stuttgart: Kohlhammer, 2002.

Fokkelman, Jan. "Stylistic Analysis of Isaiah 40:1–11." In *Remembering All the Way: A Collection of Old Testament Studies*, edited by Bertil Albrektson et al., 68–90. OtSt 21. Leiden: Brill, 1981.

Foley, John Miles. *How to Read an Oral Poem*. Urbana: University of Illinois Press, 2002.

Follis, Elaine R., ed. *Directions in Biblical Hebrew Poetry*. JSOTSup 40. Sheffield: JSOT Press, 1987.

Fox, Everett, trans. *Now These Are the Names: A New English Rendition of the Book of Exodus*. New York: Schocken, 1986.

Franke, Chris A. "'Like a Mother I Have Comforted You': The Function of Figurative Language in Isaiah 1:7–26 and 66:7–14." In *The Desert Will Bloom: Poetic Visions in Isaiah*, edited by Joseph A. Everson and Hyun Chul Paul Kim, 35–55. SBL: Ancient Israel and Its Literature. Atlanta: SBL, 2009.

Freedman, David Noel. *Pottery, Poetry, and Prophecy: Studies in Early Hebrew Poetry*. Winona Lake, IN: Eisenbrauns, 1980.

Fretheim, Terence E. *Jeremiah*. Smyth & Helwys Bible Commentary. Macon, GA: Smyth & Helwys, 2002.

Frolov, Serge. *Judges*. FOTL 6B. Grand Rapids: Eerdmans, 2013.

Gafney, Wilda. *Daughters of Miriam: Women Prophets in Ancient Israel*. Minneapolis: Fortress, 2008.

Geller, Stephen A. "Notes and Observations: A Poetic Analysis of Isaiah 40:1–2." *HTR* 77 (1984) 413–20.

Ginzberg, Louis. *The Legends of the Jews*. New York: Simon & Schuster, 1956.

Gitay, Yehoshua. "The Effectiveness of Isaiah's Speech." *JQR* 75 (1984) 162–72.

———. "Reflections on the Study of the Prophetic Discourse: The Question of Isaiah 1:2–20." *VT* 33 (1983) 207–21.

Globe, Alexander. "Literary Structure and Unity of the Song of Deborah." *JBL* 93 (1974) 493–512.

Goitein, S. D. "Women as Creators of Biblical Genres." Translated by Michael Carasik. *Prooftexts* 8 (1988) 1–33; orig. publ. in *Iyyunim bamiqra* [Studies in Scripture] (1957).

Goldberg Nathan. *The Passover Haggadah.* New York: Ktav, 1987.

Goldin, Judah. *The Song of the Sea.* Philadelphia: Jewish Publication Society, 1990.

Goldingay, John, ed. *Uprooting and Planting: Essays on Jeremiah for Leslie Allen.* Library of Hebrew Bible / Old Testament Studies 459. T. & T. Clark Library of Biblical Studies. New York: T. & T. Clark, 2007.

Goldingay, John, and David Payne. *A Critical and Exegetical Commentary on Isaiah 40–55.* ICC. London: T. & T. Clark, 2006.

Good, Deirdre, ed. *Mariam, the Magdalen, and the Mother.* Bloomington: Indiana University Press, 2005.

Gordis, Robert. *The Song of Songs and Lamentations.* New York: Ktav, 1974.

Gordon, Robert P., ed. *"The Place Is Too Small for Us": The Israelite Prophets in Recent Scholarship.* Winona Lake: Eisenbrauns, 1995.

———. "Present Trends and Future Directions." In *The Place Is Too Small for Us": The Israelite Prophets in Recent Scholarship*, edited by Robert P. Gordon, 600–605. Winona Lake, IN: Eisenbrauns, 1995.

Gottwald, Norman K. *Studies in the Book of Lamentations.* Studies in Biblical Theology 14. London: SCM, 1954.

Grabbe, Lester L. *Priests, Prophets, Diviners, Sages: A Socio-historical Study of Religious Specialists in Ancient Israel.* Valley Forge: Trinity, 1995.

Graetz, Naomi. "Did Miriam Talk Too Much?"In *A Feminist Companion to Exodus to Deuteronomy*, edited by Athalya Brenner, 231–42. FCB 6. Sheffield: Sheffield Academic, 1994.

Gruber, Mayer I. "Feminine Similes Applied to the LORD in Second Isaiah." *Beer Sheva* 2 (1985) 75–84 (Hebrew).

———. "The Motherhood of God in Second Isaiah." *Rev Bib* (1983) 351–59.

———. "Women's Voices in the Book of Micah." *Lectio difficilior* 1 (2007). http://www.lectio.unibe.ch/.

Hackett, Jo Ann. "In the Days of Jael: Reclaiming the History of Women in Ancient Israel." In *Immaculate and Powerful: The Female in Sacred Image and Social Reality*, edited by Clarissa W. Atkinson et al., 15–38. Harvard Women's Studies in Religion Series. Boston: Beacon, 1985.

Halpern, Baruch. *The Emergence of Israel in Canaan.* SBLMS 29. Chico: Scholars, 1983.

Hauser, Alan. "Judges 5: Parataxis in Hebrew Poetry." *JBL* 99 (1980) 23–41.

Heffelfinger, Katie M. *I Am Large, I Contain Multitudes: Lyric Cohesion and Conflict in Second Isaiah.* BibIntSer 105. Leiden: Brill, 2011.

Henderson, Joseph M. "Who Weeps in Jeremiah viii 23 (ix 1)? Identifying Dramatic Speakers in the Poetry of Jeremiah." *VT* 52 (2002) 191–206.

Hillers, Delbert R. *Lamentations.* 2nd rev. ed. AB 7A. New York: Doubleday, 1992.

Holladay, William L. *Jeremiah 1: A Commentary on the Book of Jeremiah, Chapters 1–25.* Hermeneia. Philadelphia: Fortress, 1986.

———. "A New Suggestion for the Crux in Isaiah I 4B." *VT* 33 (1983) 235–37.

———. "Style, Irony, and Authenticity in Jeremiah." *JBL* 81 (1962) 44–54.

Huffmon, Herbert B. "A Company of Prophets: Mari, Assyria, Israel." In *Prophecy in Its Ancient Near Eastern Context: Mesopotamian, Biblical, and Arabian Perspectives*, edited by Martti Nissinen, 47–70. SBLSymS 13. Atlanta: SBL, 2000.

Hyatt, J. Philip. *Commentary on Exodus*. NCB. Grand Rapids: Eerdmans, 1971.

Jacobs, Joseph, ed. *The Jewish Encyclopedia*. Vol. 1. New York: Funk & Wagnalls, 1906. http://www.jewishencyclopedia.com/.

Jacobs, Mignon R. "Bridging the Times: Trends in Micah Studies since 1985." *Currents in Biblical Research* 4 (2006) 293–329.

———. *The Conceptual Coherence of the Book of Micah*. JSOTSup 322. Sheffield: Sheffield Academic, 2001.

Jaffee, Martin S. *Torah in the Mouth: Writing and Oral Tradition in Palestinian Judaism 200 BCE—400 CE*. New York: Oxford University Press, 2001.

Jakobson, Roman, and Linda R. Waugh. *The Sound Shape of Language*. 3rd ed. Berlin: Mouton de Gruyter, 2002; orig. pub. 1979.

Janzen, J. Gerald. *Exodus*. Westminster Bible Companion. Louisville: Westminster John Knox, 1997.

———. "The Root *pr'* in Judges V 2 and Deuteronomy XXXII 42." *VT* 39 (1989) 393–406.

———. "Song of Moses, Song of Miriam: Who Is Seconding Whom?" *CBQ* 54 (1992) 211–20.

Kaiser, Barbara Bakke. "Poet as 'Female Impersonator': The Image of Daughter Zion as Speaker in Biblical Poems of Suffering." *JR* 67 (1987) 164–82.

Kaiser, Otto. *Isaiah 1–39: A Commentary*. Translated R. A. Wilson. OTL. Philadelphia: Westminster/John Knox Press, 1974.

Kaltner, John, and Louis Stulman, eds. *Inspired Speech: Prophecy in the Ancient Near East; Essays in Honor of Herbert B. Huffmon*. JSOTSup 378. T. & T. Clark Biblical Studies. London: T. & T. Clark, 2004.

Kessler, Rainer. "Miriam and the Prophecy of the Persian Period." In *The Prophets and Daniel*, edited by Athalya Brenner, 77–86. FCB 2/8 London: Sheffield Academic, 2001.

Klein, Lillian R. *The Triumph of Irony in the Book of Judges*. Bible and Literature Series 14. JSOTSup 68. Sheffield: Almond, 1989.

Knauf, Ernst Axel. "Vom Prophetinnenwort zum Prophetenbuch. Jesaja 8,3f im Kontext von Jesaja 6,1–8,16."' *Lectio difficilior* 2/2000. http://www.lectio.unibe.ch/00_2/v.htm/.

Kraemer, Ross Shepard. *Her Share of the Blessings: Women's Religions among Pagans, Jews, and Christians in the Greco-Roman World*. New York: Oxford University Press, 1992.

Kramer, Phyllis Silverman. "Miriam." In *Exodus to Deuteronomy*, edited by Athalya Brenner, 104–33. FCB 2/5. Sheffield: Sheffield Academic, 2000.

Kugel, James. *The Idea of Biblical Poetry: Parallelism and Its History*. Baltimore: Johns Hopkins University Press, 1981.

Lanahan, William F. "The Speaking Voice in the Book of Lamentations." *JBL* 93 (1974) 41–49.

Lange, Armin et al., eds. *From Qumran to Aleppo*. FRLANT 230. Göttingen: Vandenhoeck & Ruprecht, 2009.

Lee, Nancy C., and Carleen Mandolfo, eds. *Lamentations in Ancient and Contemporary Cultural Contexts*. SBLSymS 43. Atlanta: SBL, 2008.

Lee, Nancy C. "Exposing a Buried Subtext in Jeremiah and Lamentations: Going after Baal and . . . Abel." In *Troubling Jeremiah*, edited by A. R. Pete Diamond et al., 87–122. JSOTSup 260. Sheffield: Sheffield Academic, 1999.

———. *Hebrew Sound Patterns and Women's Biblical Composing* (Kindle Book (originally published in 2014).

———. "Prophet and Singer in the Fray: The Book of Jeremiah." In *Uprooting and Planting: Essays on Jeremiah for Leslie Allen*, edited by John Goldingay, 190–209. Library of Hebrew Bible / Old Testament Studies 459. T. & T. Clark Library of Biblical Studies. New York: T. & T. Clark, 2007.

———. "Prophetic 'Bat-'Ammî' Answers God and Jeremiah." *Lectio difficilior* 2 (2009). http://www.lectio.unibe.ch/09_2/lee.html/.

———. *The Singers of Lamentations: Cities under Siege, from Ur to Jerusalem to Sarajevo*. BibIntSer 60. Leiden: Brill, 2002.

———. "The Singers of Lamentations: (A)Scribing (De)Claiming Poets and Prophets." In *Lamentations in Ancient and Contemporary Cultural Contexts*, edited by Nancy C. Lee and Carleen Mandolfo, 33–46. SBLSymS 43. Atlanta: SBL, 2008.

Leuchter, Mark. "'Why Tarry the Wheels of His Chariot?' (Judg 5, 28): Canaanite Chariots and Echoes of Egypt in the Song of Deborah." *Bib* 91 (2010) 256–68.

Linafelt, Tod. *Surviving Lamentations: Catastrophe, Lament, and Protest in the Afterlife of a Biblical Book*. Chicago: University of Chicago Press, 2000.

Loewenstamm, Samuel E. "The Lord Is My Strength and My Glory." *VT* 19 (1969) 464–70.

Løland, Hanne. *Silent or Salient Gender? The Interpretation of Gendered God-Language in the Hebrew Bible, Exemplified in Isaiah 42, 46, and 49*. FAT 2/32. Tübingen: Mohr/Siebeck, 2008.

Lundberg, Marilyn J. et al., eds. *Puzzling Out the Past: Studies in Northwest Semitic Languages and Literatures in Honor of Bruce Zuckerman*. Culture and History of the Ancient Near East 55. Leiden: Brill, 2012.

Lundbom, Jack R. *Jeremiah 1–20*. AB 21A . New York: Doubleday, 1999.

Maier, Christl M. *Daughter Zion, Mother Zion: Gender, Space, and the Sacred in Ancient Israel*. Minneapolis: Fortress, 2008.

Margalit, Baruch. "Alliteration in Ugaritic Poetry: Its Role in Composition and Analysis." *UF* 11 (1980) 537–57.

Matthews, Victor H. *Judges and Ruth*. New Cambridge Bible Commentary. Cambridge: Cambridge University Press, 2004.

Mays, James Luther. *Micah*. OTL. Philadelphia: Westminster, 1976.

McCabe, Elizabeth A., ed. *Women in the Biblical World: A Survey of Old and New Testament Perspectives: Volume 2*. Lanham, MD: University Press of America, 2011.

McEvenue, Sean. "Who Was Second Isaiah?" In *Studies in the Book of Isaiah: Festschrift Willem A. M. Beuken*, 213–22. BETL 132. Leuven: Leuven University Press, 1997.

McKane, William. *A Critical and Exegetical Commentary on Jeremiah*. Vol. 1, *Introduction and Commentary on Jeremiah* I–XXV. ICC. Edinburgh: T. & T. Clark, 1986.

Melugin, Roy F., and Marvin A. Sweeney, eds. *New Visions of Isaiah*. JSOTSup 214. Sheffield: Sheffield Academic, 1996.

Meyers, Carol L. "*B'shalah (Exodus 13:17—17:16)*." In *The Torah: A Women's Commentary*, edited by Tamara Eskenazi, 379–99. New York: Women of Reform Judaism, 2008.

———. *Discovering Eve: Ancient Israelite Women in Context*. Oxford Paperbacks. New York: Oxford University Press, 1991.

———. *Exodus*. New Cambridge Bible Commentary. Cambridge: Cambridge University Press, 2005.

———. "Miriam, Music, and Miracles." In *Mariam, the Magdalen, and the Mother*, edited by Deirdre Good, 27–48. Bloomington: Indiana University Press, 2005.

———."Miriam the Musician." In *A Feminist Companion to Exodus to Deuteronomy*, edited by Athalya Brenner, 207–30. FCB 6. Sheffield: Sheffield Academic, 1994.

———. "Of Drums and Damsels: Women's Performance in Ancient Israel." *BA* 3 (1991) 16–27.

———. *Rediscovering Eve: Ancient Israelite Women in Context*. New York: Oxford University Press, 2013.

Miller, J. Maxwell, and John H. Hayes, *A History of Ancient Israel and Judah*. Philadelphia: Westminster, 1986.

Miller, Patrick D., Jr. *The Divine Warrior in Early Israel*. HSM. Cambridge: Harvard University Press, 1973.

Miller, Robert D., II. "When Pharaohs Ruled: On the Translation of Judges 5:2." *JTS* 59 (2008) 650–54.

Muilenburg, James. *Isaiah 40–66*. In *Interpreters Bible*. Vol. 5. New York: Abingdon, 1957.

———. "A Liturgy on the Triumphs of Yahweh." In *Studia Biblica et Semitica*, edited by Martinus A Beek, 233–51. Wageningen: Veenman, 1966.

Nachmanides (Ramban). *Commentary on Torah*. Vol. 2, *Exodus*. 5 vols. Translated by Charles B. Chavel. New York: Shilo, 1999.

Nasuti, Harry P. "The Once and Future Lament: Micah 2:1–5 and the Prophetic Persona." In *Inspired Speech: Prophecy in the Ancient Near East; Essays in Honor of Herbert B. Huffmon*, edited by John Kaltner and Louis Stulman, 144–60. JSOTSup 378. T. & T. Clark Biblical Studies. London: T. & T. Clark, 2004.

Newsom, Carol A., and Sharon H. Ringe, eds. *The Women's Bible Commentary*. Expanded ed. Louisville: Westminster John Knox, 1998.

———, eds. *The Women's Bible Commentary*. 3rd ed. 20th anniversary ed. Louisville: Westminster John Knox, 2012.

Newsome, James D., Jr. *The Hebrew Prophets*. Atlanta: John Knox, 1984.

Niditch, Susan. "Eroticism and Death in the Tale of Jael." In *Gender and Difference in Ancient Israel*, edited by Peggy L. Day, 43–57. Minneapolis: Fortress, 1989.

———. *Judges: A Commentary*. OTL. Louisville: Westminster John Knox, 2008.

———. *War in the Hebrew Bible: A Study in the Ethics of Violence*. New York: Oxford University Press, 1995.

Nissinen, Martti, ed. *Prophecy in Its Ancient Near Eastern Context: Mesopotamian, Biblical, and Arabian Perspectives*. SBLSymS 13. Atlanta: SBL, 2000.

Noll, K. L. *The Faces of David*. JSOTSup 242. Sheffield: Sheffield Academic, 1997.

O'Brien, Julia M. *Challenging Prophetic Metaphor: Theology and Ideology in the Prophets*. Louisville: Westminster John Knox, 2008.

O'Connor, Kathleen M. *Lamentations*. In *The New Interpreter's Bible*, vol. 6. Nashville: Abingdon, 2001.

———. *Jeremiah: Pain and Promise*. Minneapolis, Mn.: Fortress Press, 2012.

———. "Lamentations." In *The Women's Bible Commentary*, edited by Carol A. Newsom and Sharon H. Ringe, 278–82. 3rd ed. Louisville: Westminster John Knox, 2012.

———. *Lamentations and the Tears of the World*. Maryknoll, NY: Orbis, 2002.

Okpewho, Isadore. *African Oral Literature: Backgrounds, Character, and Continuity.* Bloomington: Indiana University Press, 1992.

Petersen, David L. "Defining Prophecy and Prophetic Literature." In *Prophecy in Its Ancient Near Eastern Context: Mesopotamian, Biblical, and Arabian Perspectives*, edited by Martti Nissinen, 33–44. SBLSymS 13. Atlanta: SBL, 2000.

———. *Late Israelite Prophecy: Studies in Deutero-Prophetic Literature and in Chronicles.* SBLMS 23. Missoula: Scholars, 1977.

Petersen, David L., and Kent Harold Richards. *Interpreting Hebrew Poetry.* GBS. Minneapolis: Fortress, 1992.

Pham, Xuan Huong Thi. *Mourning in the Ancient Near East and the Hebrew Bible.* JSOTSup 302. Sheffield: Sheffield Academic, 1999.

Pietersma, Albert, and Benjamin G. Wright, eds. *A New English Translation of the Septuagint.* New York: Oxford University Press, 2009.

Poethig, Eunice B. "The Victory Song Tradition of the Women of Israel." PhD diss., Union Theological Seminary, 1985.

Pressler, Carolyn. *Joshua, Judges, and Ruth.* Westminster Bible Companion. Louisville: Westminster John Knox, 2002.

Propp, William H. C. *Exodus 1–18.* AB 2. New York: Doubleday, 1999.

Rasmussen, Jane. "Deborah, the Woman Warior." In *Anti-covenant: Counter-reading Women's Lives in the Hebrew Bible*, edited by Mieke, Bal, 79–93. Bible and Literature Series 22. JSOTSup 81. Sheffield: Almond, 1989.

Rowley, H. H. "The Council of Yahweh." *JTS* 45 (1944) 151–57.

Ruether, Rosemary Radford, ed. *Religion and Sexism: Images of Women in the Jewish and Christian Traditions.* New York: Simon & Schuster, 1974.

Ruiten, J. van, and M. Vervenne, eds. *Studies in the Book of Isaiah: Festschrift Willem A. M. Beuken.* BETL 132. Leuven: Leuven University Press, 1997.

Runions, Erin. *Changing Subjects: Gender, Nation, and Future in Micah.* Playing the Texts 7. London: Sheffield Academic, 2001.

Sáenz-Badillos, Angel. *A History of the Hebrew Language.* Translated by John Elwolde. Cambridge: Cambridge University Press, 1996.

Sarna, Nahum. *Exodus.* JPS Torah Commentary. Philadelphia: Jewish Publication Society, 1991.

Sasson, Jack M. *Judges 1–12.* Anchor Yale Bible 6D. New Haven: Yale University Press, 2014.

———."Wordplay in the Old Testament." *IDBSup*, edited by K. Crim, 968–70. Nashville: Abingdon, 1976.

Saydon, P. P. "Assonance in Hebrew as a Means of Expressing Emphasis." *Bib* 36 (1955) 36–50.

Schmitt, J. J. "The Motherhood of God and Zion as Mother." *RB* 92 (1985) 557–69.

Schneider, Tammi J. *Judges.* Berit Olam. Collegeville, MN: Liturgical, 2000.

Scoggin, B. Elmo. "An Expository Exegesis: Micah 6:6–8." *Faith and Mission* 2 (1985) 50–58.

Seitz, Christopher R. "The Divine Council: Temporal Transition and New Prophecy in the Book of Isaiah." *JBL* 109 (1990) 229–47.

———. *Isaiah 1–39.* IBC. Louisville: Westminster John Knox, 1993.

———. *Zion's Final Destiny: The Development of the Book of Isaiah.* Minneapolis: Fortress, 1991.

Shaw, Charles S. "Micah 1:10–16 Reconsidered." *JBL* 106 (1987) 223–29.

———. *The Speeches of Micah: A Rhetorical-Historical Analysis*. JSOTSup 145. Sheffield: JSOT Press, 1993.

Shields, Mary E. "Impasse or Opportunity or...? Women Reading Jeremiah Reading Women." In *Jeremiah (Dis)Placed: New Directions in Writing/Reading Jeremiah*, edited by A. R. Pete Diamond and Louis Stulman, 290–302. Library of Hebrew Bible / Old Testament Studies 529. T. & T. Clark Library of Biblical Studies. London: T. & T. Clark, 2011.

Skehan, Patrick W. "The Hand of Judith." *CBQ* 25 (1963) 94–110.

Stone, Bebb Wheeler. "Second Isaiah: Prophet to Patriarchy." *JSOT* 56 (1992) 85–99.

Strickman, H. Norman, and Arthur M. Silver, trans. *Commentary on the Pentateuch*, by Ibn Ezra. Vol. 2, *Exodus*. New York: Menorah, 1996.

Sweeney, Marvin A. *Isaiah 1–39: With an Introduction to Prophetic Literature*. FOTL 16. Grand Rapids: Eerdmans, 1996.

Talmon, Shemaryahu. "The Desert Motif in the Bible and in Qumran Literature." In *Biblical Motifs: Origins and Transformations*, edited by Alexander Altmann, 31–63. Philip W. Lown Institute of Advanced Judaic Studies, Brandeis University. Studies and Texts 3. Cambridge: Harvard University Press, 1966.

Taylor, Joan E. *Jewish Women Philosophers of First-Century Alexandria: Philo's "Therapeutae" Reconsidered*. Oxford: Oxford University Press, 2003.

Tervanotko, Hanna. "'The Hope of the Enemy has Perished': The Figure of Miriam in the Qumran Library." In *From Qumran to Aleppo*, edited by Armin Lange et al., 156–75. FRLANT 230. Göttingen: Vandenhoeck & Ruprecht, 2009.

Tiemeyer, Lena-Sofia. *For the Comfort of Zion: The Geographical and Theological Location of Isaiah 40–55*. VTSup 139. Leiden: Brill, 2011.

Tiemeyer, Lena-Sofia, and Hans M. Barstad, eds. *Continuity and Discontinuity: Chronological and Thematic Development in Isaiah 40–66*. FRLANT 255. Göttingen: Vandenhoeck & Ruprecht, 2014.

Trebolle Barrera, Julio C., and Luis V. Montaner, eds. *The Madrid Qumran Congress: Proceedings, 1991*. STDJ 11. Leiden: Brill, 1992.

Trible, Phyllis. "Bringing Miriam out of the Shadows." *BRev* 5/1 (1989)14–25, 34.

———. *God and the Rhetoric of Sexuality*. OBT 2. Philadelphia: Fortress, 1978.

Tull, Patricia K. *Isaiah 1–39*. Smyth & Helwys Bible Commentary. Macon, GA: Smyth & Helwys, 2010.

Volz, Paul. *Der Prophet Jeremia*. Kommentar zum Alten Testament 10. Leipzig: Deichert, 1922.

Watson, Wilfred G. E. *Classical Hebrew Poetry*. JSOTSup 170. Sheffield: Sheffield Academic, 2009.

Webb, Barry G. *The Book of Judges*. NICOT. Grand Rapids: Eerdmans, 2012.

Wegner, Paul D. "A Re-examination of Isaiah IX 1–6." *VT* 42 (1992) 103–12.

West, Gerald O., and Musa W. Dube, eds. *Semeia 73: "Reading With": An Exploration of the Interface between Critical and Ordinary Readings of the Bible: African Overtures*. Atlanta: Scholars, 1996.

Westermann, Claus. *Isaiah 40–66: A Commentary*. Translated by David M. G. Stalker. OTL. Philadelphia: Westminster, 1969.

———. *Praise and Lament in the Psalms*. Translated by Keith R. Crim and Richard N. Soulen. Atlanta: John Knox, 1981.

Williamson, H. G. M. *The Book Called Isaiah: Deutero-Isaiah's Role in Composition and Redac-tion*. Oxford: Clarendon, 2005.

———. "Prophetesses in the Hebrew Bible." In *Prophecy and Prophets in Ancient Israel: Pro-ceedings of the Oxford Old Testament Seminar*, edited by John Day, 65–80. Library of Hebrew Bible / Old Testament Studies 531. T. & T. Clark Library of Biblical Studies. New York: T. & T. Clark, 2010.

Wilson, Robert R. "Current Issues in the Study of Old Testament Prophecy." In *Inspired Speech: Prophecy in the Ancient Near East; Essays in Honor of Herbert B. Huffmon*, edited by John Kaltner and Louis Stulman, 38–46. JSOTSup 378. T. & T. Clark Biblical Studies. London: T. & T. Clark, 2004.

Yee, Gale A., ed. *Judges and Method: New Approaches in Biblical Studies*. Minneapolis: For-tress, 1995.

———. "A Form-Critical Study of Isaiah 5:1–7 as a Song and a Juridical Parable." *CBQ* 43 (1981) 30–40.

# Index of Subjects and Authors

# Index of Ancient Documents

## Old Testament

## Exodus (continued)



## Numbers



## Deuteronomy



## Joshua



## Judges

## Psalms *(cont.)*



## Proverbs



## Song of Songs (Solomon)



## Isaiah

## Jeremiah



## Lamentations



## Ezekiel



## Daniel



## Hosea

## Joel



## Amos



## Micah



## Nahum



## Habakkuk



## Zechariah



# New Testament

## Luke



# Dead Sea Scrolls



# Septuagint

## Isaiah



# Talmud

27801444R10147

Made in the USA
Middletown, DE
21 December 2015